THE PRODUCTION OF GLOBAL WEB SERIES IN A NETWORKED AGE

This book tells the story of diverse online creators – women, ethnic and racial minorities, queer folk and those from hardscrabble backgrounds – producing low budget, high cultural impact web series which have disrupted longstanding white male domination of the film and TV industries.

Author Guy Healy addresses four burning problems faced by creators in the context of digital disruption (along with potential solutions), namely: the sustainability of monetizing digital content and the rising possibility of middle-class artistic careers; algorithmic volatility; the difficulty of finding people to share jealously guarded industry knowledge as traditional craft-based mentoring and expertise-sharing mechanisms break down; and the lack of diversity and authenticity in high-profile storytelling. It includes nine case studies, five drawn from a second wave of outstanding YouTube-developed talent, transitioning to longer form narrative, most collaborating with established TV producers working across the divide between online and established television culture, and all from under-represented and/or minority backgrounds. The balance are film-school and industry professionals leveraging YouTube in the same way, including two Writers Guild of America new media award-winners. These storytellers leverage their social networks and chase sustainable careers by reaching audiences of subscription video-on-demand platforms and mainstream online broadcast in Australia and North America. *The Production of Global Web Series in a Networked Age* is the first longitudinal study of this historic rapprochement between online and television cultures. Four of the cases are in Emmy-winning contexts, and one in an Emmy nominated context.

Covering 2005–2021, the book reveals distinctive new forms of screen industry convergence with profound implications for creators' careers, the screen industry in general, new media theory, and broader cultural and social change.

It is essential reading for students, academics and industry professionals working on the production and distribution of web series.

Dr Guy Healy works as a researcher on an Australian Research Council project investigating the role of the web series globally. Healy worked for about a decade at *The Australian* newspaper, mainly as a higher education writer; and for BBC Wildlife magazine as a freelance correspondent investigating species-level threats to wildlife. His most important story reported on calls from zoologists warning that research funding into, and surveillance of bat-borne viruses in Asia, Africa, and elsewhere, had to be prioritized, in 2009.

THE PRODUCTION OF GLOBAL WEB SERIES IN A NETWORKED AGE

Guy Healy

Routledge
Taylor & Francis Group

LONDON AND NEW YORK

Cover image: © Getty Images

First published 2022
by Routledge
2 Park Square, Milton Park, Abingdon, Oxon OX14 4RN

and by Routledge
605 Third Avenue, New York, NY 10158

Routledge is an imprint of the Taylor & Francis Group, an informa business

© 2022 Guy Healy

British Library Cataloguing-in-Publication Data
A catalogue record for this book is available from the British Library

Library of Congress Cataloging-in-Publication Data
Names: Healy, Guy, 1962- author.
Title: The production of global web series in a networked age /
Guy Healy.
Description: London ; New York : Routledge, 2022. | Includes
bibliographical references and index.
Identifiers: LCCN 2021040857 (print) | LCCN 2021040858 (ebook) |
ISBN 9781032022369 (hardback) | ISBN 9781032022352 (paperback) |
ISBN 9781003182481 (ebook)
Subjects: LCSH: Internet television--Production and direction. |
Television authorship. | YouTube (Electronic resource)
Classification: LCC PN1992.926.P76 .H43 2022 (print) |
LCC PN1992.926.P76 (ebook) | DDC 791.4509/051--dc23/
eng/20211118
LC record available at https://lccn.loc.gov/2021040857
LC ebook record available at https://lccn.loc.gov/2021040858

ISBN: 978-1-032-02236-9 (hbk)
ISBN: 978-1-032-02235-2 (pbk)
ISBN: 978-1-003-18248-1 (ebk)

DOI: 10.4324/9781003182481

Typeset in Bembo
by KnowledgeWorks Global Ltd.

CONTENTS

vi Contents

9 Bending algorithmic culture to serve post-TV storytelling   198

10 Tina Cesa Ward: The New York film director who
     fell into web-series   216

11 The garden in YouTube's machine   240

Appendix 1: Career mobility paths of Skip Ahead alumni,
          2014–2019   *250*
Appendix 2: Three keys to sustainability for web-series makers,
          2005–2021, based on Murdock and Goldings'
          (2016, p. 764) three economies   *252*
Index   *254*

ACKNOWLEDGEMENTS

The author's sincerest gratitude is extended to Stuart Cunningham and John Banks for their unflagging illumination on this five-year project, as well as to Mark Deuze and Ramon Lobato for their helpful comments on earlier versions of Chapters 2 and 4, respectively. Heartfelt appreciation also goes to Susan Turnbull and Steinar Ellingsen, Marion McCutcheon, and Nicola Evans without whose introductions to Erin Good, Julie Kalceff, Taylor Litton-Strain, and Rosie Lourde, Chapters 7 and 8 would not have been possible. This book also benefited from the inspiration of the work of Emilia King in Canada, Joel Bassaget in Germany, and Meredith Burkholder in New York. The author gratefully acknowledges the role of the rich intellectual village of peers in which this book was grown, QUT's Digital Media Research Centre, led by Jean Burgess and Michael Dezuanni. My PhD and post-doctoral research were also supported by Australian Research Council grants DP160100086 and LP180100626. The assistance of librarians Alice Steiner and Ellen Thompson also much appreciated. Sincere appreciation is also extended to Dr Paul Williams, reader Louise Gillian and to John and David Healy, Sarah Casey, and Suzanne Bauer for their moral support.

PREFACE

Every art form starts with the physical tools with which to create that particular art form. Without these tools, the artist is nothing more than a person filled with creative ideas unable to communicate them to the world. But once the artist has their tools, the inner world that they spend their time living in meets with reality and the perception of others.

My tool from an early age was a pencil I used to write simple stories, and later into my teens, movies became my outlet of escape. But it wasn't until my 20s that I, as a young woman, left the Ohio multiplex, discovered cinema, and fell in love with the idea of writing and directing film. Film was my path; it was all I wanted to do. I thought it was all I would ever do. I had no idea what new technology was coming nearly a decade later that would change everything for me as an artist and give me new tools to make my mark.

I have always considered myself lucky to be a creator at this time in our creative human history. I was given the opportunity to work in a new art form that no one had before me. It was short form episodic storytelling displayed on computer. I jumped onto the scene in 2008 when there were no rules, only good storytelling and technological restrictions. And those restrictions or obstructions only fuelled the creativity while forcing us to stretch our imaginations past the forms that seemed etched in stone by film or television. It was as exciting to be a web series creator as it was a struggle. I am an unabashed advocate for web series. Web series changed my life as a storyteller and gave me a chance to tell stories that would likely never have been told. Healy's examination of web series seeks and succeeds to explain why so many of us have taken to this new way to tell stories. But more than that, it validates an art form that from day one has had to explain and defend itself.

The web series is truly a product of technology. The evolution of web series runs parallel to that of technology. Once restricted by running time and attention spans, the web series has moved past its restrictions because technology has moved past its restrictions – from micro series found on social media platforms such as Instagram, Snapchat, and the like, to large Hollywood offerings on Netflix, Amazon, and their ever-growing competition. What we see today in digital/streaming entertainment can all trace their roots back to web series. Now is a perfect moment for Healy's examination of the form, its evolution, and its potential sustainability for the independent creator.

The journey towards independent storytelling on the web, in part, started with the unions in Hollywood trying to figure out how to police the work created there. Hollywood was no longer the gatekeeper of episodic storytelling. Hollywood moved quickly to close up ranks, but the in-fighting with unions gave time to independent creators and sometimes frustrated Hollywood creators to tell often rejected stories. And in the process, creators could build audiences of their own. Hollywood veterans no longer had to struggle through endless pitch meetings and long development processes. For the first time since the studio system was formed nearly a century prior, creators had the ability to distribute directly to their audience around the world, for free. And what did that mean? Everything. One specific benefit was that many of the voices and audiences that had been overlooked or frankly ignored were now being heard, proving their eagerness to support stories told by them and for them. Chris McCaleb, Emmy nominated editor with roots in web series, put it best when interviewed for the International Academy of Web TV Awards when honouring the industry's pioneers: 'When you remove the wall between yourself and the audience, you can do almost anything'. A web series, especially those made independently, is at its best and most successful when it serves a niche audience. Which again, made the web a much-needed home for all those 'misfits' who struggled to get stories financed with characters that were of a minority group.

A wave of independent web series creators pioneered the space from the mid-2000s and the decade that followed. There had been web series prior to then that carved a path, but the first wave that I was also a part of, really set the pace forward. Not only was there a sudden surge of series being made, there was also a comradery in the space amongst all creators. We were all learning and sharing information about the latest technological breakthroughs. Together we went from standard definition to HD, to cameras with unremarkable fixed lenses to cameras that allowed us to use top notch interchangeable lenses. We went through the rise of the DSLR, which made the web series even more affordable. We also travelled the changes of video players, from the need to use early video players for a price, such as Brightcove, on our websites, to the ability to embed players from other sites such as blip.tv and YouTube for free, cutting our costs down even further. With every technological breakthrough, another creator was able to push the form of web series even further.

The evolution of the web series also coincides with the launch of social media. Strong and dedicated use of social media is one of the biggest reasons for the success of a web series. The boom of web series exists because of the access to the loyal fans that support them, and most often than not, fans find shows through social media. Not only did creators have access to distribution but they also had access to marketing, again for free.

Once Hollywood squared away its union contracts for the web it was time for them to jump hard into the game. But even before Hollywood moved with full force, brands were pushing out scripted and unscripted content at a good clip. Microsoft was one of the first to see promise in the medium when they put money behind Felicia Day's megahit *The Guild*. American Express endowed Hollywood veteran and early web adopter John Avnet with enough funds to create WIGS, a YouTube channel with stories with women in the lead and starring Hollywood actors. There were also smaller brands like Spherion that backed *The Temp Life* from producer Wilson Cleveland, one of the web's biggest connectors of web series talent and brands. I worked with Cleveland on a series called *Bestsellers* with my *Anyone But Me* partner Susan Miller (see chapter 10).[1] The brand SFN Group couldn't have been easier to work with and at the time I had a bigger budget than we had on our own series.

Brands found the web an appealing way to reach potential customers at a fraction of what ads or television commercials were costing them. Brands such as 7-Eleven teamed up with web series platforms like blip.tv (which was later bought by Maker which was later bought by Disney and neither exist today) who tapped indie creators to do what they have been doing so successfully on their own, getting views and views by the millions. The partnership between web series creators and brands served both their needs perfectly. Brands cared only about getting as many views as possible and creators cared even more about getting funding to create content. Creators jumped at the chance to get in the good graces of brands and many of the early pioneers, such as creator Yuri Baranovsky, started to find their niche in branded entertainment. The budgets for many early branded series were considerably low by Hollywood standards, some even getting an hour worth of content for $50,000. The word on the street in the early years was that web series didn't have to look good. Many series that were getting an audience and bringing in views had minuscule budgets to create their series. Because their budgets were barely in the thousands due to self-funding many creators cut corners on talent for key positions. Instead, many adopted the model of grab a camera and go, ignoring even the basic fundamentals of filmmaking and creating series that often looked more amateurish than artistic. Because of that, no brand needed to spend a lot of money. That kind of thinking created an early dismissive stigma against web series here in the United States of America and it has taken the better part of a decade to lose that reputation.

Some of Hollywood's earlier adapters such as former Disney head Michael Eisner and his studio Vuguru and Sony's platform Crackle took a shot on independent creators, handing them the reins to modest budgets to create content. And soon the rest of Hollywood caught on and even agents to the stars no longer thought of web series as that pesky kid that just makes cute little cat videos.

Much like the independent film movement of the early 1990s, web series was about to travel the same path. Just like the independent film movement, new voices were being heard and reaching an audience. But just as Hollywood created 'indie' film studios in 1990s, closing the door on the movement, it seemed web series could suffer the same fate. But unlike indie film, indie web series still has the advantage of creating content and immediately reaching an audience without a middleman. So the potential to thrive without gatekeepers is still possible, although there are still great disadvantages when it comes to budget.

During the years, I have spent a great deal of time travelling to speak on panels all over the world and have also taught producing web series for a couple of institutions and the number one question asked is, how do you make money? My answer has always been, if you are getting into web series for the money, get out now. Today, there are additional avenues for creators to bring in revenue, thanks again to the evolution of technology. Because there are so many digital channels looking for content, there are opportunities. But the problem still lies in the running time of web series. In order to get digital distribution on most channels you need at least 50 hours of content, a very hard reach for web series but when paired with other series the hour restriction seems possible to overcome and so revenue beyond ad-rev share is possible. And with more channels discovering the niche audience is the way to success, the web series could see better monetization days ahead.

Even with a potential of better revenue ahead, web series have never been about the money, it's always been about artistic freedom and never having to ask permission. In the pages that follow, I think you will find that Healy balances the business of storytelling with the passion of the creator to tell stories, no matter the budget or obstructions. Not all creators have travelled the same path – our countries of origin have given each of us different advantages and obstacles – but we all share the same desire to push forward our voices and for someone like Healy to examine and celebrate them.

Tina Cesa Ward

Note

1 For their scripted web drama, *Anyone But Me* (2008–2012; 2019), Miller and Ward won the Writers Guild of America inaugural Award for Original New Media, 2011. *ABM* has attracted about 100 million views to 2020, being one of the few indie web series to platform to the Hollywood studios', Hulu, via a license deal.

1

INTRODUCTION

> The history of the field [of cultural production] arises from the struggle
> between the established figures and the young challengers…it results from
> the struggle between those who have made their mark (*fait date* – 'made an
> epoch') and who are fighting to persist, and those who cannot make their
> own mark without pushing into the past those who have an interest in
> stopping the clock, eternalizing the present stage of things.
>
> Pierre Bourdieu (2005), *The field of cultural production:*
> *Essays on art and literature*

Storytelling in algorithmic culture

One of the biggest mysteries in the arts are the Muses, the wellsprings of creativity and originality storytellers have drawn upon across the ages to entertain,
edify, inspire, and console. During the Renaissance, historian Giorgio Vasari
explained creativity as 'divinely inspired', while acknowledging 'an element
of savagery and madness' in the artists he knew (Bull, 1987, p. 67). During
the 1800s, creative inspiration was reconceptualized from 'historical, dead and
mythological muses such as Sappho or the Virgin Mary', to the 'living con-
temporaries' of poets, especially lovers, says Sarah Parker (2015). Updating our
understanding of creativity during the modern era, Larry Briskman (1980)
refers to creativity as the defining human drive, where 'mysterious and miraculous' psychological processes occur within the mind of the individual artist.
More recently, creative industries advocate, John Howkins, has focused on the
importance to jobs and wealth generation of the individual creative entrepreneur who draws upon 'the wealth that lies within themselves' (Ghelfi, 2005,
p. 6). By contrast, present-day approaches emphasize the inherently social nature
of the creative impulse driven by *frisson*, as talented people brainstorm with

DOI: 10.4324/9781003182481-1

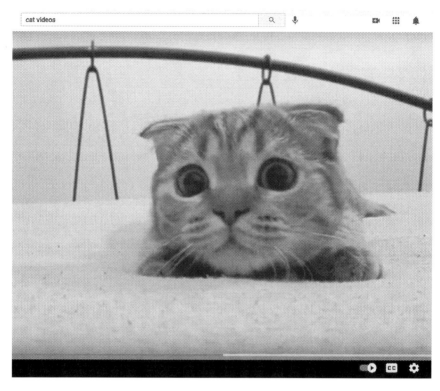

FIGURE 1.1 Content clash: Everyday content posed a challenge to pioneering web-series makers.

each together, say scholars of creativity, Paisley Livingston (2009, p. 12) and Mihaly Csikszentmihalyi (2014, p. 51). This book tells the stories of how today's most influential storytellers on the small screens are finding their Muses in the unlikeliest of places: the now ubiquitous social network of YouTube. YouTube is the world's second most popular search engine, after parent Google (Allgaier, 2020) – the basis of its appeal as a discovery platform for creators and producers. By 2007, YouTube's impact on youth pop culture was so profound that TV writers were ordered 'to make things more YouTube-able' (Banks, 2010a, p. 22), so broadcast TV could attempt to retain younger generations. Just as matter is understood to curve space-time, the US$8 billion YouTube says it distributes to creators from its US$15 billion annual advertising haul (Kafka, 2020), can curve the creative process among those doing good and the commercially ruthless alike. Via high-level access to nine outstanding creative teams, I investigate what this proto-industry means for the livelihoods of web-series makers, whose stories are told, how they are told, how fan communities are mobilized to help sustain them online, and what this means for cultural progress. Above all, by bending algorithmic culture to serve their needs, these storytellers solved the notorious problem of interference in scripts by powerful Hollywood film and

TV executives, and held fast to their creative visions. They are not making family shows for prime-time TV. These Gen Xs, Millennials, Gen Ys, and Gen Zs have long moved the zeitgeist on.

Ultimately, this book is about what happens when the young challengers and established figures put aside their differences and collaborate to best adapt to the post-TV-broadcast era that Cunningham and Craig (2019, p. 14) characterize as 'frictionless'. Such has been the growth of all forms of series outside 'TV' (broadcasters), some influential European policymakers no longer use the term 'TV series' since it is 'too restrictive' (Baujard et al., 2019, p. 34). Covering the period 2005–2021, this book reveals distinctive new forms of screen industry convergence with deep implications for the careers of creators, the screen industry itself, and more equitable social change. It is the first longitudinal study of veteran YouTubers and established TV producers making highly popular serial narrative web-series together, and it maps the professional outcomes from their rapprochement in cases 1–5. Cases 6–9 map the reverse of the coin – outcomes for film school graduates and established professionals. Long smarting from its reputation as a giant 'cat video' archive, YouTube has struggled to raise the professionalism of the creators it hosts. The platform spent US$100 million on its Original Channels initiative in 2011, has built state of the art studios – the YouTube Spaces – in seven capital cities worldwide, now largely shuttered due to the pandemic, and hosts an online Creator Academy. One largely unexamined YouTube professionalization initiative though is Skip Ahead, a hybrid collaboration between the old school of Screen Australia – which invested in independent Australian films such as *The Babadook, Red Dog, The Sapphires,* and *The Dressmaker* – and the platform the cultural establishment loves to hate, Google's YouTube. Under Skip Ahead, grant winning YouTubers were encouraged to collaborate with established TV producers to make low-budget web-series, a hybrid format usually comprising serial videos that tell a bigger story, for YouTube first release. The globally rare initiative was conceived by Kristen Bowen, now Head of Global Activation – FameBit at YouTube's San Bruno, California headquarters; Mike Cowap, a former UK Film Council Shorts coordinator; and Felicity McVay, former Head of Content Partnerships for YouTube, Australia/New Zealand. In his roles, Cowap financed and managed four Emmy-winning and one Oscar-winning project. Skip Ahead represents a natural experiment in how creativity and storytelling-based careers are adapting, or failing to adapt, at best practice level, to digital disruption in our 'platform society' (Van Dijck & Poell, 2015, p. 1).

This book is for those seeking the lessons from the creative journeys and struggles of the veteran YouTubers, established TV producers, and film & TV school graduates whose trajectories I track. Here I show, for the first time in detail, how they rejected the traditional routes to a screen career as no longer fit for purpose, and whose narratives are exhausted culturally, to leverage YouTube. Edgy web-series and high YouTube views were leveraged to break into where contemporary screen storytelling is often most authentic, progressive, and diverse: broadcast video-on-demand (BVOD) and subscription video-on-demand

(SVOD) services in Australia and North America (Healy, 2019, p. 116). Indeed, the first lesson was the tendency for more Skip Ahead creators to pursue longer formats off YouTube where they started – particularly among these hybrid VOD services – the longer they are exposed to algorithmic volatility on the endemically short-form YouTube. Where these exceptional web-series were created, they acted as an adaptive genre able to show craft and storytelling skills sufficient to secure license deals with BVODs and SVODs, and thus effect a transition to sustainable creative labour. This investigation has lessons globally for how new and old media can come together for contemporary storytelling.

Cunningham and Craig (2019, p. 200) argue social media entertainers (SME), YouTubers, are engaged in subcultural appropriation from the margins to the mainstream: '(SME) creators are like the punk musicians, if they owned their clubs and released their music on their own record labels'. Similarly, Robert Kyncl, YouTube's chief business officer, describes YouTube's mostly shortform personalities and performers as 'streampunks'. The nine cases in this book reveal the world of the streampunk storytellers, their career trajectories, and the strategies and choices they made to produce, in most cases, shortform episodic web-series with views ranging from the millions to the scores of millions, up to 170 million (*Starting from Now*, Chapter 7). These 'streampunk' storytellers – some of whom started as big personalities and performers – have stolen a march on legions of their peers. But their lessons were hard-won: they shed blood, sweat, and tears on their journeys in pursuit of their creative visions. Many waited years for traditional TV gatekeepers to greenlight their productions in the hope of breaking into a TV industry they rejected anyway as not speaking to their cultural identities in authentic ways. Many – such as Taylor Litton-Strain and Erin Good, and Tina Cesa Ward – first made numerous short films, before turning to the exceptional web-series to supersede their peers, and fulfil their passion projects among the BVODs and SVODs that exemplify post-broadcast TV. In just the space of a decade, the web-series has been reframed from professionally damaging to highly desirable, 'almost hot', Tina Cesa Ward, chair of the International Academy of WebTV (IAWTV) and co-creator, *Anyone But Me* (2008–2012; 2019) (100 million views), told me (Ward, 2019). Single episodes of web-series featured in the cases, for example, Julie Kalceff's (*Starting from Now*; 2014–2016) (pictured 1.2), and Ward's *Anyone But Me*, have each alone attracted almost 40 million and 20 million views, respectively[1]. These makers are cultural forces to be reckoned with.

For 100 years creative professionals have wanted to create and own their own IP, but have fallen short (Christian, 2018, p. 157). Unlike those still using short films few ever see, or making 'calling card' scripts that are usually never made (Ashton, 2011, p. 49), or pilots never seen again unless they air (Banks, 2010a, p. 31), or are unpaid (Baujard et al., 2019, p. 71), the teams in these nine cases discovered the web-series to be a hard and fast career shortcut, and intellectual property (IP) generator. Crucially however, equitable IP share still remains contested. The evidence from these cases also shows significant career acceleration

FIGURE 1.2 Marginalized storytellers prove a hit on YouTube: Sarah de Possesse and Rosie Lourde[3] in Starting from Now (SFN) (170 million views) (Chapter 7). This episode alone was viewed almost 40 million times by 2021.

by effective use of multiple social networks, or multiplatform labour for their storytelling (Healy, 2019), on average shaving four years from the usual decade or more to 'break in'. To build sustainable careers, these creators and writer-producers collectively published 1,257 videos to first attract the 'deep niche' attention of 2.35 billion views among themselves on YouTube alone. Then, being in an Australia concerned to protect its own culture, they won modest grants of up to AU$100,000 such as through Google/Screen Australia's Skip Ahead, provided they had 50,000 followers and could pitch a killer narrative to Screen Australia investment managers. This lean and mean subvention meant they could access a combination of Obi Wan-style narrative mentors and the sort of competitive grant scheme that fired up the early Renaissance[2].

Information disorder has made trustworthy storytelling more important than ever. My investigation centres on the unprecedented opportunities represented by YouTube for creative labour beyond what Tarleton Gillespie (2010, p. 358) describes as 'the tidal wave' of shortform user-generated content. I do not condone the dark side unleashed by participation, and advocate algorithm reform to enhance the new capacities of online storytellers to do more of the good creative work they love. The Internet was originally promised to users as 'an Athens without the slaves' and 'an age as golden as that of Greece' (Robins & Webster, 1988, p. 8). I am no such Pollyanna. After five years investigating content on YouTube, my experience instead reflects the observation of Microsoft researcher, danah boyd: 'the internet mirrors and magnifies the good *and* the bad *and* the ugly' (Turner, 2012, p. 180). For example, the performance of dangerous media 'idiocy' (Goriunova, 2012, p. 223), such as Tide Pod challenges, egregious user-generated-content (UGC) videos claiming mass shootings in the United States are staged by 'crisis actors' (Ortutay, 2018), Facebook, Twitter, and YouTube amplifying and 'platforming' racism and hate speech (Matamoros-Fernández, 2017, p. 930), and 'information disorder' generally (Krafft & Donovan, 2020, p. 195). Amazon, Facebook, Google and YouTube have also faced regulatory action over their power asymmetry (Culpepper & Thelen, 2020, p. 293), manifested in their alleged 'take it or leave it' approach to negotiations with smaller businesses. Platforms have addressed these public interests with varying degrees of effectiveness, usually via resistance to state regulation (Culpepper & Thelen, 2020, p. 288). Importantly, Newcomb and Alley (1983, p. 23), who interviewed US TV producers of the 1970s Golden era of TV, argue the best fictional TV storytelling has a special 'liminal' or reflexive quality that promotes the sorts of imagination and cognition in participants necessary for 'cultural survival', and even renewal. Addressing the dark side of participation is beyond the scope of this book except in one crucial way: that the rich participatory online communities brought into being by these diverse serial narratives, offer hope of a sorely needed, renewed public sphere to help push back the dark. Skip Ahead mentor, and Emmy-nominated script editor Mike Jones, suggests episodic storytelling – by virtue of the gaps they open up in the narrative – allow for immersion and 'cognitive processing'.[4] As JS Mill reminds us in *On Liberty* (1885), exposure to countervailing opinions greatly benefits the human race via 'the clearer perception and livelier impression of truth' (Riley, 2003, p. 57).

Ironically, given YouTube's reputation for the quotidian and demotic, storytelling has been reinvigorated by creatorship on parts of YouTube, by being made more diverse and authentic. A new breed of hybrid creators is drawing on ancient and folkloric traditions of audience participation in a phenomenon which parallels to Gutenberg's invention of the printing press almost 600 years ago[5]. This is a bold claim. Storytelling is regarded as a defining characteristic of humans, originally developed as a strategy to 'sustain a sense of agency in the face of disempowering circumstances' (Maggio, 2014, p. 92), convey essential information about the 'environment, behaviour of wildlife and the availability of food', and 'shape and form [human] experience' (Miller, 2014, p. 4). Digital storytelling predates the rise of social media platforms and was developed as a way for ordinary people to use computer tools to cease having professional media 'done to' them, and instead take 'the power (of storytelling) back' (Meadows, 2003, p. 192).

Importantly, YouTube users have evolved the platform into a creative primal soup. In post-industrial economies, innovation stemming from the mediated interactions of people and rapidly advancing socio-technologies, for example YouTube, are best understood as 'co-evolution' (Potts et al., 2008, p. 183). However, the originator of cyberpunk fiction, and the term 'cyberspace', William Gibson, captured this innovative process best '...the street finds its own uses for things' (*Burning Chrome* 1986, p. 199). Similarly, YouTube's now ubiquitous socio-technological infrastructure originally began as a failed dating app, but its video-sharing affordances are now so prized, and so vast, it must be run by two deep neural networks or AI (Covington et al., 2016, p. 192). This socio-technology is nevertheless 'hackable' or simply 'useable' enough (Burgess & Green, 2018, p. 100), to be adapted by ordinary folk in culturally significant, but unexpected ways. For cultural anthropologist, Michael Wesch (2010), YouTube enabled the revolutionary moment of 'universal film-making' where 'millions of little cameras have been linked together for the first time in history'. Indeed, Gibson's point was later echoed by YouTube's Kyncl, who said: 'it's an open platform, a lot of things happen in an unexpected manner…Ultimately, YouTube will become what its users want it to be. It's not really us deciding in the end' (Shields, 2017).

Yet, YouTube is poorly resourced for longer form, independent projects despite being among the best resourced of all media, social or otherwise. YouTube generated US$15 billion in annual ad revenue in 2019 (Alphabet, 2020), the legacy of the platform offering 'one of the oldest monetization schemes': its Partner program dates to 2007 (Kopf, 2020, p. 1). YouTube offers creators a 55/45 per cent split of ad revenue in favour of creators (Calacanis, 2013), a major motive force continuing to drive disruption to film and TV. YouTube is arguably the most innovative of the platforms, given its role in accelerating Netflix's pivot to streaming (Kyncl, 2017). YouTube is also richest in the most precious resource in the platform society: people's attention. With 70 per cent of the attention people spent on their phones watching the top five entertainment apps in 2019, YouTube is characterized as the 'frontrunner in the mobile streaming wars', far ahead of even China-based Tencent News, or the world's biggest SVOD, Netflix (Alexander, 2020). Nevertheless, in the nine cases in this book, I show how the much-critiqued algorithmic culture of YouTube (Gillespie, 2010, p. 358; Napoli, 2013, p. 10; Striphas, 2015, p. 395) – while often severely stressing many creators – paradoxically stimulated novel experimentation that better captured the zeitgeist. Principally a new co-creative, audience-centric, networked video production methodology that enabled publication of diverse, authentic stories to where hundreds of millions of viewers have fragmented to: in deep niches globally online. Difficult to be inauthentic when the online community you have built from zero is effectively present – via channel comment streams – during production.

I introduce the metaphor of the 'garden in the machine' to best capture two aspects of this newly adapted style of storytelling in algorithmic culture. When Postigo (2016, p. 333) was categorizing the nature of the digital labour of gameplay commentators on YouTube, he likened conditions to the 'machine in the garden': as commentators and channels use the platform's affordances to make a living, and their channels rise and fall, and are replaced by other hopefuls, YouTube's machine-like architecture – like the casino – always 'gets its share of the cash'. However, my deep dive among the platform's digital storytellers yielded two distinct new themes: first, crossover publication success based upon collaboration with like-minded creatives across the cultural, and often generational, divides.

As multi-Emmy-winning US web-series creator James Bland learnt after his first season of web-series crossover, *Giants* (2017–): 'If you want to go fast, go alone. If you want to go far, go together' (Ifeanyi, 2018). Second is a creator-led revival of audience participation in cultural production, I liken to that Peter Arnott (1989, p. 11) has described of ancient Greek theatre audiences. For example, Arnott says historical evidence points to these audiences being 'talkative and unruly', indeed 'participatory': 'the public was an active partner, free to comment, to be commented upon, to assist or to intervene', even reciting the lines of popular plays from memory when the memories of actors failed them. Based on these themes arising from the nine cases, I argue the assemblage of cheap, increasingly miniaturized video cameras and the YouTube algorithms, can be likened to Gutenberg's printing presses in two main ways: first, Gutenberg intended the press for one purpose, to homogenize the Catholic missal so he could sell more religious trinkets, but the powerful new technology was adapted by printers across Europe for their own individual publication interests (Epstein, 2008, p. 8). Second, the press led to a 'flood' of publication of classical texts and cross-cultural translations in the form of cheap books (Abel, 2011, p. 77), and thus the clash of ideas that drive innovation (Csikszentmihalyi, 2014, p. 107).

This book uncovers and shows the role of active audiences, web-series fans making reaction, and tribute videos, in enhancing creator and writer-producer sustainability. This evidence suggests lingering scepticism (Napoli, 2016, p. 342; Duffy et al., 2019, p. 4) towards Anderson's (2004) important new media theory of the long tail – which promised a democratization and diversification of

FIGURE 1.3 Prefiguring Tik Tok: YGmoA, a 2015 reaction video itself seen over 21 million times, radically spreading SketchSHE's original Mime through Time meme

cultural production – needs re-evaluation. For example, YGmoA's *Mime Through Time (Japanese ver.)* pictured above is a SketchSHE fan video, itself seen 21 million times since 2015. Prefiguring one of the biggest new youth apps of 2019, the lip-syncing Tik Tok, I argue these SketchSHE fans were 'writing themselves' into the *Mime Through Time* super-meme, for the aesthetic pleasures of collaboration, for monetization, skills acquisition, and peer recognition, and in the process, rising up the long tail of YouTube channel small businesses worldwide. Crucially, ethnic, cognitive, and cultural diversity has been strongly associated with the clash of ideas that can drive productive creativity (Higgs et al., 2008, p. 25), intercultural connections (Podkalicka, 2008, p. 332), cultural evolution (Csikszentmihalyi, 2014, p. 107), and political participation and citizenship (Burgess & Green, 2018, p. 124). The cultural power of this new source of trained and diverse creators cannot be over-estimated.

Hollywood

Traditionally, for screen storytellers, careers were exemplified by the paradigm defined by Joseph Conrad, the Polish-English author best known for *Heart of Darkness* (1899): 'Art is long, life is short, and success very far off'. Creatives aspiring to excellence and glory looked to Hollywood, but had to fight their way up through gatekeepers, and routinely compromise, in often egregious ways, during the career climb. Denise Bielby and William Bielby (2002, p. 21) describe Hollywood as the cultural system that has dominated production and reflected and shaped mass culture globally for 80 years. But 'young White men' wrote about three-fourths of the film and TV scripts. For Sullivan (2009, p. 46), Hollywood was best understood via sociologist Leo Rosten's conception of three concentric rings: tens of thousands of movie-workers; 'the colony' of thousands of above-the-line actors, producers and directors; and at the pinnacle of cultural and financial power and prestige, 'the movie elite, some 250 persons'. For film authority David Thomson, Hollywood produced three of the world's six most 'profound' cinematic works of art: Orson Welles's *Citizen Kane* (1941) and *The Magnificent Ambersons* (1942), and David Lynch's *Mulholland Drive* (2001). For Thomson (2012, p. 12), films represented an improved version of reality, where the medium's ultimate core was 'a way of realizing desire on the big screen'. But the price for creatives trying to make a living was high. Caldwell (2013, p. 162) characterized the industry as racialized, sexualized, gendered, and 'aesthetically salaried'. His fieldwork revealed a paradox: despite showing the industry was 'alienating, stressful and exploitative', hopefuls still flocked to Hollywood's gates. Younger workers especially were underpaid, underemployed, and 'paid' via a 'symbolic payroll systems' that allowed workers to 'stylize their public personas with trappings of artistry or legitimacy'. By 2016, the landmark University of Southern California Annenberg report on diversity in entertainment, concluded Hollywood still operated as a 'straight, White boys club' that marginalized women, ethnic, racial and sexual minorities, especially in decisive above-the-line production roles (Smith et al., 2016, p. 16). By 2019, Oscar- and multi-Golden Globe-winning director Martin Scorsese likened Hollywood's highest profile output, the Marvel cinematic universe, to 'theme-parks. It isn't the cinema of human beings trying to convey emotional, psychological experiences to another human being' (De Semlyen, 2019).

Silicon Valley

A day's drive north of Southern California's Hollywood, lies Silicon Valley near San Francisco in Northern California. Manuel Castells (2010, p. 5) credits Silicon Valley with ushering in a new technological paradigm in the 1970s, the information technology revolution, the most successful companies of which drove the formation of today's network society, reshaping global social organization and practice. For Alice Marwick (2018, p. 314), Silicon Valley is the 'global centre for venture-backed technology start-ups', the culture of 'disruption and innovation' of which gave rise to social media companies such as Twitter, Facebook, Pinterest, Snapchat, Reddit, YouTube, Instagram, and Tumblr. In contrast to the premium talent, longform narrative, and IP rights protection model of Hollywood, social networks are based in 'user-generated content, peer-production marketplaces, collaboratively generated information and datafication', the model for today's most successful start-ups (Marwick, 2018, p. 314). Indeed, YouTube founders, Chad Hurley, Steve Chen, and Jawed Karim conceived the social network at Hurley's Menlo Park, California home in 2005, developing the software to more easily share digital home videos (Keith, 2007), especially for content shot on mobile phones, and as a catalyst for online connections such as dating (Burgess & Green, 2018, p. 3). Consequently, Cunningham and Craig (2019, p. 4) argue a power shift occurred as a set of newly prominent online screen entertainment platforms, pre-eminently Alphabet/Google/YouTube, but also Apple, Amazon, and Netflix have increasingly represented a greater value proposition to the advertising industry, which has bankrolled TV since early last century. During 2021, venture capital firms had reportedly invested $US2 billion into '50 creator-focused start-ups' (Lorenz & Woo, 2021).

But business models using YouTube for community-building, monetization, and the quest for labour sustainability are only 12 years old. For example, the first indie artist to break through on the platform was Portuguese singer/songwriter Mia Rose in 2007–2008, followed by then unknown teen guitarist, Justin Bieber (Burgess & Green, 2018, p. 33, 85). Around this time in Australia, the Van Vuuren brothers, who would go onto create the longform *Bondi Hipsters* and *SoulMates* for the ABC, and the Skip Ahead-funded, Canneseries-winning web-series, *Over & Out*, first broke out on YouTube with the viral, *Fully Sick Rapper*. However, most YouTube videos are under four minutes (Cheng et al., 2013, p. 1186). Crucially, YouTube industry leader Hank Green suggests narrative 'has been nearly impossible to make work' (Cunningham & Craig, 2019, p. 148).

Meanwhile, in the shadows of cyberspace, the very first web-festivals emerged, still an unattached fraction of the dominant 6000-strong film festival circuit, but growing dramatically each decade. First was AOL's The Webby's of the mid-1990s. During the 2000s, the festivals and awards grew to three: the Indigenous Canadian Reelworld WebFest (RWF) in 2002; the Writers Guild of America's award for new media following the 2007 strike; and the Tubefilter and the International Academy of Web TV's Streamy's of 2009. The 2010s saw the rise of 14 webfests mainly in Europe, the Americas, Australia, Russia, and the most recently the United Kingdom. The first meeting of a dozen webfests, Festival Forward hosted by Canada's Dr Emilia King and Dan Speerin, occurred in early 2021, represented the avant garde of indie streaming. Nine festival directors attended via zoom to take stock of the fallout from the pandemic, and in generous public spirit, contribute to a new Australian Research Council-led longitudinal project on the web-series, to which this author contributes. Among the directors, there was general agreement producers had to be inventive to adapt to endemically low-budget packages; they had low visibility; online audiences did not want to pay for web-series; and there was a tendency for makers to hold a too-hopeful belief a distributor would lift them from the shadows, and commission a second series. However, the discussion showed just how vibrant and generative these volunteer festivals had become. Different festivals emphasized parallel missions of craft, talent, and business model development; the generation of IP in their series; their challenge to traditional structure; and their role as a 'freedom island' in helping marginalized communities find their voices. Significantly though, most festivals limited series entries to 20 minutes, preferably 12 or even just 6 minutes, to make awards selection manageable on judges. Overall, the view of the directors was immediate, direct financial returns are rarely there, but down the line, web-series potentially do a lot for creators' careers.

FIGURE 1.4 Indie film-maker Theo Saidden aka SuperWog uses cheaper, lightweight networked video technologies to get closer to their audiences online

Cable, and the rise of over-the-top (OTT) streaming services

Meanwhile, by contrast, quality longform storytelling – especially the serial narrative pioneered by Charles Dickens' serialization of *Great Expectations* (1861) – was occurring in one of the most surprising places: the former backwaters of American cable TV. Perren (2011, p. 138) traces the rise of paradigm-definers, HBO's *Oz* (1997–2003), *The Sopranos* (1997–2007), and Showtime's *Queer as Folk* (2000–2005), *The L-Word* (2004–2009), to this 'explicit', non-family-friendly originality in programming. Cable, which morphed into digital cable and the backbone supporting the present-day OTT streamers, offered writers 'greater creative autonomy, and minimal executive interference'. Crucially, in what is still a touchstone motivation for the creators in my nine cases, this tradition of creative latitude continues to pervade these hybrid digital outlets. Lotz (2018, p. 38) has shown how the most scrappy but innovative US cable TV outlets – HBO, Showtime, USA, FX, and AMC – upset the four-decade dominance of US broadcast networks, via a renewed focus on 'distinctiveness'. Distinctiveness, especially in the form of gritty, psychologically layered characters, attracted the news media 'buzz' required to cut through in the increasingly hyper-technologized, hyper-saturated media ecology, what Richard Lanham (2006) describes as the 'economy of attention' of the Internet. Consequently, what some regard as the latest Golden Age of TV Drama[6] was ushered in by the niche success of character-driven series such as HBO's *Sex in the City* (1998–2004) and *The Wire* (2002–2008). In 2013, the investment of $100 million by Netflix in *House of Cards*, made it 'the first web-based series' to win an Emmy (Ellingsen, 2014, p. 107). By 2017, the TV business – long regarded as a 'cultural wasteland' (Minow, 2003) – was producing record numbers of scripted series, a surprising number of which were 'excellent, and artistically ambitious shows', according to FX Networks chief executive, John Landgraf (Lotz, 2018, p. 11). This new rewarding of creative autonomy by the streamers quickly attracted the interest of creatives internationally. In Australia, one of the directors who put the country on the world stage, Gillian Armstrong (*My Brilliant Career, Last Days of Chez Nous, Oscar and Lucinda*), told the story of a colleague who went onto write and produce *Homeland* (2011–2020) for Showtime. In recruiting Ron Nyswaner, Armstrong said Showtime told Nyswaner: 'We want you to write something you really believe in: to go out on the line and be as brave as you want' (Donald, 2017, p. 111). For Landgraf, now is one of those rare periods where some platforms support artists 'to be truly brave, to resolutely follow their Muses in pursuit of Truth and Beauty'.

Hybridity

Hybridity – the offspring of different antecedents – explains the contending, generative, and adverse forces driving the evolution of mass media over recent decades. For Yochai Benkler (2006, p. 57), a hybrid media ecology has arisen as the participatory 'networked information ecology' has appropriated for its own ends the exclusive rights-protected content of the 'industrial information economy', the latter represented by Hollywood and the recording industry. For Henry Jenkins and Mark Deuze (2008, p. 9), networks like YouTube – where 'some videos themselves develop cult followings getting referenced through mainstream media' – are corporately created 'hybrid spaces' where 'grassroots media makers' share their creations with peers. Lawrence Lessig (2008, p. 205) observed a 'collaborative hybridity' as Hollywood slowly included audiences 'in the process of building, spreading and remaking its product', but 'the story is not always pretty'. In Australia, 'hybrids' emerged as broadcasters combined appointment-based and stored media features through 'catch-up' streaming services (Screen Australia, 2012, p. 2). In the United Kingdom, Mark Banks (2010b, p. 315) described workforces as increasing 'hybrid': lightweight video technologies had led to the specializations of 'writing, directing, camera work, editing and promotion for distribution', being performed by the one 'all-rounder'. This all-rounder was attractive to capital, but Banks argues the 'downside is a weakening of accumulated knowledge [as] there are few mechanisms for sharing and spreading expertise'. For Caldwell (2016, p. 35), 'hybrid forms of imaginative/economic speculation', such as web-series, are part of the 'deregulated creative labour herd', which TV industries seek to exploit and monetize. For Cunningham and Craig (2019, p. 22), YouTube represents hybridity writ large, the 'interdependent clash of two world-leading industrial cultures': the old school of Hollywood in Southern California (So-Cal) and the entrepreneurialism of Silicon Valley in Northern California (No-Cal). Indeed, as Eurovision Australia producer, Byran Moses told me:

> An eye-opening moment was to see the YouTube Space in LA pushing towards a traditional old school: a huge studio set, pre-built sets, great camera gear. YouTube is trying to disrupt the mainstream market and help its content creators produce more professional quality content. YouTube is pushing to be the future of content.
>
> *Moses, 2018*

Drawing these strands of Hollywood, YouTube, and the streamers together, I argue the essentials from each tradition are expressed in the hybrid format of some of the biggest and most transnational web-series to date. From Hollywood, social media entertainment (SME), draws on the core skills of acting, screenwriting and directing (Cunningham & Craig, 2019, p. 104), in turn, key web-series skillsets. From YouTube, successful creators learn algorithmic traction via Audience Growth Hacking, by understanding the very human – rather than merely instrumental – aspects of what motivates people to share creators' content widely. From the streamers, web-series makers pursue the all-important creative autonomy won by proven audience-builders, especially where they draw on diverse heritages to tell distinctive and authentic stories. Indeed, The Verge reported preeminent streamer HBO considered the social-media born web-series as 'the new

TV pilot', which for creators, represented 'a step towards the majors for this age of Peak TV'. HBO executive, Amy Gravitt, says web-series distinguish themselves from merely 'reading scripts', since the creators have 'the ability to go one step further than the page in conveying their tone' (Liao, 2017).

Five burning problems

In their drive to have their stories heard internationally – necessary to make a living since views alone usually pay so poorly – the creators and writer-producers in these nine cases went a long way to solving the problems bedevilling YouTube creators and TV producers alike.

Lack of monetization

Creators and TV producers who want to adapt faster to the new screen ecology are caught between a rock and a hard place. The lack of monetization of digital content is seen as the screen industry's 'most pressing problem' (Judah, 2015, p. 123), a challenge entwined with the sustainability of their labour itself. Indeed, the cases show lack of monetization has resulted in a distinctive, accelerated tempo of production that TV producer, Julie Byrne, in Chapter 4 on RackaRacka dubs 'fast and furious film-making' (Byrne, 2017). On YouTube, any effective creator must also deal with the platform's tendency to change rapidly and unpredictably, especially for the worse, over time. The period I consider is one especially marked by algorithmic volatility, and thus ever fluctuating platform-derived creator income. YouTube has adopted the mainstream advertising industry standard of Clicks Per Mille (CPM), where Mille is French for thousand. These CPMs have fluctuated from a healthy $7.60 in 2013 (Gutelle, 2014), but collapsed to $2 in 2015 (Dredge, 2015), although views from the Global South are not rewarded as well as those from the Global North (Britton, 2014). During the COVID-19 pandemic, and heightened screen consumption during shelter-in-place in the United States, CPMs varied from $4, to as high as almost $8 for some US creators (Weiss, 2020). Successful YouTube creators learn to deal with volatility via lucrative brand deals, but the commercial strings attached to deals means they do not work for most storytellers.

Volatility of algorithmic culture

Inside 'the black box'

Online creator precariousness is exacerbated by the socio-technological assemblage of the maths-based sets of codes, or algorithms, constituting the YouTube Recommender. The Recommender generates over 70 per cent of total platform views, estimated at 700 million hours of human attention daily (Algotransparency, 2019). Increasingly, scholarly and creator discourse has rightly focused on the 'shadowy', 'black box' nature of the YouTube algorithms (Bishop, 2018, p. 71; Burgess & Green, 2018; Cunningham & Craig, 2019, p. 103; Brevini & Pasquale, 2020, p. 1, p. 120). However, the argument in this book about the generative, but stressing role of algorithms on online creative labour, is based on explanations from Google software engineers, explanations unused by previous researchers. We now know from Google engineers' rights to publish their research on Google's AI blog, the Recommender is built on 'collaborative filtering' (Covington et al., 2016, p. 192). This filtering instantaneously matches a user's deep data history with a small corpus of hundreds of videos preferred by a demographically like-minded set of users, to rank and ultimately recommend a handful of videos tailored to the user. Crucially, these algorithms privilege 'fresh' content, and 'bootstrap and propagate viral content' (Covington et al., 2016, p. 193), a fact essential for better understanding the assemblage governing algorithmic traction, and thus the fate on which a video rises or falls and is monetized. The evidence from the cases shows this 'collaborative filtering' principle undergirds one of the five[7] key skillsets needed to succeed in the new hybrid screen ecology: Audience Growth Hacking. The Silicon Valley concept of 'growth hacking' was first promoted by former Dropbox marketer Sean Ellis. For Ellis, growth hacking is not platform instrument-driven, but traditional word-of-mouth virality based on 'making the experience of sharing the product with others must-have' (Ellis & Brown, 2017). Justifiably, Google machine intelligence designer Paul Covington et al. (2016, p. 191) describes the Recommender as 'one of the largest scale and most sophisticated industrial recommendation systems in existence'. The sheer anthropomorphic labour[8] involved in winnowing down billions of hours of video to the few instantaneously recommended to individual YouTube users' screens is so vast it must be run by two deep neural networks, or AI: Candidate Generation and Ranking (Covington et al., 2016, p. 192).

Many of the creators in the following nine cases launched their channels during the formative days of YouTube – some as early as 2006, the year Google bought it. Consequently, they have all have experienced at least two major YouTube algorithm changes, while four have experienced the most notable four algorithm changes: changes to promote older viral videos in 2016 (Alexander, 2019, p. 4; Cox, 2016); the brand safety reforms known as the 'Adpocalypse' of 2017 (Pottinger, 2018); and the subscription feed change in 2018 (Fox, 2018). Additionally, we will see in the SME-based stories how the algorithms prioritize new, trending, copied, collated, and controversial content, which clashes with creators' innate drive to originality and edginess. As YouTube veteran Ann Reardon wryly observes in Chapter 5: 'YouTube gets what it rewards'.

Divide between old and new media

Industry professionals are sceptical about the benefits of YouTube as either art or sustenance, and rightly so. An industrial rift between professional labour and new media workers drives a deep cultural divide where at the level of professional livelihoods, the stakes are existential. Importantly, younger producers and new media creators consistently report feeling blocked in finding people to share jealously guarded industry know-how (Cameron et al., 2010, p. 93; Ryan et al., 2012). Moreover, this blockage is occurring as traditional mentoring and expertise-sharing mechanisms had broken down during 'craft disaggregation' (Banks, 2010b, p. 315; Caldwell, 2010, p. 222). In Australia, producer surveys highlight a significant, systemic knowledge transfer blockage, especially for those under 45. Regarding how professional labour is faring, the scholarship also emphasizes the collision of traditional craft, with its existential enemy, speed, but also resistance: some creators taking the time to do good creative work for its own sake. Craft as a traditional industrial labour input must cope with the capitalist mode of production based on speed, argues Mark Banks (2010b, p. 314). For Neff et al. (2005, p. 309), the costs of craft acquisition and mastery of technology in 'cool jobs' in hot media industries were shifted to workers' own time, with an emphasis on individual, rather than craft skills. For Banks (2010b), as production moved from workshops to laptops, craft in film and TV production became obsolete. Caldwell (2010, p. 222) contends as professional craft groups and labour conditions were 'disaggregated' by digitization, the traditional mentoring maintaining 'proficient, collective, creative knowledge', was also disrupted. Moreover, the traditional ways of 'distributing cognition and creativity across groups of workers and crews' had become 'confused'.

Yet, mastery of craft is considered crucial to the optimal creator experience, especially the sacrosanct concept of 'flow'. According to Csikszentmihalyi (2014, p. 173), 'the optimal feeling of flow' is the motivation driving creativity. From his years of observations of artists and scientists, including a dozen Nobel winners, Csikszentmihalyi coined the term 'flow' to describe the feeling people report when 'skills become so second nature that everything one does seems to come naturally, and when concentration is so intense that one loses track of time'. Where artists traditionally operated in analogue environments with the same 'ethos of other craftsmen to do the work well for its own sake' (Sennett, 2008, p. 12), now creatives seeking flow must adapt to this networked, algorithmic environment. As YouTube's Kyncl, says, 'this is an incredibly fast-moving world. The amount of things that happen on YouTube and the amount of work we have to get done in a year … it's like dog years' (Hale, 2018).

The A List/B List problem

Fourth, Caves (2003, p. 80) identified one of the bedrock principles of the creative industries, the 'A list/B list property', to explain the great range of artists' earnings, and the 'legendary riches' of superstars. Cunningham and Flew (2019, p. 3) describe as A/B list as 'the wildly successful few and the many getting by or struggling'. The problem is notorious on YouTube. The role of influencers in the attention economy was defined by Bärtl (2018, p. 16), who found most views (85 per cent), go to a fraction – just 3 per cent – of channels. As Kyncl writes in his

book, *Streampunks: YouTube and the Rebels Remaking Media* (2017, p. 144) companies such as YouTube, and popular crowdfunding platform Patreon, are 'creating
a space between superstardom and obscurity that allows people to thrive, even if
they don't find stratospheric success'. This is a truly laudable goal and stands to
make a real difference to the prospect of middle-class creative careers, especially,
if, as Piketty (2013, 1) argues, global wealth inequality continues to deepen, as
'seems quite likely' in the 21st century. In Australia at the top level, 100 creators
with revenue-sharing deals with YouTube earned more than A$100,000 in 2017
(Cooley, 2018). These creators are concentrated in highly popular verticals or
genres such as children's entertainment.

Discrimination and lack of authenticity

Just as important as the Muses, are whose stories get told, who tells them and
how. The fifth and final burning problem, the lack of diversity in high-profile
and popular screen storytelling, is epitomized by the social media fuelled backlashes of #OscarsSoWhite and #BAFTASoWhite. These controversies were
driven by back-to-back all-white acting nominations for the 2015 and 2016
Oscars, and all White acting nominations, and no female director nominations
since 2013, for the English equivalent, the BAFTAs (Bushby, 2020; Vary, 2020).
Diversity and inclusion in decision-making is considered important on two
grounds, one moral the other pragmatic: first, the basic fairness of empowering
all people, regardless of background, to reach their full potential, an attribute classically known as 'human flourishing'. To highlight the stakes involved,
Bourdieu (2001, p. 245) draws on Bishop George Berkeley, who said 'to be, is
to be perceived'. Second, to leverage the generative power of the differing perspectives that arise in diverse, inclusive workplaces (Roberson, 2006, p. 234).
In this regard, the 10 major US media companies 'failed on their film scores',
but, by contrast, their TV/digital scorecards were positive on inclusivity (Smith
et al., 2016, p. 15). Walt Disney and The CW Network were 'top performers'
in representing women and underrepresented characters on screen, and for balanced hiring practices for writers and show creators. Hulu and Amazon 'performed strongly' due to inclusivity of women, with Amazon the only company
rated fully inclusive for hiring female directors. Regarding the potential for more
authentic voices being heard in popular culture, two of these majors, Disney and
Warner Bros, also acquired two YouTube-focused production businesses that
emerged from the primal soup of YouTube, Maker Studios and Machinima in
2014 and 2016, respectively.

The lay of the land

I situate myself within the following five key debates. From a scholarly perspective, this book shows the momentous shifts in the behaviour of younger
audiences, the increasing volatility of platform governance, the heightened

collaborative nature of creative labour within algorithmic culture, and greater content diversity led by a thoroughly diverse range of storytellers.

Disrupted screen labour

Unhappily, John Caldwell (2016, p. 46) indicts the web-series as a 'self-defeating labour practice' that undercuts traditional craft labour. Caldwell was most concerned contemporary screen labour had devolved into a blended system of three warring labour regimes: the traditional 'craft world' of film and television; the 'brand world' of high-concept features and reality TV; and the 'spec world' of external IP harvesting, where 'indies learn ever more sophisticated ways to give it (IP) away for free', such as beta-web-series. Moreover, this blockage is occurring as traditional mentoring and expertise-sharing mechanisms had broken down during 'craft disaggregation' (Banks, 2010b, p. 316; Caldwell, 2010, p. 222). For Caldwell (2016, p. 38) 'old media labour somehow keeps adapting to new-media technologies even as new-media entrants disrupt the resulting blended media labour field'. The nine cases reveal the 'somehow'.

Conditions of precarious labour

Tiziana Terranova (2000) is best known for originally interrogating the nature of 'free labour' online and then the making of websites, the compiling of mailing lists, and the development of open-source software. For Terranova (2000, p. 3), what was most striking was the ambivalence about the uses to which ordinary users and corporate actors put 'free labour': did it retain the tradition of the Internet 'gift economy', based upon the 'interactive creativity' of ordinary users, or was this free labour appropriated by late-stage capitalism for its own commercial imperatives? The informed view in broadcast TV at the time was no-one thought online content could be profitable (Kramer in Caldwell, 2004, p. 41). Political economy scholars, Murdock and Golding, propose a schema of how the world's economies are constituted by the tripartite economies of commodities, public goods and gifting and collaboration. Significantly, Murdock and Golding (2016, p. 765) argue the burgeoning of the Internet 'has drawn renewed attention to the third cultural economy of gifting and collaboration'. Their schema is tested for relevance against diverse revenue streams of the teams in the nine cases. The compelling and positive result of the test will be of interest to creative industries lecturers concerned for the precariousness awaiting graduates.

Convergence

Jenkins and Deuze (2008, p. 7) characterize the convergence of traditional media and the power of bottom-up consumers demanding recognition in cultural production as a 'collision' of sometimes aligned, and sometimes warring, interests. The technological shift has driven media convergence across technologies, industries, markets, genres, audiences, appliances, fandoms, and even 'the brain of the consumer', contends Jenkins (2004, p. 34). However, rather than the transition to convergence playing out as 'a fully integrated system', Jenkins argues it is a 'kind of kludge – a jerry-rigged relationship' between technologies. Moreover, von Rimscha et al. (2018, p. 265) report, at the media production level, that convergence is resisted as an extra burden by staff. Moreover, 'truly converged production processes do not seem to exist, let alone converged processes that would raise the chances for success in the media market'. Contrastingly, this book reveals a majority of the web-series made with cross-cultural, cross-generational 'two-way mentoring' proved effective in crossing talent and storyworlds over to BVODs and SVODs (Appendix 1). Overall, the nine cases suggest the 'rock band' model is the best defence against the hostile ecology of networked video.

Authenticity

Jean Burgess (2006), who wrote *YouTube* (2009), was originally best known for her ethnographic and observational work within the social movement of 'ordinary', untutored people turning to the new communications technologies of the late 20th century for digital storytelling. These user-led short autobiographical films could be streamed on the web or broadcast on television and were found to be 'deeply felt, poignant and gently humorous' and concerned the serious business of human experience: life, loss, belonging, hope for the future, friendship and love'. The 'vernacular creativity' of this storytelling possessed a surprising agency, 'power of social connection' and 'authentic self-expression'. In her book *AuthenticTM*, Banet-Weiser heads a chapter, 'Clamouring for Authenticity'. Banet-Weiser (2012) argues the notion of authenticity – debated passionately for millennia no less than now – remains integral to how individuals organize their lives and shape themselves: 'Moreover, in a culture increasingly understood and experienced through the logics and strategies of commercial branding and in a culture characterized by postmodern styles of irony, parody and the superficial, the concept of authenticity seems to carry even *more* weight, not less'. The nine cases exemplify grass-roots authenticity.

Social network markets

Jason Potts and colleagues (2008, p. 169) proposed a new definition of creative industries to better recognize the webification of creative and cultural industries, traditionally defined by the creative nature of inputs, and the IP nature of outputs. Instead of traditional incentives driving consumer choices, Potts et al argued that social networks had taken over the organizing role of creative industries. Due to the novelty and uncertainty of creative industries, decisions to produce and consume had become increasingly determined 'by the choice of others' in 'social network markets', replacing the usual price signals. Indeed, Hartley et al. (2015, p. 3) argue for an expansive definition of creative industries as not restricted to elite, trained artists and firms, but encompass, or should encompass 'everyone'. Moreover, this 'everyone' is highly culturally diverse and have their own agency, ingenuity, and inventiveness, which is 'the arbiter of uptake' of any novel content, thus determining whether a piece of content rises or falls. For example, China-based videographer Corndog produced an acclaimed hour-long video co-created with 100 fans and celebrity musicians and bloggers, who contributed to the storyline and post-production. Co-creativity was found to be important to creator sustainability.

Methods

My nine ethnographic-style cases track the creator/producer teams on their obstacle-laden creative journeys at deep level, especially over the past five years. The cases adopt the approach of Bourdieu (2005, p. 32), who urged researchers to understand the domain and field of artists to best understand their texts: 'What were they doing, how were they trained, where did they study, whose pupils were they, who were they writing against, in other words, what was the field in which they were embedded?' As Bourdieu observes, 'to exist in a field – a literary field, an artistic field – is to differentiate oneself'. In the context of the challenge by US technology corporations to Hollywood and TV networks, and the disruptive fallout to production and distribution, my study was initiated by Distinguished Professor Stuart Cunningham's Australian Research Council-funded Discovery Project, *The New Screen Ecology and Innovation in Production and Distribution*. To immerse myself in this new artworld, I attended VidCon, and numerous lunches and dinners and hung out late at awards nights and after-parties and got to know these creators and producers. I did 35 of my own interviews with creators, TV producers, and world-leading web-series creators, seven of them using longitudinal methodology of Hermanowicz (2013). Five of the cases are in Emmy contexts. As suggested by Yin (2009, p. 2), a multi-case approach investigating distinctive circumstances allows for cross-case analysis, essential for deepening analytical insight into 'a broad topic of contemporary interest'. These cases about storytellers are a synthesis of my serial interviews with individual creators and producers at different turning points of their journeys[8], supplemented by trade press, and my new channel data tracing revealed the sophisticated symbolic work the best creators do to cut through on YouTube, a platform now so crowded 82 years equivalent content was uploaded daily in 2019. Finally, I adopted Yin's (2009, p. 156) recommendation that findings from the now longitudinal cases be aggregated into one large word table according to a uniform framework. Overall patterns became immediately apparent: most strikingly the way SME-origin creators in cases 1–4, and professionally trained producers in cases 5–7, fell towards each other's skillsets and converged on hybrid digital outlets such as BVODs and SVODs.

Outcomes

Crucially, internationally, the screen industry literature shows a blockage occurring as traditional mentoring and expertise-sharing mechanisms have broken down, and younger producers and new media creators are stymied in finding people to share jealously guarded industry know-how. Also as established above, the true convergence of screen media production processes is not apparent, let alone supports success. Contrastingly, the core of my five-year investigation has shown the street itself has independently evolved its own elegant solution: 'two-way mentoring' ushered in by rapprochement, enabling both sides to make their marks together. The term 'two-way mentoring' is not my own. Skip Ahead producer, Margie Bryant (*Who Do You Think You Are?* [Australia]), coined the term to characterize her collaboration with YouTuber, Vanessa Hill aka Braincraft, and their *Mutant Menu*, which became PBS Digital's first long-form video in the United States. Moreover, in the context of the post-broadcast era of streaming, former ABC head of comedy, Rick Kalowski, told me the benefits of these informal, intergenerational collaborations between old school TV producers and YouTube creators flow two ways:

> The younger team learns from the more experienced producers the craft involved and creative elements in stepping up from what is often short form to longer form: the realities of dealing with a network, contracting, dealing with [production] notes from a network, the commissioning process at a network.

The more experienced producers learn about the technology younger program and video makers use at a level of mastery. More experienced producers learn just how quickly good things can be made, and possibly ways to make some types of fully scripted programmes in a leaner, more efficient cost-effective way (Kalowski, 2018).

Kalowski himself was a co-writer of *At Home with Julia,* a series that was the most watched Australian scripted comedy series of 2011 and a 2012 Australian Academy of Cinema and Television Arts Awards nominee. The series is now on Hulu. Thus, a major finding from my Skip Ahead study was the phenomenon, whereby TV producers and YouTube creators fell towards each other's skillsets during their productions. Established producers were exposed to the YouTubers' expertise in Audience Growth Hacking, while the YouTubers benefitted from the producers' craft in storytelling. This rapprochement – the establishment or resumption of formal relations between opposing entities is a very important and particularly useful pathway to viability. This finding is set against Cunningham and Craig's (2019, p. 90) investigation of SME, which stresses a lack of rapprochement between the traditional screen industry and SME. Significantly, I found the collapse in the division of labour that characterized the jack-of-all trades YouTube creators saw them gravitate to their desired specializations. Conversely, the professionals, already specialists, had to diversify to accommodate the audience growth hacking demanded of online audience-building. Surprisingly, a theme of deft experimentation with multiple genres, *in the one work,* emerged across the cases. Innovation in genre has become critical to help cut-through the hyper-saturation that characterizes the increasingly dominant paradigm of networked video.

Moreover, for the 19 Skip Ahead teams I tracked, 17 of these web-series, storyworlds, or talents crossed over to BVODs and SVODs – nine of which had established producers or above-the-line creators – including SBS Viceland, ABC iView, Stan, and Foxtel in Australia; Netflix, Discovery Channel, PBS Digital, and YouTube Originals in the United States[9]. Not all rapprochements are necessarily aimed at cross-over. Four collaborations – despite their quality and niche appeal – have recorded no sales yet. Similarly, the Skip Ahead mentors, Emmy-winning Julie Kalceff, Rosie Lourde (Chapter 7), and Emmy-nominated Mike Jones (Chapter 3), and Mike Cowap, published to Netflix, BBC Children's, Hulu, Adult Swim, and broadcasters across Scandinavia. Similarly, of the film school graduates/professionals leveraging YouTube and niche OTTs such as Vimeo in cases 6–9, their web-series crossed over to SBS Viceland in Australia and CBC Gem in Canada and Wilde. TV, Here.TV on Amazon Prime, Hulu, and Amazon Prime in the US. Critically, I found the web-series, where exceptional like these cases, was acting not just as the time-honoured calling card, but the nascent series pilot for the Networked Age. Indeed, Connor Van Vuuren, director of the post-Apocalyptic, Skip Ahead-funded, Canneseries-winning, web-series *Over and Out,* told me having 'a great web-series as proof of concept for a longer-form show' was vital:

> The fact Adele and Christiaan's idea now exists online in a form we are proud of not only helps us to sell it, seeing as tone is so hard to communicate, but it also helps us hang onto a bigger slice of the IP, given it is a pre-existing thing.
>
> *Van Vuuren, 2019*

Internationally, IP rights are the key definitional goal of the creative industries (Cunningham & Flew, 2019, p. 3), rights long sought by writer-producers, and which the highly viewed web-series has put in faster reach. Crucially, Skip Ahead represents an adaptive model for the knowledge transfer so lacking in the traditional industry, cruelling progress to sustainability. Nevertheless, I show in over half the cases herein, they developed licensable IP in their new characters and storyworlds, in a valuable iterative fashion, in these situated domains. Tellingly, as Emmy-nominated Skip Ahead mentor, Mike Jones, observes, writers in both traditional and new media increasingly view 'their central creative IP as not a Plot, or a Character, but rather as the Storyworld from which numerous plots and characters across numerous media may spawn' (Chan, 2012).

Unexpectedly, these nine cases[10] emerged inductively from underrepresented and/or minority backgrounds. The diversity of these YouTube creators is explained via the ubiquity of cheap socio-technologies free of white male gatekeepers and pent-up demand among generations of previ-ously marginalized storytellers. However, through years of experimentation, mentoring by Emmy-winning screenwriters, and sheer persistence, the crea-tors and writer-producers distinguished themselves internationally via critical and/or popular acclaim, three within the context of Emmy-winning pro-duction houses, and one on a multi-Emmy winning web-series. Crucially, unlike short films and calling card scripts, web-series also generate valuable, if modest, IP, which, licensed to streamers, provided revenue to help fund new productions. For example, we see in Chapter 10 how Tina Cesa Ward partly funded *Producing Juliet*, her 11-part web-series about playwright Juliet, from her *ABM* royalties (Ward, 2019). Significantly, the most successful web-series were strategic in their development and distribution, not scattergun. The best web-series built their own online communities as they iterated, avoiding the widespread fatal flaw of simply uploading a series to the hyper-saturated web and expecting an audience to appear magically. Instead, those who pre-build an audience experience a receptive landing, with a BVOD or SVOD sometimes commissioning new seasons from the very best. This belief in the strategic nature of the web-series is sustained in the face of only handfuls of examples of the format operating in this manner in the United States, and my evidence from Australia.

Regarding the precariousness of the intellectual professions, and their loss of autonomy, Bourdieu wrote about the power of advertisers over cultural pro-duction as long ago as the mid-1990s (Benson & Neveu, 2005, p. 42). Crucially for policy-makers and film-school lecturers concerned about the precariousness in store for most media-based graduates, I extend the work of political econ-omists of media, Murdock and Golding (2016, p. 765), to conceptualize the patterns of sustainability I found exemplified in these nine new media cases. Regarding media production, Murdock and Golding (2016, p. 765) argue 'dig-ital capitalism', driven by 'the meta-technology of digitized communications systems', is becoming well integrated into the post-industrial economy at every level. Importantly for sustainability, the growth of the Internet has focused much needed attention on 'gifting and collaboration', one of three cultural economies that sit alongside 'public goods', and the best-known economy of 'commodities' (Murdock & Golding, 2016, p. 764). Significantly, in varying combinations in different parts of the world[11], I found the web-series makers in the following nine cases, especially if they can build extremely large online communities, have developed patterns of sustainability that straddle two, and sometimes even three of these markets. For example, crowdfunding via Patreon and Kickstarter, crowdsourcing, online fan sharing, and fan art falls into Murdock and Golding's cultural economy of 'gifting and collaboration'. In non-US Western economies like the UK, Canada, and Australia, grants pro-grammes run by these countries' screen agencies fall under their cultural econ-omy of public goods. Modest private revenue streams based on license deals with SVODs, income from TVODs such as Apple iTune's, Amazon Prime, and the Vimeo OTT, and AdSense from AVODs such as YouTube and 'angel investment' fall under the market of commodities. If artists really are 'pioneers of the new economy' as McRobbie (2004) suggests, these nine cases suggest workers will increasingly sustain themselves from a mix of these three cultural economies.

Conclusion

The book raises lessons globally. For example, YouTube's Kyncl – who originally worked for HBO and Netflix – says the acquisition of storytelling and show running skillsets is challenging and 'a different kind of enterprise' to YouTube creatorship (Popper, 2015). Kyncl's observation underscores the significance of the adaptive methodology developed by the Skip Aheaders and elaborated in the first five cases herein, which detail their most important struggles and successes. The chapters proceed as follows:

In Chapter 2, I show how veteran YouTuber, Chris Voigt aka SexuaLobster aka Greasy Tales, engaged the generation of Millennials 'lost' to TV, with Absurdism and collaborative online longform writing. Voigt has since abandoned YouTube as a living, working as a storyboarder on Emmy-winning Australian cartoon series*, Bluey*. In Chapter 3, I present the case of the collaboration between SuperWog, the young Saidden brothers, and Paul Walton (actor on *Heartbeat* 1992–2010: unit director, *Touch of Frost* 1992–2010), to produce the hit YouTube-to-ABC crossover web-series, *SuperWog Series Pilot* (9.3 million views). This web-series exemplifies the new paradigm. With an IP-able storyworld and high views, and thus in Silicon-Valley-like terms, 'proof of concept', it was licensed to a BVOD hungry for series to better attract younger generations. In Chapter 4, I present the case of Variety's #7 Famechangers of 2016, RackaRacka, and their collaboration with Emmy award-winning studio, Ludo, and Triptych Pictures, on *Stunt Gone Wrong (Live)*. The edgy 'livestream' drew on creators' insider knowledge of culturally sanctioned platform trickery of YouTube audiences, and was innovative in its edgy comedy-to-gore genre-bending, as well as livestream flipping via pre-shot long-form content. RackaRacka are now collaborating with the makers of one of the most terrifying horror films of 2014, the critically acclaimed, *Babadook*, to make horror film, *Talk to Me*. Stephen King praised *Babadook*. In Chapter 5, I show how the world's #3 online dessert chef, Ann Reardon, used sophisticated symbolic work to cut-through in algorithmic culture and make a sustainable living, and transition to a popular interview-style show with influential socially progressive guests. In Chapter 6, I show how Shae-lee Raven, whose distinctive lip-syncing car videos with SketchSHE were among the most viewed on YouTube at one time, prefiguring Tik Tok, secured the attention of Paramount and Hulu and other major streamers for her web-series and longer form projects. Crucially, however, negotiations broke down over conflicting positions on share of IP (House of Raven, 2020; Shackleford, 2021).

The final four cases present the reverse of the coin: how traditionally trained writer-producers learn to embrace participatory social network markets – to varying degrees – to step up to hybrid platforms in Australia, Europe, and North America. In Chapter 7, one of the world's pre-eminent web-series makers', Julie Kalceff, reveals how she used co-creativity with her under-represented lesbian audiences on YouTube and Facebook, to reshape her narrative arcs to better reflect the desires of her audiences worldwide, authentically, in the aforementioned *SFN*. Kalceff went onto make the now Emmy-winning *First Day* (2019) for the ABC, and licenced the series to the BBC, Hulu, and Scandinavian TV. Kalceff's co-producer on *SFN*, Rosie Lourde, explains the role the web-series played in her step up to Netflix director on her rom-com, *Romance on Menu* (2020). In Chapter 8, I show the ultimately successful struggle of Taylor Litton-Strain and Erin Good to get their multi-award-winning *Jade of Death* (2018) launched on YouTube, and crossed over to Canada's CBC Gem. Like Lourde, Litton-Strain explains the role *Jade* played in her step up to producer's assistant on *The Invisible Man* (2020). Chapter 9 presents the case of master hybrid web-series maker, Ric Forster, who co-creatively developed millions of views to his edgy LGTQ teen soap, *Flunk* (2017–2019), first on YouTube, Instagram, and Twitter and then parlayed the audience attention of an initial 11 million views to Here TV, which has a channel on Amazon Prime. Chapter 10 presents the first known longitudinal study of any pioneering US web-series makers, in this case, Writers' Guild of America award-winners, Susan Miller, and Tina Cesa Ward. Set in New York in the post-911 era, their *Anyone But Me* (2008–2012; 2019) has since attracted over 100 million views and shows how they adapted drama, one of humanity's oldest performance artforms to its newest, algorithmic culture, professionalizing the web-series as the shift to the post-broadcast era accelerated.

Based on the salient lessons of these cases, I suggest William Gibson's observations from the 1990s about the future of the hybrid format of digital video at a private 'filmless film' festival at 1920s Hollywood era, Chateau Mamont, hold up well. Gibson (1999) wrote about the massive disintermediation ushered in by cheap digital cameras, but could not foresee the rise of social network markets six years later. Gibson's piece centred on one of his unrealized characters, the Garage Kubrick, 'a stone auteur, an adolescent near-future Orson Welles, plugged into some unthinkable (but affordable) node of consumer tech in his parent's garage', single-handedly making a feature film. Gibson's predictions about future film-makers, such as the Garage Kubrick, as being unconcerned about speed of production, and the purely individual nature of creativity, are not reflected in the nine cases, in fact, the cases reflect the opposite. Crucially, however, the film-makers in these cases would find much common ground with Gibson's visionary Garage Kubrick, especially his sidestepping of 'what Hollywood puts people through', his collapse of the division of labour, his commitment to 'narrative tension' and 'unforgettable characters', and above all, his pursuit of authorship, or creative autonomy. Having dealt with the meta-analysis, we now turn into the field with the nine cases.

Notes

1 Subscriber and view numbers for the creatives featured in this book increase over time, overall. Every effort has been made to ensure these figures were up to date as of October 2021.
2 Specifically, the Calimala, or merchants' guild, ran a competition for the doors of the Florence cathedral; what would become Ghiberti's 'Gates of Paradise', and paid the production costs and living expenses of the artists competitively selected for the works (Csikszentmihalyi, 2014, p. 57).
3 Creators Hayley Adams and Michelle Melky have since adapted episodic narrative to Tik Tok with *Love Songs* and *Scattered,* where episodes are just one minute. This works since young people have a strong grasp of narrative, Adams (2020) told me.
4 Newcomb and Alley (1983, p. 4) identify the zenith of the independent TV producers' creative power as occurring in the mid-1970s, as 'the brightest glow of the network era'.
5 This idea sprang from a lively discussion during a walk with Dr Paul Williams, and I gratefully acknowledge his role in this insight.
6 Based on thematic analysis of the daily work activities of 35 Silver and Gold Play Button level (100,000–1M subscribers) YouTube creators, I suggest the other four skillsets are social analytics, business/entrepreneurship, video production, and creative content strategies.
7 I draw on Latour's (2001, p. 154) theoretical exercise about how to understand the labour performed by non-human actors and then apply it to YouTube algorithms. Latour argues non-human actors or devices can be considered anthropomorphic if the device or machine was designed by humans, and if it performs the work of humans and shapes human behaviour. I did Latour's exercise listing such 'labour' as uploading videos, tagging, sorting, archiving, ranking, and recommending. This starkly showed the effectiveness and ubiquity of YouTube as a globe-spanning, real-time, searchable video archive would not be possible without the heavy-lifting and structuring work of algorithms. I suggest creators are in unavoidable, asymmetrical collaboration with these algorithms, which I argue are performing 'anthropomorphic labour'.
8 For full list see Appendix 1, Career mobility paths of Skip Ahead alumni, 2014–2017.
9 The ninth case, Chapter 10, used the same method, was begun in early 2019 and completed in 2021.
10 Significantly, the evidence from this book suggests in the new paradigm of networked video, indie web-series makers from countries without even modest subvention, most notably the United States, are at a severe competitive disadvantage in terms of production funds.
11 Rosie Lourde (right) co-produced *SFN,* helped oversee Skip Ahead, and later directed *Romance on the Menu* (2020), released on Netflix Australia & New Zealand.

References

Abel, R. (2011). *The Gutenberg revolution: A history of print culture.* Transaction Publishers.
Adams, H. (2020). Producer of Love Songs. Interview with Guy Healy.
Alexander, J. (2019). The golden age of YouTube is over: The platform was built on the backs of independent creators, but now YouTube is abandoning them for more traditional content. The Verge, 5 April. https://www.theverge.com/2019/4/5/18287318/youtube-logan-paul-pewdiepie-demonetization-adpocalypse-premium-influencers-creators
Alexander, J. (2020, February 13). YouTube is the frontrunner in the mobile streaming wars, and it's not even close. *The Verge*, Vox Media. Washington DC. https://www.theverge.com/2020/2/13/21136335/youtube-streaming-wars-mobile-android-tiktok-netflix-quibi

Algotransparency (2019). Homepage. https://algotransparency.org/index.html?date=13-06-2019&keyword=

Allgaier, J. (2020). Science and medicine on YouTube. In Hunsinger J., Allen M., Klastrup L. (eds.), *Second international handbook of internet research* (pp. 7–27). New York: Springer, Dordrecht.

Alphabet (2020, Feb 3). Alphabet announces Fourth Quarter and Fiscal Year 2019 results. *Alphabet*, Mountain View, California. https://abc.xyz/static/2019Q4

Anderson, C. (2004). 'The long tail', *Wired*, October, https://www.wired.com/2004/10/tail/. Accessed 26 November 2016.

Arnott, P. (1989). *Public and performance in the Greek theatre*. Routledge.

Ashton, P. (2011). *The calling card script: A writer's toolbox for screen, Stage and Radio*. Bloomsbury.

Banet-Weiser, S. (2012). *AuthenticTM: The politics of ambivalence in a brand culture* (Vol. 30). NYU Press.

Banks, Miranda. (2010a). The picket line online: Creative labor, digital activism, and the 2007–2008 writers guild of America strike. *Popular Communication*, *8*(1), 20–33.

Banks, Mark (2010b). Craft labour and creative industries. *International Journal of Cultural Policy*, *16*(3), 305–321.

Bärtl, M. (2018). YouTube channels, uploads and views: A statistical analysis of the past 10 years. *Convergence*, *24*(1), 16–32.

Baujard, T., Tereszkiewicz, R., & de Swarte, A. (2019). *Entering the new paradigm of artificial intelligence and series. A study commissioned by the Council of Europe and Eurimages*. Peacefulfish.

Benkler, Y. (2006). *The wealth of networks: How social production transforms markets and freedom*. Yale University Press.

Benson, R., & Neveu, E. (Eds.). (2005). *Bourdieu and the journalistic field*. Polity.

Bielby, D. D., & Bielby, W. T. (2002). Hollywood dreams, harsh realities: Writing for film and television. *Contexts*, *1*(4), 21–27.

Bishop, S. (2018). Anxiety, panic and self-optimization: Inequalities and the YouTube algorithm. *Convergence*, *24*(1), 69–84.

Bourdieu, P. (2001). Television. *European Review*, *9*(3), 245–256.

Bourdieu, P. (2005). The political field, the social science field, and the journalistic field. In E. Neveu & R. Benson (Eds.), *Bourdieu and the journalistic field*. Polity Press.

Brevini, B., & Pasquale, F. (2020). Revisiting the Black Box Society by rethinking the political economy of big data. *Big Data & Society*, Jan–Jun, 1–4.

Briskman, L. (1980). Creative product and creative process in science and art. *Inquiry*, *23*(1), 83–106.

Britton, S. (2014). *Interview with Chris Voigt* [blog]. *ScreenPro*. https://soundcloud.com/screentalks/screenpro-interview-chris

Bull, G. (1987). *Giorgio Vasari: Lives of the artists* (Vol. 11). Penguin Books.

Burgess, J. (2006). Hearing ordinary voices: Cultural studies, vernacular creativity and digital storytelling. *Continuum*, *20*(2), 201–214.

Burgess, J. & Green, J. (2009). *YouTube*. 1st edition. Polity Press.

Burgess, J., & Green, J. (2018). *YouTube: Online video and participatory culture*. John Wiley & Sons.

Bushby, H. (2020). Bafta Film Awards 2020: 10 things we learned at the ceremony. *BBC News*, 3 February. https://www.bbc.com/news/entertainment-arts-51351472

Byrne, J. (2017 and 2021). Principal producer, Triptych pictures, interview with Guy Healy. Brisbane.

Calacanis, J. (2013). I ain't gonna work on YouTube's farm no more. *Launch*, June, 2.

Caldwell, J. (2004). Convergence television: Aggregating form and repurposing content in the culture of conglomeration. In Jan Olsson and Lynn Spigel (Eds.), *Television after TV: Essays on a Medium in Transition* (pp. 35–74). Duke University Press.

Caldwell, J. (2010). Breaking ranks: Backdoor workforces, messy workflows, and craft disaggregation. *Popular Communication, 8*(3), 221–226.

Caldwell, J. (2013). Para-industry: Researching Hollywood's blackwaters. *Cinema Journal, 52*(3), 157–165.

Caldwell, J. (2016). Spec world, craft world, brand world. In M. Curtin, & K. Sanson (Eds.), *Precarious creativity* (pp. 33–48). University of California Press.

Cameron, A., Verhoeven, D., & Court, D. (2010). Above the bottom line: Understanding Australian screen content producers. *Media International Australia, 136*, 90–102.

Castells, M. (2010). The rise of the network society, second edition with a new preface.

Caves, R.E. (2003). Contracts between art and commerce. *Journal of Economic Perspectives, 17*(2), 73–83.

Chan, S. (2012, October 2). On storyworlds, immersive media, narrative and museums – An interview with Mike Jones [Blog]. http://www.freshandnew.org/2012/10/storyworlds-immersive-media-narrative-interview-mike-jones/

Cheng, X., Dale, C., & Liu, J. (2013). Understanding the characteristics of internet short video sharing: YouTube as a case study. https://arxiv.org/pdf/0707.3670.pdf

Christian, A. J. (2018). Open TV. New York University Press.

Cooley, M. (2018). *Updated calculations for economic impact of YouTube. Submission to the Australian content on broadcast, radio and streaming services inquiry.* Alphabeta.

Covington, P., Adams, J., & Sargin, E. (2016). Deep neural networks for YouTube recommendations. In *Proceedings of the 10th ACM Conference on Recommender Systems.* ACM.

Cox, E. (2016). Did YouTube's algorithm change? Reactions from big, small YouTubers. [Web-blog]. https://heavy.com/tech/2016/12/youtube-algorithm-change-reactions-pewdiepie-jacksepticeye-delete-channel-new-algorithm-how-to-boost-views-revenue

Csikszentmihalyi, M. (2014). *The systems model of creativity: The collected works of Mihaly Csikszentmihalyi.* Springer.

Culpepper, P. D., & Thelen, K. (2020). Are we all amazon primed? consumers and the politics of platform power. *Comparative Political Studies, 53*(2), 288–318.

Cunningham, S., & Craig, D. (2019). *Social media entertainment: The new intersection of Hollywood and Silicon Valley.* New York University Press.

Cunningham, S., & Flew, T. (Eds.). (2019). *A research agenda for creative industries.* Edward Elgar Publishing.

De Semlyen, N. (2019, November 6). The Irishman week: Empire's Martin Scorsese interview empire, Bauer Consumer Media, Hamburg, Germany. https://www.empireonline.com/movies/features/irishman-week-martin-scorsese-interview/

Donald, E. (2017). Her brilliant career: Gillian Armstrong on the Australian screen then and now. *Metro Magazine: Media & Education Magazine 194*, 111.

Dredge, S. (2015). YouTube: Hank Green tells fellow creators to aim for '$1 per view'. The Guardian, 8 April. https://www.theguardian.com/technology/2015/apr/08/hank-green-youtube-1000-cpm-vlogbrothers

Duffy, B., Poell, T., & Nieborg (2019, October-December). Platform practices in the cultural industries: Creativity, labor, and citizenship. *Social Media + Society, 5*(4), 1–8.

Ellingsen, S. (2014). Seismic shifts: Platforms, content creators and spreadable media. *Media International Australia, 150*, 106–113.

Ellis, S., & Brown, M. (2017). Hacking growth: How today's fastest-growing companies drive breakout success. Currency.

Epstein, J. (2008). The end of the Gutenberg era. *Library Trends*, *57*(1), 8–16.

Fox, C. (2018). YouTube stars' fury over algorithm tests. *BBC News*, 28 May. https://www.bbc.com/news/technology-44279189

Ghelfi, D. (2005). *Understanding the engine of creativity in a creative economy: An interview with John Howkins*. World Intellectual Property Organization.

Gibson, W. (1986). *Burning Chrome*. Gollancz, Orion Publishing.

Gibson, W. (1999). William Gibson's Filmless Festival, WIRED, Conde Nast, San Francisco, California. https://www.wired.com/1999/10/gibson-5/

Gillespie, T. (2010). The politics of 'platforms'. *New Media & Society*, *12*(3), 347–364.

Goriunova, O. (2012). New media idiocy. *Convergence*, *19*(2), 223–235.

Gutelle (2014, March 2). The average YouTube CPM is $7.60, but making money isn't easy, Tubefilter, Tubefilter Inc. Los Angeles. https://www.tubefilter.com/2014/02/03/youtube-average-cpm-advertising-rate/

Hale, J. (2018). Robert Kyncl sits down with Caspar Lee to address YouTuber concerns about monetization changes, burnout. Tubefilter, 20 September. https://www.tubefilter.com/2018/09/20/robert-kyncl-caspar-lee-interview-youtuber-concerns

Hartley, J., Wen, W., & Li, H. S. (2015). *Creative economy and culture: Challenges, changes and futures for the creative industries*. Sage.

Healy, G. (2019). 'Fast and furious film-making': YouTube's prospects for budding and veteran producers. *Metro Magazine*, *202*, 100–105.

Hermanowicz, J. C. (2013). The longitudinal qualitative interview. *Qualitative Sociology*, *36*(2), 189–208.

Higgs, P., Cunningham, S., & Bakhshi, H. (2008). Beyond the creative industries: Mapping the creative economy in the United Kingdom.

Ifeanyi, K. C. (2018, April 13). 'Giants' is the 'very black' digital series everyone should watch. [Blogpost] Fast Company, New York. https://www.fastcompany.com/

Jenkins, H. (2004). The cultural logic of media convergence. *International Journal of Cultural Studies*, *7*(1): 33–43.

Jenkins, H., & Deuze, M. (2008). Editorial. Convergence Culture, Convergence.

Judah, T. (2015). Place your bets: Unknown odds at the 2014 Screen Forever Conference. *Metro*, *184*, 123.

Kafka, P. (2020, February 4). YouTube makes $15 billion a year from ads – and pays more than half of that to video makers, Vox Media, Comcast. https://www.vox.com/recode/2020/2/4/21122309/youtube-revenue-7-billion-paid-media-advertising

Kalowski, R. (2018). Then head of ABC comedy. Skype interview with Guy Healy.

Keith, B. (2007, September 13). YouTube millionaires front camera, Sydney Morning Herald, *Nine Entertainment*. https://www.smh.com.au/business/small-business/youtube-millionaires-front-camera-20090619-co61.html

Kopf, S. (2020). 'Rewarding Good Creators': Corporate social media discourse on monetization schemes for content creators. *Social Media+ Society*, *6*(4), p 1–12.

Krafft, P., & Donovan, J. (2020). Disinformation by design: The use of evidence collages and platform filtering in a media manipulation campaign. *Political Communication*, *37*(2), 194–214.

Kyncl, R. (2017). The inside story of how Netflix transitioned to digital video after seeing the power of YouTube. Vox, Vox Media, Washington DC. https://www.vox.com/2017/9/13/16288364/streampunks-book-excerpt-youtube-netflix-pivot-video

Kyncl, R. & Peyvan, M. (2017). *Streampunks: YouTube and the rebels remaking media*. HarperCollins.

Lanham, R. A. (2006). *The economics of attention: Style and substance in the age of information*. University of Chicago Press.

Latour, B. (2001). Where are the missing masses? *Organizational Studies: Evil Empires, 4*, 1842.

Lessig, L. (2008). Making art and commerce thrive in the hybrid economy. https://archive.org/stream/LawrenceLessigRemix/Remix-o.txt

Liao, S. (2017). In 2017, the web series may be the new TV pilot, The Verge, Vox Media, New York. https://www.theverge.com/2017/10/27/16145498/insecure-broad-city-high-maintenance-web-series-hbo-comedy-central

Livingston, P. (2009). Poincaré's 'Delicate Sieve': On creativity in the arts. In M. Krausz, Denis Dutton, & K. Bardsley (Eds.), *The idea of creativity*, 28, pp. 129–146. Brill.

Lorenz, T., and Woo, E. (2021, July 17). *Smart money on creators*. Australian Financial Review, Nine Entertainment Co.

Lotz, A. D. (2018). *We now disrupt this broadcast: How cable transformed television and the internet revolutionized it all*. MIT Press.

Maggio, R. (2014). The anthropology of storytelling and the storytelling of anthropology. *Journal of Comparative Research in Anthropology and Sociology, 5*(02), 89–106.

Marwick, A. (2018). Silicon Valley and the social media industry. In J. Burgess, A. Marwick, & T. Poell (Eds.), *The sage handbook of social media* (pp. 314–329). Sage Publications.

Matamoros-Fernández, A. (2017). Platformed racism: The mediation and circulation of an Australian race-based controversy on Twitter, Facebook and YouTube. *Information, Communication & Society, 20*(6), 930–946.

McRobbie, A. (2004). *Everyone is creative: Artists as pioneers of the new economy*. Routledge-Cavendish.

Meadows, D. (2003). Digital storytelling: Research-based practice in new media. *Visual Communication, 2*(2), 189–193.

Miller, C. H. (2014). *Digital storytelling: A creator's guide to interactive entertainment*. Focal Press.

Minow, N. N. (2003). Television and the public interest. *Federal Communications Law Journal, 55*(3), 1–13.

Moses, B. (2018). Eurovision Australia producer. Skype interview with Guy Healy, 19 January 2018.

Murdock, G., & Golding, P. (2016). Political economy and media production: A reply to Dwyer. *Media, Culture & Society, 38*(5), 763–769.

Napoli, P. M. (2013). *The algorithm as institution: Toward a theoretical framework for automated media production and consumption*. Fordham University Schools of Business Research Paper.

Napoli, P. M. (2016). Requiem for the long tail: Towards a political economy of content aggregation and fragmentation. *International Journal of Media & Cultural Politics, 12*(3), 341–356.

Neff, G., Wissinger, E., & Zukin, S. (2005). Entrepreneurial labor among cultural producers: 'Cool' jobs in 'hot' industries. *Social Semiotics, 15*(3), 307–334.

Newcomb, H., & Alley, R. S. (1983). *The producer's medium: Conversations with creators of American TV* (p. 33). Oxford University Press.

Ortutay, B. (2018, July 10). *YouTube aims to crack down on fake news, support journalism, Associated Press*. Non-profit cooperative Associated Press. Retrieved from: https://apnews.com/article/north-america-technology-business-journalism-media-a3b9b5a518f247b8a2ebbf4fb5c2d9ed

Parker, S. (2015). The lesbian muse and poetic identity, 1889–1930. Routledge.

Perren, A. (2011). In conversation: Creativity in the contemporary cable industry. *Cinema Journal, 50*(2), 132–138.

Piketty, T. (2013). *Capital in the 21st century*. President and Fellows, Harvard College.

Podkalicka, A. (2008). Public service broadcasting as an infrastructure of translation in the age of cultural diversity: Lessons for Europe from SBS Australia. *Convergence, 14*(3), 323–333.

Popper, B. (2015). Red dawn: An inside look at YouTube's new ad-free subscription service. *The Verge*, 21 October. https://www.theverge.com/2015/10/21/9566973/ youtube-red-ad-free-offline-paid-subscription-service

Postigo, H. (2016). The socio-technical architecture of digital labour: Converting play into YouTube money. *New Media & Society, 18*(2), 332–349.

Pottinger, N. E. (2018). Don't forget to subscribe: Regulation of online advertising evaluated through YouTube's monetization problem. http://dx.doi.org/10.2139/ ssrn.3149984

Potts, J., Cunningham, S., Hartley, J., & Ormerod, P. (2008). Social network markets: A new definition of the creative industries. *Journal of Cultural Economics, 32*(3), 167–185.

Riley, J. (2003). *Routledge philosophy guidebook to Mill on liberty*. Routledge.

Roberson, Q. M. (2006). Disentangling the meanings of diversity and inclusion in organizations. *Group & Organization Management, 31*(2), 212–236.

Robins, K., & Webster, F. (1988). Athens without slaves … or slaves without Athens?: The neurosis of technology. *Science as Culture, 1*(3), 7–53.

Ryan, M., Cunningham, S., & Verhoeven, D. (2012) *Second Australian Producer Survey 2012: Understanding Australian screen content producers: Wave 2.* ARC Centre of Excellence for Creative Industries and Innovation, QUT.

Screen Australia (2012). *What to watch? Audience motivations in a multi-screen world.* Screen Australia.

Sennett, R. (2008). *The craftsman.* Yale University Press.

Shackleford, S-L. (2019). Writer/director of SketchSHE. Pers comm with Guy Healy, 3 September.

Shackleford, S-L. (2021). Writer/director of SketchSHE. Pers comm with Guy Healy, 3 September.

House of Raven (2020). Why we really left LA | This is us, House of Raven [YouTube vlog]. Retrieved from: https://www.youtube.com/watch?v=oc6FLeF0D30&t=5s

Shields, M. (2017, September 6). YouTube wants to go head to head with HBO on quality. *Business Insider*, New York. https://www.businessinsider.com.au/ youtube-exec-wishes-google-was-making-hbos-acclaimed-show-insecure-2017-9

Smith, S. L., Choueiti, M., & Pieper, K. (2016). Inclusion or invisibility? Comprehensive Annenberg report on diversity in entertainment. *Institute for Diversity and Empowerment at Annenberg, 22,* 1–27.

Striphas, T. (2015). Algorithmic culture. *European Journal of Cultural Studies, 18*(4–5), 395–412.

Sullivan, J. L. (2009). Leo C. Rosten's Hollywood: Power, status, and the primacy of economic and social networks in cultural production (pp. 47–61). Routledge.

Terranova, T. (2000). Free labour: Producing culture for the digital economy. *Social Text, 18*(2), 33–58.

Thomson, D. (2012). *The big screen: The story of the movies.* Macmillan.

Turner, F. (2012). A conversation with danah boyd, Microsoft research. *Television & New Media, 13*(2), 177–185.

Van Dijck, J., & Poell, T. (2015). Social media and the transformation of public space. Social Media+ Society, *1*(2), 1–5.

Van Vuuren, C. (2019). Director, Bondi Hipsters, *Over & Out.* Personal communication with Guy Healy.

Vary, A. (2020). Academy awards barely escape a reprise of #OscarsSoWhite, Variety, 13 January. https://variety.com/2020/film/news/oscarssowhite-2020-oscars-diversity-1203463343

von Rimscha, M. B., Verhoeven, M., Krebs, I., Sommer, C., & Siegert, G. (2018). Patterns of successful media production. *Convergence, 24*(3), 251–268.

Ward, T. C. (2019). Creator, anyone but me (2008–15), chair, International Academy of WebTV, Los Angeles. Skype interview with Guy Healy.

Weiss, G. (2020, April 16). A lot of YouTube creators just disclosed their declining AdSense rates amid the coronavirus pandemic. Most are down at least 20%, with a few bright spots. https://www.tubefilter.com/2020/04/16/creators-disclose-declining-adsense-rates-coronavirus/

Wesch, M. (2010). Lessons from YouTube [web-video]. https://www.youtube.com/watch?v=lNwvPauwbFg&t=43s

Yin, R. K. (2009). How to do better case studies. In L. Bickman & D. J. Rog (Eds.), *The Sage handbook of applied social research methods* (pp. 254–282). Sage.

2

ABSURDIST YOUTUBE ANIMATOR CHRIS VOIGT'S JOURNEY TO EMMY-WINNING, BLUEY

Rise of the networked Muse

History has attributed the most novel creativity to the heroic figure of the individual 'genius', but, as shown in Chapter 1, novel creativity is increasingly recognized as springing from social foundations. The literature on creative labour over the past quarter century positions late-stage capitalism as increasingly repudiating collective approaches and job protections in favour of individual choice, risk, and reward-taking. Contrastingly, Voigt's labour stands out as resistance to individualization via distinctive co-creativity with online peers, the same phenomenon we saw in Chapter 1 with leading China-based videographers, Corndog and Shouting Beast.

The stakes are existential. For Sennett (1998, p. 284), the vision of former conservative British leader Margaret Thatcher where only 'individuals and families' would remain, undermined a polity which gave people a collective good to identify with, and which promoted psychological and ethical growth. For Beck (2000, p. 18), this second phase of modernity was characterized by a shift of risk and responsibility from the state and other institutions to the individual, 'ecological crises', the erosion of paid employment, globalization, and gender revolution. Drawing on trends in indie fashion houses, McRobbie (2002, p. 55) noted individualization had become 'full-scale' requiring 'branding the self as a commercial strategy', backed by the UK's former Blair Labour government. For Castells (2009), globalization was accelerating the tempo of production and natural resource exploitation, which, while shortening the livelihood of the human species, was extending the lifespan of individuals. Gandini and Graham (2017, p. 3) described an 'entrepreneurialization of the individual', who nevertheless carried the Romantic ideal of the artist 'into the fragmented ecosystem of the market'. For Zhang et al. (2019, p. 351), the virtual gifting practices on China's

DOI: 10.4324/9781003182481-2

live streaming platforms maximized content monetization at the expense of communitarian sensibility and reciprocity among individuals, yielding 'soulless leviathans – uncaring, impersonal, amoral'.

However, within this bleak vision of labour, scholars also uncovered a resistance to individualization and marketization of jobs, towards collective approaches. Lévy (1997) emphasized 'collective intelligence', where the more intelligent communities are formed 'as open-minded cognitive subjects capable of initiative, imagination, and rapid response, the more we will be able to ensure our success in a highly competitive environment'. In response to market domination and pervasive commodification, Boltanski and Chiapello (2005, p. 176) noted a pushback by employees for self-management, personal autonomy, and creativity. Similarly, Tedjamulia, Dean, Olsen, and Albrecht (2005, p. 2) noted motivations driving online communities included 'community citizenship, generalized reciprocity, moral obligation, and pro-social behavior'. Noyes (2006) drew a parallel between folkloristic oral tradition in Homer, where multiple actors added to these epics over generations, and the social base of inventiveness in the development of open source software. These competitive creative networks 'inhabit both the traditional and cutting edges of modernity'. For Noyes (2006), the motivator of participation, whether in 'rhapsodes, software or Carnival floats', is 'recognition of one's peer creators', which often, in the longer run, yielded better profits. For 'next generation film-makers', Ryan and Hearn (2010, p. 139) the disrupted screen ecology placed a premium on creative individuals – or 'a team as a collective' – since a range of skills were needed. For Lanham (2011, p. 9), the reason Google paid US$1.65 billion for YouTube was their recognition economic value had migrated from physical assets, to individual attention, especially 'the cultural conversation' in the ether. By 2013, Jenkins et al. foregrounded Brazilian popular music genre, Tecnobrega, where participants, some amateur, some professional, sustained the scene 'as active multipliers who contribute symbolic value' to their social dance community. For Jenkins at al. (2013, p. 193), at stake was 'the century-long struggle for grassroots communities to gain greater control over the means of cultural production and circulation'. Regarding YouTube, Burgess and Green (2018, p. 99) found the platform's socio-technological infrastructure was never originally designed for collaboration, and creative opportunities were built by online communities themselves, or by special invitation of the company. For Marwick (2017, p. 10), Silicon Valley entrepreneurs were valorized as individuals 'a breed apart', fuelled by passion and independence, 'a desire to change the world'; but also a role 'anyone can and should step into'. For their part, based on a transnational sample of 12,299 Millennial and Gen Z's, a third expect evolving technologies to replace all or part of their jobs, while a majority expect these technologies to 'augment' their roles, freeing them to pursue 'creative, human and value-added work' (Deloitte, 2018, p. 22). Time and again in the coming nine cases, we will see these themes of self-branding, entrepreneurialism, and the drive to personal creative autonomy in tension with, or augmented

FIGURE 2.1 Brisbane animator and songwriter for a hipster audience, Chris Voigt

by, collective, collaborative responses to a globalized market and participatory fan behaviour. Voigt is the first of the five Skip Aheaders profiled in this book (Figure 2.1). His fan demographics and geographics show just how international his web-series was overwhelmingly teen and young adult males in the Global North of the United States, followed by Europe, especially the UK and Germany, then Canada and Australia.

Voigt's cultural labour spans the pre-YouTube era prior to 2005 to the present day. His generosity in participating in my study thus provides a unique lens to view how this struggle between individualization and the collective manifest in algorithmic culture. I draw on six main sources: five interviews – one with Voigt by Stuart Cunningham in late 2015; the others I conducted between 2016 and 2021. Contextual information was drawn from Voigt's main SexuaLobster channel and his public Patreon channel. I also conducted ongoing correspondence with Voigt, and he provided feedback on a draft of his case as part of the iterative process outlined in Chapter 1. Surprisingly, there are no reviews of Voigt's exquisite artistry, which is symptomatic of the lack of social media entertainment coverage by media generally.

Biography

Voigt joined YouTube in early 2006, months before its purchase by Google, and so has endured all four major YouTube algorithm changes detailed in Chapter 1. With his fellow Skip Aheaders in its inaugural class, Voigt was described as representing a depth of online creative talent, and being among 'the next generation of Australian storytellers' (Screen Australia, 2014). But the intensity of his labour – his painstakingly slow animation work is the equivalent of scripted web-series – made him one of the least sustainable. He is also one of the edgiest in terms of sexual thematics. Here I trace Voigt's creative and labour journey: his formative period on proto-platform Newgrounds; his breakout with a string of YouTube 15 hits; his Skip Ahead web-series; his struggle with algorithmic volatility during YouTube's 'Adpocalypse' and intensified period of experimentation in response; and finally, his abandonment of the platform and transition to a steady income on multi-Emmy-winning Ludo Studios' *Bluey,* as a storyboarder. The fact his first storyboarding credit on the award-winning children's show was its very first episode, *Magic Xylophone* (2018), underscores his flexibility and inventiveness. In 2020, Voigt returned to YouTube as a side project and raised his career-long experimentation with co-creativity to a new level in the co-composed *Banando* (animatic).

Voigt says he has been drawing comics from 'as soon as I could clutch a crayon in my talons' (Limbrick, 2013). He became interested in Flash animation while studying 'multimedia' at college, frustrated with the slowness of scanned drawings. Voigt began uploading Flash animation to Newgrounds in 2005. Newgrounds is credited as an influential platform shaping the pre-broadband web, empowering pro-ams to create and share content, in the process building online communities and giving rise to the animated web-series as an important 'cultural form' (Fiadotau, 2020). Animation is a labour-intensive and artistically skilled occupation within a multi-billion-dollar screen industry dominated by major US studios and their runaway productions. Up until 2009, DreamWorks' *Shrek 2* (2004) was the top animated film, amassing US$920 million, the seventh-highest box office total record for all films (Yoon & Malecki, 2010, p. 250). However, computer-generated imagery and global production chains have 'opened up opportunities for artisan entrepreneurs for niche markets, including markets not controlled by media giants' (Yoon & Malecki, 2010, p. 240). Animation on YouTube dates to its earliest days, being mostly professional content in the Most Viewed category (Burgess & Green, 2018, p. 71). Voigt graduated from the Queensland College of Art with a Bachelor in Animation in 2009.

As a first-mover on YouTube, Voigt has published 116 videos, to attract 395,000 subscribers; a Silver Play button ranking. During the course of my tracking from 2016 to 2021, his views grew from 59 million to over 77 million. Voigt's breakout hits centred on the adventures of his most popular characters, Fernando and Gooseman. He went full time as an animator in 2011, achieving 21 videos attracting over 1 million views on YouTube to date.

Formative period

Voigt's online storytelling taps rich cultural heritages from both East and West. The 'integration of perspectives from more than one domain' is known to yield creative insights (Csikszentmihalyi, 2015, p. 96). As major influences on his 'absurdist' brand of comedy (Figure 2.2), Voigt cites *Dragonball* animator Akira

Ask Raptor Jesus

1,269,804 views · Apr 26, 2010   👍 15K   👎 363   ↗ SHARE   ⬇ SAVE   ···

FIGURE 2.2 Voigt's first breakout hit on YouTube animated the *Raptor Jesus* meme [screenshot from Voigt's YouTube channel]

Toriyama and TimeWarner's subcultural channel Adult Swim (Limbrick, 2013). Toriyama created Japanese TV show, *Dragon Ball*, based on his adaptation of 16th century Chinese book, *Journey to the West,* which told the sagas of Xuanzang, a Buddhist monk accompanied by Son Goku, a mischievous Monkey King, in search of sacred sutras (Mínguez-Lopez, 2014, p. 32). The popularity of Absurdist humour – or neo-Dada – among millennials has been attributed to their disillusionment with modern life and the often-horrifying nature of world affairs (Aroesti, 2019). Moreover, Koltun (2018, p. 102) explains the appeal of absurdism as escapism, drawing on Pew research which found millennials are 'the first in the modern era to have higher levels of student loan debt, poverty and unemployment, and lower levels of wealth and personal income than their two immediate predecessor generations'. Adult Swim grew from an obscure cable channel to a transmedia empire based on its appeal to an anti-hegemonic aesthetic of late-night TV, hip hop, nerd culture, recreational drug use, anime, para-cinema, and remix (Elkins, 2014, p. 597). Adult Swim captures a dominant cultural identity, 'young, white, heterosexual masculinity' in a fragmented US media (Elkins, 2014, p. 595).

Crucially, Voigt's practice emerges from some of the earliest manifestations of digital culture, anticipating the later feature of YouTube that distinguishes the platform from one-way TV: socio-technological affordances enabling new levels of 'cultural conversations' between creators, peers, and fans. By virtue of reading the comment streams on his channels invoked by his content, Voigt was necessarily immersed in the conversations of his fans. Being exposed to zeitgeist in rawest form, he was informed to make the most 'authentic' art. Voigt's practice originated on a bulletin board, where he first started co-composing with others online:

> I would ask for a line of lyrics from fans and then write music to that, develop verse structure, ask for more lines with same rhythm, then develop the chorus.
>
> *Voigt (2017)*

This transparent insight is striking for the contrast with US screenwriters who are not known for making admissions of creative vulnerability (de Kosnik, 2018, personal comment). Voigt's early co-creativity prefigured what would become best practice in the creator professionalization arm of YouTube – the worldwide YouTube Spaces – years later. The former head of YouTube Spaces Mumbai, Jigisha Mistry Iyengar (2015), lauded this type of practice where Twitter was used to connect fans directly to popular Indian creators, for 'fan engagement, production and collaboration' during 'Happy Hours'.

Breakout

Since animation is labour intensive and online attention fickle, Voigt had to master the art of telling a story in just one minute. Over a prolific creative period from 2010 to 2013, Voigt created 15 edgy videos (Figure 2.4) that resonated highly with his mostly US-based fans. This phenomenon exemplifies the power of what industry insiders call shortform serial narratives, to attract an audience of many millions with deep niche content.

From Voigt's approval by YouTube for advertising as a Creator Partner in 2010, crowd-writing and crowdfunding illuminated Voigt's biggest and most enduring animated characters: the bearded and buff manwhore Fernando, 'a tragic tale of crack abuse and imaginary sea-creatures' (Figure 2.3); and his urbane mate Gooseman. Six of these most popular videos are based on his Fernando and Gooseman characters, according to my tracing of video metadata. Despite their sexual thematics, these videos were able to obtain high views on Watch Time, one of YouTube's major algorithm changes detailed in Chapter 1 (Meyerson, 2012). This shows there was a time of greater creative latitude before the post-Adpocalypse policy changes – critiqued as 'Disneyfication' by RackaRacka (McCauley, 2018) – when sexually edgy content was not a bar to helping keep a creator afloat.

Despite these hits, Voigt was not making 'a decent living', and the money was just enough of 'a supplement' to cover food and rent (Britton, 2014). Voigt explained in a good month he might get 1.2 million views. But there is a catch: 'only 250,000 to 350,000 views are monetised, because there's so many different types of advertising, most aren't worth very much' (Britton, 2014). Crucially, views from the Global North such as the US and England paid more than those from the Global South, such as Uganda and Venezuela. The artists' cherished

FIGURE 2.3 *Passion of the Manwhore*, Voigt's third most popular video ever [screenshot from Voigt's YouTube channel]

creative autonomy can be preserved on YouTube due to the power of deep niche audiences, but for Voigt, the living is still precarious:

> My channel is a place for films I want to watch. Most people wouldn't like it. It's the wonder of the internet: obscure interest groups can come together.
>
> *Britton (2014)*

Skip Ahead web-series

Among participants I interviewed, Skip Ahead represented a generative antidote to the problem known to veteran YouTubers as the platform's 'speeding tread-mill', where algorithms demand preferably daily video uploads (Game Theory, 2016). The nominal AU$100,000 per team funded YouTube creators with the most narrative potential, until at least 2020, enabled these creators to step off YouTube's treadmill for a year to produce their web-series. In 2014, Voigt was in the first class of the Screen Australia/YouTube-funded Skip Ahead program with other Australian YouTube veterans[1]. His seven-part, animated, backing-tracked web-series, *Fernando's Legitimate Business Enterprise*, was approved. The story for the seven episode by three-minute web-series follows 'a singer with bound-less manly sexuality, Fernando, and his shifty business partner, Gooseman, as they struggle to transition from unknowns to C-list celebrities', in parody of the A/B List phenomenon. Skip Ahead presented an opportunity to do an impor-tant collaboration with storyboarder Peter Yong, who worked on episodes of

Dreamworks' *The Adventures of Puss in Boots* (2015), for Netflix. Yong's painting in figure occurs as Voigt sings the following absurdist lyrics:

> My love for you is wider than the widest river of yoghurt
> My bleeding heart is an open wound, I invite you to probe it
> My tears of lust shine like the sun, our love knows no eclipse
> I will love you with the frenzy of one thousand chimps.

Voigt fulfilled the requirements of Skip Ahead, producing seven episodes featuring Fernando and Gooseman. For Voigt, the grant meant financial security for a year, and a period of creativity free from YouTube's upload regime, and the classic bind of the emerging artist:

> The problem with making things for YouTube is getting the financial return that allows you to keep doing it. I spend most of my time working on commissions for other people, which is fun, but always have to scrape some time to work on my own projects. Skip Ahead gives me an opportunity to work almost exclusively on that for a fairly long period of time and make something I would not be able to make usually (Britton, 2014).

Voigt's practice raises the question, and important tension, about whether Skip Ahead drove his practice to the next level of narrativization, or whether he produced more of the same. Voigt's pre-existing Fernando and Gooseman characters featured in the seven episodes. Voigt acknowledges a continuity of practice during Skip Ahead, but says his practice was deepened:

> I probably would have made one or two of the seven Skip Ahead cartoons without the grant. But I would not have spent as much time on them.
>
> *Voigt (2017)*

Voigt's decision makes sense given YouTube's fickle audience culture. Other veteran YouTubers argue they feel typecast by their fans locking creators into continually reworking the style of content subscribers signed on for, or risking financial adversity. As Cunningham and Craig (2019) found, featuring ongoing characters is a must because the characters originally given life by creators are the foundation of their fan communities, and thus their living.

Adpocalypse

In the online video business, YouTube is regarded as an unavoidable collaborator, meaning the fortunes of YouTube impact the fortunes of creators. For Voigt (2017) was a lean year, and while the early months of 2017 were among his best, mid-March 2017 saw the 'Adpocalypse' mentioned in Chapter 1. Leading creators claimed they suffered significant losses in revenue and profits as iconic advertisers boycotted the platform. The platform responded by augmenting its automated advertising systems with thousands of human reviewers, and unnecessarily recategorizing thousands of videos 'not advertiser-friendly', or NAF (Pottinger, 2018, p. 529). In response, Voigt experimented with new forms and accelerated his production, all the while trying not to alienate his loyal fans. But the impact on his revenue from the volatile private economy of YouTube – together with a decline in gifts on his crowdfunded Patreon channel – meant Voigt's creative entrepreneurship on YouTube reached a turning point: abandonment.

Formal hybrid market period

Voigt's skills in high-end animation – especially storyboarding – were clearly valued by prototypical hybrid producers, Ludo Studio in Brisbane's Fortitude Valley. Ludo specializes in producing original stories in innovative formats across many platforms, winning three International Emmy's: #7DaysLater (2015), an unprecedentedly participatory comedy series; Doodles (2016), an interactive animation series; and *Bluey* (2020), a children's animation. So great has been *Bluey's* cultural impact the New York Times ran a feature on the show in 2020, recognizing its role in helping American parents cope with the pandemic (Sebag-Montefiore, 2020). Ludo's vertical comedy, Content (2020) was also Emmy nominated. Ludo had turned to Voigt to help animate and storyboard the studio's new children's series, *Bluey*, for ABC Kids iView and the BBC (2019). Voigt helped bring *Bluey* to life, performing the first visualization of the script:

> Storyboarding is the first visualisation of the script. You make your film language decisions, and also where character acting happens with a shot. I make some layout suggestions, but the designers and art directors have permission to throw out anything of mine they think they can improve on. But the finished episodes I have seen, have a lot of my poses, and acting suggestions … and backgrounds as well.
>
> *Voigt (2018)*

Surprisingly, Ludo did not hire Voigt for his co-creative skills with fans, but rather for his storyboarding (Voigt, 2018). Voigt has 14 storyboard artist credits on *Bluey* up to *Shaun* (2019), especially for his work on the family of main characters, pups *Bluey* and Bingo, and their sire Bandit and dam, Chilli. Such is his work ethic and robustness, that by early 2018, despite his day job and annual holidays, he released the mini-epic, *Fernando and the Disk of Chaos*. The latest instalment of the eight-year-long series of Fernando and Gooseman – which had reached a peak during his Skip Ahead funding – was, at over seven minutes, one of the longest yet. The credits show Voigt sharing the writing with another nine writers, and many more content contributors, as well as support from Patreon. By 2019, Voigt had returned to one of the characters from the formative stages of his practice, *Great Destiny Man*, for a new series. Underlining the immersion of Voigt in the flow of his online collaborators, and wider community from 2005 to

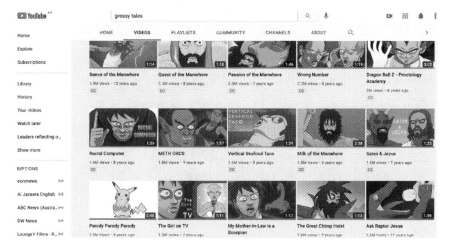

FIGURE 2.4 'Struggling with modernity'. These 15 character-driven, mainly Fernando and Gooseman adventures, have attracted cumulative views over 26 million to date [screenshot from Voigt's YouTube channel - Most popular]

2020, Voigt's *Banando* was co-written with 15 writers. The Muse from antiquity elaborated in Chapter 1 has become networked.

Burning problems

Monetization

Voigt is a walking ensemble. Like the creators in this book, and to varying degrees the professional producers, Voigt's pre-Ludo practice was as a creative entrepreneur. As indicated above, Voigt drew on six of the ten revenue streams used across the nine cases ranked in importance below in Table 2.1. Patreon crowdfunding and YouTube AdSense combined with music and merchandize sales covered Voigt's financial expenses, but left him well short of a $60,000 income (Voigt, 2017) prior

TABLE 2.1 Ten most important revenue streams for the nine cases in descending order

Sponsorship/brand deals
Patreon
Off-platform jobs, including teaching
Subvention (state grants)
IP licensing
AdSense
Merchandize
Appearance fees
Song sales
Commercial production funds

Source: (Healy, 2020)

FIGURE 2.5 Patreon is equally important to YouTube to generate creator revenue streams [screenshot from Voigt's Patreon channel]

to the 2017 Adpocalypse. Regarded as the world's biggest reward crowdfunding platform, creators on Patreon had received monthly payments of over \$1billion from over four million fans as of late 2019 (Regner, 2021, p. 2) (see Figure 2.5).

At different times and to varying degrees, Voigt's sustainability thus drew on all three of the cultural economies as defined by Murdock and Golding (2016, p. 765) as introduced in Chapter 1: gifting (crowdfunding); public goods (Screen Australia's half of Skip Ahead); and commodities (YouTube Adsense). Voigt's work life conforms to the multi-platform labour I also elaborated in Chapter 1.

A recurring narrative of the press – and arguably therefore creator imaginary – is YouTube is an overnight pathway to ostentatious wealth manifested in twenty-something YouTubers buying prestige cars such as Lamborghinis (Watkins, 2015; Anderson, 2016). My five-year investigation found no evidence to support this narrative, which suggests it is merely a powerful media frame. Indeed, a 10-year analysis of YouTube views found 'a rich-get-richer' phenomenon with the vast majority of views (85 per cent), going to just the top three per cent of channels, a tiny cohort itself split between UGC and professional videos (Bärtl, 2018, p. 18). Nevertheless, Voigt went fulltime as an artist and kept himself afloat with periods of financial security, within a few years of leaving art college. The fact Voigt's first breakout hit, *Ask Raptor Jesus,* came four years after his inception on YouTube suggests he had by then synthesized traits Csikszentmihalyi (2015, p. 24) found necessary for successful artistry: concentration, self-discipline, and high sensitivity[2]. Ultimately his living was decimated by the Adpocalypse, precipitating his transition off the endemically volatile platform and into secure artistic work; a macro trend I found among Skip Ahead teams overall. Significantly, Voigt began fulltime storyboarding of *Bluey* at Emmy-winning Ludo just eight years after leaving college, suggesting his creative practice on Newgrounds and YouTube accelerated his career. As of 2021, Voigt was still at Ludo.

One of Voigt's prime income streams is IP-based. On his Patreon channel, Voigt says he has been creating 'horrifically sensuous' cartoons since 2005 and offers tiered levels of behind-the-scenes access, ad-free viewing at the $1 donation tier, song compilations, mp3 music downloads, HD mp4 cartoon downloads, and customized credits to the most generous patrons in credit sequences for donations of up to $20 per creation.

The most important factor governing Voigt's production conditions is the intensive nature of the labour of even his scripted shortform video-making, and one he directly attributes to his ability to crowdfund:

> I aim for a minute long, because less than a minute you get a lot less ad impressions … It takes a month a minute. That's one of the reasons I am able to crowdfund. People can appreciate the fact time goes into them. Cartoons take a long time.
>
> *Voigt (2016)*

Similarly, Baym (2015) identified a cellist, Zoe Keating, with a one million-strong Twitter following, where online followers gradually became paying consumers of her concerts and albums. Keating used a non-idealized online self, presented with emotional honesty, to explain to her fans she relied on her music revenues to support her family.

Voigt also asserts his own creative autonomy alongside his distinctive co-creativity. A third of Voigt's most popular videos were crowd-written, collaborated, or funded, especially his biggest hit, *Dance of the Manwhore* (2010) (3.8 million views) Figure 2.6 above. His co-opting audiences parallels the

FIGURE 2.6 Voigt co-composers [screenshot from Voigt's YouTube channel]

co-creativity and online community-building by Baym's musicians above. Voigt told me he practises co-composition for three reasons:

> It was a means to come up with ideas for short videos because they do best on my channel, but I don't tend to have too many ideas for them. Second, it was a way to come up with successful videos, and thirdly – just sounds weird – community engagement. People really got into it; people who got their lyrics used in the song were thrilled.
>
> *Voigt (2017)*

Co-creating fans are rewarded by Voigt in two important hybrid ways: screen credits, a long-standing traditional film and TV industry practice, and artistic recognition. This insight of Voigt's directly addresses the research gap I highlighted in Chapter 1 by drawing on Banks (2009, p. 87), who argues the 'motivations, incentives and behaviours' of co-creators' needed to be better understood, especially whether these processes are transparent and participatory. Here I show co-creating fans are emotionally engaged by recognition in the art-world of Greasy Tales, in a clear and participatory way. Some people are good lyricists and would contribute more often than most – for example, wmfivethree and bigtasty67.

> These two contributors stand out. I always credit the writers in the 'About' section of the videos they contribute to, and at the end of the video.
>
> *Voigt (2019)*

Volatility

This online storyteller coped with heightened algorithmic volatility during the Adpocalypse by drawing on the heart of creativity itself: increased experimentation in the face of financial stress. We will see this generative response to the upload regime demanded by algorithmic culture, with varied strategies, in the following cases. In parallel, Csikszentmihalyi (2015, p. 313) found in his studies of artists and scientists that 'economic hardship can stimulate productivity'. Nevertheless, it remains a problematic peculiarity for YouTube creators worldwide they share what they see as an artistic domain with malevolent forces able to exploit the openness of the platform to their own dark ends. Propaganda was uploaded by extremists to YouTube, triggering the Adpocalypse that impacted creators worldwide. Subsequently, Voigt turned over work during this period enjoyed by his fans, but he does not describe this as 'good' creative work in the sense of his subjective experience. For an artist whose living was not enmeshed in a networked, algorithmic global domain such as YouTube, there would be no direct impact upon their living from global publicity about extremists using new media. So 2017 proved a major turning point for Voigt, with his videos dipping significantly in number, and the animator returning to deep artistic roots – an adaptation of an old comic he drew with friends – in his short video *Razor Blades*.

When the Adpocalypse bit hardest, Voigt stepped up his co-writing with lead fans and experimentation, but was ultimately stymied by the incongruence of the high labour intensity required, and the platform's reward system:

> I tried a few different forms: new content; a series where the crowd wrote it and I would have a fixed amount of a character asset; making conversation pieces. The first one did well, even though it was limited visually. With the second one, there was a sharp decrease in enthusiasm, and it also came out on the cusp of the ad revenue decline. So I took a plank of that idea, 'Was there something I could produce first in five days? Second one in six days?' I thought I could get assembly line going. Do a weekly cartoon four or five minutes long. Play the Watch minutes game. But I quickly realized I would lose a lot of viewers. Ad revenue suddenly became not a thing anymore. I could try my hardest and make only $200 a month from AdSense (Voigt, 2018).

Crucially, the principle of temporality as ideas develop, and the variegated career outcomes for traditional artists (Csikszentmihalyi, 2015, p. 44) and any prospect of doing 'good' creative work (Sennett, 2008, p. 12), becomes immediately apparent when artistic work is conducted in social network markets. Voigt considers himself an artist, and indeed his accounts of the wellsprings of his creative practice harken to the four-stage classical model of high art and science: preparation, incubation, insight, and revision (Livingston, 2009, p. 19; Csikszentmihalyi, 2015, p. 78):

> Most of my scripts sit around for at least a few months, sometimes three or four years, before I make them. I occasionally glance and view them as objectively as I can during that time and whittle away at them – the ones that aren't collaborations, anyway.
>
> *Voigt (2017)*

The advent of Watch Time impacted YouTuber creativity in various ways, particularly the sustainability of artistic expression. This evidence from Voigt suggests in a networked algorithmic environment, the four-stage creative process continues unabated, with socialization in the 'gaps' continuing. Crucially though, flow is problematized. At our first lunch, Voigt bluntly reported highly adverse platform effects upon creativity in the YouTube domain: 'Creativity gets killed' (Voigt, 2016). Danny Philippou, aka RackaRacka (1.04 billion views), makes the same point, just as bluntly, in Chapter 4.

This choice for the class of worker working within algorithmic culture parallels the bleak dichotomy predicted by the co-author of the Netscape browser, Marc Andreessen, who predicted the spread of computers and the Internet would put jobs in two categories: 'People who tell computers what to do, and people who are told by computers what to do' (Mullaney, 2012). New Zealand ethics professor Nicholas Agar (2019, p. 163) argues a future preferable to Andreessen's vision is Jeremy Rifkin's Collaborative Commons, where 'we will combine our creativity with powerful digital technologies' as prosumers in the maker economy. Nevertheless, this evidence of Voigt's art and commerce suggests a deep challenge for the Romantic ideal of the artist, who for Caves (2000, p. 76) 'seeks new problems of creative visualization and devises compelling solutions', when labouring in a multi-platform environment.

Cultural divide

Recall from Chapter 1 the problem of the industrial rift contributing to younger producers and new media workers feeling blocked in finding people to share jealously guarded industry know-how. To overcome this problem, Voigt benefited from three processes that helped him adapt to algorithmic culture. First, he achieved formal specialized training from a college able to provide an intellectual framework for students to absorb the best of the past and acquire the skills to master the socio-technologies of the present. For example, Voigt 'hated' doing life drawing and anatomy, a practice dating from antiquity (Bull, 1987, p. 2), but recognized it improved his drawing (Limbrick, 2013). He also stresses he read books such Williams' *The Animator's Survival Kit* (2012) on drawing for the classics to the Internet. Second, as shown in this chapter, he learnt to adapt the communication affordances of social network markets with online peers to co-composition, giving rise to what I suggest is a networked form of the Muse. According to Csikszentmihalyi (2015, p. 151), collaborators are essential for the productivity and eminence of scientists and artists, based on six key factors: they facilitate the expression of creativity; they facilitate problem finding and solving; they help prevent mistakes and screen out bad ideas; they keep one professionally informed; they impart important values; and they complement skills deficiencies, and work as effective interlocutors. Importantly, YouTube's early architecture and design sought individual participation – as exemplified in its 'Broadcast Yourself' logo (Burgess & Green, 2018, p. 101). In contrast, the case of Chris Voigt emphasizes his co-creativity with collaborators, much more get together with your peers, have fun, and *broadcast yourselves*. Third, Voigt's participation in Skip Ahead meant he attended a 'YouTube Bootcamp' in Sydney and spent a week at YouTube Spaces Los Angeles. Since Skip Ahead was hosted by Screen Australia and Google, Voigt received a mix of perspectives from the old school domain of film and the new school domain of Silicon Valley as elaborated in Chapter 1.

A list/B list

The A list/B List is regarded by Caves (2000) as beneficial for a number of reasons, especially in ordering situated artworlds, enabling artists to acquire greater 'muscle', in turn yielding greater autonomy, better potential collaborations, as well as price signals to fans. Yet, as highlighted in Chapter 1, these informal rankings also result in what Cunningham and Flew (2019, p. 3) describe as 'the notorious gap in the creative industries between the wildly successful few and the many getting by or struggling'. The lesson from Voigt's use of YouTube and Patreon is nuanced. At different times, he was financially secure and could support himself as an artist and save. As a freelancer, he worked hard and inventively, but did not make the middle wage of AU$60,000 to $70,000 he aspired to for greater autonomy and to help support family. This status changed once he joined Ludo on *Bluey*.

The evolution of the Internet towards platforms monetizable by creative entrepreneurs, such as Voigt's exemplary use of Patreon herein, has finally made the aspiration of a middle-class creative career realistic and credible. As flagged in Chapter 1, YouTube's Robert Kyncl advocates the beliefs of WIRED founding editor, Kevin Kelly and YouTube entrepreneur Jack Conte, that artists – using YouTube and Patreon – aim for 'the much saner', more readily achievable goal of a 'middle' income using the '1000 True Fans' strategy (2017, 145). Artists no longer need to unrealistically aspire to millions of dollars or customers or fans, just 1000 true fans who 'will buy anything you produce' at $100 each, yielding a US$100,000 annual income (Kelly, 2008). The nascent platform-based creative economy enabled almost 15 million Americans to earn US$5.9 billion from their creations in 2016, especially on WordPress, Tumblr, and Instagram, with 42,000 earning over US$11,141 annually from YouTube Adsense (Shapiro & Aneja, 2018, p. 3). We will see a similar best practice pattern time and again in the following cases.

Discrimination and authenticity

As a well-educated white heterosexual male, discrimination did not come up as an issue Voigt experienced; however, authenticity was imperative. Following their deep dive among YouTubers, Cunningham and Craig (2019, p. 13) were so struck by creatives' emphasis on authenticity, the phenomenon became key to their definition of social media entertainment. I argue as a career path, YouTube is a double-edged sword: it is both a radically empowering technology, and a precarious Darwinian environment in which only the fit survive – and perhaps thrive (Healy & Cunningham, 2017, p. 114). Voigt's authenticity – he never raised the topic with me – has four elements. First, Voigt's own multi-dimensionalities are who he draws and sings and writes about: his most enduring characters are white heterosexual males. Six of his most viewed videos feature Fernando and Gooseman, for example, the sublime *Vertical Seafood Taco* (2013) (1.6 million views). Second, while he depended on crowdfunding and free-lance commissions off YouTube to sustain himself before Ludo, Voigt is among the least brand oriented, conspicuously so. Voigt says his content is not 'brand safe'. Voigt's brand-free content is thus congruent with Banet-Weiser's point from Chapter 1 that rampant commercialism and the intrusion of brands into audience spaces has left audiences 'clamouring for authenticity' (2012, p. 10). Third, Voigt's creative mode of address helps further animate an important style of expression millennials have appropriated for themselves from previous generations: absurdism. For Nagel (1971, p. 726), absurdism was a transcendent aspect of a humanity faced with a collision between pretension and reality. According to Pew Research (1998), the oldest of the millennials were the then biggest fans of *Seinfeld*, best known for its 'satirical and absurdist humour' (Pierson, 2000, p. 53). For Elkins (2014, p. 601), Time Warner's Adult Swim network was an important recognition its 'usual absurdism' was appealing to a subculture of young white males. By 2017, The Washington Post's Elizabeth Bruenig asked, 'why is millennial humor so weird?' (Bruenig, 2017) The self-identified millennial answered, faced with 'a world of the surreal and bizarre, horror mingling with humor', young people have 'a creeping suspicion the world just doesn't make sense'. Indeed. Fourth, as above, five of Voigt's top 15 videos were crowd-written, collaborated, or funded, further ensuring his content resonated with peers, and thus his largest audience, the United States. Over 90% of the views of Australian YouTube creators in 2016 came from overseas (YouTube, 2017). To make a living – just like all these other creators – Voigt had to target the territories where CPM rates were highest, the UK and the US. Critics might argue globalization threatens the cultural integrity of the creator's home territory. However, drawing on O'Regan and Potter (2013, p. 13), I suggest, similarly, that employment of creatives from their home territories 'at the helm' is what guarantees a nation's cultural integrity. In the final analysis, authenticity is enabled by Voigt's deep niche strategy. Most people would not like Voigt's content, but as he says, they do not have to since the wonder of the net is like-minded people can come together (Britton, 2014).

Notes

1 See Appendix 1 for full list, 2014–2019.
2 Csikszentmihalyi (2015, p. 24) also found successful artists shared more traits of the opposite sex than considered 'normal', giving them the advantage of 'a full range of cognitive and emotional responses' upon which to draw.

References

Aroesti, R. (2019, August 13). 'Horrifyingly absurd': How did millennial comedy get so surreal? *The Guardian*. Guardian Media Group, London. https://www.theguardian.com/tv-and-radio/2019/aug/13/how-did-millennial-comedy-get-so-surreal

Agar, N. (2019). *How to be human in the digital economy*. MIT Press.

Anderson, K. (2016). How to make a $1000 a day driving cars. *BBC*. http://www.bbc.com/autos/story/20160415-how-to-make-1000-a-day-driving-cars

Banks, J. (2009). Co-creative expertise: Auran games and fury – A case study. *Media International Australia*, *130*, 77–89.

Bärtl, M. (2018). YouTube channels, uploads and views: A statistical analysis of the past 10 years. *Convergence*, *24*(1), 16–32.

Baym. N. (2015). Connect with your audience! The relational labor of connection. *The Communication Review, 18*(1), 14–22,

Beck, U. (2000). *The brave new world of work.* John Wiley & Sons.

BBC (2019). Bluey: The Australian cartoon that's going global. BBC News, 1 August. https://www.bbc.com/news/av/world-australia-49175684/bluey-the-australian-cartoon-that-s-going-global

Boltanski, L., & Chiapello, E. (2005). The new spirit of capitalism. *International Journal of Politics, Culture, and Society, 18*(3), 161–188.

Bull, G. (1987). *Giorgio Vasari: Lives of the artists* (Vol. 11). Penguin Books.

Burgess, J., & Green, J. (2018). *YouTube: Online video and participatory culture* (2nd ed.). Polity Press.

Britton, S. (2014). Interview with Chris Voigt [blog]. *ScreenPro.* https://soundcloud.com/screentalks/screenpro-interview-chris

Bruenig, E. (2017, August 11). Why is millennial humor so weird? *Washington Post.* WP Company LLC, Washington. https://www.washingtonpost.com/outlook/why-is-millennial-humor-so-weird/2017/08/11

Castells, M. (2009). *The rise of the network society*: The information age – economy, society and culture. John Wiley & Sons.

Caves, R. E. (2000). *Creative industries: Contracts between art and commerce.* Harvard University Press.

Cunningham, S., & Craig, D. (2019). *Social media entertainment: The new intersection of Hollywood and Silicon Valley.* New York University Press.

Cunningham, S., & Flew, T. (Eds.). (2019). *A research agenda for creative industries.* Edward Elgar Publishing.

Csikszentmihalyi, M. (2015). The systems model of creativity: The collected works of Mihaly Csikszentmihalyi. Springer.

Deloitte (2018). *Deloitte millennial survey: Millennials disappointed in business, unprepared for Industry 4.0.* Deloitte.

de Kosnik, A. (2018). Associate Professor in the Berkeley Center for New Media and the Department of Theater, Dance, and Performance Studies. Pers. comm with Guy Healy.

Elkins, E. (2014). Cultural identity and subcultural forums: The post-network politics of Adult Swim. *Television & New Media, 15*(7), 595–610.

Fiadotau, M. (2020). Growing old on newgrounds: The hopes and quandaries of Flash game preservation. *First Monday,* University of Illinois, Chicago. https://journals.uic.edu/ojs/index.php/fm/article/view/10306/9585

Game Theorists (2016, Dec 11). Is YouTube Killing Pewdiepie [sic] and H3H3 … and Everyone?, YouTube, 10 December 2016. https://www.youtube.com/watch?v=tyHaMVRgBV0>

Gandini, A., & Graham, J. (2017). *Collaborative production in the creative industries* (p. 240). University of Westminster Press.

Healy, G., & Cunningham, S. (2017). YouTube: Australia's parallel universe of online content creation. *Metro Magazine, 193,* 114–121.

Healy, G. (2020) *Fast and furious film-making: Emerging hybrid online-TV production practices in Australia.* PhD thesis, Queensland University of Technology.

Iyengar, J., Head of Operations, YouTube Space (India) (2015). Interview with S. Cunningham and D. Craig.

Jenkins, H., Ford, S., & Green, J. (2013). *Spreadable media: Creating value and meaning in a networked culture.* New York University Press.

Kelly, K. (2008). 1,000 true fans [Blogpost]. *The Technium.* https://kk.org/thetechnium/1000-true-fans/

Koltun, K. (2018). Rick, Morty, and absurdism: The millennial allure of dark humor. *The forum: Journal of History*, *10*(1), 12.

Kyncl, R., & Peyvan, M. (2017). *Streampunks: YouTube and the rebels remaking media.* HarperCollins.

Lanham, R. A. (2011). The two markets. *Library Resources & Technical Services*, *52*(2), 3–11.

Lévy, P. (1997). *Collective intelligence.* Plenum/Harper Collins.

Limbrick, A. (2013). Interview: Chris Voigt, creator of Space Adventure Legend Quest. GeekGirlWorldBlog. https://geekgirlworld.com/2013/01/19/interview-chris-voigt-creator-of-space-adventure-legend-quest

Livingston, P. (2009). Poincaré's 'delicate sieve': On creativity and constraints in the arts. In K. Bardsley, D. Dutton, & M. Krauz (Eds.), *The idea of creativity* (pp. 129–146). Brill.

Marwick, A. (2017). *Silicon Valley and the social media industry. Sage handbook of social media.* Sage.

McCauley, D. (2018). Brothers' grim tale: 'Disney-fied' YouTube bans RackaRacka videos. The Australian, 4 June, https://www.theaustralian.com.au/business/media/brothers-grim-tale-disneyfied-youtube-bans-rackaracka-videos/news-story

McRobbie, A. (2002). Fashion culture: Creative work, female individualization. *Feminist Review*, *71*(1), 52–62.

Meyerson, E. (2012). YouTube now: Why we focus on watch time. YouTube Creator Blog. https://youtube-creators.googleblog.com/2012/08/youtube-now-why-we-focus-on-watch-time.html

Mínguez-López, X. (2014). Folktales and other references in Toriyama's *Dragon Ball. Animation*, *9*(1), 27–46.

Mullaney, T. (2012, September 14). Marc Andreessen: Venture Capitalist. *USA Today.* Virginia, US. https://www.pressreader.com/usa/usa-today-us-edition/20120914/282729109092360

Murdock, G., & Golding, P. (2016). Political economy and media production: A reply to Dwyer. *Media, Culture & Society*, *38*(5), 763–769.

Nagel, T. (1971). The absurd. *The Journal of Philosophy*, *68*(20), 716–727.

Noyes, D. (2006). From homeric epic to open-source software. Toward a network model of invention. *Con/texts of Invention: A Working Conference of the Society for Critical Exchange* (Vol. 22). Case Western Reserve University.

O'Regan, T., & Potter, A. (2013). Globalisation from within? The de-nationalising of Australian film and television production. *Media International Australia*, *149*(1), 5–14.

Pew Research (1998, May 10). Mixed reaction to post-Seinfeld era: Fans Say Yada survey findings. Pew Research Centre, Washington, US. https://www.pewresearch.org/politics/1998/05/10/mixed-reaction-to-post-seinfeld-era/

Pierson, D. P. (2000). A show about nothing: Seinfeld and the modern comedy of manners. *The Journal of Popular Culture*, *34*(1), 49–64.

Pottinger, N. E. (2018). Don't forget to subscribe: Regulation of online advertising evaluated through YouTube's monetization problem. http://dx.doi.org/10.2139/ssrn.3149984

Regner, T. (2021). Crowdfunding a monthly income: an analysis of the membership platform Patreon. Journal of Cultural Economics, 45(1), 133–142.

Ryan, M. D., & Hearn, G. (2010). Next-generation 'filmmaking': New markets, new methods and new business models. *Media International Australia*, *136*(1), 133–145.

Screen Australia (2014). Creative teams selected to Skip Ahead with Screen Australia and YouTube. Media release. https://www.screenaustralia.gov.au/sa/media-centre/news/2014/mr_140319_skipahead

Sebag-Montefiore, C. (2020). Stuck inside? Here's an Australian kids' show every parent can love. The New York Times, 1 April. https://www.nytimes.com/2020/04/01/arts/television/bluey-cartoon-dog-australia

Sennett, R. (2008). The craftsman. Yale University Press.

Shapiro, R., & Aneja, S. (2018). Unlocking the Gates: America's new creative economy. The Routledge Companion to Global Television, Routledge. www. recreatecoalition. org/wp-content/uploads/2018/02/ReCreate-Creative-Economy-Study-Report. pdf

Tedjamulia, S. J., Dean, D. L., Olsen, D. R., & Albrecht, C. C. (2005, January). Motivating content contributions to online communities: Toward a more comprehensive theory. In Proceedings of the 38th Annual Hawaii International Conference on System Sciences (pp. 1–10). IEEE.

Watkins. N. (2015). YouTuber lands Lamborghini. The Sun, 1 September. https://www.thesun.co.uk/motors/2739258/supercar-vlogger-buys-160k-lambo-with-youtube-cash

Voigt, C. (2017, 2018, 2019, 2021). Creator of SexuaLobster channel. Interviews and personal communications with Guy Healy.

Yoon, H., & Malecki, E. J. (2010). Cartoon planet: Worlds of production and global production networks in the animation industry. *Industrial and Corporate Change, 19*(1), 239–271.

YouTube (2017, November 15). YouTube – The Australian Story. Google Australia Blog. YouTube, Sydney. https://australia.googleblog.com/2017/11/youtube-australian-story.html

Zhang, X., Xiang, Y., & Hao, L. (2019). Virtual gifting on China's live streaming platforms: Hijacking the online gift economy. *Chinese Journal of Communication, 12*(3), 340–355.

3

RAPPROCHEMENT ACROSS THE DIVIDES

The Saidden brothers aka Superwog and Emmy-nominated Princess Pictures

Introduction

Democratized access to publication via social networks Twitter, YouTube, and Facebook has been implicated in 'platforming racism', especially via subscribers using humour to cloak prejudice (Matamoros-Fernández, 2017, p. 938). This chapter considers the reverse of the coin.

This case exemplifies what has been happening for the past decade as talented minorities have been confronted with a homogenous broadcast TV industry and instead pivot to the new paradigm of networked video. Narratively gifted YouTubers are seen to collaborate with established TV producers to generate IP in licensed web-series, make a middle-class living, and significantly depower prejudice on their journeys. With over 2.7 million subscribers, the Saiddens are Silver level YouTubers whose skits and web-series have attracted over 423 million views on YouTube alone (Figure 3.1). Their journey is especially important in three ways: first in terms of crossover from YouTube to BVODs and SVODs via the professional web-series; second, the role of rapprochement between YouTubers and established TV producers in effecting crossover; and third, for exemplifying a power shift as talented minorities hold up racial and other stereotypes to the 'disinfectant of sunlight' through satire, and so invalidate them. For critics, Superwog 'are not politically correct, but it is damn funny' (Lallo, 2018a). By contrast, Starke (2013) said the humour of Superwog was too 'controversial' by mainstream TV standards. Season One of their Skip Ahead web-series, *Superwog Series*, achieved 16 million views two months after launch, and internationalized their audience. Just 14 days after launch Australia accounted for 72 per cent of views, the United Kingdom 9.4 per cent, New Zealand 6 per cent, and the United States 5 per cent. Making a middle-class living from multiplatform labour is a significant achievement. Based on the latest mapping

DOI: 10.4324/9781003182481-3

FIGURE 3.1   Leveraging YouTube: anti-clockwise from the top, Theo and Nathan
            Saidden aka superWog, and John Luc and Mychonny, Athenaeum
            Theatre, Melbourne, 2013

of YouTube's 36 million channels by Rieder et al. (2020, p. 14), the Saiddens
2.7 million subscribers place them among the most elite cohort of just 15,
496 channels worldwide over 1 million subscribers, and who collectively account
for 37 per cent of both platform subscribers and views. These makers are robust.
These elite channels attract disproportionate exposure, but as the top tier they
have three times more videos than the next lower tier, an average of 940 compared to 294 (Rieder et al., 2020).

Lay of the land

Web satire is an increasingly important site in the formation of cultural citizenship for minorities, scholarship suggests. Popular culture – increasingly mediated
by media conglomerates, and fans, rather than nations – forms cultural citizenship (Hermes 2008, p. 1). Simultaneously, hegemonic media, which has long
enjoyed a monopoly on cultural narratives, is now having to compete with the
representations of influential minority celebrities and media activists, especially
regarding cultural citizenship and prospects for social change (Lopez, 2016,

p. 142). For Hermes (2008, p. 10), cultural citizenship is defined as 'the process of bonding and community-building, and reflection on bonding, implied in par-taking of text-related practices of reading, consuming, celebrating, and criti-cizing in the realm of popular culture'. For Lopez (2016, p. 4), Asian American activists, for example, are engaging in a fight for cultural citizenship – empow-ering themselves via collective rather than individual approaches – to achieve 'a deeper sense of belonging and acceptance within a nation that has long rejected them'. As for the long tradition of satire itself, Hodgart (1969, p. 3) regards sat-ire as 'an alternative form of power' where the crimes committed escape the scrutiny, or inhabit, the worlds of law, religion and politics. However, for satire to be art, 'aggressive denunciation' must be combined with some 'aesthetic fea-tures which can cause pure pleasure' in the audience. Ultimately, satire, while not necessarily noble, nevertheless requires 'a high degree of commitment to and involvement with the painful problems of the world' and is fundamentally human and social (Hodgart, 1969, p. 1).

Demographic realities are such Western democratic nations like the United Kingdom, the United States, and Australia were settled by waves of immigrants, and socio-political means had to be found to peacefully reconcile the newly dominant culture with contending minorities. Lippman (1965, p. 21) argued to cope with the swirl of information constituting 'the world outside', humans naturally categorized the people they encountered via a process of stereotyping: 'the pictures inside the heads of human beings, the pictures of themselves, of others, of their needs, purposes'; and these stereotypes shaped public opinion. Drawing on Lippmann, Berg (1990, p. 287) argued stereotyping was a basic cognitive process and was only bad or racist when people chose to turn it 'into a hateful tool used by one people to segregate and ultimately dominate others'. For Berg (1990, p. 292), in the context of US film, the expression of stereo-types reinforces, and thus validates and perpetuates these pre-existing cultural categories, slipping 'effortlessly into the existing hegemony', thus contributing 'to the naturalizing way the ruling class maintains its dominance over subor-dinated groups'. Significantly, Berg (1990, p. 293) draws on feminist theory to argue minority groups, which are under-represented and typed as outsiders in film to begin with, were categorized as 'the bearers rather than the makers of meaning'. In the context of US TV, Mastro and Greenberg (2000, p. 690) argue representation of ethnic minorities are understood as 'perpetuating or dimin-ishing racial stereotypes', thus influencing the way Whites and even non-Whites themselves perceive minorities. Thus, historically, multicultural approaches were prioritized, but have been contested, at times severely. Australia, where for example about a third of the population was born overseas, regards itself as 'a highly successful and well-functioning multicultural society' based on 'the fair go' (Ozdowski, 2013, p. 1). However, surveys and self-reporting show 'a substantive degree of racism' (Dunn, 2003).

So what happens to cultural production when ethnic minorities turn to social media and flip from being the mere 'bearers of meaning', to *the makers* of the 'pictures in our heads'? Ethnic humour has acted as an important intercultural circuit-breaker, but has at times had to contend with claims of being either 'politically correct' ('PC') or, conversely, politically incorrect. 'PC' is language intended to give the least offence in the context of race, gender, culture, or sexual orientation. For Fairclough (2003, p. 24), claims of 'PC' against feminists and anti-racists and other groups publicly seeking social change, have been an effective and damaging strategy used by the Right as part of a covert neoliberal project to widely inculcate flexibility and individual responsibility; successfully disorienting the Left. Political actors have known since antiquity the most persuasive rhetoric is brief. A carefully crafted phrase of two-to-three power words, principally metaphors, is enough to shape public opinion, especially when used on an often 'under-informed or disengaged' public in a 'post-truth' political milieu (Healy & Williams, 2017, p. 151). The term 'wog' is believed to stem from the British idea of a 'western oriental gentleman', first heard by Australian troops abroad in the first World War (Tsolidis & Pollard, 2009, p. 430), a slur against those of southern European, Turkish, or Lebanese heritage. While 'wog' initially reflected the alienation and racism migrants encountered, Tsolidis and Pollard (2009, p. 430) argue the term has changed meaning over the generations, being reclaimed by the children of migrants 'as both a statement of belonging and as an ironic counter-racist strategy'. Moreover, based upon their work with migrant children in Australia, they found 'wog' was linked to 'gangsta rappers' in US pop culture, which speaks to transnational agendas of oppression and alienation (Figure 3.2).

For Marx (2011, p. 15) web comedy can act as a bridge between 'the competing impulses of the trangressive and the conservative', creating space for innovation in the barely regulated online domain, while offering low-budget talent development. Gillota (2013) argues race still has the power to divide and cause controversy in the United States, even in an era some claim as 'post-racial'. Humour has an important role to play in promoting conversation about race and

FIGURE 3.2 Theo and Nathan Saidden aka Superwog [Photo credit: Princess Pictures]

ethnicity, indeed public protest. Gillota (2013, p. 154) suggests TV producers have learnt 'unthreatening and harmonious visions of diversity' can be highly profitable. Importantly, ethnic humourists respond to 'real world' events, drawing on the discourse of race itself. Comedians in the United States have used the nation's multiethnic demographic 'to interrogate and explore intercultural dialogue' in fuller and more complex ways (Gillota, 2013). Importantly, Flux (2015, p. 51) argues the priority challenge in redressing longstanding under-representation of minorities involves 'the dominant group recognizing lifestyles and worldviews beyond their own'. In the United States, Lopez (2016, p. 143) argues Asian-Americans such as lifestyle influencer, Michelle Phan, have so successfully used YouTube to build audiences, their subscriber numbers 'have frequently eclipsed even mainstream stars like Rhianna, Lady Gaga and Justin Bieber – himself discovered and brought to fame on YouTube'. Significantly, Lopez (2016, p. 152) criticizes YouTubers overall for failing to call out racism sufficiently, but concedes their cultural work 'renders Asian American identities legible and disseminates Asian American narratives', so creating important networks of cultural citizenship that impact broader communities. In her study of Australian YouTube comedy makers, Tofler (2017, p. 826) found they were able to tap into the zeitgeist of Australian popular culture. Moreover, content that elicited 'responses of laughter, shock, surprise and anger' was the most easily shared online.

Parody and self-mockery are highly distinctive, even emblematic, social practice among YouTube creators (Lange, 2007, p. 11; Morreale, 2014, p. 122). Indeed, parody and its 'producerly' quality of being manipulable enough to evoke shared experiences is regarded as one of the most 'spreadable' forms of content online (Jenkins et al., 2013, p. 207). However, comics have to contend with volatile flashes of so-called 'cancel culture', what Ng (2020, p. 623) defines as online collectives withdrawing support for those assessed to have said or done something problematic or unacceptable in the social justice realm, especially bullying, racism, homophobia, heterosexism, and sexism. These periodic eruptions – originally known as 'brigading' by creators in early YouTube days – can be high-risk events for entertainers using social media, since their livings are so bound up in what Graham and Gandini (2017, p. 21) categorize as 'the reputation economy' that structure artworlds. As an antidote to the brevity and rapidity of online exchanges powering the frame of 'cancel culture', Ng (2020, p. 621) suggests renewed focus on message boards and comment threads 'which foster more long-form engagement'.

Biography

The 'integration of perspectives from more than one domain' that proved so generative in Chapter 2 is a rich thread that again weaves through the case of Superwog. Theo and Nathan Saidden, born in Sydney in the late 1980s, are the children of a Greek-Egyptian mother and an Egyptian father. Theo said his mother had 'a crappy camcorder' and the young boys made videos to entertain themselves in their early teens:

> We'd re-enact scenes of our Mum and Dad fighting. We derive a lot of observational comedy from their arguments. They are just over the top. Shoes flying. Getting offended. All wogs get offended...it's a very big thing. They are very emotional and loud and make big deals out of little things.
>
> *Galvin, 2014*

Like the children of many parents who fought, Theo says the siblings were very close – inseparable. They attended the prestigious Trinity Grammar school, which Theo describes as 'colonial and regimented and also socially elite' (Galvin, 2014). Theo and Nathan hung out at school even though Nathan was a year younger. Some of the cultural clash and misunderstanding that drives their humour stems for their early years:

> As we were born into quite a dysfunctional household, it also meant we would look at the outside world through that lens. For example, we would compare the order we observed at the private school we attended with the madness at our house – this might've helped also.
>
> *Saidden, 2021*

Theo describes Nathan as the physical brother, full of bravado, who used to stand up for other kids against the bullies: 'He was almost like the protector of the nerds' (Galvin, 2014). Nathan says where Theo was studious, he was more interested in gadgets and cars. He had a dark period at school, but came out of it. His father was intrigued by Trinity's elitism and would come to school sports 'with his big belly and hair coming out of his chest and shaved balding head', to scream encouragement to his sons. But on the other hand, Theo told me he attributes to his father an inspiration for the future Superwog: 'Our Dad fed us a lot of comedy as kids from a young age. He'd play *Monty Python* skits in the car as we were driving, so we were laughing' (Saidden et al., 2017). The highest profile ethnic humour broadcast on Australian TV includes *Acropolis Now* (1989–1992), *Housos* (2011), and *Here Come the Habibs* (2016–2017), but the Saiddens only watched *Housos*.

Theo Saidden said their comedy influences growing up were also Sasha Baron Cohen's *Da Ali G Show* (2000–2004), *Chappelle's Show* (2003–2006), *Borat* (2006), Chris Lilley, Laura Waters, and Princess Pictures' *Summer Heights High* (2007), and, significantly, *Fat Pizza* (2000–2007; 2019-). *Fat Pizza* is best known internationally for the breakout success of Rebel Wilson (*Pitch Perfect*, 2012-2017), who played Toula in the Australian series. Struck at the time by *Fat Pizza's* 'lewd, crude and utterly insensitive' representations, The Age asked how Paul Fenech, the show's creator, got away with it? 'We thrive on stereotypes...

We don't want to admit we have people like that in Australia...We do attack everyone' (McManus, 2007). Theo says home life and school life provided rich material for their later observationally based comedic practice. Nathan's 'wog dad' character resonates with audiences since he was imitating their angry wog dad (Galvin, 2014). He said Trinity – established soon after Australian nationhood in 1901 – also provided 'a perfect analysis' for social mores among dominant Anglos and minorities:

> Wogs are not wired for sport like Aussies...at Trinity swimming was a big part of the curriculum and you had to wear (extremely brief) Speedos and all the wogs would be sick on swim day, whereas the Aussies were comfortable around each other half naked.
>
> *Ongaro, 2013*

Theo did well enough in Year 12 to enter University of Technology, Sydney, where he completed a law/business degree and became a paralegal. Nathan says he did not bother with school and ran an online furniture business. Theo and Nathan continued to do imitations for their friends, who, in a turning point, wanted more, so they kept doing parody videos from their social milieu.

Their early TV work proved a formative experience regarding traditional TV gatekeepers, screen representations in multi-ethnic Australia, and later pivoting to YouTube. Theo enrolled at the Actors Pulse in Redfern, which counts among alumni Vietnamese-born Australian, Anh Do, actor and author of *The Happiest Refugee* (2010). The Saidden's signed up with an extra's agency, taking roles in TV shows, *Gangs of Oz* (2009–2010), *Underbelly: The Golden Mile* (2010), and *Home & Away* (1988-). Theo Saidden said 'a massive filtration process' in mainstream media at the time tended to disallow the appearance of 'ethnics' on TV in substantive roles. Years later, he told me 'diversity is now in for TV' (Saidden, 2021). However, back then, if ethnics did get roles, they were stereotyped:

> Every job we got was related to crime, holding a gun, doing drugs. It was always playing these stereotypes on TV. Which is ironic because then I turn around and say, 'we're going to do our own thing and see how it goes'.
>
> *Starke, 2013*

Ironic indeed. The Saiddens were co-opted by traditional TV into performing the stereotypes they would later invert in social media production culture. By 2010, the Saidden's met veteran Australian YouTuber, John Luc aka Mychonny (154 million views), at a YouTube Creator Day. John Luc is best known for and had just released his own parental parody, *Justin Bieber is a Gay Baby* (2010; 19.5 million views). These informal collaborations, such as between the Saiddens and Luc, are vitally important and characteristic of creative alliances on YouTube.

We will see them time and again in coming cases, and their role in hacking audience growth for both parties. The livings these creators were making online did not escape the notice of Screen Australia. These disruptive creatives, specifically, John Luc, who began YouTube uploading in 2008, together with Natalie Tran, and her community channel (2006; 173 million views), and the Janoskians (2011; 276 million views), helped inspire Screen Australia and YouTube's Skip Ahead (Cowap, 2017). Crucially, these Saidden/Luc collaboration videos, or 'collabs' in creator vernacular, show how they solved the most urgent problem with doing ethnic humour for a living: protecting themselves against blowback, physically or online. They learnt to 'tread the thin line between entertaining and offending' (McNicholas, 2013): 'We're playing on a stereotype I think is very real, on both sides, so we'll make fun of the Aussies and then we'll make fun of the wogs just as much', says Theo Saidden. Theo was admitted as a lawyer in 2011 and would continue to balance legal work – to pay the bills – with comedy – his passion, until 2015. Their hard work on YouTube saw their peers claim they halved the years required to make their marks (Humphries, 2015).

Breakout

The comedic vision of the Saiddens became wildly popular and critically acclaimed. In 2011, they uploaded their first YouTube hit *Phone Operators* (2011; 1.6 million views). This proto-skit foreshadowed their oeuvre of even-handed parody exploiting the friction points in the schools, workplaces, roads, houses, and back fences constituting multicultural Australia. From 2012 to 2020, the pair made about 60, mainly short YouTube skits, including an extraordinary 28 with over five million views, including their Skip Ahead web-series, 25 over three million, and seven over one million:

> The most important thing for us is writing the scripts. We cannot stress, rush, or do any of this if it is going to be worthy of production. Writing is a private activity done with extreme care. The madness really only starts with production.
>
> *Saidden, 2021*

In 2012, they uploaded eight skits, the most popular being *Childhood* (4.9 million views). Superwog also did their first formal 'collab' with a veteran YouTuber, John Luc, *Asian and Wog Parents on driving (ft Superwog1),* which has since attracted 2.7 million views. In 2013, they leveraged their growing YouTube profile to put on *Superwog and Mychonny* in shows at the Melbourne International Comedy Festival, and the Sydney Opera House in their hometown. This would be among the first of their later 50 live shows. They also licensed Superwog content to Time Warner's absurdist network, Adult Swim. In a reflexive observation reflecting the candour of YouTube creator culture,

Theo Saidden acknowledged their stage humour would play with stereotype, like their online work:

> It's a show based around race comedy. We are not trying to do something totally different. This is what we are here for. So, it's going to have stereotypes and a bit of irony. We are celebrating the differences. That's got a positive ring to it.
>
> *McNicholas, 2013*

Tellingly, the Saidden's differentiation as a hybrid storyteller compared to YouTube performers and personalities was already evident, as they adapted their YouTubing to live audiences:

> We are not doing stand-up…We are not just having a conversation between two characters; we are having a narrative behind it as well. You have to listen. You have to understand, and you will laugh because of the situations, how it starts and how it finishes.
>
> *McNicholas, 2013*

Consolidation

In 2013, they uploaded nine skits, the most popular being *The Difference Between Wogs & Aussies* (6.3 million views), as well as another five over five million views, including *Wogs visit Aussies on Australia Day*. Six years hence the skit would be drawn by the Murdoch press into Australia's protracted culture wars, a rhetorical struggle between the Right and Left still preoccupying the public sphere Fairclough (2003, p. 20) argues dates back to the Reagan and Thatcher eras. The year 2014 saw Superwog upload just seven skits, but they included two of their most highly viewed videos of their decade-long oeuvre, within just months of each other. The first was *America v China: RAP BATTLES* (16 million views). The second was with fellow future 2016 Skip Aheaders, the Philippou twins, aka RackaRacka, on *Ronald McDonald on Cheaters (ft. Superwog)* (16.5 million views) (Figure 3.3). The collaboration brought together four of Australia's most popular, narratively gifted, and physical performers in an arc of escalating chaos and gore, but was too much for YouTube, and was subsequently age-restricted for violating the platform's self-regulated community guidelines. However, Superwog were exposed to what RackaRacka's Skip Ahead producer, Julie Byrne, describes in Chapter 4, as the Philippous' 'fast and furious film-making methodology'. Collaboration, as ever, enables skills exchange:

> RackaRacka are amazing, we were honoured to work with them. They have a ridiculously large following and manage to create high production value content with very low budgets with their extensive knowledge of film techniques. They are also the authority on fight sequences. We

FIGURE 3.3 Hacking growth via 'collabs': from left, Theo Saidden, Michael Philippou (RackaRacka) and Nathan Saidden (right)

participated in a few videos on their channel and they even helped direct a fight sequence on our channel.

Saidden, 2021

In 2015, they produced seven videos, two of which, a parody of a global reality TV franchise, and another on 'differences' in camping, each attracted over five million views. Also that year, Theo Saidden reported other comics would tell the pair 'we've had to work 10 to 15 years to do the places you are performing in' (Humphries, 2015). Superwog again leveraged their online profile for second national tour, *'Talk Shit Get Hit'*.

Skip Ahead

The year 2016 was a major turning point and represents a master class in the development of a web-series story world into indie IP. Moreover, in line with the role of ethnic humour in promoting intercultural conversation, the web-series inadvertently featured in a debate about the role of racial stereotypes in comedy, on the Left and Right of Australia's national press. Just five years after *Phone Operators,* the satire of Saiddens was recognized by Screen Australia, adding evidence to the YouTube career acceleration argument. The Saiddens became successful participants in the third annual class of Skip Ahead, with their pitch reprising their established online characters. The choice was their own, but they accepted the suggestion of Screen Australia for applicants to partner with an established production company. Ultimately, they wanted to make a TV sitcom,

FIGURE 3.4   Nine years after starting on YouTube, Superwog Series Pilot (2017) (11 million views) is launched [screenshot from Superwog's YouTube channel]

so chose the more traditional route and Princess Pictures, 'who are very famil-
iar with edgy comedy' (Saidden, 2021). Ultimately, this meant they received
AU$220,000 (Saidden, 2021), to bridge the Valley of Death-like script develop-
ment process that breaks so many writers. After being shortlisted for Skip Ahead,
the pair were inculcated into shortform episodic narrative at workshops run out
of Google Australia's Sydney headquarters. Classes were run by professionals
such as Mike Cowap and Mike Jones, script producer on Emmy-nominated
Wrong Kind of Black (2018). Oscar, BAFTA and Golden Globe winning director,
George Miller (*Babe* 1996; *Happy Feet*, 2007), also mentored those shortlisted.
Skip Ahead funded the pilot, while season one was funded by the ABC, Screen
Australia, Film Victoria, and Google (Figure 3.4).

Crucially, in an example of the argument supporting the career-enhancing
value of rapprochement between new and old media in this book, the born-
online Saiddens opted to collaborate with established TV producers. The
Saiddens had proved that they could hold deep niche attention online for an
average of three to four minutes for their irreverent stand-alone skits, but could
they step up their storytelling to sustain attention longer than even a feature film,
a six by 24-minute web-series? 'It's raw and blue and dirty. But the crassness
isn't a substitution for comedy. It's always funny', said then ABC comedy chief,
and Superwog executive producer, Rick Kalowski. Their pitch to the Screen
Australia and YouTube gatekeepers centred on the struggle of the highly dysfunc-
tional Superwog family as they navigate life in Australian suburbia. Superwog
(Theo) is a fast food and girls-obsessed teenager attending a private school, with
best friend Johnny (Nathan). Their misadventures stress Superwog's 'emotionally

primitive, highly-strung father' (Nathan) as he attempts to keep his 'delusional, but fiercely loyal' wife (Theo in cross-dress) happy. The series was written by the pair, directed by Theo Saidden and produced by then Princess Pictures producer Paul Walton. Walton was a child actor in the United Kingdom before turning to producing on shows including *Heartbeat* (1992–2010) and *A Touch of Frost* (1992–2010), and first assistant director on *Charlie & Boots* (2009) and *McLeod's Daughters* (2001–2009). The pair were inculcated into the mysteries of the serial narrative under the specialized guidance of experienced above-the-line creatives: executive producers at Princess Pictures, Elia Eliades, and Emma Fitzsimons would go onto produce the Emmy-nominated *Wrong Kind of Black* (2018) and ABC executive producers, Rick Kalowski (*Double Take Julia Gillard 9 to 9*) (2010); (*At Home with Julia*) (2011), and Lauren Metrolli.

To cope with the problem of cut-through in a hyper-saturated online screen environment, these streampunk storytellers turn to the format long left in the shade of longform: the serial narrative. Smith (2018, p. 1) contends that different cultural systems impose different industrial requirements on storytellers or narrative designers, which influence the formation and conveyance of narratives. For example, Dickens' *Great Expectations* (1860–1861) was first published as a serial narrative in the magazine, *All the Year Round*. Smith (2018, p. 13) argues that this condition imposed on Dickens the need to 'anticipate the division of his novel into discrete instalments, each with a predetermined length, and to account for the weekly interval that separated the publication of each new instalment from the last'. In the modern era, Smith argues that the modified soap structure – where episodes are organized around 'multiple distinct storylines' – was driven by cable TV's need to shift from mass to niche audiences, exemplified by TV series like *Hill Street Blues* (1981–1987). The Saiddens learnt many narrative models during the Skip Ahead workshops. However, they decided 'to stick with the classic sitcom format of weaving multiple comedic storylines' which best suited their writing:

> As comedians, we are primarily concerned with making our audience laugh and we let this dictate everything we do, including the storylines.
>
> *Saidden, 2021*

After an eight-month script development process, *Superwog Series Pilot* was released in mid-2017, and attracted over 500,000 views within 24 hours (Bizzaca, 2017). In addition to their standard multiplatform labour of posts to their Facebook, Instagram, and Twitter, crowd-speaking platform Thuderclap, where fans authorize one message to be shared across their own peer networks, was used to create extra buzz. The *Pilot* episode alone has since attracted 9.3 million views. With about 54 million views for the seven episodes, the Saiddens' Skip Ahead series became the most successful in terms of views across the six years of the initiative so far. In describing the success of *Pilot*, Australia's influential wire service characterized Superwog as 'irreverent' (AAP, 2017). Superwog also appeared on

FIGURE 3.5   The 60 videos of Superwog's oeuvre reduced for thematic analysis.
Photo: Guy Healy

SVOD Foxtel's *The Slot*. Later the following year, the six episodes were released, the first, *Breaking Dad*, subsequently attracting 12 million views.

Overnight success is a fantasy. The pair credit the success of the series to 'hard work, conviction and dedication', having so many so people and organizations backing them, but 'most importantly we spent almost 10 years developing and working on our craft before we made the series' (Film Victoria, n.d.) (Figure 3.5). In 2018, the Sydney Morning Herald reported Superwog were among comedians who insist 'there's an essential truth to their "offensive" stereotypes'. Kalowski, overseeing the series at the time, pushed back on accusations of stereotyping: 'There are endless examples of godawful Australian films that seem custom-built to get five-star reviews or be included in a festival. They are just as stereotypical as so-called "wog" comedy and its interesting no-one singles them out' (Lallo, 2018b). In late 2019, a year following the record-breaking success of the *Superwog* web-series, The Weekend Australian's Richard Guilliatt posed the question: 'Is call-out culture killing comedy?" For example, Guilliat highlighted the apparent absurdity of Kate Hanley Corley's *Aisha The Aussie Geisha* (2019) being subjected to 'call-out culture' sufficiently to pull her shows, while Theo and Nathan Saidden 'were packing out theatres on their Superwog tour, a cavalcade of racial stereotypes that has earned them a million fans on YouTube and an ABC comedy series'. Tellingly, the clip of the skit embedded in Guilliat's feature was Superwog's *Wogs invite Aussies for Australia Day* (2015) (4.1 million views). The skit exhibited Superwog's s typically fearless choice of real-world event for the story and their strategically even-handed approach to their parody of their representations of the 'Wogs' and the Aussies.

New heights

Also in 2019, they released three videos, one of which, *Going to the Gym*, attracted over five million views. In 2020, they released another three videos including their first absurdist animation, *If Kangaroos Could Talk* (1.5 million views). In late 2020, the ABC announced Superwog would be renewed for a second season, this time with Princess Pictures' Mike Cowap and Antje Kuple producing. In the interim had Walton left to found his own company, 360 Creative.

Critical reception

The 'Greek-Egyptian Saiddens skewering Australian multiculturalism' are 'crass and frequently hilarious' (Bastow, 2018). In reviewing their Skip Ahead web-series for the Sydney Morning Herald, Lallo (2018a) said people might assume Superwog was just focused on ethnic humour, when in fact, 'many gags are aimed at uptight white people'. One of their 60s kits that attracted controversy was, *If Superwog was on The Bachelor* (2015) (4.9 million views). Film-maker Koraly Dimitriadis (2015) said the skit highlighted a gender problem with migrant comedy generally. While Superwog was 'funny', and she understood the character was satire, she still felt the skit was 'sexist'. Significantly, Dimitriadis was pragmatic about the perpetuation of stereotypes in ethnic comedy: 'when that's the closest you can get to characters that represent your own experience, you join in and have a laugh, especially when your Anglo counterparts are too'. Dimitriadis challenged Superwog to put their power to good use and collaborate with migrant women who challenge their ideas: 'so we can level the playing field and promote change. It all begins with art'. But for the art to have social impact, the commerce supporting it must also be effective.

Burning problems

Monetization

Demonstrable views of multi-millions in storyworlds developed on YouTube, for example, cut investment risk for long-form platform gatekeepers, especially for BVODs and SVODs. There is no written record of this requirement, but I have established from Screen Australia that Skip Ahead teams retain copyright in their web-series, and it is very rare for third parties to be involved in Skip Ahead IP ownership (Healy, 2019). The IP arrangements under Skip Ahead are confidential; however, the IP rules for grant receivers are clear. Screen Australia requires producers to retain all underlying rights to make the project and exploit any sequels, or tell them otherwise. Similarly, the ABC (2015, p. 3) says creators and rights-holders control the exploitation of their content to reward their creativity, risk, and investment. As we saw in Chapter 1, first-mover YouTube-born creators first crossed over to the ABC in 2015–2016: for example, the *Bondi Hipsters* and the *Katering Show*, but ad hoc. In the past few years, an institutional and creator maturation has occurred due to 'underbelly' professionalization initiatives like Skip Ahead. This book tracks this significant change. Crucially different now is the innovation of funded story development to diverse creators who have not done it before; their acquisition of craft skills due to the new collaborations with established producers; and a levelling of the playing field in creators' favour when negotiating IP share against platforms, provided they have pre-built large online audiences. Emmy-winner and Skip Ahead mentor, Julie Kalceff, told me IP and the moral rights of creators are essential to creator sustainability from their early projects:

> It is important to see young creators keep their IP. It's essential since they are the ones who have built up the IP and audiences. If both parties respect each other, they can create fantastic synergies. That doesn't always happen. It will be interesting to see the long-term benefits.
>
> *Kalceff, 2019*

The lessons from the Saiddens about making a living are twofold. First, they used the affordances of the traditional economy of commodities to leverage the economy of public goods, and thus IP licensing. Second, their prodigious efforts in these two economies, inadvertently engaged the third economy, gifting and collaboration, via fan reaction videos and remixes, due to the voluntary digital labour brought into being by the Internet. Of the ten most important revenue streams from Table 2.1 in Chapter 2, the Saiddens used off-platform pay (legal work and driving), and AdSense and appearance fees (live shows) from the economy of commodities, to leverage the economy of public goods, that is subvention (Skip Ahead) and resulting IP licensing (Superwog web-series). Theo Saidden said they were fortunate enough not to have to adopt the two-track production strategy that seems endemic to emerging artists, commercial products to pay the bills, and passion projects to feed their souls: 'We are fortunate not to have to do this. We focus purely on writing, performing and making what we love in order to make our audience laugh' (Saidden, 2021).

Algorithmic volatility

Crucially, the Saiddens did not struggle with algorithmic volatility like we saw Voigt in Chapter 1, or will see with the Philippous in Chapter 4, Shackleford in Chapter 6, or Reardon in Chapter 5. The Saiddens also did not fall into the burn-out inducing trap of many YouTubers of uploading daily, weekly, or even monthly videos. They produced just 60 scripted YouTube videos over the decade from 2011, yet attracting 410 million views. The Saiddens' capacity to resist the time pressures on their creative flow appears to stem from two sources, one commercial, the other philosophical. First, they were never fully exposed to algorithmic, and thus CPM volatility, since the brothers always had either day jobs, live shows, subvention, or licensing. Second, as we saw in Breakout above, they have a striking degree of discipline over how they manifest their creativity in scripting.

Aside from their ethnic humour resonating so strongly with fans, the Saiddens also struck up three key collaborations: two with veteran YouTubers with their own mass fan bases, especially in the United States, Mychonny and RackaRacka; and finally with Emmy-nominated Princess Pictures, which produced both their web-series. Superwog's content also inspired many scores of fan and super-fan reaction and remix videos on YouTube and Tik Tok, themselves attracting hundreds of thousands of views in total. The most significant fan videos in this regard are US-based Strugglenation's, *Ronald McDonald on Cheaters (ft Superwog) Reaction* of 2016, which itself attracted 82,000 views; and *Superwog: Classroom comebacks Sparta Remix* of 2010, with 42,000 views. In terms of the impact of this UGC on overall Superwog views, the spreadability is likely modest to date, especially when compared with the extraordinary impact from the same co-creative UGC phenomenon we will see in Chapter 4 with RackaRacka, and Chapter 6 with SketchSHE.

Divide between old and new media

Where some traditional media have perpetuated racial stereotypes, this case shows their long overdue disruption via new media. In Chapter 1, I flagged this significant finding: the much-critiqued algorithmic culture of YouTube – while often stressing leading creators – nevertheless stimulated experimentation, and an audience-centric, networked production methodology that enabled publication of authentic stories in web-series to many hundreds of millions of viewers in under-represented deep niches online, globally. Based on my analysis of thumbnail meta-data and themes of Superwog's oeuvre (Figure 3.5), most striking is their five-year long 'proof of concept' of the representational strategies and characters in their short skits, that would ultimately find their fullest expression in their Superwog web-series under Skip Ahead. Indeed, their innovation in networked video of self-parody combined with even-handed parody of dominant Anglo and contending Asian minority culture, is evident from their first official videos, *Phone Operators* (1.6 million views), *Wog Girls vs Aussie Girls* (3 million views), and *Asian visits the Superwog family* (3.4 million views), of 2011 and 2012. Crucially, Superwog's representations of racial stereotypes – from which they get some of their best comedy – hold stereotypes up to the sunlight, long considered the best

FIGURE 3.6   Theo Saidden and John Luc aka Mychonny, in Asian visits the Superwog family; Interrogating Mum (3.4 million views) (August 2012) [screenshot from Superwog's YouTube channel]

'disinfectant' (Aftergood, 2008, p. 399). For example, at 0:50 minutes in the 'Interrogating Mum' beat within *Asian visits the Superwog family,* Superwog's mother cannot articulate why she assumes her son's Vietnamese friend (John Luc), must get good grades and be a doctor, and can only lamely indicate his face (Figure 3.6).

The Superwog case has important takeaways for screen industry policy makers internationally, and the question of whether they can customize the Skip Ahead model for their own nationals. The long development of Superwog's innovative and distinctive tone parallels what (Csikszentmihalyi, 2015 p. 54) argues is the long gestation of creative ideas in art and science generally: 'the folk view of the creative idea as a bolt of lightning is least realistic'. Creative insight is contextualized within a four-stage creative process characterized by *preparation* or hard work and research preceding the insight; *incubation* or a period of idle time alone; *illumination*, the moment of insight itself; and *verification*, the hard work and elaboration needed to bring the insight to bloom (Csikszentmihalyi, 2015, p. 75). Crucially regarding the distinctively temporal nature of creativity (Csikszentmihalyi, 2015, p. 66), Skip Ahead teams were accorded 'creative autonomy' informed by the understanding that 'pitch ideas change over the course of development'.

One of the most important problems in creative labour solved by Skip Ahead, as foreshadowed in Chapter 1, was younger producers and new media creators reporting feeling blocked in finding people to share jealously guarded industry know-how. It is to this problem I now turn. Overall, I found creators and established producers fell towards each other's skillsets, thus leveraging collaborating partners' strengths, allowing them to create award-winning web-series in social network markets, and, where they attracted extremely high views, enabled them to platform to upfront paying hybrid digital services of BVODs and SVODs. Crucially, as regards coping with algorithmic volatility and collaborating across the cultural divide, Cowap envisaged Skip Ahead as involving knowledge transfer – in principle – from the start. Cowap said he was only too aware of the divided 'camps' of old and new media. Even the professionals who ensured they were 'au fait' with the new platforms and new talent had little sense of the sheer scale of young creators who had been 'pushing out content since they were teenagers'. On the other side, creators had been making content without any support from Screen Australia, who they may have regarded 'as a faceless organisation that only deals with older folk and traditional TV' (Cowap, 2015). Cowap (2017) foresaw that Skip Ahead could 'be a really nice beneficial relationship' if the two camps could work together. Creators would benefit from the budgetary rigor, on-set expectations and the political experience of producers who could 'help them exploit their talent with traditional broadcasters'[1]. Crucially, for solving the problem of re-engaging lost, fragmented audiences, these 'switched-on' producers would be exposed to 'the world of online video', and in cases such as Superwog and Princess Pictures, Triptych Pictures, and Ludo and RackaRacka (Chapter 4), brought an 'extraordinary audience and talent [that was] eminently financeable'. Accordingly, Skip Ahead applicants were encouraged to team up from the start:

> To help them (YouTube creators) move towards a sustainable career, I try to instil an understanding and respect for craft skills. How to structure a longer, more ambitious piece of narrative content. How to create sympathetic characters. How to include twists and turns in the story. How to have character arc and have that reflected in theme. Things that really are instinctual, but also require a lot of study to truly understand.
>
> *Cowap, 2017*

Two hybrid collaboration models were brought into being by Skip Ahead: the first elaborated here is the *do-it-yourself* model; the second, the *hire-in-a-famous-writer* model, is elaborated in Chapter 4 with RackaRacka's Skip Ahead web-series. My core argument centres on Skip Ahead becoming an adaptive mechanism for the knowledge transfer lacking in the traditional industry, cruelling its progress to sustainability, as identified in the comprehensive surveys of producers cited in Chapter 1. Contrastingly, I argue that the problem of knowledge transfer – in the context of adapting to digital screen disruption – is respect for each other's accomplishments as creators and producers and shared senses of humour. They respond with two-way mentoring towards each other. I saw this respect first hand when interviewing the Saiddens and Walton in a green room at a VidCon. Both Walton and RackaRacka, collaborating producer Julie Byrne (Chapter 4), stressed that they shared the same sense of humour with their collaborating Skip Aheaders, the Saiddens, and the Philippous, respectively. Walton said genuine mutual respect for the artistry of both sides was essential, together with a principle of no censorship of the content:

> There's something subversive and renegade about their channel. We didn't want to water it down in any way. It was important to get to the core of who they were, and for these guys to get an understanding of my world, so we could mould these two worlds together.
>
> *Walton, 2017*

Theo Saidden attributes much of the success of the pilot, and ultimately their series commission, to the complete creative control they were afforded by the funding bodies and Princess Pictures 'guaranteeing authenticity'. This meant the extended work could sit comfortably within their oeuvre on YouTube. The production process was daunting:

> Paul took us through every step. He said it was a marriage between old and new, but every step was a multitude of steps. 'You are going to see a lot of emails now as we build up to shoot. Don't freak out!'.
>
> *Saidden, 2017*

As I show in the nine cases, the imperative to creative autonomy, wherever that journey leads, is paramount. In the end, the pre-existing material from their Skip Ahead pitch had to be abandoned in favour of a blend of two YouTube videos they had already been writing, *If SW worked at Drive Thru* and *Marriage Therapy* (Saidden, 2021). This became *Superwog Series Pilot*, a 'fish-out-of-water model' that arose from their collaboration with Elia Eliades, writing mentor and Egyptian Australian stand-up comic, Akmal Saleh, and character writing workshops at Princess Pictures. But the pressures put on social relations and work communications between collaborators engaged in any collision of production cultures, should not be underestimated:

> Fireworks, mate! Fireworks. No, it was good. For us, we really respected Princess. We respected their history, the stuff they'd done and thought we'd love to work with them.
>
> *Theo Saidden, 2017*

Crucially, established producers had as much to learn, as the YouTubers:

> I learnt not to hold onto things. Just because that's the way we always do it, doesn't mean that's the way you have to do it. We learnt what's important to that process.
>
> *Walton, 2017*

On the basis of greater creator IP retention, this path to monetization would apply when, for example, Kalowski, then head of ABC Comedy, commissioned the Saidden brothers. He saw their 23-minute Skip Ahead project *Superwog Pilot* on YouTube, and commissioned the pair to make six new half-hour series for *Superwog*, the first full-series collaboration between YouTube and the ABC, and ABC Comedy's first original scripted series. Kalowski says the make-or-break social analytics of the pilot were decisive, and he could see how the production skills of the creators had been honed during the pilot:

> I thought *SuperWog* was incredibly funny; it's hard to be funny for a long time. It was much more polished than their previous short form videos. They stepped up successfully to telling a really funny story across almost a half-hour – more than just five to 10 minutes. The production and creative quality had improved as well. Millions of people were watching, and they were watching right across the video. The story held them.
>
> *Kalowski, 2018*

Discrimination and authenticity

Creativity in art is defined as the conceptualization and solving of longstanding problems in a domain in new ways (Livingston, 2009, p. 20; Csikszentmihalyi, 2015, p. 24). Similarly, the Saiddens, in trying to solve the problem of how to get extremely high views to make a living from ethnic comedy, without social media-fuelled blowback, solved an old and deep problem: how to overturn the corrosive stereotypes of cultural Othering, by speaking their own representations independently. For Edward Said (1985, p. 2), the West had long projected its own 'suppositions, images and fantasies' on a region of the world called the Orient, but the Orient 'was not Europe's interlocutor, but its silent Other', left 'mute' and 'frozen', despite being in 'perpetual flux'. For Stuart Hall (2019, p. 360), popular culture only matters insofar as it is the terrain characterized by the struggle between the people and the power-bloc, and only where makers empower the oppressed and excluded: 'That is why 'popular culture' matters. Otherwise, to tell you the truth, I don't give a damn about it'. The impact of the Saidden's video skits and web-series is significant in both the parallel universe of content creation elaborated in this book, and the mainstream press. The Saiddens have been officially recognized for their satire jointly by Screen Australia and YouTube under Skip Ahead; they have attracted 410 million views worldwide on YouTube alone; and, by 2022, would have had a two-season web-series based on their YouTube characters and storyworlds on the national public broadcaster, the ABC. Moreover, their skits and web-series provoked mainstream debate about the role of ethnic humour and the use of racial stereotypes in satire (Starke, 2013; Galvin, 2014; Lallo, 2018; Guilliatt, 2019). As one of the Saiddens key collaborators, John Luc, aka Mychonny, said at the time: 'We've never had a real physical backlash. We're playing on a stereotype that I think is very real on both sides.

So, we'll make fun of the Aussies and then we'll make fun of the wogs just as much. It's an equal playing field'. The significance of this strategy – arguably a best practice in social-media-based ethnic humour – is underlined by the view of Cunningham and Craig (2017, p. 80), that this social media entertainment, and its discursive drivers, 'is what television is now', especially for younger viewers.

For screen storytellers, such as Superwog, authenticity may act as an inoculant against social media brigading. 'The thing about our videos is that they are reality', says Nathan Saidden (Galvin, 2014). Authenticity is crucial to screen business models going forward. The longstanding struggle over media representation has become increasingly acute. In collision are two historical forces, one cultural, one technological. The first, longstanding white male domination of Hollywood story rooms became apparent to any observer of the picketers at the Writers Guild of America strike of 2007–2008 (Banks, 2010, p. 96). This gender and racial disparity had an inevitable result 'on the production of the final product, translating to what we see on screen' (Banks, 2009, p. 96). The second, ubiquitous social media – the democratization of publication – has meant 'access to the master's machine' is effectively available to all (Caldwell, 2008, p. 329). As flagged in Chapter 1, in response to rampant commercialism and the intrusion of brands deep into audience spaces, Banet-Weiser (2012, p. 10) describes vocal audiences as 'clamouring for authenticity'. On the side of benefits, the role of diversity in screen storytelling is not mere 'political correctness'. Words and 'the pictures in our heads' matter: the more diverse and inclusive the creators and writer-producers, the more that diverse stories can be authentically told and heard. Indeed, the senior executive in charge of Netflix's content for Australia and New Zealand, Que Minh Luu, has indicated that her role involves a lens of inclusion: 'Netflix, it's all about that. Hyper-locality is what gives you authenticity. And leaning into that and having a good story can transcend borders'. Significantly, Luu is a child of Vietnamese refugees who fled in the 1970s by boat to Australia. Luu told Tadros (2021) that screen media to date has been too 'homogenous', and more points of view contributing to the conversation' are needed, 'because we haven't had ourselves reflected on screen'. Of blowback from reasonable industry inclusion initiatives that has nevertheless seen people being labelled 'diversity hires', Luu is forthright: 'I get called a diversity hire and its like, F – you. I do my job' (Tadros, 2021).

However, on the side of risk, recent years have seen an increasing premium on authenticity in screen storytelling and reputational damage when it fails. The Anglosphere has a big ongoing problem with screen representation, and, as Tina Cesa Ward argues in Chapter 10, little sense of an effective implementation plan to solve it. As explained in Chapter 1, social media fuelled backlashes, #OscarsSoWhite, and #BAFTASoWhite, surrounded these peak annual award events in the United States in 2015 and 2016 and in 2020 in the United Kingdom (Nwonka & Saha, 2021). Acclaimed Netflix Original *Orange is the New Black* (2013–2019), based on a white woman's year in a US jail with fellow people of colour and elderly inmates, was nevertheless criticized by activists as 'trauma porn written for white people' (Shackelford, 2016). Instigated by Banet-Weiser, the landmark Comprehensive Annenberg Report on Diversity in Entertainment of 2016 reported 'disturbing patterns around the lack of media representation concerning females and people of color in film'. By contrast, digital and TV led by Walt Disney and The CW Network were recognized by the University of Southern California's Annenberg report for their strong progress on screen representations of women and underrepresented characters generally. Hulu and Amazon were recognized for their inclusivity of women, while Viacom performed well for inclusion of female and underrepresented characters (Smith et al., 2016, p. 15). Multiple strategies were required to counter media inequality, especially recognition and altering of 'stereotypical thinking' and various accountability measures. But in mid-2020, George Floyd was killed in police custody. Under the #Hollywood4Blacklives movement, hundreds of creative people of colour called for an end to the glorification of 'brutal and lawless' police and agents as heroes. The wake of the convulsion over the killing continues to impact. In a wave of self-correcting and self-regulation, some major outlets and producers are reviewing high profile titles in response to changing community attitudes and the power to express it on social media (Bekiempis, 2020; Carras, 2020; Frater, 2020; Schuessler, 2020). If the historical reproduction of 'Othering' via stereotypes underpins hegemonic power as Hall contends (Molina-Guzmán, 2016, p. 441), the parody of stereotypes in culturally impactful ways indicates a momentous shift in power has been underway for a decade or more.

Note

1 Ultimately, Cowap was right about everything, except traditional broadcasters publishing Skip Ahead web-series. As I showed in Chapter 1, my longitudinal evidence is Skip Aheaders gravitated to SVODs and publicly funded BVODs, not commercial broadcasters.

References

AAP (2017, December 6). Aussie brothers behind 'Superwog' take out top YouTube spot [Wire release], Australian Associated Press, Sydney. https://www.9news.com.au/national/aussie-duo-takes-out-youtube-top-spot/

ABC (2015). *Intellectual property arrangements. Submission to Productivity Commission.* ABC. At our current pace of roughly 930,000 doses a week, we can expect to reach the 40 million doses needed to fully vaccinate Australia's adult population in early March 2022.

Aftergood, S. (2008). Reducing government secrecy: Finding what works. *Yale Law & Pololicy Review, 27,* 399.

Banet-Weiser, S. (2012). *AuthenticTM: The politics of ambivalence in a brand culture* (Vol. 30). NYU Press.

Banks, M. (2010) The Picket Line Online: Creative labor, digital activism, and the 2007–2008 writers guild of America strike, *Popular Communication, 8*(1), 20–33.

Bekiempis, V. (2020, January 19). Simpsons actor Hank Azaria says he'll no longer voice Apu. *The Guardian,* The Guardian Media Company, London. https://www.theguardian.com/tv-and-radio/2020/jan/18/simpsons-actor-hank-azaria-says-he-will-no-longer-voice-character-of-apu

Bastow, C. (2018). Wengie to RackaRacka: Navigating the world of Australia's YouTube superstars. *The Guardian*, The Guardian Philanthropic trust. https://www.theguardian.com/technology/2018/apr/02/wengie-to-rackaracka-navigating-the-world-of-australias-youtube-superstars

Berg, C. R. (1990). Stereotyping in films in general and of the Hispanic in particular. *Howard Journal of Communications, 2*(3), 286–300.

Bizzaca, C. (2017, July 21). Superwog: Leaping from sketches to a TV pilot [Blogpost]. *Screen Australia*, Sydney, Australia. https://www.screenaustralia.gov.au/sa/screen-news/2017/07-21-superwog-leaping-from-sketches-to-tv-pilot

Caldwell, J. T. (2008). *Production culture: Industrial reflexivity and critical practice in film and television.* Duke University Press.

Carras, C. (2020, June 23). Tina Fey under scrutiny after requesting '30 Rock' blackface episodes be removed, *Los Angeles Times*, Nant Capital LLC, Los Angeles. https://www.latimes.com/entertainment-arts/tv/story/2020-06-23/30-rock-blackface-tina-fey-episodes-nbc

Cowap, M. (2015) Development management, Screen Australia. Interview with Stuart Cunningham and Adam Swift, Sydney, 4 March and 4 September.

Cowap, M. (2017). Then Screen Australia multi-platform investment manager. Phone interview with Guy Healy, Brisbane, March.

Csikszentmihalyi, M. (2015). *The systems model of creativity: The collected works of Mihaly Csikszentmihalyi.* Springer.

Cunningham, S., & Craig, D. (2017). Being 'really real' on YouTube: Authenticity, community and brand culture in social media entertainment. *Media International Australia, 164*(1), 71–81.

Dimitriadis, K. (2015, October 15). When will migrant culture stop making jokes at the expense of women? [Blog]. *Daily Life, Sydney Morning Herald*, Fairfax Media, Sydney. http://www.dailylife.com.au/news-and-views/dl-opinion/when-will-migrant-culture-stop-making-jokes-at-the-expense-of-women

Dunn, K. M. (2003). Racism in Australia: Findings of a survey on racist attitudes and experiences of racism, National Europe Centre paper No. 77. In 'The Challenges of Immigration and Integration in the European Union and Australia Conference.

Fairclough, N. (2003). Political correctness': The politics of culture and language. *Discourse & Society, 14*(1), 17–28.

Film Victoria (n.d). Q&A with Superwog, [Blog] Film Victoria, Melbourne. https://www.film.vic.gov.au/showcase/qa-with-superwog

Flux, E. (2015). Battling with stereotypes: 'Maximum choppage' and Asian representation. *Metro Magazine: Media & Education Magazine, 185*, 46–51.

Frater, P. (2020, June 10). Netflix permanently pulls four Chris Lilley shows over racial depictions, Variety, Penske Media Corporation, New York. https://variety.com/2020/streaming/asia/netflix-removes-chris-lilley-shows-racial-depiction-

Galvin, N. (2014, June 7) Two of us: Theo and Nathan Saidden. *Sydney Morning Herald*, Fairfax Media, Sydney. https://www.smh.com.au/lifestyle/two-of-us-theo-and-nathan-saidden

Gandini, A., & Graham, J. (2017). *Collaborative production in the creative industries* (p. 240). University of Westminster Press.

Gillota, D. (2013). *Ethnic humor in multiethnic America*. Rutgers University Press.

Guilliatt, R. (2019, November 22). Is call-out culture killing comedy? *The Weekend Australian*, News Corp Australia. https://www.theaustralian.com.au/weekend-australian-magazine/is-callout-culture-killing-comedy/news-story/

Hall, S. (2019). *Essential essays* (Vol. 1), Foundations of cultural studies. Duke University Press.

Healy, G. (2019). Fast and Furious filmmaking: YouTube's prospects for budding and veteran screen content producers. *Metro Magazine: Media & Education Magazine, 202,* 114–120.

Healy, G., & Williams, P. (2017). Metaphor use in the political communication of major resource projects in Australia. *Pacific Journalism Review, 23*(1), 150–168.

Hermes, J. (2008). *Re-reading popular culture.* John Wiley & Sons.

Hodgart, M. J. C. (1969). *Die Satire* (Vol. 42). Transaction Publishers.

Humphries, G. (2015, July 29). Shortcut to stardom for Superwog. Illawarra Mercury, Fairfax Media. https://www.illawarramercury.com.au/story/3244027/shortcut-to-stardom-for-superwog/

Jenkins, H., Ford, S. & Green, J., 2013. *Spreadable media: Creating value and meaning in a networked culture* (Vol. 15). NYU Press.

Kalceff, J. (2019). Julie Kalceff, founder and director of Common Language Films. Skype interview with Guy Healy.

Kalowski, R. (2018). Head of ABC Comedy. Skype interview with Guy Healy.

Lallo, M. (2018a, October 11). Superwog is not politically correct – but it is damn funny. *Sydney Morning Herald,* Fairfax Media, Sydney. https://www.smh.com.au/entertainment/tv-and-radio/superwog-is-not-politically-correct-but-it-is-damn-funny

Lallo, M. (2018b, July 7). Australia's new wave of 'wog humour' is about class as much as race. *Sydney Morning Herald,* Fairfax Media, Sydney. https://www.smh.com.au/entertainment/tv-and-radio/australia-s-new-wave-of-wog-humour-is-about-class-as-much-as-race

Lange, P.G. (2007). Fostering friendship through video production: How youth use YouTube to enrich local interaction. In *Proceedings of annual meeting of the International Communication Association* (Vol. 27). ICA.

Lippmann, W. (1965). Public opinion (1922). http://infomotions. com/etexts/gutenberg/dirs/etext04/pbp nn10. htm

Livingston, P. (2009). Poincaré's "Delicate Sieve": On creativity in the arts'. In M. Krausz, D. Dutton, & K. Bardsley (Eds.), *The idea of creativity* (pp. 129–146). Brill.

Lopez, L. K. (2016). *Asian American media activism: Fighting for cultural citizenship* (Vol. 10). NYU Press.

McManus, B. (2007, October 18). Still taking the Pizza. The Age, Fairfax Media Group, Melbourne. https://www.theage.com.au/entertainment/still-taking-the-pizza

McNicholas, H. (2013, June 2). Superwog and Mychonny share their experiences to stardom, Grapeshot, Macquarie University Student Publication, Sydney. https://grapeshotmq.com.au/2013/06/superwog-and-mychonny-share-their-experiences-to-stardom/

Marx, N. (2011). 'The missing link moment': Web comedy in new media industries. *The Velvet Light Trap, 68,* 14–23.

Mastro, D. E., & Greenberg, B. S. (2000). The portrayal of racial minorities on prime time television. *Journal of Broadcasting & Electronic Media, 44*(4), 690–703.

Matamoros-Fernández, A. (2017). Platformed racism: The mediation and circulation of an Australian race-based controversy on Twitter, Facebook and YouTube. *Information, Communication & Society, 20*(6), 930–946.

Molina-Guzmán, I. (2016). # OscarsSoWhite: How Stuart Hall explains why nothing changes in Hollywood and everything is changing. *Critical Studies in Media Communication, 33*(5), 438–454.

Morreale, J. (2014). From homemade to store bought: *Annoying Orange* and the professionalization of YouTube. *Journal of Consumer Culture, 14*(1), 113–128.

Ng, E. (2020). No grand pronouncements here…: Reflections on cancel culture and digital media participation. *Television and New Media, 21*(6), 621–627.

Nwonka, C., & Saha, A. (Eds.). (2021). *Black film British cinema II*. Goldsmiths Press.

Ongaro, D. (2013, December 28). Superwog creators see their comedy skit become a YouTube sensation, *The Sunday Telegraph*, News Corp Australia, Sydney. https://www.dailytelegraph.com.au/superwog-creators-see-their-comedy-skit-become-a-youtube-sensation/news-story/

Ozdowski, S. (2013). Australian multiculturalism. The roots of its success. Promoting Changes in Times of Transition and Crisis: Reflections on Human Rights Education. https://doi. org/10.12797/9788376383651.10

Rieder, B., Coromina, Ò., & Matamoros-Fernández, A. (2020). Mapping YouTube. First Monday.

Said, E. W. (1985). Orientalism reconsidered. *Race & Class*, *27*(2), 1–15.

Saidden, T. (2021, March). Director of Superwog season two, and co-creator, writer, producer. Personal Communication with Guy Healy, Brisbane.

Saidden, T; Saidden, N. and Walton, P. (2017). Theo and Nathan Saidden, actors, writers and producers of Superwog, and Paul Walton, producer Superwog. Face-to-face Interview with Guy Healy, VidCon Melbourne, September, 2017.

Shackelford, A. (2016, June 20). 'Orange is the New Black is Trauma Porn Written for White People [spoilers]'. Wear Your Voice. wearyourvoicemag.com

Schuessler, J. (2020, Jun 14). The long battle over 'Gone with the wind'. *New York Times Company*. https://www.nytimes.com/2020/06/14/movies/gone-with-the-wind-battle.html

Smith, A. (2018). *Storytelling industries: Narrative production in the 21st century*. Springer.

Smith, S. L., Choueiti, M., & Pieper, K. (2016). Inclusion or invisibility? Comprehensive Annenberg report on diversity in entertainment. Institute for Diversity and Empowerment at Annenberg.

Starke, P. (2013, April 4). Australia's hottest YouTube stars Jason Pinder, Theo and Nathan Saidden and Louna Maroun. News Corp Australia Network, News Corp, Surry Hills, Sydney.

Tadros, E. (2021, February 27–28). How Netflix channels diversity. *Weekend Financial Review*, Fairfax Media Group, Sydney. https://www.afr.com/companies/media-and-marketing/netflix-s-local-content-boss-talks-diversity-and-inclusion

Tofler, M. (2017). Australian made comedy online – Laughs, shock, surprise and anger. *Continuum*, *31*(6), 820–832.

Tsolidis, G., & Pollard, V. (2009). *Being a 'wog' in Melbourne – Young people's self-fashioning through discourses of racism. Discourse: Studies in the Cultural Politics of Education*, *30*(4), 427–442.

Walton, P. (2017). Theo and Nathan Saidden, actors, writers and producers of Superwog, and Paul Walton, producer Superwog. Face-to-face Interview with Guy Healy, VidCon Melbourne, September, 2017.

4

THE DARK CINEMATIC DREAMS OF THE PHILIPPOU TWINS, AKA RACKARACKA

When Danny and Michael Philippou met George Miller, the director of *Mad Max* (1979–) at a Skip Ahead workshop for Google on longform, Miller talked about 'how not to sacrifice your creative vision, and how he didn't bend to the rules. Stand your ground' (Philippou, 2017). This touchstone principle from the rapprochement between the Oscar and BAFTA winning director of *Happy Feet* (2006), and the enfant terrible YouTubers, illuminates the twins' oeuvre, and their cinematic background story. As I argue in Chapter 1, rapprochement is occurring as the most narratively gifted Youtubers converge with the SVODs and BVODs that most value diversity, authenticity and creative autonomy, via exceptional web-series. This chapter tells the story of the Philippous' journey, as their fans and collaborators saw it, and of the twins' web-series and features development occurring simultaneously behind the scenes. In explaining their oeuvre of horror-comedy to US audiences, *Variety* said RackaRacka (Figure 4.1) came 'from Down Under (with) a disquieting blend of homemade slasher pics, gruesome film-and-video-game parodies, and a homicidal Ronald McDonald doppelganger' (Spangler, 2016).

The public-facing side of the story of how they leveraged over one billion YouTube views for their longform projects, emerges from my analysis of their 171-video oeuvre from 2013 to 2021 (Table 4.1). However, their longerform process is informed by interviews I conducted separately with then collaborators Danny Philippou, and producer Julie Byrne of Triptych Pictures, as the Adpocalypse broke on the YouTube creator world in early 2017, and longitudinal interviews with both now four years later. By then they were working on separate projects, and the twins had abandoned their RackaRacka-style production to re-prioritize their longstanding web-series and film ambitions, sustained by their lucrative new 'roast' channel, Left on Red. When we spoke, Danny Philippou had been in one his 'full horror zone

DOI: 10.4324/9781003182481-4

FIGURE 4.1   The Philippou brothers in their extensive home DVD library

moods' rather than a comedy mood, 'bingeing horror films' to help the twins write 'this straight horror movie, '*Talk to Me*', with filming to start later in 2021 (Philippou, 2021). Just months previously more videos were demonetised, as they 'got black-listed from the algorithm' for being too violent (Philippou, 2021).

Regarding Skip Ahead and deepening their narrative skills, Byrne introduced the Philippous to multi-Emmy-winning producers Daley Pearson and Charlie Aspinwall of Ludo Studios, who in turn brought in Andrew Ellard, a writer and script editor who worked for different periods on *Red Dwarf* (1988–2020) and *The IT Crowd* (2006–2010). Collectively, the collaborative trio delivered the Skip Ahead project, *Stunt Gone Wrong LIVESTREAM* (2017) in under a year. The demographics were 80 per cent male, 20 per cent female, while the geographics were 43 per cent US, 11 per cent UK, and Australia just 8.6 per cent, followed by Canada, Mexico, and Norway. The 43-minute *SGW Live* is as yet unreviewed by critics, and at 1.7 million views over three years later, only achieved a fraction of the views of most RackaRacka videos. I argue the seamless warping of *SGW Live's* three-act narrative structure into at least three distinct genres, faux livestream, thriller, and horror, represents a novel innovation for longform networked video in the endemically shortform culture of YouTube. *SGW Live* retained 80 per cent of its audience across the video (Philippou, 2021). Revealed also beneath the wild ride of *SGW Live* is a significant moral dimension that warns teenagers about the threat of online predation, crucially, in the field of networked video into which their attention has fragmented.

In terms of creativity and storytelling in algorithmic culture, RackaRacka matters especially for two reasons. First, with over billion views on YouTube

TABLE 4.1 RackaRacka's 171+ video oeuvre, 2013 to 2021*

Year	Videos total	Views total (millions)	Top Three (millions)
2013	4	22	Attacked by McDonalds Manager (8.7); Knife trick (5.7); Teaching kids fighting (5.5)
2014	31 including eight in the Top 15, 2013-2021	421.7	Ronald tastes Burger King (76); Chicken Store Massacre (60); Potter vs Star Wars #1 (31)
2015	10 including five in the Top 15	195	Marvel vs DC (71); Halo vs CoD (44); Ronald Playground slaughter (21)
2016	17 including one of Top 15	108.5	Naruto (18); Ronald WWE Beatdown (15); Ronald Beatdown #2 (13)
2017	33 including one of Top 15	140	Star Wars in Public (35); It – McDonalds' Version (14); Ronald vs Cookie Monster (11)
2018	35	72.7	Ronald plays Fortnite (8.2); Ronald fired (7.7); *deep web* (Ash vlogs)
2019	27	51.2	Potter vs Star Wars #2 (7.7); Ronald meets Riley (5.5); Dirty Talk w Riley (4)
2020	11	16.7	Recreating WWE moments (6.6); Ronald Extreme Muckbag (2.3); Ronald vs Batman (2)
2021 (until March*)	3	0.9	Ronald meets Dr Phil (0 6); Pokémon rampage (0.2); No reach…no views (.1)
		1,027	

Source: Healy's own analysis.

ALT Table summarises RackaRacka's views from 2013 to 2021, showing how their views dramatically declined after the 2017 Adpocalypse, even as they uploaded ever more videos

alone since 2013, RackaRacka have had a significant impact on popular culture, especially among their Millennial peers and Gen Z's worldwide. For 'a great many especially younger viewers', SME is what television is, now' (Cunningham & Craig, 2017, p. 80). Second, the twins also have 'a serious side' with arthouse influences, especially South Korean director Bong Joon-Ho (*Parasite*, 2019), particularly his crime thriller, *Memories of Murder* (2003), and obscure Russian writer-director, Andrey Zvyagintsev's films, *The Return* (2003) and *Loveless* (2017):

> My brother and I are big fans of Russian and Korean films in terms of the films we are writing. For RackaRacka it's a mess of popular culture. Joon-Ho is one of our favorite directors, even before he blew up with *Parasite*. I really love all of Zvyagintsev's films. His films are really tense and beautifully shot, drawn out relationship dramas, yeah.
>
> *Philippou, 2021*

RackaRacka - Flex - Official Music Video- Reupload - (if it ever gets deleted)

I KNOW I'VE GOT NO TALENT

0.23 / 2.56

FIGURE 4.2 Capturing the zeitgeist: Women in bikinis sit and straddle a limousine while the RackaRacka crew perform a rap song titled Flex

But when these masters of SME, who have lived within the maelstrom of net-worked video for the past eight years reveal what they really think and feel, they produce the searing critique of social media culture, *Flex* (Dec 2018) (Figure 4.2)[1]. The three-minute rap video achieved 2.4 million views before it was removed from YouTube in unknown circumstances. However, the rap has since been posted on channels other than RackaRacka's and appears to have been looped by fans to 30 minutes as a party mix. Despite its high production values and confrontational address, *Flex* appears also yet to have been reviewed.

The messaging of *Flex* occurs in an effective rap song that addresses, self-reflexively, six burning issues in contemporary popular culture scholars and thought leaders have been grappling for a decade. For example, the Philippous lines *'we are not people, we are brands'*, with parallels Banet-Weiser's (2012, p. 3) concerns young people feel pressured to 'self-brand': 'as a dominant way to express our politics, our creativity, our religious practices – indeed, our very selves'. The lines *'where are the spending parents, the ones who don't care what their children stare at'* and *'until you pop on Victory Royale'*, parallels Carter et al.'s (2020, p. 461) analysis of single-person-shooter game, Fortnite, highly popular with 8-12-year-old children. Despite Fortnite's *Lord of the Flies*-style narrative, Carter et al critiqued parents for letting their children download the game because of an apparent lack of visible violence or blood. The lines *'worth measured by my followers…I do it for the clicks'*, parallels research among emerging adults, 'Generation Validation', by Stapleton et al. (2017, p. 148), about the risks of psychological harm of social media's comparison culture, especially among those with low esteem. Moreover, the lines *'are you Gen Z or Gen Sheep, make your brain demented'*, arguably echoes

Millennial and Gen Z concerns about social-media fuelled tribalism (Deloitte, 2019, p. 1). The line *'the message is this, if somebody fucken dies, then their death is for clicks'*, came in the year US authorities reported 86 poisonings related to the Tide Pod challenge, with YouTube recasting its content guidelines 'to ban videos of people doing dangerous shit for views' (Weisenstein, 2019). Finally, *'not Nature, not nurture, it's a helluva lure, girls only worth are their breasts'*, parallels research by Davis (2018, p. 5) about the objectification and pacification of women's bodies in social media posts. RackaRacka's use of the corporately owned, but UGC-dominated YouTube for their indictment of social media in *Flex*, is arguably 'culture jamming'. For Caldwell (2008, p. 329), this counter media, counter conglomerate strategy calls for workers 'to throw a wrench in the machine', with conditions now ripe for 'culture jamming', since everyone has access to the master's machine. The twins operate in two narrative worlds, one the RackaRacka and Left on Red world they have built with fans and superfans respectively, and 'the more serious subject matter' which 'we lightly touch on, we started looking at in *Flex*' (Philippou, 2021). For Byrne (2021), *Flex* is next level excellence: 'they are commenting on pop culture constantly in a way that satisfies their fans with gore and crudeness and sexual stuff, but the messaging underneath is just extraordinary'. This moral dimension parallels the 'tendency towards idealism among Australian producers' (Cameron et al., 2010, p. 90).

Genre, horror, comedy, horror-comedy, and screenwriting canon

Before we explore how the Philippous and their mentors and collaborators broke so many of the rules, but stuck by others in important ways, we need to briefly consider what the pre-eminent rules, or canons are relevant to this case. For example, concern for genre, the way stories are organized so we know what to read and expect, dates back to antiquity. For Aristotle, the classical arts were understood as 'modes of imitation', each differing regarding medium, objects and manner of imitation, but in each case distinct (Altman, 1999, p. 62). Mode of address also varied such as switching from narration to being in character, staying in the same narrative mode, or imitating the whole story dramatically as if it were real. For Todorov (1990, p. 18), genres function as 'horizons of expectation' for readers, and as 'models of writing' for authors. Genres are thus essential to mass marketing, especially in the Golden Age of SVOD series. For example, George RR Martin's *Games of Thrones* became marketed as '*The Sopranos* meets Middle-earth' (Hughes, 2014).

With the webification of culture, the meta-genre of digital video was broken up to better understand participatory culture, and its role in driving innovation in cultural production. Based on the tidal wave of videos emanating from K-pop musician Psy's, *Gangnam Style* (2012), viewed over four billion times, Xu et al. (2016, p. 110) categorized these cultural creations into five genres: official, original, remix, participation, and evaluation. For example, remixes recreated elements of the original *Gangnam Style (GS)*; participation involved users moving rhythmically to the song, parodies and covers, while evaluation involved formal critiques and, importantly, reaction videos. Xu et al's taxonomy, based in the eighth highest viewed networked video to 2021, will be applied to better understand the different forms of participatory videos to the creators, writers, and producers in this book: RackaRacka below, SketchSHE's in Chapter 6, Kalceff's *Starting From Now* in Chapter 7, Forster and Rowland's *Flunk* in Chapter 9 and Miller and Ward's *Anyone But Me* in Chapter 10. Importantly, Xu et al. (2016, p. 120) concluded while virality ensures mere dissemination, elevation to meme status ensured longevity of the innovation since the video content was supported by a community of creators. Dawkins (1989, p. 192) coined the term 'meme', defined 'as a unit of cultural transmission, or unit of imitation', such as tunes, ideas, catch-phrases, fashions, or building arches.

Drawing on Dawkins, Csikszentmihalyi (2015, p. 55) argues in relation to artistic and scientific pursuits 'a domain is a system of related memes that change through time, and what changes them is the process of creativity'. These participatory processes and innovation in networked video's long tail arise time and again across the cases of this book and are increasingly important to the sustainability of creative labour.

The horror genre traces its ancestry back to the Gothic literature of late 1700s England, amid condemnations about the impact of the 'sordid taste and depraved morals' of these 'un-natural horrors' and 'gross improbabilities' on 'impressionable' young imaginations (Davison, 2009). Significantly, 'many of the first Gothic romances are simply moral tales in supernatural dress' (Napier in Davison, 2009). Stephen King (2011, p. xii), naturally, defends young horror fans as mostly healthy people with over-active imaginations who better recognize the fragility of existence, and who see and feel 'in darker spectrums'. Since the mid-1980s, scholars have tried to fathom why people, mainly young men, seem to voluntarily enjoy graphic violence and getting terrified, with Tamborini and Stiff (1987, p. 416) suggesting horror can provide psychic relief to internal conflict, and Phillips (2005) arguing such films capture the deep anxieties and grave concerns of the day. Australia has made a rich contribution to the genre. Horror or horror-related titles include the Australian Gothic-influenced *Mad Max* (1979-) films (Dermody & Jacka, 1987, p. 47); and terror in outback settings, what Ryan (2021) terms 'the monstrous landscape' such as *Picnic at Hanging Rock* (1975), *Razorback* (1984) and *Dead Calm* (1989). Recent research has lent some credibility to what has been regarded as one of the most disreputable genres of film. Scrivner et al. (2021) tested the effects of horror and disaster media on viewers a month into the 2020 pandemic, and, surprisingly, found they were beneficial regarding coping strategies. Research on media effects date to concerns about the propaganda of contending militaries last century, but are generally regarded as inconclusive unless rigorous studies of effects can be traced to individual behaviour.

Conversely, the origins of staged comedy are so ancient they have been lost, with the genre effectively starting with genius Greek playwright, Aristophanes

(Sifakis and Sephakes, 1971), whose plays on topics concerning the battle of the sexes and parodies of tragedies, still resonate (Austin & Olson, 2004). Where tragic drama functioned to account for humanity's past, comedy featured 'magic coincidences which could be justified by the arbitrary ways of fortune' (Sifakis and Sephakes, 1971, p. 9). Campbell (1993, p. 28) argues in the ancient world, comedy held a higher status than tragedy on account of its capacity for deeper revelations of the human condition, and reflection of 'inexhaustible joy of life invincible'. Indeed, Campbell argues tragedy and comedy, in their mythological aspects, are bound together, and to the extent they are loved, help people navigate 'the dark interior from tragedy to comedy'. Greek comedy was direct address of jokes to the audience which took their reactions into account (Sifakis and Sephakes, 1971, p. 11). Modern screen comedy is situational, with the actors having to believe in what they are doing, or risk appearing contrived, and therefore, unfunny (Field, 1979, p. 139). Burgess and Green (2018, p. 6) attribute the breakout of YouTube into the mainstream to *Lazy Sunday* (2005), two New York comics' rap about getting together for cupcakes and watching *Chronicles of Narnia*. Tofler et al. (2019) suggested for broadcasters, the comedy web-series, by for example, Australian writer-producers the Bondi Hipsters and The Katering Show, had become a new form of script development as online audiences replaced broadcast executives as gatekeepers. Carroll (1999, p. 145) argues the seemingly paradoxical subgenre of horror-comedy, for example, *Beetlejuice* (1989), had gained increasing prominence: 'Horror turns the screw; comedy releases it. Comedy elates; horror stimulates depression paranoia and dread'. To explain the apparent contradiction, Carroll argued as a genre, comedy had always been 'stridently amoral', and within the comedic frame, injury, pain, and death are often elements in a joke.

As the second decade of the 21st century turns into the third, the design of longform narrative structure – already a wicked problem for screen storytellers – has become both more challenging and open to new subversions. Writers are now designing storyworlds and populating them with characters and plots in a context where generations of film, TV, and VOD viewers, courtesy of *Star Wars* (1977), have familiarity with the dominant paradigm of Joseph Campbell's hero's journey, or the monomyth. Campbell (1993, p. 11) drew on religious, mythological, and folk sources from both the East and West, many of which pre-date the Hellenistic period in which Aristotle articulated storytelling canon, to argue the human spirit is driven forward by mythologies which exhibit a profoundly constant set of basic truths, to navigate our journeys and metamorphoses. For Campbell (1993, p. 30), the mythological adventure of the hero is an enlarged version of the rites of passage, based on the tripartite 'separation-initiation-return' model: 'a hero ventures forth from the world of the common day into a region of supernatural wonder: fabulous forces are there encountered and a decisive victory is won: the hero comes back from this mysterious adventure with the power to bestow boons on his fellow man'. For example, the proto-story of romance and betrayal where Theseus slays the

Minotaur, with the aid of Ariadne's clever red thread, but whose love Theseus ultimately spurns (Mills, 1997, p. 251). Hundreds of years later comes Aristotle ([335BCE] (Armstrong, 1998, p. 452)), who defined the well-constructed plot as a whole 'which has a beginning, middle and end'. Jumping forward to the 1800s, Coleridge (1817) articulates how he writes engaging supernatural and romantic characters for his own lyric ballads to: 'transfer a human interest and a semblance of truth sufficient to procure for these shadows of imagination that willing suspension of disbelief for the moment'. In the modern era, Field (1998, p. 11) promulgates an alternative to drawing on myth to power compelling narrative. Inspired by American novelist, Henry James, writers should determine characters' 'dramatic need' and ask: 'What is character but the determination of incident? And what is incident but the illumination of character?'

Nevertheless, the power of the Campbellian hero proves strong. For Disney, 20th century Fox and Paramount story analyst and development executive, Christopher Vogler (2017, p. 15), the spirit of the hero's journey pervaded his contribution to *Aladdin* and *Hercules* and helped drive films such as *Indiana Jones*, some 28 sci-fi films, *The Matrix*, *Harry Potter*, *The Chronicles of Narnia*, *Lord of the Rings*, *The Hobbit*, and more. Vogler (2017, p. 17) argued viewers' understanding of the classic forms represented 'an opportunity for artists to shock, challenge and delight by constantly questioning assumptions about what is a hero and what is a hero's journey'. *Star Wars* director George Lucas himself acknowledged his use of the monomyth metaphor, saying Joseph Campbell had 'become my Yoda' (Campbell, 2003, p. 187). For his part, Campbell (2003, p. 187) said *Star Wars* had updated the hero's journey for modernity, which is the existential struggle between man and machine: 'Is the machine going to be the servant of human life? Or is it going to be master and dictate? And the machine includes the totalitarian state, whether its Fascist or Communist it's still the same state'. Finally, Csikszentmihalyi (2015, p. 103), underlines the stakes for artists in relation to understanding tradition: 'Without rules, there cannot be exceptions, and without tradition there cannot be novelty'.

Biography

The nine years from 2013 to 2021 was a creative whirlwind unprecedented on YouTube as the Philippous adapted horror to algorithmic culture (Table 4.1). The Philippous' artistic career has evolved through distinct phases: formative, breakout, rehearsal for longer forms, dissent, and leveraging, all grounded in their outer suburban roots.

In terms of career trajectory, Table 4.1 shows how the Philippous built a formidable online profile over 1.047 billion views strong and leveraged this body of 171 videos into behind-the-scenes collaborations with Triptych Pictures and Ludo Studios; as well as a funded film production deal with Causeway, the official producer of *The Babadook*. Byrne, the Philippous' 'film mother', was line

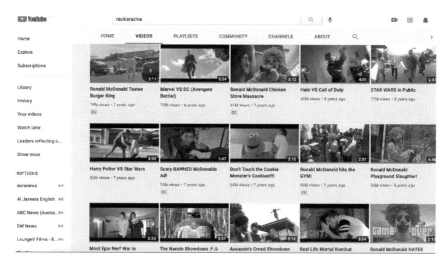

FIGURE 4.3 Screenshot from RackaRacka's YouTube channel – Most popular

producer on *The Babadook,* marketed as 'psychological horror' film. For New York Times bestseller and author of *Danse macabre (2011),* Stephen King, *The Babadook* was 'highly recommended' (King, 2014). The 'cinephile' twins were forever talking about *The Babadook* and wanted to make their own mark with a horror feature of the same calibre (Byrne, 2021). Moreover, the view numbers and top three videos show just how well RackaRacka understood the tastes of their mostly young US and European male audiences for violence, comedy and gore, especially when these genres were mixed (figure 4.3). Audience tastes for graphic violence are as old as the prototypical hero's journey itself, for example the blood-soaked final act of Homer's *The Odyssey* (750BCE) (Butler, 2013, p. 703). Shown also in two of their four most popular videos to date, *Marvel vs DC* and *Halo vs Call of Duty,* was their first significant rapprochement with mainstream screen storytelling conventions: these two videos were produced with Byrne with subvention from Screen Australia. In SME terms, we also see most dramatically how their views declined after the 2017 Adpocalypse, even as they uploaded ever more videos. In the press, RackaRacka characterized the platform's post-Adpocalypse policy changes as the 'Disney-fication' of YouTube (McCauley, 2018). Indeed, 'a stricter regime of demonetizing videos found not to be advertiser friendly' was among a raft of post-Adpocalypse policy changes by the platform (Kumar, 2019, p. 3).

Formative period

'Of course we got hurt', they say of their constant efforts to 'out-hard-core each other' as children (Gutelle, 2015). By the first decade of the 21st century, the video camcorder had become ubiquitous household technology, putting 'the means of producing video within the reach of the everyday consumer' (Willett, 2009). So the twins made 130 'films and tapes' of their 'violent, over-the-top' childhood, a montage of which, *Our Epic Childhood* (Philippou, 2020), strikingly foreshadows the oeuvre they carved out on YouTube as twenty-something adults. The twins attended Para Hills High School and Media Arts Production School and were *Harry Potter* fans. Inspired by mid-1990s cult-fantasy TV hit, *Zena: Warrior Princess,* and World Wrestling Entertainment (WWE), they made their earliest YouTube clips at their father's house at Pooraka, but moved out to spare him further anguish from all the wall and ceiling damage. For the Philippous', their earliest videos were sampled by US TV and pirated (Joshi, 2016).

> They kept going really viral and ending up on massive TV shows like *Conan O'Brien* and *Jimmy Kimmel.* Everyone kept on using them and re-uploading them without knowing where they came from.
>
> *Joshi, 2016*

RackaRacka thus pivoted to YouTube to counter the piracy, due to perceived better copyright protection.

Meanwhile, fatefully, Byrne employed the pair as runners and assistant electrics on film projects and was impressed by their award-winning directorial debut, the short horror film, *Deluge* (2014) (Byrne, 2017). Written with Michael Beck, Danny's future co-writer on *Talk to Me,* the logline for *Deluge* prefigured their early talent for dark narrative: 'The world is flooding, it's been raining for weeks on end and 12-year-old Briggs is the last in line of kids to be sacrificed in a ritualistic drowning'.

Breakout period

However, their distinctive oeuvre of horror parodying the McDonald's iconic corporate mascot Ronald McDonald, scenes of escalating dramatized violence and superhero mashups broke them out, proving highly popular with teens and twenty-somethings, especially in the densest viewing market in the world, the United States.

Given the precarity of AdSense and the 'six-figure' paydays available via brand sponsorships, Danny Philippou explains their business model:

> There's two sides to RackaRacka (pictured): there's the violent stuff we have for one half of the audience, and then there's the PG videos: *Harry Potter VS Star Wars,* or focus on fight scenes. We can work with gaming and films companies because there are violent films and violent games.
>
> *Danny Philippou, 2017*

Danny Philippou attributed its breakout popularity to the same strategy fellow Skip Aheader Shae-Lee Shackleford explains drives the popularity of

SketchSHE's *Mime Through Time* in Chapter 6: the mass mobilization of niche fandoms via the one online video. Philippou explains:

> We thought it was pretty decent because of the massive audience already behind *Harry Potter* and *Star Wars*, but we didn't imagine this!
>
> *Galletly, 2014*

In less than a month in 2014, the twins produced two of their most famous, and bloodiest, videos ever: *Ronald McDonald Tastes Burger King* and *Ronald McDonald Chicken Store Massacre*. As mentioned in Chapter 1, emergent YouTubers often form on-screen collaborations, especially symbiotic 'rat-packs' (Relis, 2015). Frank Sinatra, Dean Martin, and Sammy Davis Jnr led the original 'rat pack', a singing and comedy collaboration at a Las Vegas casino at the turn of the 1950s (Levy, 1999).

In 2015, Byrne and the Philippous made three YouTube videos funded by Screen Australia as online TV drama: *Marvel VS DC (Avengers Battle!)*, *Halo VS Call of Duty* and *Walking Dead VS Last of Us*, which so resonated with lower ranked YouTubers – especially in the United States – lead fans produced tribute and reaction videos in such numbers they ran many pages deep on YouTube (Figure 4.4). Crucially for our re-conceptualization of co-creativity, however, YouTubers such as the Philippou use them to fine-tune their uploads:

> I watch reaction videos to see where the jokes hit (pictured). Film-makers sit in the back of cinemas and listen to the audience, or do test screenings with audiences. We don't have that with YouTube. It just goes straight out there.
>
> *Philippou, 2021*

FIGURE 4.4 American teenagers sitting on a couch reacting to a RackaRacka video

During 2015, they also shot their bloodiest video, *Real Life Mortal Kombat Fatalities*, categorized as being of such graphic violence and horror, it has since fallen foul of YouTube's Community guidelines, being displayed and only accessible beneath an official 'Offensive material' warning. Nevertheless, RackaRacka is clearly serving audience tastes, since the video is the twins' 13ᵗʰ most popular, with 18 million views by late 2019. Personally, I cannot 'unsee' this video.

Meanwhile, behind the scenes, Triptych received script subvention for an action comedy, *Concrete Kings,* which referenced cult US skating film, *Lords of Dogtown* (2005). With Byrne as the producer, the Philippous were listed as directors, collaborating with local writers, Word Ninjas. Just as the trajectories of creators and producers have their own twists and turns, so to do stories under development, as collaborators come together to craft lead characters and journeys into an effective script, see it through to production and distribution, or not, take their leaves, and recombine on new narratives. This was especially true of *Concrete Kings,* under development for six years. Danny Philippou regrets deprioritizing the project's scripting due to the twins' SME commitments, but Michael Philippou is still talking with Byrne about it (Byrne, 2021; Philippou, 2021).

In 2016, RackaRacka's public efforts to cross over to long-form narrative triggered a debate in the United States about increasing roles for traditional screenwriters as 'ghost screenwriters' for YouTubers. In 2016, RackaRacka only produced two highly popular videos, *Meet the McDonalds* and *Naruto Showdown,* but they won such rapidly increasing recognition from the mainstream industry in Australia and the United States they were a cultural force to be reckoned with. Indeed Platinum-level creator Ryan Higa, who created for Wong Fu Productions, ruefully acknowledged RackaRacka's *Naruto Showdown* had rendered his own version 'irrelevant' (Higa, 2019). In April, *LA Screenwriter* blogger Fin Wheeler (2016) likened the Philippous to the Oscar-winning writer-directors the Coen Brothers, assessing their *Don't Touch the Cookie Monster's Cookies* video was 'distinctly noir'. Wheeler predicted ghost screenwriting would become a major growth industry, since the skillset required to be 'Instafamous and/or a YouTube sensation is quite different to the screenwriter's range of skills'. Wheeler's claim parallels Kyncl's: the acquisition of storytelling and showrunning skillsets is 'a different kind of enterprise' to YouTube creatorship (Popper, 2015). Crucially, Wheeler's and Kyncl's observations underscore the significance of the adaptive methodology developed by Skip Ahead designers, participants, script mentors and collaborating TV producers, as elaborated in Chapters 2–6.

Taking RackaRacka's brand of hair-raising, escalating stunt violence, and parody live in 2016 was a big view winner, as audience participants with their own networked smartphones became live micro-narrowcasters, further leveraging spreadability at the grassroots. Two of their most significant videos in terms of richness of their YouTube platform practice are their *Ronald McDonald WWE Beatdown* (15 million) and *Ronald McDonald WWE Beatdown 2* (13 million) (figure 4.5). These videos intuitively manifest key insights media scholars have

FIGURE 4.5 Fans shown using smartphones to film a RackaRacka wrestling match

used to explain YouTube creatorship and the online sociality. Brand parody (Fournier & Avery, 2011) is seen in the presence of Ronald McDonald, co-creativity with fans (Banks & Deuze, 2009), wildly dangerous stunts (Lange, 2007), collaborative circulation (Jenkins et al., 2013), and improvisational per-formativity (Cunningham & Craig, 2019, p. 279). For its part, the YouTube Creator Academy recommends 'hero content'.

By mid-year, Hollywood's *Variety* had nominated RackaRacka as among the world's top 10 Famechangers, 'digital stars changing the nature of fame'. *Variety* said RackaRacka came 'from Down Under (with) a disquieting blend of home-made slasher pics, gruesome film-and-video-game parodies, and a homicidal Ronald McDonald doppelganger'.

Extension to long-form narratives off YouTube

During 2016, work began on Triptych and RackaRacka's ultimately success-ful pitch to Screen Australia and YouTube for what would become *SGW Live*. The jointly funded Skip Ahead investment fund was especially rich year with four teams to share AU$725,000, a nominal AU$181,000 each. Originally, *RackaRacka: LIVE* was a livestream vlog featuring the film-makers on a rampage in a haunted abandoned theatre. At the time, YouTube Asia Pacific Head of Top Creators, Kristen Bowen said creators had the choice to make longer narratively driven films of at least 30 minutes, either being one-off films or a series of epi-sode instalments, or a pilot for a future idea (If.com, 2016). The Philippous, who were ultimately training all along for their step up to features and series, were starkly confronted with the challenge flagged by Hank Green in Chapter 1:

longerform narrative 'has been nearly impossible to make work' on the endemically shortform YouTube. To solve it, Danny Philippou told me he decided to 'mess with' the canons of dramatic film-making, genre, and character arcs:

> I was looking at it as instead of having three acts, wanting it to have three genres. I wanted the first act to feel like it was a livestream or us documenting like a typical blog or BTS breakdown of how these stunts are done. Then the second act we wanted it to be more of a thriller with this car following us and trying to run us off the road, then leading up to the final act where we went full blown horror; pretty over the top horror. She was a sexual predator turned into an actual predator a monster that rips everyone to pieces. We wanted three genres as opposed to three acts to keep the audiences engaged, because it was such a long time and we had never done anything that long before.
>
> *Philippou, 2021*

Danny Philippou's move in *SGW Live* (Figure 4.6) for Skip Ahead represents a significant rules-breaking innovation to genre itself, which cultural and critical tradition has long demanded be stable, clearly defined and belonging 'wholly and permanently to a single genre' (Altman, 1999), despite occasional mutants. Even the conflation of just two genres risks putting viewers in a dilemma: 'Where one genre seems to assure the young lovers' safety, the other offers only atrocious death', Altman argues. In contrast, first, as a vlog, *SGW* draws on 'the most emblematic form of YouTube participation', especially its 'possibilities

FIGURE 4.6 A fellow actor is comforted after an apparent accident during shooting of Stunt Gone Wrong LIVE (2017).

of inauthentic authenticity' when the character of an authentic seeming vlog is 'manufactured', a vernacular genre tracing to the earliest days of YouTube (Burgess & Green, 2009, p. 95). The livestream aspect draws on the most lucrative of all YouTube genres, the livestreamed Let's Play that, for example, made problematic figure, Felix Kjellberg aka PewDiePie, one of the world's wealthiest YouTubers. Next, the second act subverts the thriller. For Cobley (2000, p. 3), the thriller is a vast genre where male, and increasingly female protagonists, confront conspiratorial villains who threaten society, and thus become heroes and heroines as they battle to restore social order. Thirdly, for Stephen King, the best horror such as *The Strangers* (2008) involves 'an orchestration of growing disquiet' as unease builds slowly 'to terror and horror'. *SGW Live's* third act does just this, but then subverts this genre as well, by not relieving or purging the tension, leaving viewers with a chilling final scene I personally cannot 'unsee'. What started as a behind-the-scenes of another spectacular RackaRacka stunt, escalated to 'full-blown horror', and a fade-out to the final message about online predation. Indeed, the Philippous' hero film-maker, Bong, has said he will 'follow the genre conventions for a while, then I want to break out and turn them upside-down' (Klein, 2008, p. 880).

The Philippous genre-bending content creation for Skip Ahead was experimented with earlier when they did an upward collaboration with British, near Platinum-level YouTube gamer, Deji, in an apparent Let's Play, *Deji VS RackaRacka,* (9.1 million views) (2015). But in a creative twist that 'messes with the heads' of their RackaRacka fans, what started as a routine Let's Play morphed into video of their characteristic escalating stunt and parodic violence. Meanwhile, this strategy of creators bending reality has shown up in Hollywood. Credible reports show 10 minutes of Martin Scorsese's 1970s rock documentary, *Rolling Thunder Revue,* consists of prankish fake-documentary footage (Gleiberman, 2019).

Broadcast TV and film have a deep cultural problem with generations raised with socio-technologies. In 'a spirit of youthful rebellion', YouTubers are perceived to have 'really real' personalities compared to mainstream actors who are just 'a body with a script' (Cunningham & Craig, 2017, p. 4). Indeed, Philippou favoured an improvised outline.

> We made it clear from the start we didn't want any (move-based) character arcs to feel as real as possible. I wanted it to feel like a real live one hour.
>
> *Philippou, 2021*

Crucially for their narrative skills development, Skip Ahead enabled the outline to be passed back and forth from the Philippous to Bryne, Charlie Aspinwall, Daley Pearson, and Meg O'Connell at Ludo and onward to Andrew Ellard and circulated back again with accumulated notes (Byrne, 2021; Philippou, 2021). Where we saw the Saiddens use an in-house model for their Skip Ahead project, Byrne and the Philippous used a hybrid, a combination of in-house and hire-in-a-famous writer model.

For Byrne, *SGW Live* was 'a brilliant project' for three reasons: first, for those watching live, belief was only suspended when the genre turned from thriller to horror in the third act. Second, was the moral dimension symbolized by the 'Beware Children' sign on the toilet door: 'As a producer it's very important I want to help kids be aware, but they might not even be aware. They just think they are watching a wild RackaRacka ride, but for me the message was very important' (Bryne, 2021). Third, the closest film-making has come to *SGW Live's* genre morphing was Quentin Tarantino and Robert Rodriguez's vampire Western 'mash-up', *From Dusk Till Dawn* (1996) (Prasch, 2012, p. 118).

During 2017, RackaRacka worked with writer-producer Deb Cox, a collaboration which exhibited further rapprochement and co-creativity. The producers conducted 'a unique development process' under which young people from Byron Bay's surrounds contributed stories and ideas for the series in a workshop (ABC iView, 2017). Fans were invited to follow the *Deadlock* production on the BVOD iView and the socials of Every Cloud in a sign of their recognition of the importance of audience-building prior to the launch of *Deadlock*, subsequently critically acclaimed Figure 4.7. These share buttons exemplify this BVOD's efforts to retain and build its youth audience via appeals to their participatory consumption patterns.

Discontent

Despite the high views and accolades, by mid- to late 2017, the 'Adpocalypse' had challenged the RackaRacka business model. In *McDonald's Drive Through Rejection*, the twins complained just 7 per cent of their views had been monetized in the last quarter. By late 2017, however, YouTube's censorship restrictions, or 'age-gating' of screen violence shown to teenagers, had rendered an otherwise sophisticated content methodology – and their capacity to make a living on the platform – unsustainable. Age-gating or age restriction means some videos

FIGURE 4.7 Made to share among the generation lost to TV: the Philippous (pictured) star in Deadlock [screenshot from ABC iview, a public broadcast, BVOD]

FIGURE 4.8 Exemplifying the rock band model of creative labour that excels in networked video

are not monetized, not shown in certain sections and not eligible for ads. The
'Adpocalypse' triggered a rap-style protest music video by RackaRacka in late
2017, *Ronald McDonald Drama Alert (3.5 million views)* figure 4.8.

A day later, they released their Skip Ahead project, *Stunt Gone Wrong LIVE*
(1.7 million views). Using Syd Field's touchstone book, *Screenplay* (1994, 10) as a
guide RackaRacka's 42-minute *SGW Live* was half the length of a typical European
film of 90 minutes and a third of a Hollywood film at 120 minutes. The Philippous,
who had long described themselves as 'Wannabe Film-makers on a rampage!', were
thus a major step closer to achieving their childhood dreams of cinematic glory.

Crucially, however, commercially driven algorithm reform by YouTube often
produces creator estrangement and catalysed the Philippous trajectory to longer
forms. The film proposal for *Talk to Me* 'was the first thing we wrote as soon
as we started noticing all the restrictions of reach and views from YouTube'
(Philippou, 2021). *Talk to Me* also had a journey from Ludo to Causeway and also
has a moral dimension:

> *Talk to Me* is now fully-funded. It's full-blown horror, its not Racka, its
> very serious. It's about kids using demonic possession to get high is the
> elevator pitch: it's an analogy for drugs. There's an embalmed hand, a cut-
> off hand kids can hold onto and they connect with spirits, and they can let
> these demons get inside them for a minute and they can get the greatest
> adrenaline rush and the best feeling but their spirits are left lingering for
> one of the girls who is not in the right mental state.
>
> *Philippou, 2021*

By 2018, behind the scenes, work began on the twins first web-series, *The Racka*, originally a 6 × 22-minute comedy with Ludo Studio for the ABC, with producers Triptych's Julie Byrne and Ludo's Daley Pearson. The pitch line was 'social media stars – famous for their juvenile behaviour – are rewarded with their first Hollywood movie and make up for their incompetence and dangerous innovation'. Like *Concrete Kings, TheRacka* also has had its own journey from Ludo to Causeway, and likely 'messes with' genre:

> I still like writing RR, *TheRacka* its full-blown RR, over the top, action-comedy-horror genre-bending thing a bit like RackaLIVE, but over 10 episodes, in terms of genre it's a crazy over-the-top show.
>
> *Philippou, 2021*

Leveraging

By 2021, they had parlayed their teenage enjoyment for filming their playful violence and destruction – and broken bones and stitches – into an 'upper-class' living (Philippou, 2021) and international screen careers. Netflix reached out to RackaRacka in 2021 and were considering three different pitches, especially *TheRacka* (Philippou, 2021).

> Recently we stopped doing all the YouTube stuff like RackaRacka, so all my artistic energy is going into scriptwriting just because there's such interest in the projects. We've been getting into some really good (pitching) rooms. We have new managers, specialist Hollywood film representatives.
>
> *Philippou, 2021*

At the creative level, the twins may appear to be pivoting to longerform, but the reality is they are returning to the genre and style of their first short film:

> What we watch is not what we make at all. I was always scared to upload *Deluge* to my audience. I don't think RackaRacka would embrace *Deluge*, it seems like two different worlds to me.
>
> *Philippou, 2021*

Burning problems

Monetisation

'I am an artist as often as I can be', said Gary Marshall, creator of *Happy Days* (1974–1984) and *Mork and Mindy* (1978–1982) (Newcomb & Alley, 1983). Marshall captures the bind of the artist caught between the competing drives of feeding their souls, and others with their art, but having to pay their bills with commerce. The twins have had nine financially turbulent years: 'there's been years we made a million-plus dollars, but we put a lot back into the videos, so one year we made a million dollars, but the next we were bankrupt'. They are now on 'AU$100,000 a year easy' (Philippou, 2021).

An overview of the twins' income streams, based on interviews with Danny Philippou and public-facing data over the past eight years, shows they sustained themselves from a combination of all three of Murdock and Golding's economies: commodities, public goods, and gifting and collaboration, in order. Although the market of commodities is central to the function of capitalism, two other cultural economies 'are in play': public goods such as public service broadcasting paid out of taxation; and gifting, constituted by voluntary collaborations via civil society (Murdock & Golding, 2016, p. 765). 'Collaborative patronage', rather than the creative urge, has been credited with driving artistic production since the early Renaissance (Csikszentmihalyi, 2015, p. 56) and this is a defining characteristic of successful YouTube creators. RackaRacka's most lucrative, sustaining stream was brand deals with sponsors who produce their own narratives that include violent fare, including Netflix, Village Roadshow Pictures and Warner Brothers Games. References in the videos to Netflix and Online Fight Pits for Tolkien-inspired *Middle Earth* – the web-series and games products being spruiked by RackaRacka– are minimal, which deflect brigading. These sponsored videos are notable for triggering fan reaction videos of their own, and much positive – even celebratory – commentary. RackaRacka's brand deal videos stand on their own as entertainment, as attested by their 3.2 million view numbers for their Netflix brand deal (Figure 4.9).

FIGURE 4.9 Netflix pay day: RackaRacka (pictured) made *TV Spoiler Rage!* for Netflix as the global subscription streamer launched in Australia, March 2015 [screenshot from RackaRacka's YouTube channel]

The second revenue stream, gifting and collaboration, was hard won and evolved over the medium term. First, RackaRacka has had high levels of co-creativity with fans, which manifests especially in reaction videos, dares, provision of film locations, and public stunts. For example, 'Ronny Mac' inspires not just fan reaction videos, but reaction mashups such as *Meet the McDonalds Reactions Mashup (RackaRacka)* by Bronze-level creator Subbotin. Importantly, in this *Reactions Mashup*, we see a confluence of principles, practices, and technologies of YouTube creatorship – for example, parody by the creator (Lange, 2007); co-creativity between creators and fans (Banks & Deuze, 2009); brand parody (Fournier & Avery, 2011) by RackaRacka; many scores of response videos with views in the millions as opposed to the 'tens of thousands' for Annoying Orange (Morreale, 2014); and fans entering the 'art worlds' of creators (Baym, 2018). The twins were also able to use Superchat, a direct to creator tipping/gifting method during vlogged livestreams. Moreover, after six years of suffering demonetization of their videos, while experimenting with 'diss' or insult videos, the Philippous hit on a solution to sustainability for YouTubers of high profile. They bent algorithmic culture back to their needs for funding their cinematic dreams via lucrative second channel, Left on Red:

> Left on Red is a small audience for superfans, the friends and personalities we have around us. I am not doing Left on Red each day. I'll be gone for four months (to write our scripts), then come back for 20 days straight... On RackaRacka everything is demonetised, its age-gated, its covered in blood, it's so violent and edgy, they just don't make any money. Whereas for a fraction of the views, Left on Red can make eight to 10 times as much money.
>
> *Philippou, 2021*

The third revenue stream, subvention from Screen Australia's former Multiplatform Fund, and Skip Ahead, has been modest. However, crucially, the evidence of this chapter has shown even modest funding has driven RackaRacka's longform narrative development and the foundations of new IP. The development of RackaRacka has fed into and driven new projects among Australia's indie production houses, in RackaRacka's case alone, Triptych Pictures, Ludo Studios, and Causeway.

Volatility of algorithmic culture

Artists have long used multiple simultaneous projects as hedge against precarity. The Philippous had four additional strategies to deal with platform volatility: insider access, increased experimentation, fan cooption videos, and trade press lobbying. But, in hindsight, experimentation was the most important to their cinematic and ambitions, since the quintessentially creative practice yielded the insight their fans loved 'diss', or disrespectful talk. This fruit of experimentation led to their lucrative 'diss' channel, Left on Red, a genre now 'notorious for off-colour and cutting jokes', but traceable to the Friars Club of 1900s New York where comics gathered to honour a beloved peer (Kies, 2021, p. 3).

YouTube censored many of RackaRacka's early violent videos by removing them upon upload (Philippou, 2017). However, one of the platform's most attractive affordances for successful creators is so-called 'insider access' to YouTube channel-optimisation experts, now known as partner managers:

> When we first started RackaRacka, videos were getting removed because of how violent they were. When I got my manager, we could combat that. We could use the age-gating rules to show mature content.
>
> *Philippou, 2017*

Evidence of increasingly experimental, creative responses to platform volatility, which we first saw with Voigt, also applies to RackaRacka, as well as to SketchSHE, as we will see in the case after next. At a time when their channel was under some of its greatest pressure from the twofold blow of declining views due to age-gating and platform advertising, it is instructive to consider the Philippous' response. The RackaRacka collective dug deep and turned to its most enduring, distinctive, and popular formats: collaboration videos with fellow Gold and Platinum peer creators SuperWog, Logan Paul and KSI, *VS* fights, mass superhero fights in public, a sponsored mass cage fight (*Orc Fight Club, Dec 2017*) and a prank at one of their most enduring locations, any local McDonalds (from which they say they are banned nationwide). The twins talent for dissing, especially other high-profile YouTubers and others, runs throughout their oeuvre, but is most evident in *Drama Alert* (2017; 3.5 million views), *RackaRacka Diss Track* (2019; 1 million views), and *Riley Reid and RackaRacka diss track* (2019; 3.6 million views).

Danny Philippou copes with the artistic drive to creative flow by writing late at night and editing during the day (Philippou, 2017).

> Things we want to take out to market, we get different producers attached. We are simultaneously doing 10 in segments. We'll work on this, then 'Oh' that reminds me of that, and I'll jump over to horror projects, then I'll jump over to comedy projects. That's my creative process. Whatever mood I am in is the project we'll focus on.
>
> *Philippou, 2021*

The online economy of gifting and collaboration has matured such that this community of Left on Red superfans are the sort of people who Bruns's original produsers have evolved into.

> We got lucky in building an audience we can rely on a bit. We can focus on scripting without worrying. If YouTube is blacklisting us, and our films

aren't making any money in a few years' time, when I'll be completely broke. These are fans we know and talk to and I really like the group and the community. We'll go with their suggestions.

Philippou, 2021

Old and new media

Until a future doctoral candidate manages to persuade Netflix to let her shadow a powerful Netflix buyer, we will have to take the Philippous pitching as an example of how rapprochement might work between otherwise contending YouTube and Netflix cultures. The prospects of success with Netflix for the Philippous were too early to tell as this book went to print. But just the fact of Philippou-Netflix pitch negotiations means Caves (2003, p. 74) bedrock principle of the creative industries, Nobody Knows, is recast to *both parties informed*. As in Biography above, rapprochement in this book has so far centred on the process of collaboration between veteran YouTubers and established TV producers, how I found their skillsets fall towards each other and how more of them gravitate to longerform BVODs and SVODs, the longer they are exposed to algorithmic volatility. A new edge of rapprochement now though is exemplified in the Philippou-Netflix negotiations. What does this mean for pitching and commissioning when both sides come to the table informed? The narratively gifted YouTuber has their own social analytics; the other, Netflix, has its own famed Recommender that uses algorithms in production to predict ratings (Gomez-Uribe & Hunt, 2015, p. 2). Over the years, Netflix leaders have sent mixed signals about the balance of authority in its human/non-human assemblage: between its empowered 'buyers' on 'rock-star pay' (Hastings & Meyer, 2020, p. 77), and their 'projection models' that evaluate the attributes of series (Whittock, 2018).

Prima facie, such a process might be assumed to be overly automated, far from the reassuring guidance of human minds and hands. After all, storyteller YouTubers only get to the coveted position of pitching to major SVODs after years of being in unavoidable collaboration, with what I argued in Chapter 1, was the anthropomorphic labour of the YouTube algorithms. Conversely, Netflix success is seen as founded in its 'fusing of technology and subscriber information in a complex alchemy of audiovisual matchmaking' (Hallinan & Striphas, 2016, p. 117). Netflix's proprietary algorithms are so influential that they were credited with powering the cultural shift to media marathoning or binge-watching (Perks, 2014, p. 24). But concerns were raised about the increasingly influential role of algorithms in displacing human decision-making about culture, defined by Matthew Arnold as 'the best which has been thought and said' (Hallinan & Striphas, 2016, p. 118). Early on Netflix itself fed the narrative of the socio-technological magic of its algorithms in personalizing content choices for subscribers: a cross-section of most demographics in the US middle-class and English-speaking elites transnationally, further broken down to 'deep niche' micro-audiences. As Netflix moved into Originals, co-founder, Ted Sarandos, said they had confidence in their major investments in *Lilyhammer* (2012–2014), *House of Cards* (2013–2018), and *Arrested Development* (2013–2019), 'because the algorithms on Netflix will put it in front of the right people' (Karpel, 2012). However, the evidence suggests culture, 'the best which has been thought and said', at least in the case of Netflix, is retained in the best human hands, since, as we saw in Chapter 1, algorithmic processes are best thought of as Latourian assemblages of humans and non-humans. The leaders of Netflix, former maths teacher turned co-founder of Netflix, Reed Hastings, vice-president of Original programming, Cindy Holland, and Sarandos, have emphasised their buyers – individually empowered to greenlight films and series – were recruited at double market rates for their 'judgement'. Hastings acknowledges Netflix has invested heavily in algorithms, 'to ensure the right content gets to the right people', but has emphasised the behind-the-scenes deliberative processes of their buyers: 'You can't just run on algorithms; it's a mix of judgement' (Anderson, 2018). For Hastings, the test was what movies and series viewers could recall after a year, 'that has moved them'.

Better understanding how humans and algorithms interact in dominant assemblages such as Netflix, especially where the balance of authority sits between the buyers and the Netflix algorithms, is more important for creative industries and storytelling than ever. Netflix and the Philippous are both hybrids in new media. The twins have their own social analytics from the longerform *SGW Live*. They are both steeped in algorithmic culture, based as it is in collaborative, crowd-informed filtering (Gomez-Uribe & Hunt, 2015, p. 14; Covington et al., 2016, p. 192; Lobato, 2019, p. 40). The film industry may still function 'as a straight, White, boy's club' (Smith et al., 2016, p. 16), but, constrastingly, the Philippous and Netflix are both living, not just paying lip-service to diversity. For example, the latter's 'ethnically and sexually diverse' sci-fi offering, *Sense8* (2015–2018) (Shimpach, 2020, p. 3). The top 20 leaders of Netflix are finally evenly gender balanced, and comprise 25 per cent people of colour (Anderson, p. 2020). The Philippous are algorithmic traction masters with hard-won know-how, their own screenwriters, and years of mentoring by Byrne, Emmy-winning writer-producers at Ludo, and the Emmy nominated, Mike Jones (*Wrong Kind of Black*, 2018). But YouTube is a shortform platform, while Netflix is a longform, to super-longform platform, given its prevalence of almost novelistic length series. The twins are all too aware of the challenge:

> (Joseph Campbell's *The Hero with a Thousand Faces,* 1993) is one of those foundation things. If you are going to bend the rules you have to be familiar with all the rules before you start to try and break them. It's pivotal. Even the most obscure films are good at hiding those original structures; those bones are still in everything. They are still relevant today. You can hide them and break them. I wouldn't know it by heart, but I have Bill Hinzman who does. I could never make the movie I originally wrote

because it was just too all over the joint. It's all the way through Netflix, all those big projects still have those themes.

Philippou, 2021

However for Philippou, the reality is multiplatform labour does not allow for periods of either quiet or extended periods for intense preparation. For creativity scholar Paisley Livingston (2009, p. 6), the key to creative inspiration, is 'recombination of ideas' enabled by 'the unconscious mental machine', where novel ideas emerge during periods of quiet only after intense preparation. This reality underlines the importance of the insights from the Skip Ahead mentors. Crucially, Kalowski describes these collaborations, such as RackaRacka and Triptych Pictures and Ludo, which were facilitated under Skip Ahead, as 'incredibly vital. They are a great way for experienced producers to engage with these new creatives'. Similarly, Mike Jones underlined the position of Cowap and Kalowski (2018) regarding the skills acquisition required and the means of acquisition for creators to cross over into the hybrid digital services elaborated above:

> The bottom line is YouTubers most often need a lot of traditional screenwriting and story-development support from established industry professionals to successfully transition to longer-form narrative projects.
>
> *Jones, 2018*

Authenticity and discrimination

As regards authenticity, the twins are Australians of Greek heritage from a hardscrabble suburb of Adelaide. They explain much of their over-the-top violence, as they reveal in *Our Epic Childhood*, as due to loose parental controls given their father suffered serious illness, and they had an absent mother. There is a striking consistency, in terms of their literally shedding blood, sweat, and tears between their boisterous childhoods and their style of expression on screen. Danny Philippou told me 'the YouTube stuff we ran with and brand isn't exactly what we enjoy watching. We are drawn to more serious subject matter' (Philippou, 2021). But then the twins have never made a secret of their ultimate cinematic dreams and use of YouTube, without monetizing ads until their first 1 million subscribers, to develop as writers and directors (Hawker, 2014).

On discrimination, however, the Philippous have alleged YouTube has unjustly and selectively applied the platform's content guidelines to RackaRacka, yet not to the graphic dramatized violence of acclaimed and popular YouTube Originals series, *Wayne* (2019-). The storyline is 'Wayne, a 16-year-old Dirty Harry with a heart of gold, sets out on a small two stroke road bike from Boston to Florida with his new friend Del to get back the shit-hot 79' Trans-Am stolen from his father before he died' (Wayne, 2019). 'Don't make rules if they don't apply to yourselves' Danny Philippou said in a rare two-hander vlog, *YouTube hates RackaRacka* (2019). In a further example of the power and freedom of

YouTuber advocacy, their protest video has now been seen over 645,000 times and prompted an interview with the twins on Platinum YouTuber Logan Paul's own vlog, ImPaulsive, *Mother YouTube hates RackaRacka twins, Ep 48* (2019). The twins say they love *Wayne,* but their reaction video samples *Wayne* doing dangerous stunts and being subjected to a graphic beating, which the Philippous claim would have triggered age-gating, poor reach, and subsequent demonetization of any such video of their own. For its part, Hale (2019) reported YouTube had responded by age-restricting Wayne to an 18+ account. In response to RackaRacka's callout of YouTube, the platform said in a statement: 'All videos uploaded to YouTube must comply with our Community Guidelines. The Guidelines prohibit violent or gory content primarily intended to be shocking, sensational, or gratuitous. We remove videos that violate our policies and age-restrict content that, while not violating our Guidelines, may not be suitable for all ages'. For their part, co-writers of *Wayne*, Rhett Reese and Paul Wernick (*Deadpool*, 2016), say they are not interested in stereotypical fight scenes, but rather action that is either memorable or comes from character (Countryman, 2019). YouTube gave the pair notes that made the show better, and the creative 'freedom to think outside the box of networks or even cable networks', said Reese (Wojnar, 2019). The journey of these lead creatives in relation to arguably the world's two most important streaming platforms YouTube and Netflix, highlights how platforms are co-evolving content standards with lead creatives.

Note

1 Despite young people and social media being synonymous, vast numbers of Millennials and Gen Z's report social media 'does more harm than good' (Deloitte's Global Millennial Survey of 2019)

References

Altman, R. (1999). *Film/genre*. Bloomsbury.

Anderson, C. (2018, July 13). How Netflix changed entertainment – and where its headed | Reed Hastings [Interview] TED, *TED Conferences LLC*, Vancouver, Canada. https://www.youtube.com/watch?v=LsAN-TEJfN0&t=773s

Anderson, C (2020, September 9). 3 secrets of Netflix's success: Reed Hastings and Chris Anderson [Interview], TED, *TED Conferences LLC*, Vancouver, Canada. https://www.youtube.com/watch?v=9w0PL2_-oAE

Armstrong, JM. (1998). Aristotle on the philosophical nature of poetry. *The Classical Quarterly, 48*(2), 447–455.

Austin, C., & Olson, S. D. (2004). *Aristophanes thesmophoriazusae*. OUP.

Banet-Weiser, S. (2012). *AuthenticTM: The politics of ambivalence in a brand culture* (Vol. 30). NYU Press.

Banks, J., & Deuze, M. (2009). Co-creative labour. *International Journal of Cultural Studies,* 12(5), 419–431.

Baym, N. K. (2018). *Playing to the crowd: Musicians, audiences, and the intimate work of connection* (Vol. 14). NYU Press.

Bruns, A. (2007). The future is user-led: The path towards widespread produsage. In *Proceedings of perthDAC 2007: The 7th international digital arts and culture conference* (pp. 68–77). Curtin University of Technology.

Burgess, J., & Green, J. (2009). *The entrepreneurial vlogger: Participatory culture beyond the professional/amateur divide* (pp. 89–107). National Library of Sweden.

Burgess, J., & Green, J. (2018). *YouTube: Online video and participatory culture*. John Wiley & Sons.

Butler, S. (2013). *Translation of Homer's The Iliad and The Odyssey*. Barnes & Noble.

Byrne, J. (2017 and 2021). Principal producer, Triptych Pictures, interview with Guy Healy. Brisbane.

Cobley, P. (2000). *The American thriller: Generic innovation and social change in the 1970s.* London: Palgrave Macmillan.

Caldwell, J. T. (2008). *Production culture: Industrial reflexivity and critical practice in film and television.* Duke University Press.

Cameron, A., Verhoeven, D., & Court, D. (2010). Above the bottom line: understanding Australian screen content producers. *Media International Australia, 136*(1), 90–102.

Campbell, J. (1993). *The hero with a thousand faces.* Fontana Press.

Campbell, J. (2003). *The hero's journey: Joseph Campbell on his life and work.* New World Library.

Carroll, N. (1999). Horror and humor. *The Journal of Aesthetics and Art Criticism, 57*(2), 145–160.

Carter, M., Moore, K., Mavoa, J., Horst, H., & Gaspard, L. (2020). Situating the appeal of fortnite within children's changing play cultures. *Games and Culture, 15*(4), 453–471.

Caves, R. E. (2003). Contracts between art and commerce. *Journal of Economic Perspectives, 17*(2), 73–83.

Coleridge, S. T. (1817). Biographia literaria, chapter XIV. In Vincent B. Leitch (gen. Ed.), *The Norton anthology of theory and criticism* (pp. 677–682).

Countryman, E. (2019, January 13). Upcoming YouTube series 'Wayne' uses violence thoughtfully based in character, [Blogpost], Daily Bruin, University of California Los Angeles. https://dailybruin.com/2019/01/13/upcoming-youtube-series-wayne-uses-violence-thoughtfully-based-in-character

Covington, P., Adams, J., & Sargin, E. (2016, September). Deep neural networks for YouTube recommendations. In *Proceedings of the 10th ACM Conference on Recommender Systems* (pp. 191–198).

Csikszentmihalyi, M. (2015). The systems model of creativity: The collected works of Mihaly Csikszentmihalyi. Springer.

Cunningham, S., & Craig, D. (2017). Being 'really real' on YouTube: authenticity, community and brand culture in social media entertainment. *Media International Australia, 164*(1), 71–81.

Craig, D., & Cunningham, S. (2019). *Social media entertainment: The new intersection of Hollywood and Silicon Valley.* NYU Press.

Davis, S. E. (2018). Objectification, sexualization, and misrepresentation: Social media and the college experience. *Social Media+ Society, 4*(3), 1–9.

Davison, C. M. (2009). *Gothic Literature 1764-1824.* University of Wales Press.

Dawkins, R. (1989). *The selfish gene.* Oxford University Press.

Deloitte (2019). *Deloitte global millennial survey:* Deloitte.

Dermody, S., & Jacka, E. (1987). *The screening of Australia* (Vol. 1, p. 158). Currency Press.

Field, S. (1998). *The Screenwriter's Problem Solver,* Dell Publishing.

Eds Buckingham, D., and Willett, R. (2009). In the frame: Mapping camcorder cultures. In Video cultures (pp. 1–22). Palgrave Macmillan.

Fournier, S. & Avery, J. (2011). The uninvited brand. *Business Horizons, 54*(3), 193–207.

Galletly, J. (2014). SA filmmakers Danny and Michael Philippou create a YouTube sensation with Harry Potter vs Star Wars, *The Advertiser,* 5 May.

Gleiberman, O. (2019). Why did Martin Scorsese prank his audience in Rolling Thunder Revue? Even he may not know. *Variety,* 15 June. https://variety.com/2019/film/columns/why-did-martin-scorsese-prank-his-audience-in-rolling-thunder-revue-1203243856

Gomez-Uribe, C. A., & Hunt, N. (2015). The Netflix recommender system: Algorithms, business value, and innovation. *ACM Transactions on Management Information Systems, 6*(4), 1–19.

Gutelle, S. (2015). YouTube millionaires: For RackaRacka, 'the whole process is chaos'. Tubefilter, 4 June. https://www.tubefilter.com/2015/06/04/racka-racka-youtube-millionaires.

Hale, J. (2019, January 28). RackaRacka claims YouTube is breaking its own content policies and community guidelines with new original 'Wayne' [Blogpost]. *Tubefilter,* Los Angeles. https://www.tubefilter.com/2019/01/28/youtube-breaking-its-own-content-policy-rules-with-new-original-wayne-rackaracka/

Hallinan, B., & Striphas, T. (2016). Recommended for you: The Netflix Prize and the production of algorithmic culture. *New Media & Society, 18*(1), 117–137.

Hastings, R., & Meyer, E. (2020). *No rules rules: Netflix and the culture of reinvention.* Random House Large.

Hawker, P. (2014). Harry Potter vs Star Wars YouTube hit wins Australian Online Video Award for twins. *Sydney Morning Herald,* Nine Entertainment Co., Australia. https://www.smh.com.au/entertainment/harry-potter-vs-star-wars-youtube-hit-wins-australian-online-video-award-for-twins-20141015-116d9k.html

Hughes, S. (2014, March 23). 'Sopranos meets Middle-earth': how Game of Thrones took over our world. *Guardian,* UK. https://www.theguardian.com/tv-and-radio/2014/mar/22/game-of-thrones-whats-not-to-love

If.com (2016). Skip Ahead gifts $725,000 to YouTube creators, if.com, Intermedia Group, Sydney Australia. Retrieved from: https://www.if.com.au/skip-ahead-gifts-725000-to-youtube-creators/

Jenkins, H., Ford, S., & Green, J. (2013). *Spreadable media: Creating value and meaning in a networked culture,* NYU Press.

Jones, M. (2018). Skip Ahead story consultant. Personal communication with Guy Healy, Brisbane.

Joshi, K. (2016). From lab rats to online superstars: The twins behind RackaRacka. MediaWeek, 5 May.

Higa, N. (2019, October 1). RackaRacka's $130K YouTube Video (Ft. Danny Philippou) – Off the Pill Podcast #34, Los Angeles. https://www.youtube.com/watch?v=fkIys904f7s

Hughes, S. (2014, March 23) 'Sopranos meets Middle-earth': How Game of Thrones took over our world. *Guardian News Media.* https://www.theguardian.com/tv-and-radio/2014/mar/22/game-of-thrones-whats-not-to-love

Kalowski, R. (2018). Then Head of ABC Comedy. Skype interview with Guy Healy.

Karpel, A. (2012). Netflix's head of content Sarandos queues up an original programming Strategy. *Fast Company.* https://www.fastcompany.com/1679595/netflixs-head-of-content-sarandos-queues-up-an-original-programming-strategy

Kies, B. (2021). Remediating the celebrity roast: The place of mean tweets on late-night television. Television & New Media, 22(5), 516–528.

King, S. (2011). *Danse macabre.* Simon and Schuster.

King, S. (2014, November). Tweet. https://twitter.com/stephenking/status/535984981219479552?lang=en

Klein, C. (2008). Why American studies needs to think about Korean cinema, or, transnational genres in the films of Bong Joon-ho. *American Quarterly*, *60*(4), 871–898.

Kumar, S. (2019). The algorithmic dance: YouTube's Adpocalypse and the gatekeeping of cultural content on digital platforms. *Internet Policy Review*, *8*(2), 1–21.

Lange, P. G. (2007). Fostering friendship through video production: How youth use YouTube to enrich local interaction. In *Proceedings of annual meeting of the International Communication Association* (Vol. 27). Annenberg Center for Communication University of Southern California.

Levy, S. (1999). *Rat pack confidential: Frank, Dean, Sammy, Peter, Joey and the Last Great show biz party*. Broadway Books.

Lobato, R. (2019). *Netflix nations*. New York University Press.

Livingston, P. (2009). Poincaré's 'Delicate Sieve': On creativity in the arts'. In M. Krausz, D. Dutton, & K. Bardsley (Eds.), *In e idea of creativity* (pp. 129–146). Brill.

McCauley, D. (2018). Brothers' grim tale: 'Disney-fied' YouTube bans RackaRacka videos. *The Australian*, 4 June, https://www.theaustralian.com.au/business/media/brothers-grim-tale-disneyfied-youtube-bans-rackaracka-videos/news-story.

Mills, S. (1997). *Theseus, tragedy, and the Athenian Empire*. Oxford University Press.

Morreale, J. (2014). From homemade to store bought: Annoying Orange and the professionalization of YouTube. *Journal of Consumer Culture*, *14*(1), 113–128.

Murdock, G., & Golding, P. (2016). Political economy and media production: A reply to Dwyer. Media, Culture & Society, 38(5), 763–769.

Newcomb, H., & Alley, R. (1983). *The producer's medium: Conversations with creators of American TV*. Oxford University Press.

Perks, L. G. (2014). *Media marathoning: Immersions in morality*. Lexington Books.

Phillips, K. R. (2005). *Projected fears: Horror films and American culture: Horror films and American culture*. ABC-CLIO.

Popper, B. (2015, October 21). Red dawn an inside look at YouTube's new ad-free subscription service, Vox Media, New York. https://www.theverge.com/2015/10/21/9566973/youtube-red-ad-free-offline-paid-subscription-service

Philippou, D. (2017 and 2021). Phone interviews with Guy Healy, Brisbane, March.

Philippou, D & M. (2020, April). Our epic childhood, Philippou twins home movie cut. https://www.dailymotion.com/video/x234ahb

Prasch, T. (2012). Blood on the Border. In *Undead in the West: Vampires, Zombies, Mummies, and Ghosts on the Cinematic Frontier*, Eds Cynthia Miller and A Van Riper, Scarecrow Press, 113-130.

Relis, A. (2015). Head of YouTube Spaces. New York, interview with Stuart Cunningham, Australia.

Ryan, M. D. (2021). A monstrous landscape filled with killer animals and madmen: Tropes of contemporary Australian horror movies. In: K. McWilliam, & M. D. Ryan (Eds.), *Australian Genre Film* (pp. 90–108). Routledge.

Shimpach, S. (Ed.). (2020). *The Routledge companion to global television*. Routledge.

Scrivner, C., Johnson, J. A., Kjeldgaard-Christiansen, J., & Clasen, M. (2021). Pandemic practice: Horror fans and morbidly curious individuals are more psychologically resilient during the COVID-19 pandemic. *Personality and Individual Differences*, *168*, 110397.

Sifakis, G., & Sephakes, G. (1971). *Parabasis and animal choruses: A contribution to the history of attic comedy*. GM Sifakis.

Smith, S. L., Choueiti, M., & Pieper, K. (2016). Inclusion or invisibility? Comprehensive Annenberg report on diversity in entertainment. *Institute for Diversity and Empowerment at Annenberg*, *22*, 1–27.

Spangler, T. (2016, Jun 22). Racka Racka: Australian Brothers' Gory videos lead to film deal, Variety, Penske Media Corporation, New York. https://variety.com/2016/digital/news/racka-racka-youtube-film-deal-1201797416/

Stapleton, P., Luiz, G., & Chatwin, H. (2017). Generation validation: The role of social comparison in use of Instagram among emerging adults. *Cyberpsychology, Behavior, and Social Networking, 20*(3), 142–149.

Tamborini, R., & Stiff, J. (1987). Predictors of horror film attendance and appeal: An analysis of the audience for frightening films. *Communication Research, 14*(4), 415–436.

Todorov, T. (1990). *Genres in discourse.* Cambridge University Press.

Tofler, M., Batty, C., & Taylor, S. (2019). The comedy web series: Reshaping Australian script development and commissioning practices. *Australasian Journal of Popular Culture, 8*(1), 71–84.

Vogler, C. (2017). Joseph Campbell goes to the movies: The influence of the hero's journey in film narrative. *Journal of Genius and Eminence, 2*(2), 9–23.

Wayne (2019). Wayne TV Series. IMDb, Amazon.com, Seattle, US. Retrieved from: https://www.imdb.com/title/tt7765404/?ref_=ttpl_ql

Weisenstein, K. (2019). How YouTube's ban on dangerous stunts will affect creators. *Vice News.* https://www.vice.com/en_au/article/9k4epy/how-youtubes-ban-on-dangerous-stunts-will-affect-creators

Wheeler, F. (2016, April 1). RackaRacka: From YouTube to features, LA screenwriter [Blog].https://www.la-screenwriter.com/2016/04/01/rackaracka-from-youtube-to-features/

Whittock, J. (2018, April 25). Netflix originals exec reveals how streaming giant makes commissioning decisions. *Screen Daily,* Media Business Insight, London. https://www.screendaily.com/news/netflix-originals-exec-reveals-how-streaming-giant-makes-commissioning-decisions/5128552.article

Wojnar, Z. (2019, Jan 16). Rhett Reese and Paul Wernick interview: Wayne. [Interview]. *Screenrant,* Valnet Inc., St Laurent, Quebec. https://screenrant.com/wayne-rhett-reese-paul-wernick-interview/

Xu, W., Park, J., Kim, J., & Park, H. (2016). Networked cultural diffusion and creation on YouTube: An analysis of YouTube memes. *Journal of Broadcasting & Electronic Media, 60*(1), 104–122.

5

THE WORLD'S #3 ONLINE DESSERT CHEF AND DEVELOPMENTAL ACTIVIST, ANN REARDON 'STUCK IN THE ALGORITHMS'

Millennial mother of a growing family, Ann Reardon (Figure 5.1), is an award-winning, 11-year social media veteran whose How To and cultural activism videos have attracted 825 million views and 4.7 million subscribers, placing her halfway between a Gold and Diamond Play button YouTuber. As an early Skip Aheader, Reardon also produced a global web-series about desserts that has attracted over 7.8 million views, mainly in the Global North, but also the Philippines, Indonesia, Malaysia, Taiwan, and India. Reardon's case in relation to web-series is not one of studied narrative design like that of Voigt, the Saiddens and the Philippous in previous chapters. However, her case is nevertheless extremely valuable regarding the following: her more doable, autobiographical model of a web-series; her content innovation in one of the most competitive SME verticals, style tutorials; her symbolic work to cut through the hyper-saturation of web-content; her new model for cultural activism web-series; and her audience-participation debunking web-series. Moreover, as we will see below, Reardon started her social media career to keep herself awake while nursing a sick child who needed night feeds. Reardon's case shows an alternative to the women in their 20s and 30s in micro-enterprises who had to delay having children due to precariousness (McRobbie, 2011, p. 72); the wives who worked as reality TV editors but could not have children due to six-day-a-week work-loads and a lack of insurance (Caldwell, 2013, p. 160); and the showrunner who found it tough to manage her relationship with her husband and children since she had to shoot on cheaper runaway productions interstate: 'We're people. We're creative people. We're not robots.' (Akil in Curtin & Sanson, 2017, p. 31).

Audience growth hacking know-how is prized (Gielen, 2019), but leaves most creators and writer-producers nonplussed. As a YouTuber from 2011, Reardon's on-platform experience pre-dates all four of YouTube's major algorithm changes, including the platform's attempt to clean up clickbait via the shift to Watch Time

DOI: 10.4324/9781003182481-5

MAGICAL ICE DROP PANNA COTTA DESSERT RECIPE How To Cook That Ann Reardon

0:01 / 9:36

FIGURE 5.1 Veteran YouTuber and mother Ann Reardon has experimented with documentary style web-series

that rewarded viewer time on the platform in 2012. Accordingly, Reardon's insights and strategies and experiences shared in four email interviews with me since 2017, are particularly valuable regarding how she coped with algorithmic volatility, while protecting her passion for content originality and autonomy. As a small business-woman with a family to support, and a livelihood in the field of creative entre-preneurship to protect, her stakes could not have been higher. Reardon's insights in this regard have helped shape my conceptualizations of the collision between algorithms and creativity in this book. This chapter suggests Reardon exemplifies the kind of 'lead user' that von Hippel (2006, p. 4) contends are ahead of mar-ket trends and the bulk of users in their domains, and who expect high benefits from their innovative solutions to the needs they encountered. Importantly, this case shows how YouTube's revenue-prioritizing algorithms are contributing to the wider information disorder undermining trustworthy storytelling as elaborated in Chapter 1, building further on the case for renovation of the algorithms established with Voigt in Chapter 2. Nevertheless, I find in this chapter that creative entre-preneurship in algorithmic culture is quite capable of enabling a fulfilling middle-class career, especially in the context of deft symbolic-work and socially led cross-channel collaboration. But this small business model is not for the faint-hearted.

Creative entrepreneurship

For the past 20 years, the cultural and creative industries have been a field of struggle between late-stage capitalism and the remnants of unruly collec-tivism centring on the new media figure of the creative entrepreneur. The democratization of cultural production, gatekeeper-less creative autonomy, and independent audience-building enabled by socio-technologies have been enclosed by the profit-taking logics of the neoliberal project, scholarship suggests. For Murdock (2011, p. 19), ever increasing commodification is a 'generalized form of enclosure' extended to more kinds of resources, a modern manifestation first begun in Tudor times when agricultural entrepreneurs fenced off commons used by villagers to graze livestock and collect firewood and wild foods.

For McRobbie (2002, p. 52), aggressive neoliberal approaches cruelled an otherwise promising UK fashion industry of the 1980s and 1990s of female self-generated work centred in collaboration and cooperation, but little labour representation. A culture of individualization led to people being expected to act as their own micro-structures, without reliance on welfare or subsidy, exacerbating class and social division, especially among young workers who bore the brunt of the shift. Conversely, for Bruns (2008, p. 85), the hyper-distribution technologies of the Internet gave rise to participatory evaluation of user-generated content, produsage, and the prototyping of new content genres such as machinima and mashups, and the revitalization of older forms such as short films. Importantly, Potts et al. (2008, p. 183) theorized that socio-cultural and economic systems 'co-evolve'. By 2011, McRobbie suggested micro-entrepreneurs – many of them white women better able to afford start-up business loans – were exhibiting enjoyment, even passionate commitment in this new style of career, but their work was characterized by speeded-up, intensified work and significant periodic change.

Meanwhile, Castells (2010, p. xxiv) argued that the new-networked-based shift to entrepreneurship and innovation was thriving on the margins of corporations, but the transformation was most intense, and society most profoundly modified, where humans were best defined, by conscious communications. For de Peuter (2011, p. 418), policy-makers and their allies, in their push to prioritize the cultural and creative industries as sites of market growth and new jobs, had 'sugar-coated' the precariousness of the sector of which they had championed. In frustration, the creative economy vaunted by the neoliberal project was showing significant signs of collective responses, such as low-cost, co-working offices, and co-ops. Nevertheless, a universal guaranteed income[1] sufficient to provide a dignified existence, and smooth out irregular pay, was needed to help rebalance workers' control over their lives, he argued. Also, the first of three major studies on ongoing attention inequality on YouTube was published. Ding et al. (2011, p. 361) found the top 20 per cent of uploaders contributed 72 per cent of the videos and attracted 97 per cent of views.

Indeed, in his deep dive into YouTube gamer culture, Postigo (2016, p. 345) concluded that creation of stars was essential to the revenue generation model of YouTube. The platform's socio-monetizing architecture meant all forms of socio-cultural practice traversing across the platform were 'captured and converted' to revenue'. Miller (2016, p. 27) warned that precarious artistic labour had become the 'shadow-setter of conditions of labour' pointing to thousands of small content firms – with unorganized workforces – on the outskirts of Los Angeles making video content for games, DVD commentaries and reality TV. Meanwhile, Healy and Cunningham (2017, p. 115) reported that post-broadcast TV labour was increasingly multiplatform labour, for example, the go-to YouTube-Patreon model of many creators in this book, given 'the small sums per 1000 views' from Google's automated advertising. Indeed, YouTube's own chief business officer, Robert Kyncl, in his book with Maany Peyvan, Streampunks: YouTube and the rebels remaking media, signals *the combination* of YouTube, and gifting and collaboration platform Patreon, is needed to achieve a middle-class living (2017). For Christian (2018, p. 248), algorithms were the means by which advertisers were able to follow audience attention to where it was now concentrated online, but these algorithms had also become extremely valuable IP driving the way YouTube, Amazon, Disney and Netflix understood and served their customers.

For McRobbie (2018, p. 11), the term creative industries had come to represent too pragmatic a focus on the creative capacity of the individual on whom risk had been imposed in service to a talent-led economy. While this enterprise culture appeared to represent upward mobility to young people, especially young women, this was a mere ideological effect of giving entrepreneurs 'the feeling of being middle class and aspirational', while the reality was, they had to run several jobs at once to make ends meet. For Arthurs et al. (2018, p. 10), awareness was increasing in some scholarly quarters that YouTube's Recommender was founded on 'collaborative filtering', the crucial socio-technological principle elaborated in Chapter 1. Recommendations were thus not wholly artificial, but had 'an eminently social logic'. Meanwhile, Carah and Angus (2018, p. 188) showed how the Instagram posts of festival-going Splendour in the Grass fans were captured to better train the platforms' algorithms. As fans became part of the ever-encroaching social media assemblage, this capitalization of participatory culture disproportionately served attending brands and influencers, they found. Ominously, with the increasing sophistication of algorithmic systems, Carah and Angus contended this capitalization was only limited by human attention, a limitation others suggested could be rectified by new machines that made these decisions for us.

Indeed, at the creative frontline, veteran creators said YouTube's social analytics had become 'information overload' and responded with old-fashioned trial and error (Cunningham & Swift, 2017). Finally, in another major piece that surveyed research contributors, Duffy et al. (2019, p. 3) questioned whether the 'unbridled creativity and diversity' promised by the rise of niche tastes enabled by the digital age, had been fulfilled for creative entrepreneurs? The conclusion? 'Collectively, the contributors are ambivalent. Although new fangled genres and hybrid business models are emerging, platforms simultaneously exert constraints that steer the creative process' (Duffy et al., 2019, p. 6).

Algorithms, deep neural networks, hybrid AI platforms, and creativity

Algorithms need to be better understood since they increasingly structure creative labour. The role of deep neural networks embedded in hybrid human/AI-run platforms such as Google, YouTube, Facebook, and Netflix has been formally acknowledged by their software engineers in the past five years (Gomez-Uribe & Hunt, 2015; Covington et al., 2016; Beutel et al., 2018; Tang et al., 2019). Scholarship has increasingly scrutinized what these former 'black', but now opaque boxes mean for all aspects of citizenship, especially human attention, identity, social formation, cultural labour, power relations, and knowledge generation. However, with a few notable exceptions regarding creative entrepreneurship elaborated below, little attention has been focused on what these ubiquitous assemblages mean for online creative labour, let alone at best practice level as exemplified by Ann Reardon (825.7 M views). This chapter rectifies this gap.

Looking back into Palaeolithic pre-history, symbols on the walls of cave art have been conceptualized as the building blocks or 'mental girders' underpinning thought and action. Symbols thus help structure gender, identity, political participation, and ritual, with some scholars saying symbols merely 'represent' social realities, while others regard them as actually 'constituting' them (Robb, 1998, p. 335). In the realm of art, artistic domains are symbolic systems that define the rules. Under one prominent theory of creative processes, a circle recurs 'from person to field to domain and back to the person, paralleling the evolutionary pattern of variation (person), selection (field), and retention (domain) (Csikszentmihalyi, 2015, p. 78). The history of algorithms stem from algebra itself traced back to Moorish Spain and from there to Western Europe from 780CE, where they were conceptualized as defining, or alternatively concealing truth (Striphas, 2015, p. 404). Contemporary algorithms are best thought of as software, the Maths-based sets of instructions aimed at producing desired outcomes. Crucially for creator livelihoods, algorithms are 'contingent, ontogenetic (always becoming) and performative' (Kitchin, 2017, p. 18). As they are constantly fed by users, they are in a state of constant evolution, known in Silicon Valley as 'permanent beta' (Burgess & Baym, 2020, p. 25). This means human communication, online, is mediated within a trilogy of types of actors. Weight (2006, p. 414) argues this trilogy is formed when 'an apparatus mediates creative communication – the three partners in the technosocial undertaking are human programmer/artist, the executing apparatus, and the human interpreter'. Even though the apparatus is human-based[2], it appears to have 'uncanny' pseudo-agency. By 2010, the YouTube algorithms used to generate and recommend content including the most viewed, favourited, and rated, accounted for about 60 per cent of all clicks, and underpinned click through rates (Davidson et al., 2010, p. 296).

Google's algorithms, for example, provide humanity with profound benefits in education and health. However, Hesmondhalgh (2010, p. 282) noted that a theme of critiques was that user-generated cultural content involved unpaid work, 'free labour' by participants. This made questions about the quality of creators working lives and 'significant opportunities for good work' – an important political issue, 'even if celebrants and critics of digitalisation see professional cultural work as in decline'. All web users leave behind what Cheney-Lippold (2011, p. 164) terms an 'algorithmic identity' that models our gender, class, and race, irrespective of our genitalia or appearance, making suggestions, managing ourselves, and recommending ads and content. The year 2012 saw one of YouTube's periodic socially led ruptures which triggered the redesign of YouTube's algorithm to replace clicks with Watch Time. A group of savvy YouTube users 'who knew too much' about how to game the YouTube algorithm, the 'cleavage girls', used enticing thumbnails to attract greater attention and thus potential monetization. However YouTube, concerned by mounting levels of user dissatisfaction, responded with the biggest algorithm change in its short history, Watch Time, to reward length of user engagement, over clicks. However, for many established IP-rightsholders, especially in Europe, YouTube's promotion of mass piracy, despite removing nine million illegal URLs from its web-index in one month in 2012, underlined perceptions Google was gaining an unfair trade advantage from its algorithms (Bakhshi et al., 2013, p. 82).

Jenkins et al. (2013, p. 6), emphasized the socially based foundation to their influential notion of spreadability, based as it was in YouTube's embed codes that make it easier for people to spread videos across the wider Internet. Jenkins' point underlined the growing power and animal-spirits-like nature of online audiences. For Gillespie (2014), algorithms should not be regarded as discrete units because 'there are people at every point: people debating the models, cleaning the training data, designing the algorithms, tuning the parameters, deciding on which algorithms to depend on in which context'. Striphas (2015, p. 406) noted algorithms constituted Trending topics, which presented themselves as an algorithmic real, but provided no accountability if we thought they were wrong. Most algorithms used by the majors were based on collaborative filtering – or 'the wisdom of crowds' – which was a good thing, nevertheless algorithmic data processing was becoming increasingly private, exclusive, profitable. Algorithms, Striphas (2015, p. 407) argued, 'are becoming decisive, and why companies like Amazon, Google and Facebook are fast becoming, despite their populist rhetoric, the new apostles of culture'.

Indeed, soon after, Google's Covington et al. (2016, p. 192) publicly released their explanation of how two AI – Candidate Generation and Ranking – winnowed down the many hours of videos uploaded to YouTube per second to help over one billion users discover the personalized content they wanted with a high degree of precision. This software architecture prioritized 'freshness' and the 'boot-strapping and propagating viral content'. For Kitchin (2017, p. 27), this growing technosocial assemblage meant that when citizens were playing or working, their behaviour was being 'subtly reshaped through engagement', a process that urgently needed to be better understood through, for example, comparative case studies[3].

Google chief executive, Sundar Pichai, said Google was leading the shift to AI-driven computing, with the aim to 'make people's lives easier ...powered by machine learning', a process itself increasingly automated in design (Alphabet, 2017). Uricchio (2017, p. 125) contends the age of the algorithm is so advanced as to have reached a tipping point where these networked non-human actors are capable of directly generating machine-readable data. Likening the assemblage to the printing press in its generative powers, Uricchio nevertheless warns bad actors can also be empowered to control and stabilize a master narrative that perpetuates traditional and iniquitous power dynamics. Nevertheless, the potential of algorithms to enable collaboration and creativity needed to be better understood, he says.

Indeed, in their deep dive among veteran Australian YouTubers, Healy and Cunningham (2017) concluded that for creators, the platform was a double-edged sword: paradoxically both a radically empowering, contingent technology, but also evolving a precarious Darwinian environment in which only the fit survive – and perhaps thrive. Quality content got lost on a platform so vast its reach and depth were regarded as 'incalculable', presenting major challenges to business models and creativity itself. Veteran creators such as Ann Reardon, told us that the algorithms favoured collation and copying over originality. Some artists such as Chris Voigt and Danny Philippou said, 'creativity gets killed'. Tim O'Reilly (2017), who coined the term Web 2.0, contends that while a positive aspect of algorithmic culture was the delivery of right results and lower-cost goods, financial markets were run by a master algorithm designed to maximise efficiency and corporate profits, at the expense of jobs and livelihoods. Truly intelligent machines were very far off and the real danger lay in major 'hybrid AI platforms', 'human-machine hybrids', that were mining the links people made and their intelligence, to feed and train algorithms. For example, the Facebook disinformation convulsion during the 2016 US Presidential election (Guess et al., 2019), showed how dangerous hybrid AI platforms could be when they 'went amok' (O'Reilly, 2017). Moreover, this information disorder is also manifested on YouTube via the phenomenon of over 1 million 'flat-Earth' videos, often amplified by other YouTube creators; but countered by fewer, but highly popular debunking videos. While this disparity in numbers may reflect the zeal of the flat-Earthers, Mohammed (2019, p. 96) argues that the globe-Earthers, 'with the full force of history and science at the ready, probably see little point in trying to respond to flat-Earthers'.

By 2018, content was diversifying and accelerating such that the Recommenders of Facebook, Netflix, YouTube, and Twitter had to become increasingly sophisticated to cope with the burgeoning demands of citizens and consumers. Collaborative filters and Recommender algorithms had to understand not just the user profiles of billions of individuals, but the type of content they all preferred at different times of day, locations, and type of devices and browsers used such as iOS, Android, Roku and Chromecast (Beutel, 2018, p. 5). In an echo of Minow's (2003)[4] excoriating critique of US commercial broadcasters' 'cultural wasteland' 40 years earlier, Gillespie (2018, p. 201) contended popularity-based algorithms had replaced relevance, merit, and newsworthiness, feeding a toxic culture. Without social pressure, platforms were unlikely to consider their public obligations beyond legal liability to uphold higher public standards encouraging compassion and just participation. In relation to threats of violence and intimidation, and hate speech, platforms were making choices that 'affect livelihoods, elections, and even life or death' (Gillespie, 2018, p. 58; Rosenberg, 2018).

By 2019, the conservative Australian Morrison government made world news when it proposed to form a new special branch of the country's consumer watchdog to investigate the algorithms of Google and Facebook (BBC, 2019). The BBC reported Australia's world first followed the announcement of similar plans by the US government to investigate the tech giants. The Australian proposal – which appears to be on the backburner – would investigate instances of anti-competitive conduct and harm to consumers, especially news outlets such as News Corp and others, run for five years, and have the power to compel information release (ACCC, 2019, p. 31). That same year, one of YouTube's earliest scholars Lange (2007), returned to her theme of how YouTube fostered meaningful relationships among youth *offline*. Lange (2019, p. 176) contended the moderation of sexist, racist, and homophobic comments on YouTube remained its greatest challenge: the assemblage merely enabled the formation of discursive communities, but civil and meaningful discussion had to be sustained through participation of like-minded individuals. As an antidote to online toxicity, designers of automated algorithms should aim to build what US cultural anthropologist, Michael Wesch, describes as 'communities of truth' to promote productive discourse (Lange, 2019, p. 181). Indeed, YouTube is capable of meaningful change driven by social pressure. The platform was reportedly working on a new metric 'quality Watch Time', to reward constructive, responsible content, but designing software that could emulate human judgement was even a challenge for YouTube (Bergen & Shaw, 2019). By the same token, wildly popular ephemera in the form of 15 second video snippets are diverting a significant proportion of the attention of the world's youth to YouTube Shorts. In a democratization of Computer Graphic Imagery on YouTube Shorts, the one short, *Turning Statues into Food!! Delicious* (2020), by veteran UK YouTuber Brandon Baum, has attracted 339 million views alone. As an important signal for the future of human attention, Baum encourages fans to remix his shorts by promising the best will be featured on his own Gold Play level channel. YouTube Shorts, the platform's response to shortform platform Tik Tok, attracted over 6.5 billion daily views as of early 2021, according to Alphabet and Google chief executive, Sundar Pichai (Alphabet, 2021). The world's population stood at 7.8 billion as of late 2021 (UNPA, 2021).

Regarding another of the dominant platforms, Twitter, Burgess and Baym (2020, p. 15) argued platform companies, their technologies and their user cultures 'co-evolve over time', for example, two of Twitter's primary features, @, created to hail other users, and the #, created to organize topics and groups.

These powerful symbols mediate discussion, but users also 'often resist, subvert or creatively work around the intended uses of such features' (Burgess & Baym, 2020, p. 35). Rieder et al. (2020) found YouTube remained heavily dominated by elite channels of 100K+ subscribers, who attracted 70 per cent of all subscriptions, and 62 per cent of all views. Arguably underlining the importance of Audience Growth Hacking know-how demonstrated by Reardon below, Rieder et al found more than half of all YouTube videos failed to reach over 550 views. Soon thereafter, Baym (2021) contended the unions and guilds that had fought for acceptable working conditions for generations of their mass-media counterparts had been marginalized in the creative economy. Despite the rhetoric of democratization and examples of youths who used their phones to climb out of poverty, an intervention was necessary to rebalance worker power in relation to platform recommendation systems and algorithmic discrimination. 'People's very selves become products in this economy, as regardless of what they produce, being 'authentic' and forming relationships that feel intimate to audiences become germane to making a living' (Baym, 2021, p. ix).

Cultural activism

Over a decade ago, Seo et al. (2009, p. 124) noted that non-government organizations had begun to adapt to new media, especially via websites and blogs, but struggled with their two-way affordances to interact with the public. NGOs tackle the burning issues of the biosphere via advocacy that helps shape international and domestic policies. However, NGOs are regarded as being less sophisticated in their mobilization strategies than electoral campaigners or social movements such as the Arab Spring, Occupy, #BlackLivesMatter, #MeToo, or #FridaysForFuture (Hall et al., 2020, p. 161). Indeed, drawing on Castells concept of the networked society, and Ramo's notion that billions of connected lives are now joined to tens of billions of linked sensors and machines, Slaughter (2017, p. 161) contends power has been realigned in the Networked Age. For Slaughter, 'the emerging networked world of the twenty-first century...exists above the state, below the state, and through the state. In this world, the state with the most connections will be the central player, able to set the global agenda and unlock innovation and sustainable growth'. Slaughter (2017, p. 10) argues that despite the future being unknown, humanity needs the skills and means to function in this very different age, 'where states still exist and exercise power, but side by side with corporate, civic and criminal actors enmeshed in a web of networks'. Meanwhile brands have been quick to capitalize on the capacity of some social media entertainers to market brand information to their circle of influence (Sng et al., 2019, p. 301), despite the risks of public relations disasters from influencer flame-outs. For example, the Australian government banned the use of influencers in marketing campaigns, however, later reneged using influencers following the devastating Australian bushfires of 2020 (Abidin et al., 2021, p. 117).

Nevertheless for activists, Hall et al. (2020) argue that participatory digital technologies are merely a potential capability, not an emergent property. The better NGOs were able to move along the continuum of the newly decentralized networks to coordinate supporter-led decision-making, the better NGOs would be able to tap into the new forms of networked power (see Figure 5.5 below). For example, 87 per cent of NGO websites were mobile-capable, an important consideration in attempting to reach audiences in the Global South who primarily use smartphones.

Biography

Reardon earliest inspiration for the channel sprang from necessity. Reardon had qualified as a food scientist, dietitian and pastry chef, but importantly, had worked as a youth pastor in a low socio-economic area of Western Australia. Now a mother of three, she had a sick baby and had to stay awake during night feeds. To keep herself awake, she started a cooking website, also typing out recipes one-handed while breastfeeding. To engage local youth in announcements and games, she taught herself video shooting on an early digital camera as iPhones had not yet been developed. Reardon uploaded her first video to YouTube in 2011, and was soon surprised to receive her first monetization: a cheque for $20, 'which to us made a big difference'. Reardon started thinking that the only reason people would watch these how-to genre videos was because they wanted to know how to make desserts. From listening to her comment streams, Reardon was surprised to discover people also watched them for very different reasons: to learn how to make desserts, just to be entertained, because they loved her Australian accent, or even for anger management, as they calmed people down (Reardon, 2017).

Between 2012 and 2020, Reardon made well over 400 videos, 45 videos of which have since each attracted up at least four million views, 18 of which were her trademark How To genre desserts, 17 of which featured iconic symbols, and nine of which were debunking videos that exposed fakery, and dangerous cooking methods. Starting in 2013, Reardon sprang to global digital media attention with the prototype of what would become a highly popular content concept for her channel: social media logo-themed cakes. Reardon's *Instagram Dessert Chocolate Mousse Recipe Dessert How to* video was likened by *The Huffington Post* to another 'creatively constructed cake: the Mondrian cake by pastry chef Caitlin Freeman for the Blue Bottle Café at San Francisco's Museum of Modern Art' (Tepper, 2013).

Reardon's nine-minute Instagram cake video has since attracted 11.5 million views. Once she achieved over 770,000 subscribers and over five million views, a *Forbes* profile on her small social media business followed. Three and a half years after launching HTCT, Reardon posted her most famous video to date, a highly fan requested iPad cake (Figure 5.2) (pictured).

With HTCT the world's third most popular baking channel, the *Sydney Morning Herald* described Reardon as 'Australia's baking Queen' in 2014. The

FIGURE 5.2 Three years' experimentation finally resulted in Reardon's famous iPad cake video

following year she was reported to have almost twice as many monthly views as celebrity chef Jamie Oliver. Tubefilter recognized her in 2015 in its YouTube Millionaires column. Reardon also participated in Skip Ahead, making a four by 10-minute documentary series, *The Sweetest Thing*, which 'uncovered the weird, wild and wonderful world of extreme desserts and cakes'.

The year 2016 was especially busy for Reardon. The first few months saw the staggered release of her 4-by-10-minute online Skip Ahead documentary, *The Sweetest Thing*. Reardon said the year she secured Skip Ahead, the initiative did not place as much emphasis on narrative as it did soon after (Reardon, 2021). Nevertheless, Reardon managed to weave together her own backstory including the role of her mother in creating themed cakes for birthdays, her continuation of the tradition with her own children, and the work she and her husband, Dave, did with troubled youth and gangs in Perth, with dessert creation by expert chefs. Despite the four series since attracting almost 8 million views, Reardon said three of the four performed 'very poorly' compared to her other uploads at the time which were averaged 2.6 million views (Reardon, 2021). Only one video in the web-series, *Magical Ice Drop* (2016) performed above average, since attracting 4.4 million views. Importantly regarding her ongoing sustainability, however, pre- and mid-roll ads continue to run on her YouTube videos, attracting modest AdSense, all these years later. Reardon learnt the low-budget, fast tempo-style film-making required in networked video:

Skip Ahead made me realize what we do every week to produce our show has given us years of experience in filming, sound, lighting, editing, production and direction, to the same level as people working in television. Also, increasing the budget and getting more people involved does not necessarily equate to more views.

Reardon, 2021

Later that year, Reardon's channel won The Taste Awards for 'Best Food Program: Web'. The following year, her channel was inducted into The Taste Awards Hall of Fame alongside CNN Style, E! Entertainment, and VICE Media. In 2017, of her two most viewed videos, *Chocolate Tools* and *Teeny Weeny* challenge, have since attracted a combined 14 million views. In 2018, she made three videos which have since attracted a combined 23.6 million views, being dessert, debunking, and symbol videos. In 2019, Reardon, increasingly alarmed by the information disorder being promulgated by disproportionally influential content farms on YouTube and Facebook, and the threat to the legitimate business model of YouTuber bakers, made three debunking videos since attracting 26 million views. The same year family priorities led her 'to put her work into perspective', such that she eased off the pace of weekly videos to fortnightly uploads instead. The shift enabled her to have weekends off, and work on off-platform projects such as a cookbook, now in its second print run.

By 2020, Reardon moved to step up the pressure on YouTube to enforce its own Community Guidelines against DIY content farms, for example, TheSoul Publishing's 5-Minute Crafts, by appealing to her viewers to lobby the platform directly. Reardon turned to her Twitter-enabled followers to tell YouTube leadership in San Bruno, California, subscribers were not happy with the business model of dumbed-down content farms via *#SaveYouTubeBaking*. Reardon urged her four-million-plus subscribers to tell YouTube they wanted a living for their favourite creators who were making complex videos in their own voices. Indeed, the Wall Street Journal had denounced the so-called home remedies and short cuts – or life hacks – as 'impractical, inadvisable or downright dangerous' (Horwitz, 2019). Tragically, an online star had to pay compensation to the families of two teenage girls – one of whom died and the other injured – in what one of the families said was an attempt to copy a viral video, the BBC (2019) reported. Six of Reardon's debunking videos, in a genre that effectively became a popular new series for her, have since attracted over 37 million views in their own right. In an important audience participation phenomenon, many of the targets of Reardon's debunking videos were initiated by her own fans.

Lead users leveraging their influence – in concert with their fans – to reform YouTube's reconstitution of the public sphere, is a promising and significant collective response that needs to be better understood. Indeed the importance of the presence of responsible, scientifically literate creators on search-based streamers such as YouTube, committed to promoting informed choices, is exemplified by Reardon's own efforts to counter misinformation in the early months of the COVID-19 pandemic. Her *Debunking Viral Covid-19 Videos* (May, 2020) used US Centres for Disease Control advice about the high levels of alcohol needed to make effective hand-sanitizer, to debunk viral hacks about home-made disinfectants on YouTube. Again, the importance of Patreon in enabling creators to fund themselves while they make videos on topics important to them, but that are labour-intensive, was emphasized. As of 2020, YouTube demonetized videos on sensitive news topics involving loss of life, such as shootings and COVID-19, as not appropriate for advertising, but allowed them to stay up (Alexander, 2020). 'Without Patreon I would not have been able to tackle this topic' (Reardon, 2021).

Burning problems

Monetization

In their pursuit of sustainable livelihoods in the absence of an effective template for success, different creators rely on different combinations of different revenue streams at different times[5]. However, a theme of these cases is the way Voigt, the Saiddens, the Philippous, and now Reardon rely in varying degrees at different times on the original schema of the three political economies advanced by Murdock and Golding (2016, p. 765), commodities, gifting and collaboration, and public goods. Cunningham and Craig (2019, p. 104) found that working across multiple platforms was 'the basis for the more lucrative practices of influencer marketing and sponsorship'. In terms of commodities, Reardon's high view-based profile thus attracted AdSense and sponsorship from Breville, KitchenAid, Wix, Candy Crush, YouTube, and LG. Crucially for web-series maker sustainability in future, Reardon says she has opted not to license her Skip Ahead documentary, *The Sweetest Thing*: 'We get lots of queries wanting to license the whole channel for SVOD, but the payments are so low that it is not worth it' (Reardon, 2021).

In terms of gifting and collaboration, Reardon initiated her social media journey uploading videos, but spent hours immediately chatting with viewers who became fans who became subscribers, and many of whom became audience participators. Specifically, fans contributed requests for recipe ideas, and fodder for Reardon's highly popular debunking videos, and supported her channel directly via crowdfunding on one of the most important platforms for all YouTubers, Patreon. Crucially, of the nine cases in this book, seven of the cases, born-online SME's and film school graduates alike, emphasized significant to very significant levels of co-creativity with fans, especially Voigt, the Philippous, Reardon here, Shackleford in the next chapter, Kalceff, Forster and Rowland and Ward. Importantly, the principle of co-creativity in these case studies is associated with high views, and since high views enable entrepreneurial opportunity, co-creativity promotes sustainability.

Significantly, the model of audience participation practised by Reardon and to a greater degree by SketchSHE – as expressed in a consensus of requests from fans – is a lighter, nimbler version, quite distinct from the formal, industrially based, directly collaborative models of co-creativity increasingly applied in games development such as elaborated by Banks and Humphreys (2008, p. 402) (Figure 5.4).

Coping with algorithmic volatility and doing good creative work

Reardon does 55 hour-plus weeks (Reardon, 2017), which has significant implications for her creativity, but is confident she has preserved work–life balance. Creative artists are known for their 'intrinsic motivation' (Csikszentmihalyi, 2014, p. 119), which sees them unable to distinguish work from enjoyment: 'I come up with my ideas usually on my day off when I shouldn't do any work!' (Reardon, 2017).

However, strongly supported by her symbol-laden creative practices, I argue that Reardon, and Shackleford as we will see in Chapter 6, cope with algorithmic volatility via three main strategies: increased experimentation, including surveillance of the channels of peers to see what succeeds and what fails, enhanced peer collaboration, and the direct lobbying of the platform that we saw with RackaRacka.

First, experimentation is an important response to platform volatility. For this level of creator, uploading a YouTube video is a high-stakes gamble, given the perceived risks to channel momentum from poor reception by audiences:

> We watch everything everyone does to see if it's going to help us. You put out a new video every day, which sounds exhausting, and decreases the creative content of what you can do.
>
> *Reardon, 2017*

Despite the family-friendly nature of HTCT, and Reardon's good behaviour on the channel, reformulation of the YouTube algorithms adversely impacted this creator's business model, foreshadowing a new round of experimentation, or channel abandonment like we saw with Voigt earlier:

> Finances drop when the views drop. I'd like to know what happens in six months? Will it stabilize or will it keep dropping? If it keeps dropping we must do something completely different even if the audience hates it, or stop uploading altogether which will be the interesting choice at some point.
>
> *Reardon, 2017*

But evidence from Reardon suggests YouTube algorithms adversely shape creative novelty. Reardon observes that if creators are driven solely by the need to make a living and are capable of producing original creative work, they may nevertheless succumb to the temptation to produce fresh videos that merely hook into topics that are trending:

> Copying something that is currently trending will get more promotion by the algorithm than creating something new. People are trying to get views, so even if they could come up with their own ideas, they don't.
>
> *Reardon, 2019*

Reardon explains that creators are necessarily deeply enmeshed in the algorithms:

> It's a difficult situation because what do we actually do? We are stuck in the fact that we are in the algorithm. If you don't please the algorithm, you don't get viewed. It's a tricky one.
>
> *Reardon, 2019*

Second, in addition to increased experimentation, peer collaborations are a very important creator response to platform volatility. Reardon's collaboration with Jos Brooks, Jamie & Nicki, and Jayden Rodrigues, *DIY Prank Chocolate Truffles* (Figure 5.3) was cross-posted on all four creators' channels, leveraging a combined viewership of over 6mn subscribers:

> Collaborations can take ages to plan and organise. Filming with multiple creators at once means you have four different channels shouting out for you for only one lot of planning and filming.
>
> *Reardon, 2019*

These creators show sophisticated understanding of audiencing, especially audience swapping, which can be integral to high views, and thus potential sustainability.

Third, direct lobbying is an important response to algorithmic volatility. Reardon says that prior to 2016, she had an effective creative practice where

FIGURE 5.3 To get algorithmic traction, these Gold Play YouTubers band together in face-to-face collaborations to swap audiences and build sustainability

the tenor of her comment stream was directly coherent with her views, but that congruence was broken following the 2016 change:

> With the algorithmic thing, always before I found what the audience liked and what they responded positively to, would get good views, and what the audience didn't like, would get bad views. But with the algorithm change on YouTube they are not matching up anymore and we are finding that quite frustrating. I have had this conversation with YouTube many times. The algorithm now favors collation and copying over creativity, but the audience loves creativity.
>
> *Reardon, 2017*

By 2021, algorithmic beta appeared just as permanent.

Old and new media divide

I make two related points in this section: first, creators and producers have to adapt to social analytics as a key element of their multiplatform labour; and second, as the cases of Reardon and Shackleford up-coming show, deft symbolic work is used to cut through the increasing hyper-saturation of web content.

First, the catch to creative autonomy on YouTube is social analytics, which can be a boon in identifying niche audiences worldwide, or information overload, or indeed both. The data-mining practices of social media giants have come under scrutiny in relation to increased concerns about transparency, privacy, and surveillance (Kennedy et al., 2017, p. 270). However, some of this data intensification can provide a vital resource underpinning the entrepreneurial activities of multi-platform creators, and thus creator livelihoods. Every creator has their own personalized, real-time, data-driven feedback loop in the form of the Creator Dashboard, featuring recent uploads and comments, account notifications from the platform, high-level statistics, and announcements about new features (YouTube Creators, 2021). Like all creators, Reardon can tell you her audience is still the United States, followed by the United Kingdom, Canada, and Australia, with the newcomer India now in her top five with 4.5 per cent of all her views. Social analytics have been critiqued for inducing information overload without real analytical insight (Cunningham & Craig, 2019, p. 98), but for Reardon and Shackleford, they have sent increasingly confusing signals over time.

Second, I showed in Chapter 1 that traditional, analogue-based creativity is highly socially based. In a substantial contribution to deepening our understanding of how creativity is faring in a networked, algorithmic environment, I show in these cases that creativity, in best practice form, is also highly socially based online. Of the 15 totems or icons identified, the most prominent are *Heart Cake Taylor Swift* (8.7 million views), *Lego Cake* (6.2 million views), *Frozen Elsa Princess Cake* (5 million views), *Minion Cake* (3.6 million views), *Van Gogh's Starry Night*

FIGURE 5.4 Co-creativity: Van Gogh's *The Starry Night* 1889, was rendered in chocolate after 200 fans requested the iconic painting

in Chocolate (3.3 million views – see Figure 5.4) and *Top 10 Best Books Cake* featuring Harry Potter, and books by YouTubers such as Hank Green's *The Fault in
Our Stars* (2 million views).

Authenticity and discrimination

In contrast to the perception some vloggers espouse progressive causes to merely
perform virtue, QUT Digital Media Research Centre PhD candidate, Cristel
Antonites told me Reardon's was a good example of where the creator *shares the
attention* of their subscribers with an expert organization of which viewers may
have been unaware:

> Most NGOs and social enterprises tend to struggle with sustainability and
> rarely have adequate marketing resources. Influencers often do and likely
> can do more to draw attention to their work, especially when they are
> interested in initiating projects that align with these organizations' work.
>
> *Antonites, 2021*

For example, *Giant Kit Kat Recipe* recognizes Jackson Moore, who ran one of the
largest youth groups in NSW (5.2 million views). Youth groups are regarded as
sharing some of the features of school work, for example socially shared intellectual
work and direct accomplishments, in informal settings (Dubas & Snider, 2020).
Similarly, her *Giant Twix Candy Bar Recipe* recognized the Carabez Alliance, an
Australian-based charity that distributed free hearing aids in Fiji (4.2 million

views). Among those with hearing loss, access to hearing aids is associated 'with delayed diagnosis of Alzheimer disease, dementia, depression, anxiety and falls among older adults' (Mahmoudi et al., 2019). Reardon's *Giant Ferrero Rocher recipe* recognized social enterprise, Thankyou Group's work in funding water, food, and hygiene in developing countries (4.1 million views). The Millennial and Gen-Z led enterprise reported to have delivered AU$5.2 million to social enterprise projects in 16 countries, began with bottled water with unique identifiers enabling citizens to track their impact (Brancatisano, 2016). Developing countries continue to endure 'the millennium old challenges' of microbial pollution and access to water, in addition to the new stresses of population growth, demographic shifts, and global warming (Westerhoff et al., 2019). New technologies capable of decentralized water treatment offer hope of meeting the clean water needs of this century. In a pandemic world, Thank you group managing director Daniel Flynn has challenged organizations, charities, and brands to question 'what we are taking into the future', and what else they 'can walk away from as we step into a new world' (Michael, 2020). This theme also recognized youth who performed exceptionally in sport – for example, world-circumnavigating yachtswoman and World Food Program ambassador Jessica Watson in *Giant Tim Tam Recipe* (1 million views). War and conflict, poverty, global warming, and natural disasters are regarded as the main causes of hunger and malnutrition, with undernourishment affecting about 13 per cent of the world's growing population (Pawlak & Kołodziejczak, 2020). Food production must double by 2050 to feed a world population predicted to rise from 7.6 billion in 2018, to 9.2 billion by 2050, the authors say.

FIGURE 5.5 Cut-through developmental-cultural activism via web-series featuring a symbol: Giant Ferrero Rocher recipe (2015) has attracted 4.1 million views

These public-good kinds of creative novelty generated via YouTube – for all its many faults – are among the most vivid blooms in YouTube's garden.

Notes

1 By 2021 in the United States, the combined effects of COVID-19 stimulus payments, increased unemployment benefits, and the child tax credit 'fit the definition' of guaranteed income, even if Washington did not use the language of Universal Basic Income, Guo (2021) argued.
2 The anthropomorphic nature of algorithmic action was introduced in Chapter 1.
3 The core methodology of this book is comparative case studies.
4 Newton N. Minow delivered this critique in a speech before the National Association of Broadcasters, May 9, 1961
5 The 10 most important revenue streams arising from the nine cases in this book are ranked in Table 2.1, Chapter 2.

References

Abidin, C., Lee, J., Barbetta, T., & Miao, W. S. (2021). Influencers and COVID-19: Reviewing key issues in press coverage across Australia, China, Japan, and South Korea. *Media International Australia, 178*(1), 114–135.

ACCC (2019). Digital Platforms Inquiry – Final report, Commonwealth of Australia, Canberra. https://www.accc.gov.au/publications/digital-platforms-inquiry-final-report

Alexander, J. (2020, March 4). YouTube is demonetizing videos about coronavirus, and creators are mad. *The Verge*, New York. https://www.theverge.com/2020/3/4/21164553/youtube-coronavirus-demonetization-sensitive-subjects-advertising-guidelines-revenue

Alphabet, (2017, July 25). Alphabet 2017 Q2 Earnings Call, Alphabet, Mountain View, California. Retrieved from: https://www.youtube.com/watch?v=xklBZ7W4Ox4

Alphabet (2021, April 27). Alphabet Q1 2021 Earnings Call, Alphabet, Mountain View, California. https://www.youtube.com/watch?v=B4VgDDlOaEc

Antonites, C. (2021). Personal communication with Guy Healy, Brisbane.

Arthurs, J., Drakopoulou, S., & Gandini, A. (2018). Researching YouTube. Convergence: The International Journal of Research into New Media Technologies, *24*(1), 3–15.

Bakhshi, H., Hargreaves, I., & Mateos-Garcia, J. (2013). *A manifesto for the creative economy, national endowment for science*. Technology and the Arts (NESTA).

Banks, J., & Humphreys, S. (2008). The labour of user co-creators: Emergent social network markets? *Convergence, 14*(4), 401–418.

Baym, N. K. (2021). *Creator culture: An introduction to global social media entertainment*. NYU Press.

BBC (2019, July 26). Australia to police tech giants' algorithms. BBC Tech, BBC London. https://www.bbc.com/news/technology-49125845

BBC (2019, September 20). YouTuber pays compensation after 'copycat' death, BBC News, BBC, London. https://www.bbc.com/news/49765176

Bergen, M & Shaw, L (2019, April 11). To answer critics, YouTube tries a new metric: Responsibility. *Bloomberg*, New York. https://www.bloomberg.com/news/articles/2019-04-11/to-answer-critics-youtube-tries-a-new-metric-responsibility

Beutel, A., Covington, P., Jain, S., Xu, C., Li, J., Gatto, V., & Chi, E. H. (2018, February). Latent cross: Making use of context in recurrent recommender systems. In Proceedings of the eleventh ACM international conference on web search and data mining (pp. 46–54).

Brancatisano, E. (2016, Dec 8). 'Thankyou' founder tells the story behind your bottle of water. *Huffington Post*, Australia. https://www.huffingtonpost.com.au/2016/12/07/thankyou-founder-daniel-flynn-on-eradicating-poverty/

Bruns, A. (2007). The future is user-led: The path towards widespread produsage. In Proceedings of perthDAC 2007: The 7th international digital arts and culture conference (pp. 68–77). Curtin University of Technology.

Bruns, A. (2008). Reconfiguring television for a networked, produsage context. *Media International Australia*, *126*(1), 82–94.

Burgess, J., & Baym, N. (2020). *Twitter: A biography*. NYU Press.

Caldwell, J. T. (2013). Para-industry: Researching Hollywood's Blackwaters. *Cinema Journal*, *52*(3), 157–165.

Carah, N., & Angus, D. (2018). Algorithmic brand culture: Participatory labour, machine learning and branding on social media. *Media, Culture & Society*, *40*(2), 178–194.

Castells, M. (2010). *The rise of the network society* (2nd Ed.). John Wiley & Sons.

Cheney-Lippold, J. (2011). A new algorithmic identity: Soft biopolitics and the modulation of control. *Theory, Culture & Society*, *28*(6), 164–181.

Christian, A. J. (2018). *Open TV*. New York University Press.

Covington, P., Adams, J., & Sargin, E. (2016). Deep neural networks for YouTube recommendations. In Proceedings of the 10th ACM conference on recommender systems (pp. 191–198).

Cunningham, S., & Swift, A. (2017) Over the horizon: YouTube culture meets Australian screen culture. In F. Collins, S. Bye, & J. Landman (Eds.), *Wiley-Blackwell companion to Australian cinema*. Wiley-Blackwell.

Cunningham, S., & Craig, D. (2019). *Social media entertainment*. New York University Press.

Curtin, M., & Sanson, K. (Eds.). (2017). *Voices of labor: Creativity, craft, and conflict in global Hollywood*. University of California Press.

Csikszentmihalyi, M. (2014). *The systems model of creativity: The collected works of Mihaly Csikszentmihalyi*. Springer.

Davidson, J., Liebald, B., Liu, J., Nandy, P. (2010, September). The YouTube video recommendation system. In Proceedings of the fourth ACM conference on recommender systems (pp. 293–296).

De Peuter, G. (2011). Creative economy and labor precarity: A contested convergence. *Journal of Communication Inquiry*, *35*(4), 417–425.

Ding, Y., Du, Y., Hu, Y., Liu, Z., Wang, L., Ross, K., & Ghose, A. (2011, November). Broadcast yourself: understanding YouTube uploaders. In Proceedings of the 2011 ACM SIGCOMM conference on internet measurement conference (pp. 361–370).

Dubas, J. S., & Snider, B. A. (2020). The role of community-based youth groups in enhancing learning and achievement through nonformal education. *Early Adolescence*, 159–174.

Duffy, B. E., Poell, T., & Nieborg, D. B. (2019). Platform practices in the cultural industries: Creativity, labor, and citizenship. *Social Media+ Society*, *5*(4), 1–8.

Gielen, M. (2019). Cracking The YouTube Algorithm In 2020. *Tubefilter*, Tubefilter Inc, Los Angeles. https://www.tubefilter.com/2019/07/12/cracking-the-youtube-algorithm-in-2020

Gillespie, T. (2014). Algorithm [draft][# digitalkeywords]. Culture Digitally.

Gillespie, T. (2018). What platforms are, and what they should be. In Gillespie, Tarleton. *Custodians of the Internet: Platforms, Content Moderation, and the Hidden Decisions That Shape Social Media*, (pp. 197–214). New Haven: Yale University Press.

Gomez-Uribe, C. A., & Hunt, N. (2015). The Netflix recommender system: Algorithms, business value, and innovation. *ACM Transactions on Management Information Systems (TMIS)*, *6*(4), 1–19.

Guess, A., Nagler, J., & Tucker, J. (2019). Less than you think: Prevalence and predictors of fake news dissemination on Facebook. *Science advances*, 5(1).

Guo, E. (2021, May 7). Universal basic income is here—it just looks different from what you expected, *MIT Review*, MIT. https://www.technologyreview.com/2021/05/07/1024674/ubi-guaranteed-income-pandemic

Hall, N., Schmitz, H. P., & Dedmon, J. M. (2020). Transnational advocacy and NGOs in the digital era: New forms of networked power. *International Studies Quarterly*, 64(1), 159–167.

Healy, G., & Cunningham, S. (2017). YouTube: Australia's parallel universe of online content creation. *Metro Magazine: Media & Education Magazine*, 193, 114–121.

Hesmondhalgh, D. (2010). User-generated content, free labour and the cultural industries. *Ephemera: Theory & Politics in Organization*, 10(3/4), 267–284.

Horwitz, J. (2019, Oct 9). Why Life Hack Videos Seem Too Good to Be True. *Wall Street Journal*, Dow Jones & Company, News Corp, New York. https://www.wsj.com/articles/long-story-short-my-microwave-exploded-the-problem-with-life-hack-videos-11570636955

Jenkins, H., Ford, S., & Green, J. (2013). *Spreadable media*. New York University Press.

Kennedy, H., Elgesem, D., & Miguel, C. (2017). On fairness: User perspectives on social media data mining. *Convergence*, 23(3), 270–288.

Kitchin, R. (2017). Thinking critically about and researching algorithms. *Information, Communication & Society*, 20(1), 14–29.

Kyncl, R., & Peyvan, M. (2017) *Streampunks: YouTube and the rebels remaking media*. HarperCollins.

Lange, P. G. (2007, May). Fostering friendship through video production: How youth use YouTube to enrich local interaction. In *Annual Meeting of the international communication association* (Vol. 27). Annenberg Center for Communication, University of Southern California.

Lange, P. (2019). *Thanks for watching: An anthropological study of video sharing on YouTube*. University Press of Colorado.

Mahmoudi, E., Basu, T., Langa, K., McKee, M. M., Zazove, P., Alexander, N., & Kamdar, N. (2019). Can hearing aids delay time to diagnosis of dementia, depression, or falls in older adults? *Journal of the American Geriatrics Society*, 67(11), 2362–2369.

McRobbie, A. (2002). Fashion culture: Creative work, female individualization. *Feminist Review*, 71(1), 52–62.

McRobbie, A. (2011). Reflections on feminism, immaterial labour and the post-Fordist regime. *New Formations*, 70(70), 60–76.

McRobbie, A. (2018). *Be creative: Making a living in the new culture industries*. John Wiley & Sons.

Michael, L. (2020, August). Thankyou, next: Aussie social enterprise says goodbye to bottled water. Pro Bono. https://cifal.newcastle.edu.au/thankyou-next-aussie-social-enterprise-says-goodbye-to-bottled-water/

Miller, T. (2016). Cybertarian flexibility—When prosumers join the cognitariat, all that is scholarship melts into air. In Eds Michael Curtin and Kevin Sanson, *Precarious creativity* (pp. 19–32). University of California Press.

Minow, Newton N. (2003) Television and the public interest. *Federal Communications Law Journal*, 55(3), 4.

Mohammed, S. N. (2019). Conspiracy theories and flat-earth videos on YouTube. *The Journal of Social Media in Society*, 8(2), 84–102.

Murdock G (2011) Political economies as moral economies: Commodities, gifts and public goods. In J. Wasko, G. Murdock, & H. Sousa (Eds.), *The Blackwell handbook of the political economy of communication* (pp. 13–40). Wiley-Blackwell.

Murdock, G., & Golding, P. (2016). Political economy and media production: A reply to Dwyer. *Media, Culture & Society, 38*(5), 763–769.

O'Reilly, T. (2017). The economy's running on the wrong algorithm. Tim O'Reilly on fake news, AI and the future | Wired, *Wired UK.* https://www.youtube.com/watch?v=4sM1eyt79CE

Pawlak, K., & Kołodziejczak, M. (2020). The role of agriculture in ensuring food security in developing countries: Considerations in the context of the problem of sustainable food production. *Sustainability, 12*(13), 5488.

Postigo, H. (2016). The socio-technical architecture of digital labor: Converting play into YouTube money. *New Media & Society, 18*(2), 332–349.

Potts, J., Cunningham, S., Hartley, J., & Ormerod, P. (2008). Social network markets: a new definition of the creative industries. *Journal of Cultural Economics, 32*(3), 167–185.

Reardon, A. (2017, 2018, 2019 and 2021). Creator, how to cook that, interviews with Guy Healy, Australia.

Rieder, B., Coromina, Ò., & Matamoros-Fernández, A. (2020). Mapping YouTube. First Monday.

Robb, J. E. (1998). The archaeology of symbols. *Annual Review of Anthropology, 27*(1), 329–346.

Rosenberg, S. (2018). What we're reading: How content moderation defines tech platforms. Axios, 29 July, https://www.axios.com/

Seo, H., Kim, J., & Yang, S. U. (2009). Global activism and new media: A study of transnational NGOs' online public relations. *Public Relations Review, 35*(2), 123–126.

Slaughter, A. M. (2017). *The chessboard and the web.* Yale University Press.

Sng, K., Au, T., & Pang, A. (2019). Social media influencers as a crisis risk in strategic communication: Impact of indiscretions on professional endorsements. *International Journal of Strategic Communication, 13*(4), 301–320.

Striphas, T. (2015). Algorithmic culture. *European Journal of Cultural Studies, 18*(4–5), 395–412.

Tang, J., Belletti, F., Jain, S., Chen, M., Beutel, A., Xu, C., & H. Chi, E. (2019, May). Towards neural mixture recommender for long range dependent user sequences. In *The World Wide Web Conference* (pp. 1782–1793).

Tepper, R. (2013). Instagram cake by Ann Reardon will take your breath away [Video]. The Huffington Post, 11 September. https://www.huffingtonpost.com.au/2013/09/11/instagram-cake_n_3907815.html

UNPA (2021). World population dashboard [Blog], United Nations, New York. Retrieved from: https://www.unfpa.org/data/world-population-dashboard

Uricchio, W. (2017). Data, culture and the ambivalence of algorithms.

Von Hippel, E. (2006). *Democratizing innovation* (p. 216). The MIT Press.

YouTube Creators (2021). Going Global with Shorts and Comments, Key Moments and more. [Official blog], YouTube, San Bruno, California. https://www.youtube.com/watch?v=qnmrVOaAWMU.

Weight, J. (2006). I, apparatus, you: A technosocial introduction to creative practice. *Convergence, 12*(4), 413–446.

Westerhoff, P., Boyer, T., & Linden, K. (2019). Emerging water technologies: Global pressures force innovation toward drinking water availability and quality. *Accounts of Chemical Research, 52*(5), 1146–1147.

6

THE BLOOD, SWEAT AND TEARS OF SHAE-LEE SHACKLEFORD AND SKETCHSHE

Regional Australian Shae-lee Shackleford has two authorial identities, one the social media entertainer; the other, a director working on her longerform scripts for future web-series. When I first met Shackleford over Skype in 2017, she was sitting in her Los Angeles apartment, well positioned to 'chase down her dreams'. SketchSHE had won their own production fund from 'Gen Z darling', AwesomenessTV, and Shackleford had been doing 'meetings', pitching her new funded web-series with a major legacy studio and SVOD gatekeepers. Just two years prior, inspired by the left-field career trajectories of Broad City, and Flight of the Conchords (Shackleford, 2018), the trio of three young Millennials she led, formed SketchSHE. Convinced there was a market gap for a female-centred comedy show on TV, they had spent almost a year working quietly on scripted sketches. The period of intense preparation proved generative once they began uploading. Three of SketchSHEs early lip-sync videos, *Bohemian Carsody* (March 2015), *Mime Through Time* (April 2015), and *SketchSHE Stole the Show* (January 2017) have together now attracted over 111 million views on YouTube alone. *Mime Through Time* proved such an innovative participatory meme it inspires cover videos from many corners of the world to this day: six of which, from Russia, Japan, India, Poland, Mexico and Brazil, themselves so resonate with audiences online they total 95 million views. This is the new long tail at its finest and most fun. This chapter centres on Shackleford's journey from Australian-based YouTuber and Skip Aheader to the Dream Factory of Hollywood, and her 'brutal' clash with gatekeepers over differences about who should own the IP of web-series: theirs from legacy media, her own from Silicon Valley startups; her turn to plant-based spirituality with husband and fellow creator, Russ Raven; their ultimate rejection by US authorities; her return home fleeing the pandemic in Los Angeles, and time in an Australian quarantine hotel; and finally, their new strategy of weekly, multi-genre web-series on YouTube.

DOI: 10.4324/9781003182481-6

FIGURE 6.1   From left, Shackleford, Lloyd, and Kington performing their Mime Through Time

Ninety years after 'lesser wits and playwrights' migrated from Broadway in Depression-era New York to nascent Hollywood in pursuit of their dreams, Shackleford heard the siren call of 'Westward Ho!', and made the journey to Los Angeles from Australia. With the coming of the sound film in the dark days of the Depression, writers were regarded as 'indispensable', and 'there was a good living to be made in movies, which were also magical and potentially great' (Jacobs, 1992, p. 117). The then 'little three' studios such as Paramount and Universal, became the 'Dream Factory to the world' (Marcom, 1991), churning out mass-market films and a few 'prestige' films each year, to a guaranteed theatre market during Hollywood's Golden era, but which was adversely affected by World War 11. But by the 1950s, Hollywood adapted and flourished despite the advent of new narrative entertainment technologies such as broadcast TV (Schatz, 2013), and later the video cassette and scrappy but innovative cable. Hollywood had turned to the studio saving blockbuster. However, by the mid-1990s, Hollywood's status as one of the world's leading suppliers of consumer products was challenged by the resurgent technology and aircraft industries of America's West Coast. Based on the export of semi-conductors for the nascent Internet, Silicon Valley became the 'real Dream Factory' with its vision of low-cost 'network computers' to enable networking access for Everyman (Ellis, 1997). For Cunningham and Craig (2019, p. 22) the emergent political economy for media was best understood as *an interdependent clash of cultures'*, they named social media entertainment (SME). A day's drive south to Los Angeles, Hollywood ethnographer John Caldwell (2006, p. 145) was finding industry players used sophisticated portrayals of themselves 'as simple, honest and direct men; screenwriters in touch with the universalism of Aristotle's three-part drama and well-rounded characters; producers responsively creating what the common person wants'. A key skillset for producers and executives was 'to take people to lunch for a living, and do so everyday. That's their profession'. But even Kenneth Lonergan, Oscar nominee for his *Gangs of New York* (2002), characterized pitch negotiations with studio executives as a power struggle over creative autonomy: 'I always feel like they're trying to move your original idea and make it go their cliché. And your job is to move their cliché to the nearest original idea' (Caldwell, 2008, p. 88). By mid-2021, Australia's ABC reported 'Fire, drought and real estate prices are ending the Californian dream', as the state lost migration for the first time in 170 years. Texas was fast becoming 'a new home for entrepreneurs, young families and Silicon Valley types because of the affordable lifestyle it offers' (Diss, 2021, June 13).

Musical films – often first emerging from the proving ground of Broadway such as *West Side Story* – are regarded as one of the most popularly beloved of all Hollywood genres. Musicals are the only film genre that owe their existence to Hollywood's capacity to record music and lyrics (Vogel, 2009). They often involved 'a group of young people or adults getting together to put on a show', the 'backstage' and later stardom itself during the Fred Astaire and Ginger Rogers cycle (Feuer, 1995, p. 441). Such reflexive 'verisimilitude' drew a US citizenry weary from decades of 'war and want' into something approaching an uplifting participatory experience. Backstage plots centred on rehearsal sequences detailing the evolution of the show, intercut with the off-stage affairs of the characters, while narratives suggested making musicals was the best solution to technological crisis (Feuer, 1995). Historically, film musicals are disproportionately represented among Oscar nominations for best picture award. Nine of 38 musical nominees won best picture to the early 1990s, compared to the number of winning gangster and war films, and Westerns (Vogel, 2009, p. 1). 'They gave audiences the precious gift of laughter, performers to cherish, songs to sing, dreams to dream, and welcome respites from the troubles of day-to-day living' (Vogel, 2009, p. 2). But the zeitgeist changed so 'no longer, it seemed, could 90 minutes' worth of watching and hearing pretty people perform pretty tunes suffice to insure healthy box office revenue' (Vogel, 2009). As music became webified, press critics and scholars focused on original music, but less on its commercial but influential twin, the music video. Music videos are regarded as significant sites of creativity and meaning, especially by feminists. They have critiqued some famous examples, for example the music video for Destiny Child's *Cater 2 you* (2004), for sending unhelpful and contradictory signals to teens and young women. Incongruously, the lyrics emphasize female subordination, but the video reinforces 'the image of Destiny Child as independent women who are in control of their own lives and pleasures' (Railton & Watson, 2011, p. 9).

However, as the nine cases in this book demonstrate, traditional show-business career trajectories have been radically destructured by the affordances of socio-technologies. A seductive 15-year-old world-stage is dangled before aspirants, with the Catch-22 they must master its byzantine networks. Traditionally, screenwriters take up to 15 years to achieve 'overnight success'

(Field, 1994, p. 256). Now, in about a third of the time, creative entrepreneurs can use multiplatform labour to distinguish themselves via an exceptional web-series, and parlay the resulting IP[1] and audience, into sales and licensing on a BVOD or SVOD (Healy, 2019, p. 116). For example, two of the most path-breaking Western career trajectories, and fast arcs certainly inspired Shackleford and SketchSHE, are those of pioneering New Zealanders' Jemaine Clement and Bret McKenzie, aka Flight of the Conchords, and YouTube comics from New York, Abbi Jacobson and Ilana Glazer, aka Broad City (Shackleford, 2018). Clement and McKenzie worked live comedy gigs and a BBC radio series to build a large fanbase which they leveraged into their own TV series on edgy SVOD, HBO. Much of their success was based on their own musicianship and original song parodies of pop cultural figures, combined with the enduring charm of Australian and New Zealand-style self-deprecating humour. For example, Flight of the Conchords describe themselves as 'formerly New Zealand's fourth most popular guitar-based, digi-bongo acapella-rap-funk-comedy folk duo' (Gibson, 2011, p. 606). Similarly, Broad City shows the role of YouTube in career acceler-ation, as I argued in Chapter 1 – in this case just five years to achieve their own female-centred show on a mainstream SVOD. Based on the narrative premise, 'Abbi and Ilana disagree on social etiquette', the pair used YouTube to post edgy sketches from 2009, supported by Facebook and Twitter, before transitioning to their own show on Comedy Central, which premiered in 2014. Underscoring the challenge of cut-through for aspirants, hyper-saturation of musical con-tent is just staggering: there were some 46,000 music channels with 24 billion subscribers (to multiple channels), and seven trillion views (7,200,116,048,127) (Rieder et al., 2020).

Scholars trace the origins of IP to the rights of chefs over new culinary dishes, and poets over their words and phrases in ancient Greece (Moore & Himma, 2018), and Venetian glassblowers and silk fabricators to their technologies, patterns and designs in the early Renaissance (May, 2002, p. 166). The proto-capitalist Venetian Republic, built at the crossroads of East and West, is credited with the innovations later 'codified into law' by the British Crown, spreading onward to the US and international patent experience (May, 2002, p. 159). For the Royal Society for the Arts (2006), IP law should be designed to promote human flourishing, 'now as in the past, to ensure both the sharing of knowledge and the rewarding of innovation'. However, as culture has become increasingly webified over the past generation, IP rights protection has become highly prob-lematized as socio-technologies enabled unfettered file-sharing of copyrighted stories laterally by the public. Except for a pluralism-defending Europe, much of the global architecture governing IP in the context of contemporary socio-technologies, especially transformative use and remix, stems from a landmark US suit brought by legacy media against Google. Viacom sued Google for making 160,000 Viacom-owned video clips available to YouTube users without permis-sion (VerSteeg, 2007, p. 43). Ultimately, the US Court ruled on a compromise: the 'burden of investigating infringing content' should fall on IP rights-owners, while 'the burden of removing all specifically identified content' should fall on Internet service providers (Williams & Mandell, 2013, p. 240).

The foundation of the crucially important principle of transformative use is attributed to US Justice Story who said the question of IP infringement turned on the question of whether the new expression was 'a fair and bona fide abridgement'. Accordingly, Story concluded there 'must be real substantial condensation of the materials, and intellectual labour and judgement, bestowed thereon; and not merely the facile use of scissors' (Liu, 2019, p. 222). When Australia was considering where the balance of public and private interest lay, 'fair use' was regarded as where works were transformative, such as sampling, remixes and mash-ups. The more transformative the work, the better remixers can fend off accusations of commercial purpose weighing against fair use (ALRC, 2012, p. 36). The most important example of transformative use in networked video is *Buffy vs Edward: Twilight Remixed* (June, 2009), Jonathan McIntosh's expert remix which has attracted almost 4 million views on YouTube. Subjected to a rights' claim McIntosh later won, *Twilight's* romantic heart-throb Edward Cullen is recast as an obsessive predator of a spirited Buffy. For McIntosh, the 'best mashup videos can serve as a form of critical media literacy, exploring the myths and messages embedded in media, typically masked by glossy Hollywood productions' (Burwell, 2013, p. 210).

Equitable division of IP to recognize 'blood sweat and tears'

Fair division of IP is increasingly a struggle in the fields of US West Coast subscription streamers Netflix, Amazon Video and Hulu, and Silicon Valley tech-startups. US OTT giants were found to be emulating the longstanding practice of Hollywood studios in insisting on full rights, all windows and territories in perpetuity, a high-level report for the Council of Europe found[2]. Talents needed 'fair alternatives' regarding share of IP, and subvention to help sustain writers through the important but 'fragile phase of development', especially as the international series sector expected more series to meet 'the new quality standards' set by HBO, Netflix and Amazon (Baujard et al., 2019, p. 76). Some OTTs have been starting these discussions with usually inexperienced showrunners in Europe, but talents needed fair alternatives to be independent (Baujard et al., 2019, p. 71). Equity, or the shares issued to founders, investors, employees and the public, has been a major driver of tech-startups in Silicon Valley since the late 1950s. Crucially, Don Valentine, the late founder of Sequoia Capital, which invested in Google, Facebook and Tik Tok owner, ByteDance, advocated an even split between financial backers, and entrepreneurs: 'We'll put up all the money, you put up all the blood, sweat and tears, and we'll split the company'. However, over recent years, records of initial public offers by 400 successful start-ups show investors own 50 per cent, employees 20 per cent, the investing public 20 per cent, and founders the remaining 10 per cent (Lebret, 2017, p. 2). Unless the US Teamsters form an effective coalition with YouTube creators going forward (Cunningham & Craig, 2021, p. 284), creators will be left with no collective voice since the shuttering of the three-year-old Internet Creators Guild. Former ICG executive director, Anthony D'Angelo says creators still need health care and fair contracts, but 'because the space is so atomized, it's hard to build awareness and solidarity' (Alexander, 2019). It remains an irony and paradox that despite the centrality of the collective phenomenon of YouTube 'collabs' to leverage each other's audiences shown in this book, creators remain unable to collectively bargain to better sustain their livelihoods together.

For young women over the past 20 years, identity formation has been occurring during a period of unprecedented turbulence. Radner (1999, p. 15) suggests for young women, the norm of innocence and virtue has been displaced by a commodified 'technology of sexiness', which emphasizes sexual knowledge, practice and agency. In 2004, one of the world's highest profile public relations agencies released the influential Dove Campaign for Real Beauty, which involved a participatory contest that drew young women worldwide into a discussion about creativity, empowerment, and their sense of their authentic selves. Duffy (2010) attributes the campaign's influence to its open, polysemic nature. While the campaign conflated citizenship and consumption, it nevertheless 'enabled women to conceptualize themselves in ways that mattered to them'. For Banet-Weiser et al. (2014, p. 1074), participatory culture had lost efficacy as it was 'defanged' by commercialism. The voices of producers and consumers were of over-riding importance, but had become steeped in neoliberal individualism, she argued.

However, the deadliness of 2018 appears to have marked a sea-change in terms of collective responses by young women to burning crises, and, the future nature of feminism itself, scholarship suggests. In February 2018, 17 students were killed at Stoneman High in Parkland, Florida, one of the deadliest high school shooting in US history. The tragedy provoked the national student-led March for Our Lives, described as 'one of the biggest youth protests since Vietnam' (Bent, 2020, p. 795). Bent observes, Emma González, the public face of the protest, refused to allow a framing of herself as exceptional, arguing, '[students] deserve more than Thoughts and Prayers, and after supporting us by walking out we will be there to support you by raising up your voices'. Less than six months later, Swedish teenager, Greta Thunberg, inspired by the student walkouts for gun control in Parkland, mobilized #FridaysforFuture 'the movement of movements' (Bowman, 2020). By the following year, #FFF – led by three young women in Europe including Thunberg – mobilized one of the largest, still ongoing, mass movements aimed at winning effective enough cuts in carbon emissions to sustainably protect the biosphere, and our collective futures. Girl activists, first Gonzalez and then Thunberg, were identified by mass media as the 'exceptional' leaders of the respective movements. But despite their youth, grass-roots organizational leaders in both movements exhibited significant and canny resistance to media framing of themselves as exceptional, encouraging decentralized, deliberative decision-making among their peers (Bent, 2020, p. 798; Van der Heyden et al., 2020, p. 207).

Spreadable videos are also socially based. For Burgess (2008, p. 5), the unpredictable success of videos such as Tay Zonday's famous *Chocolate Rain* (2008) so resonate in participatory culture they generate an outpouring of parodies, mashups and remixes, far exceeding the intentions of the original producers and disseminators: 'Successful 'viral' videos have textual hooks or key signifiers, which cannot be identified in advance (even, or especially, by their authors) but only after the fact, when they have become prominent via being selected a number of times for repetition'. Such videos are best understood as 'canonical' works in music in which 'layers upon layers of repetition are laid one over the other to create counterpoint', Burgess argues. For Jenkins et al. (2013, p. 19) the biological 'virus' metaphor disenfranchises the fundamentally social nature of these highly 'spreadable' videos, which are selected by active audiences for sharing with friends, family, peers and colleagues: 'Culture is a human product and replicates through human agency'. The trio explain some spreadability by drawing on Fiske's (2010, p. 84) concept of the 'producerly': text which 'offers itself up to popular production'. There is a longstanding algorithmic correlation between lip-syncing and memes going back to Israeli twentysomethings Lital Mizel and Adi Frimerman's *Hey Clip* (34.5 million views; August 2005) and Gary Brolsma's *NumaNuma* (50 million views; December 2006). Crucially, Millennials and Gen-Zs globally report feeling positive about social media overall, Deloitte's have reported 'a deeper dive' reveals a complex picture. Two-thirds of Millennials said they would be physically healthier if they spent less time on socials, and six in 10 said 'it would make them happier people' (2019, p. 20).

Biography

Shae-Lee Raven, nee Shackleford, wants 'to affect and change the world in a positive way through the stories I tell. Through comedy, through spreading joy. To me, there's enough negativity and trolling. My role is to make things that uplift people's spirits, to help them to grow, to help them discover who they are' (Shackleford, 2018). Born in Rockhampton, she grew up on Queensland's Sunshine Coast. The region, which neighbours the Coral Sea and the South Pacific Ocean, is especially vulnerable to severe climatic events, and is considered a model of community resilience (Smith & Lawrence 2014, p. 216). Shackleford trained at the Australian Acting Academy and the National Institute for Dramatic Art, and later at the Margie Haber Studio in Los Angeles. In 2013, Shackleford wrote, produced and directed the short film *The Anti-Social Network*, which has attracted over 893,000 views on YouTube. Her critique prefigured Netflix film, *The Social Dilemma*, which highlighted the addictiveness of the socio-technologies, and the need for an ethical reset in their design (McDavid, 2020, p. 1). In 2014, she teamed with Lana Kington, who grew up nearby in regional Queensland town of Biloela, who herself was already making mockumentaries in high school. At a promotional shoot in Sydney, the pair met Melbourne-born communications graduate, Madison Lloyd, and formed an all-female sketch comedy group, SketchSHE. In Australia, the SketchSHE trio made a sketch comedy pilot on sweat equity, but did not put anything online.

> Most people think we just sat in the car one day, and 'Oh My God' were viral. But (first) we did nine months' of filming sketches, trying to make a female driven TV comedy show in the lead-up.
>
> *Shackleford, 2018*

The trio were doing exactly what scientific history tells us is necessary for creative achievement. This intense preparation – albeit to attract the maximum amount of shareable attention on social networks – is one of the four parts of the process considered necessary to novel creativity. For Csikszentmihalyi (2014, p. 80), preparation involves concentrated attention 'on a problematic issue – long enough to master and understand its parameters'. For Livingstone (2009), creative achievement, most notably inspiration, is first set in motion by the four 'stages of preparation, incubation, insight and revision'. Nevertheless, frustrated by the lack of response to their pilot from local broadcasters, Shackleford flew to Los Angeles to pitch the show directly to Hollywood agents. In one of the few meetings she secured, she was fatefully advised to establish a comedy brand online, and re-pitch the show once SketchSHE had built a fan base.

Dejected, Shackleford returned to Australia and wrestled with the trio's dream to put the pilot 'into long-form comedy pieces', against the temptation to just put the pilot online 'and blow it all at once'. The pilot was edgy and 'boundary-pushing', having been influenced by the creative vision of Shackleford's then partner, *'Fully Sick Rapper'* and Bondi Hipster Christiaan Van Vuuren[3]. One sketch, *Certified Sick Cunts*, where the trio cross-dress as male gang members dropping the C-word to mark gang identity, 'will never see the light of day' as it would 'mortify fans'. But their edginess was reflected in their first posted video, *Slutguard for Sale*. Three weeks later, SketchSHE's first car choreography (not lip-synced), *Baby Got in the Back*, was posted, attracting tens of thousands of views. Then came *Gamer Girls*, which flipped gender roles for Valentine's Day. The choreographed car videos were 'resonating' with audiences worldwide who related to 'rocking out in their cars.

> A month later I had the *Bohemian Carsody* idea. I just woke up one day and it was there. We shot it in an hour on my iPhone, and the rest is history.
>
> *Shackleford, 2018*

Exemplifying the generative nature of preparation and networked video, 18 months before Douyin first launched internationally in Beijing in September 2016, SketchSHE secured worldwide attention and Internet fame with twin videos (Figure 1). *Bohemian Carsody* (March 2015, 30 million views), was followed weeks later with what would become a beloved and innovative participatory meme, *Mime Through Time* (Ap 1, 2015, 47 million views). The trio's videos would prefigure the explosive rise of shortform video remix apps for youth in pursuit of visual-audio fun, and their new status of 'Internet famous' (Tanz, 2008). Fuelling the attention economy, Tik Tok would dangle a US$1 billion fund enabling creators to cash out earnings based on the engagement of their posts (Abidin, 2020, p. 94). Significantly for creator empowerment, *Bohemian Carsody* (pictured below), epitomizes the converged creative, productive and distributive powers of the video–camera function of the iPhone, combined with the iMovie editing app, and Facebook and YouTube upload affordances:

> I thought let's do Queen's *'We Will Rock You'*, the greatest song of all time. Shot it in my car. Propped my iPhone up on a bra. Did three takes in (Sydney's) Centennial Park. Uploaded it, and it went crazy viral on Facebook.
>
> *Shackleford, 2016*

In hindsight, *Bohemian Carsody* would come to be their third most shared video (Figure 2). In quick succession, SketchSHE released *The Intervention FT Ryan Gosling*, *Girls Fight Club* and *Present-Day Princesses*. *Mime Through Time* was described by Tubular Labs as one of the most viral videos up to that time, with over 200 million views on Facebook (Jarboe, 2015). *Mime* was also shot on Shackleford's iPhone and was produced for just $1400. Queen fans complained Queen co-founder Freddie Mercury 'would be rolling over in his grave' over

FIGURE 6.2 SketchSHE's first breakout video, their first lip-sync, Queen's 'We Will Rock You'

FIGURE 6.3   'Spec world': SketchSHE perform their Mime Through Time live on Ellen

SketchSHE's lip-sync sampling of 'We Will Rock You'. But Queen guitarist Brian May shared the video, validating their sampling amplifying its spread. Weeks later, SketchSHE were interviewed by Ellen DeGeneres on her show on NBC Universal, then performed their video live on the stage (Figure 6.3). They then flew to New York to perform the Cyndi Lauper hit 'Girls Just Wanna Have Fun' for *Good Morning America* in a partly closed-down Times Square.

After their consecration in news and current affairs by US media conglomerates NBC and ABC, financial disaster struck. To fame flock opportunists, and the salient lesson for creatives about the need to do due diligence on potential collaborators. That lesson is exemplified in a major survey of Australian producers by Cameron et al. (2010, p. 100): compelling ideas and hard work are not enough for career success, but must be nested in rigorous business culture. SketchSHE signed a contract with a manager who Shackleford has publicly claimed 'pretty much managed to pocket every cent we earned in that boom period'. The loss of a 'house deposit'-sized sum under the contract left them indebted after they sued for breach of contract. The financial loss was telling. They were denied the opportunity to use the precious funds to hire a screenwriter, for example. Recovering from the blow, SketchSHE consolidated and continued to post videos to YouTube.

Skip ahead web-series

Underlining just how hard scripted creators have to work to make web-series work on YouTube, the series attracted 1.1 million views, a fraction of their breakout hits. Nevertheless, SketchSHE achieved a funded global web-series just 18 months after their channel start, underlining the career acceleration potential of networked video. Critics do not appear to have reviewed *Traffic Jam.* Like all creators, Shackleford can tell you the main audience for SketchSHE is in the US, followed by Germany, Russia and Australia, especially the capital cities, 60/40 female/male, and 18- to 24-year-olds based on her social analytics. SketchSHE's experience of Skip Ahead underlines three themes of this book. First, the web-series represented significant skills and career progression for the troupe. Up to then, Skip Ahead runner Mike Cowap said SketchSHE had been:

> making two kinds of videos with great success – lip-sync car videos and sketches like *#Instafaker Vs #InstaReality. Traffic Jam* combined those things. It was the perfect blend of their kind of music and comedy.
>
> *Bizzaca, 2016*

Importantly, Shackleford had a Hollywood vision for her ultra-low budget web-series, which prefigured the multi-Oscar, Golden Globe and BAFTA-winning *La-La Land* (2016) featuring Ryan Gosling and Emma Stone. The musical was about young lovers pursuing fame in a city 'sacrificing comfort, security and relationships for the dream' (Hill, 2016). Shackleford says she jokes 'La-La land is essentially Traffic Jam if we'd had $100,000. It was ahead of its time. (Shackleford, 2018). Drawing on the power of 'the backstage' Hollywood musical genre, *Traffic Jam* opens with the SketchSHE lip-sync trio in a car on the way to meet a film agent in the world of Hollow City off the back of a viral video.

Second, SketchSHE's first web-series, *Traffic Jam,* was achieved via a collaboration model, but without the studied narrative design and strong mentoring presence evident in SuperWog's *Pilot,* and RackaRacka's *Stunt Gone Wrong LIVESTREAM,* elaborated in Chapters 3 and 4. Importantly, no writing credits are evident for *Traffic Jam,* which was produced by Academy Award-nominated Drew Bailey (*Miracle Fish,* 2009) and directed by Marc Furmie (*Terminus,* 2015). Crucially, like RackaRacka's experience of modest subvention under Skip Ahead triggering new, hybrid, professional collaborations, so it was for SketchSHE. Now Gold-level YouTube dancer Jayden Rodrigues was brought in to choreograph *Traffic Jam,* and for a character role. Rodrigues own cover of Silento's *Watch Me,* was uploaded in 2015 and has since attracted 107 million views.

Third, crucially, SketchSHE made the transition from jack-of-all-trades division of labour typical of YouTubers to specialization that characterizes craft labour:

> On *Traffic Jam,* we used producer Drew Bailey who has worked with Screen Australia. This took pressure off the negotiations with crew so you can focus on the creative! Usually we're doing everything.
>
> *Shackleford, 2018*

FIGURE 6.4 'Craft world': Traffic Jam

The next two years involved a series of significant collaborations, especially upward with more highly viewed creators on Facebook or Instagram. The trio's biggest video in 2016 was *Best Duets*, a collaborative car video with US YouTube star Logan Paul.

The highlight of 2017 was what would turn out to be another smash-hit car video, a lip-sync of Kygo's *Stole the Show*, which has since attracted 34 million views, their second biggest ever. They did another two collaborations with social media influencers Violet Benson and Landon Moss, and returned to their popular battle of the sexes theme with the hit, *Dating 3 months vs married three years* (16 million views). Their mastery of YouTube, what Caldwell (2016, 38) would call 'spec world', and their web-series *Traffic Jam*, part of 'craft world', brought them to the attention of 'brand world' in the US, AwesomenessTV (Figure 6.4). The multi-channel network (MCN) started life as part of YouTube's professionalization of UGC-drive with seed funding from the platform in 2011 (Kyncl & Peyvan, 2017, p. 37), and evolved into a two-sided MCN to exploit the dominating convergence brands and US SME (Santo, 2018, p. 245). SketchSHE signed with AwesomenessTV, securing a dedicated production fund for a confidential sum. During 2017, Shackleford moved to Los Angeles. Picking up on their edgy style, women's health brand Canesten commissioned *Thrush: The Musical*, which has attracted 2.5 million views, and lead to a second episode a year later (Figure 6.5).

Gender matters web-series

In 2018 the troupe collaborated with future Skip Aheaders, Skit Box (*Activewear*), to win a Screen Australia Gender Matters Grant to make the eight-minute TV pilot *Posse!* Gender Matters aimed to correct the identified imbalance in lead creative roles by targeting subvention to ensure creative teams were at least 50 per cent female by 2018 (Screen Australia, 2016), a target contentiously met in 2019 (@devt, 2019). *Posse!* exhibits high production values exhibiting Shackleford's

FIGURE 6.5 'Brand world': Thrush

directorial skills, but the eight-minute story pilot has not engaged enough of an audience for the collaborative filtering mechanism of the YouTube Recommender to amplify broadly. The year also saw SketchSHE release another two battle of sexes videos, the most popular of which was *Freaky Friday* (508,000 views); a striking *Handmaid's Tale* parody featuring Katja Glieson (148,000 views); and a multi-voice 'girl power' video, *#BareAll* (190,000 views).

Just four years after SketchSHE had posted *Slutguard* on YouTube, Shackleford secured the attention of Paramount and Hulu for *Posse!!!*, and was working on production note feedback (Shackleford, 2019) (Figure 6.6). The projects later unravelled in a dispute over IP as we will explore below, but getting meetings with major streamers so soon after channel inception, is in itself an achievement for any aspiring director. Crucially, based on the nine cases in this book, I argued in Chapter 1 the web-series has evolved into a hybrid genre enabling screen storytellers to better adapt to the new paradigm of networked video. Indeed, in launching Posse! on YouTube in 2018, Shackleford herself made this clear:

> 'Posse! is the female Entourage'. A TV concept I wrote & directed! Love your feedback and if you think it should be made into a full female driven musical comedy series! Love, Shae x.
>
> *Shackleford, 2018*

HBO's *Entourage* (2004-2011) dealt with the pursuit of a screen career by a young A-List actor in the context of a share house in Los Angeles and is known for portraying a range of masculinities with a combination of fantasy and reality

FIGURE 6.6 In LA, Shackleford fronts her Posse! web-pilot alone

(Click et al., 2015, p. 403). Showrunner, Doug Ellin, has since defended the multi-Emmy and Golden Globe nominated show against accusations of celebrating toxic Hollywood culture. Ellin argues while not high art, *Entourage* was 'a pretty accurate portrayal of how people [acted] at that time in Hollywood' (Alter, 2021). Shackleford said *Traffic Jam* had provided an effective platform to step up to her next professional challenge of moving to Los Angeles and pitching her next web-series pilot, *Posse!* (2018; 47,300 views) to the major streamers. *Posse!* was funded by Screen Australia and shot at YouTube Spaces Los Angeles. The web pilot started life as *Manifest,* set in a storyworld called 'the Grotto, a multicultural Burning Man-esque camp filled with creatives in Hollywood, Los Angeles'.

The new Gender Matters grant helped Shackleford to advance in directing, and bring other women with her:

> It's always about platforming into the next stage of my career. I am writing a pilot, *Posse!!!* to take that next step. You don't always have to be what the industry tells you.
>
> *Shackleford, 2018*

Six years after the inception of their channel on YouTube, SketchSHE announced their last video as a trio. Feeling burnt by Hollywood, Shackleford and long-time partner and collaborator, Russ Raven, were turning back to YouTube to make multiple web-series pursuing their passions. Kington and Lloyd would continue SketchSHE on their Facebook and Instagram channels. In a three-hander vlog in September 2020, released a follow-up vlog of their experiences *Why we really left LA* (House of Raven, 2020). The vlog was shot back in Australia, and after a side-trip to Peru, homeward bound from Los Angeles. Released under a rebrand, House of Raven, they foreshadowed their new experiment in releasing an episode of one of their four new web-series on different topics each week, plus a mid-week vlog, centred on YouTube. The pair would build out a popular theme of their SketchSHE work, battle of the sexes videos such as *Dating three months VS married three years* (2017; 16 million views), as well as travel, animal education, performance sports, and dance. The pair explained after four years living in Los Angeles in pursuit of sustainable screen careers, they hit 'a massive roadblock' when they could not secure the green cards that would enable them to continue to live and work legally in the United States.

> I never thought Los Angeles was going to be easy, but I never really knew how insanely brutal it was going to be.
>
> *House of Raven, 2020*

The experience of shooting *Posse!* and their hard-edged musical parody of *Handmaid's Tale* at YouTube Spaces LA was invaluable for Shackleford. But for Raven, the Los Angeles acting scene also came with tough screen business lessons. He explained the manager and agent-led process of pitching himself for acting roles was so stressful he had sought professional help. Ultimately, he joined an alternative lifestyle community, and participated in 'plant medicine' ceremonies in Los Angeles. Shackleford observed their own lives had taken 'a surprising twist', since they went to LA driven by career dreams, but got diverted to a spiritual community. The lifestyle change became important to their growth as individuals and a couple, and helped sustain themselves during feelings of defeat. Nevertheless, this raw and 'really rough' experience had brought with it an epiphany: 'It's helped us align what our passions are; you are seeing the fruits of all of that. We didn't pull these five different shows out of nowhere'. Importantly, the pair explained despite securing a studio agreement from which major streamers became involved, negotiations over the division of the IP became a dealbreaker. By early 2021 the pair had released five videos on relationships and dance attracting 71,000 views in all. As the COVID-19 pathogen started to exact its deadly toll worldwide, and New York went into shelter-in-place, Shackleford fled the US. However, on her return home she went into mandatory quarantine in Australia, an experience she captured in *14 Day Hotel Quarantine – the Mashup.*

Burning problems

Monetization

Shackleford and SketchSHE are on the cutting edge of contemporary content creation, but edges cut both ways. Over the past seven years, the trio have made their livings from YouTube AdSense, sponsorships and a creative grant from

Awesomeness TV; Shackleford won two Screen Australia grants to make web-series; and they collaborated with fellow creators, while legions of fans gifted them via Kickstarter, sharing their content and participatory memes worldwide. Cunningham and Craig (2019, p. 83) found working across multiple platforms was 'the basis for the more lucrative practices of influencer marketing and sponsorship'. Shackleford is no exception, exhibiting a host of sponsorships including HP Spectre, Ministry of Sound, Red Nose Day, Disney, YouTube, Canesten and Vibe Israel. Arguably, the business model underpinning the creative entrepreneurship of Shackleford and SketchSHE draws directly on Murdock and Golding's schema of how the world's economies are constituted by the tripartite economies of commodities, public goods and gifting and collaboration. Indeed, Murdock and Golding (2016, p. 765) argue the burgeoning of the Internet 'has drawn renewed attention to the third cultural economy of gifting and collaboration'. The tripartite strategy of SketchSHE provides a solid model for sustainable creative entrepreneurship, but with the most crucial of caveats, a solid grounding in business skills for the creative economy.

> [After their breakout], the next 12 months were a crash course in music licensing and business. It's not something I talk about because its not in line with the SketchSHE brand of fun. We had an horrific experience after our viral videos.
>
> *Shackleford, 2016*

One person's copyright is another's transformative remix. If, at the time, SketchSHE had been able to monetise just their two most spreadable infringing videos, *Bohemian Carsody* (30.4 million views) and *Mime Through Time* (43.4 million views) at the going CPM rate of $1 (Batty, 2017), the trio would nominally have reaped AU$73,800. Crucially, this money could have been invested in paying script mentors to better help them achieve their original vision for a female-driven TV comedy show. For her part, Shackleford has a fatalistic to negative attitude to Content ID regarding SketchSHE's most popular videos:

> Yes [we get caught up in Content ID]. Luckily, only once or twice we've had issues where our videos have been taken down. Those bigger videos have matched Content ID but have been allowed to stay up. We could only monetise for a short period before the record companies got wind of it, and then they steal the monetization.
>
> *Shackleford, 2018*

The web-series genre is the hybrid child of Silicon Valley being web-based; pioneering US cable, with their creative autonomy in common; and Hollywood, since they draw on traditions of scripting and acting. To help better address creator sustainability, and drawing on Shackleford (2016), I argue ambitious web-series should be re-conceptualized as tech-startups (Figure 6.7). For Hamel (1999,

FIGURE 6.7   Now a veteran creative entrepreneur, Shackleford gives workshops like this

p. 75), tech-startups are characterized by the 'proof of concept' that the 'unending stream of entrepreneurs on the make' in Silicon Valley must create to attract seed funding of at least US$100,000. Shackleford has likened SketchSHE's early channel to the start-up model of development (Shackleford, 2016): 'We realised we were following the essence of any start-up. We had ambition; innovation in what we were doing; scalability; and what every start-up dreams of massive growth'.

In the manufacturing industry, a funding gap – or 'Valley of Death' – was found to exist in the early stage of research, but manifests as a valley at the intermediate stage – in the commercialisation of a new product (Beard at al., 2009, p. 345). The development phase of series writing is also considered a high financial risk, and does not receive enough public funding in Europe (Baujard et al., 2019, p. 77)[4]. The roadblocks between basic research and commercial development in the technology start-up industry, are paralleled in the risky development phase of series writing, for example, we will see Litton-Strain's unpaid development work in Chapter 8, Forster's 'Step 2' for series monetisation in Chapter 9, and Ward's 'big void' for development and discovery in Chapter 10. Moreover, it is 'not a stretch to equate investment in TV and film content projects with investment in start-up businesses', argues Deanne Weir, chair of Hoodlum, an Australian production company that has won an Emmy for *The Bourne Legacy – Lost*, and BAFTAs for *Spooks*. The risk profile is matched and would allow the screen industry to 'productize' investment in content products, 'giving them a common language' with which to speak to the investment community, Weir says. A frame of cultural impact philanthropy would be most effective: 'Many of the same people who have been willing to donate funds to content projects may also be willing to consider investment in more commercial content projects under the umbrella of 'Impact Investing' (Weir, 2020, p. 3). Indeed, just how much cultural impact a web-series can have, for example, is shown in the case of Tina Cesa Ward's *Anyone But Me* (100 million views) in Chapter 10, which was supported by an angel investor (Ward, 2019).

Coping with algorithmic volatility

For web-series makers, the most important decision facing them is whether, and if so how, to solve a Catch-22-style dilemma: winning huge enough algorithmic traction for their web-series to achieve licensing, which takes fulltime labour; while writing a compelling script, which requires fulltime labour. Shackleford does 55 hour-plus weeks which has implications her creativity. But these heavy workloads necessarily conflict with the periods of idleness and leisure scholars Bourdieu and Csikszentmihalyi, cited in Chapter 5, say are essential to creative novelty in high art:

> I have been working as a writer director in Los Angeles creating online videos and developing other ideas. That would be a 50- to 60-hour week. It can interfere. People in the social media business have to know when to shut off, because otherwise you can be up to midnight writing comments back to people.
>
> *Shackleford, 2018*

At a deeper level, these signals reinforce Andreessen's argument, mentioned in Chapter 5, that the world would increasingly be divided into 'people who tell computers what to do, and people who are told by computers what to do':

> Our YouTube audience just loves to see us doing stuff in the car. But as a creator that's like banging your head against a wall, because you do that on your ear. I am going to be 32. I don't want to be singing and dancing in the car for the rest of my life. But the analytics show that's what the people respond.
>
> *Shackleford, 2018*

In addition to this *algorithmic typecasting*, during the second and third interviews with Shackleford in 2018 and 2019, she acknowledged making a living on the platform had become 'harder'. She attributed this to the crowding-in effect, at both the bottom and top ends, exemplified by the rise of the creative economy among nearly 15 million indie Americans cited above. As Shackleford explained:

> There's a handful of people really blitzing it like Liza Koshy (17.8 million subscribers; 2.4 billion views).[5] For everyone else it's harder to break through because it's so saturated. The average video doesn't quite get the traction.
>
> *Shackleford, 2018*

YouTubers collaborate with like-minded friends, but there is a strategic aspect to such face-to-face creativity by leveraging off each other's subscribers on different platforms in a complementary way:

> I just collaborated with Violet Benson from Daddy Issues, *Why I Hate Halloween* (38,000 views). Violet has a big Instagram account (3.7 million followers), so that was about trying to share each other's audience.
>
> *Shackleford, 2018*

The solution to algorithmic typecasting is suggested by best practice multiplatform labour itself. For example, the SME creators Cunningham and Craig (2019, p. 95) describe as the most prominent in the US, the Vlogbrothers, Hank and John Green, have 'several different playlists, formats and verticals [genres] and operate multiple channels'.

Divide between old and new media

The YouTube creators in this book not only expect and demand their IP be respected, but they can 'sweat the asset' to the full via the multiple, *but non-exclusive licenses* we will see in the remaining four cases. OTT platforms such as Netflix, Amazon Video and Hulu are regarded as continuing the US studio tradition of claiming full rights, all windows and territories. This dominance leaves the indie producer to negotiate with powerful platforms to secure enough residual IP ownership to receive a margin from the production budget, and later potential international sales (Baujard et al., 2019, p. 70). The state of play, or really struggle over IP, is also a theme in the next chapter, when the book turns to the career trajectories of professional above-the-line creatives. For example, *Starting From Now* co-producer and later Netflix director, Rosie Lourde, emphasizes the importance of these conversations, producers – with platforms on one side, and creators on the other – must have over IP. Indeed, Shackleford and Raven attribute the collapse of their longerform project with Hollywood SVODs to just such a struggle over a division of the rewards from their IP; proportionate to who performed the majority of the creative labour, themselves (House of Raven, 2020).

Ultimately, all the cases of this book focus on how creativity is faring in a networked, algorithmic environment. In this case, creativity, in best practice form, is also highly socially based online. Shackleford's videos exhibit an exploitation of powerful totems, symbols or icons to cut through and mobilize fandoms in the crowded attention economy, a mastery of platform vernaculars and, importantly, continuities with traditional notions of creativity – but of a stressed kind. Scholars theorize that since the time of Palaeolithic cave art, symbols have acted as important 'mental girders', orienting people and helping them to think and act, especially regarding art, ritual, identify formation, social agency and technological knowledge (Robb, 1998). Arguably, spreadable videos such as *Mime Through Time* act as 'mental girders' for Gen Z and Millennials.

Shackleford and SketchSHE's 100-plus videos shows a strategy with four main categories: the icon strategy; identity play and gender politics; platform vernaculars, and girl power. Shackleford also has sought to distinguish herself via SketchSHE with web-films such as *The Anti-Social Network*, *If People Were Apps!*, *Posse!* and *The L-Bomb*. The powerful cultural symbol or icon strategy is shown in lip-synced videos referencing iconic popular songs and films such as Queen's '*Bohemian Rhapsody*', the 14 pop song-strong *Mime Through Time*, *Baby in the Back*, *Ice Ice Baby*, *Star Wars Parody* and *Pitch Perfect*. Identity play and gender politics is strongly exhibited in videos such *Gamer Girls*, *Girls Fight Club*, *Sexcuses*, *Break-ups*, *Break-up #2*, and *Dating 3 Months vs Married 3 Years*. Just like the US teenagers Fiske studied in relation to *Married With Children*, these videos enable teen and twenty-something viewers to engage in 'age politics with their absent parents', or engage in gender politics with their present partners (Fiske, 1992, p. 350).

Platform vernacular-inspired videos include *#NeverHappens*, *Shit You Do When You're Home Alone* (Figure 7.16), *Romantic Movie Mash-up*, *Hotel Mash-up* and *Versus* videos such *Girls vs Guys Getting Ready* and *Girls vs Guys Car Moments*. Videos such as *Break-up Mash-up* combine gender politics and platform vernacular strategies with what Fiske (1992, p. 353) might describe as audiencing, where parody is often used to differentiate youth culture then as opposed to now.

Authenticity and discrimination

Shackleford's re-invention of the participatory meme in *Mime Through Time* via hooks that authentically appealed to multiple demographics in just 3.5 minutes, was serendipitous. But like all the best innovation and creativity, it was proceeded by a period of hard work focused on understanding the problems confronting networked creators in the first place. This evidence further supports Jenkins et al.'s (2013) conception of spreadability as socially based rather than informational 'virus'-based. Shackleford emphasizes the importance of tapping people's love for nostalgia, authentically:

> There's a big difference between liking and sharing. If you want to create something that has this mass explosion, it has to be one of those relatability things: I want to tag my friend; that reminds me of someone I know; or a blog (like Mashable) will share and comment on it.
>
> *Shackleford, 2016b*

The genesis of a participatory meme such as *Mime Through Time* lay in YouTube's most valuable affordance of all: the drive to experimentation:

> There are 14 songs in that video, so you are giving yourself 14 chances to resonate with different fans. Okay, I love Britney Spears; so did me (sic) and

FIGURE 6.8 Pre-Tik-Tok: The co-creation of a super-meme via format innovation: SketchSHE's Mime Through Time lip-sync (2015)

that person. We wanted to do sketch comedy, and stumbled on a format that resonated.

Shackleford, 2016a

Analysis of the SketchSHE covers around the world does show adoption of the Western-produced lip-synced SketchSHE format (Figure 6.8). Crucially however the cover videos feature locally created choreographies celebrating locally indigenous songs, culture and national dress, such as the *Mime Through Time (Japanese ver)* SketchSHE cover:

The most significant remixes of SketchSHE's remix – are *Za Molokom* by Russians, Bonya, and Kuzmich (45.4 million views); *Mime Through Time (Japan ver SketchSHE cover)* (22.4 million views); the *Bollywood Mime Through Time Madhuri Dixit* (10 million views); and a Polish version by a YouTube book reviewer, *Mime Through Time and Books (SketchSHE Cover)* (9.4 million views). Latin Americans Carolitho and Summer Girls also contributed their own covers of *Mime Through Time*, attracting a total of three million views. Even British health workers got in on the fun with *Mime Through Time: NHS edition* (2017, Apr 21). Underlining the importance of the vernacular appropriation, remix principles and play-to-platform vernaculars, YGmoA's Japanese cover of SketchSHE's *Mime* also lip-synced in its closing sequence the Internet meme *Numa* (2004) shown in Figure 6.9.

Like their fellow creator, Reardon, Shackleford and SketchSHE show a strong social concern, as well as a post-feminist activism, in videos such as *#BareAll Challenge* (Figure 6.10), *Honest Social Media* and *Handmaid's Tale Fancy Parody*.

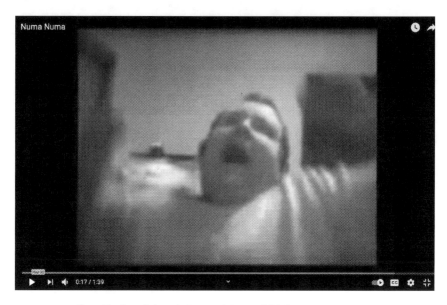

FIGURE 6.9 Gary Brolsma's iconic Numa Numa (2004)

On one hand, this looks like 'commodity activism', which describes 'the prom-ise and perils of consumer-based modes of resistance as they take shape within the dynamics of neoliberal power' (Mukherjee & Banet-Weiser, 2012, p. 2). On the other, they could constitute the genuine empathic spaces that encourage cultural citizenship by the sharing of intimate personal stories, thus promoting 'greater understanding of oneself and others' (Lange, 2007) (Figure 6.10).

FIGURE 6.10 'Girl power' in social media, 2018: Shackleford shares her SketchSHE attention with many other diverse female voices, for example US Instagrammers

Notes

1 We will see with Susan Miller and Tina Cesa Ward in Chapter 10 that retaining their IP in the hit web-series, *Anyone But Me*, is one of their proudest achievements.
2 This squares with the new convention known as 'cost plus a percentage' instigated by Netflix. Netflix acquires the rights for a long time, if not perpetuity, but pays the full production costs of a series plus a percentage typically 25 per cent (Lotz, 2018, p. 123).
3 Christiaan's brother, Connor, emphasized to me the role of the web-series as an IP-bearing 'proof of concept' for a longer form show, and one that helps creators 'hang onto a bigger slice of the IP, since it is a pre-existing thing'.
4 Best practice countries with exceptional series creative environments are Denmark, the UK, Israel, Belgium, and France (Baujard et al 2019, p. 55).
5 Koshy's web-series, *Liza On Demand* (52 million views), is among the few Originals projects for YouTube Premium to achieve both critical and popular acclaim.

References

@devt (2019, Nov 7). #GenderMatters Returns! https://medium.com/womens-film-activism/gendermatters-returns

Abidin, C. (2020). Mapping internet celebrity on TikTok: Exploring attention economies and visibility labours. *Cultural Science Journal*, *12*(1), 77–103.

Alexander, J. (2019, July 11). YouTubers' first organizing attempt, the Internet Creators Guild, is shutting down. The Verge, Vox Media, New York City. https://www.theverge.com/2019/7/11/20688929/internet-creators-guild-shutting-down-hank-green-youtube-copyright-claims-monetization

Alter, E. (2021, April 28). 'Entourage' creator Doug Ellin on how 'wave of righteous PC culture' impacted HBO show's legacy. Yahoo Entertainment, Verizon Media, New York. https://www.yahoo.com/entertainment/entourage-doug-ellin-culture-wars-controversy-metoo-hbo-reboot

Australian Law Reform Commission. (2012). Copyright and the digital economy: issues paper. Commonwealth of Australia, Canberra. https://www.alrc.gov.au/wp-content/uploads/2019/08/whole_ip_42_4.pdf

Banet-Weiser, S. Baym, N. K., Coppa, F., Gauntlett, D., Gray, J., Jenkins, H., & Shaw, A. (2014). Participations| Part 1: Creativity. *International Journal of Communication*, *8*, 1069–1088.

Baujard, T., Tereszkiewicz, R., de Swarte, A., & Tuovinen, T. (2019). Entering the new paradigm of artificial intelligence and series: A study commissioned by the Council of Europe and Eurimages. https://rm.coe.int/eurimages-entering-the-new-paradigm

Batty, D. (2017) Creator, Black As. Phone interview with author.

Beard, T. R., Ford, G. S., Koutsky, T. M., & Spiwak, L. J. (2009). A valley of death in the innovation sequence: An economic investigation. *Research Evaluation*, *18*(5), 343–356.

Bent, E. (2020). This is not another girl-power story: Reading Emma González as a public feminist intellectual. *Signs: Journal of Women in Culture and Society*, *45*(4), 795–816.

Bizzaca, C. (2016). Australia: Multi-platform storytelling pioneer. *Screen Australia*. https://www.screenaustralia.gov.au/sa/screen-news/2016/12-13-australia-multi-platform-storytelling-pioneer

Bowman, B. (2020, August 28). Fridays for future: How the young climate movement has grown since Greta Thunberg's lone protest. *The Conversation*, Melbourne. https://theconversation.com/fridays-for-future-how-the-young-climate-movement-has-grown-since-greta-thunbergs-lone-protest

Burgess, J. (2008). *'All Your Chocolate Rain Are Belong to Us?' Viral Video, YouTube and the Dynamics of Participatory Culture*. In: UNSPECIFIED, (ed) Video Vortex Reader: Responses to YouTube. Institute of Network Cultures, Amsterdam, pp. 101–109.

Burwell, C. (2013). The pedagogical potential of video remix: Critical conversations about culture, creativity, and copyright. *Journal of Adolescent & Adult Literacy*, *57*(3), 205–213.

Caldwell, J. (2006). Cultural studies of media production: Critical industrial practices. *Questions of method in cultural studies*, 109–153.

Caldwell, J. T. (2008). Trade Rituals and Turf Marking In Caldwell, J. T. (2008). *Production culture*. Duke University Press.

Curtin, M., & Sanson, K. (Eds.). (2016). *Precarious creativity: Global media, local labor* (p. 336). Oakland, CA: University of California Press.

Cameron, A., Verhoeven, D., & Court, D. (2010). Above the bottom line: Understanding Australian screen content producers. *Media International Australia*, *136*(1), 90–102.

Click, M. A., Holladay, H. W., Lee, H., & Kristiansen, L. J. (2015). "Let's hug it out, bitch" HBO's entourage, masculinity in crisis, and the value of audience studies. *Television & New Media*, *16*(5), 403–421.

Cunningham, S., & Craig, D. (2019). *Social media entertainment*. New York University Press.

Cunningham, S., & Craig, D. (2021). *Creator culture: An introduction to global social media entertainment*. New York University Press.

Csikszentmihalyi, M. (2014). Society, culture, and person: A systems view of creativity. In Csikszentmihalyi, M. (2015). *The systems model of creativity: The collected works of Mihaly Csikszentmihalyi*. (pp. 47–61). Springer.

Deloitte. (2019). The Deloitte global millennial survey 2019. *Deloitte Touche Tohmatsu Limited*.

Diss, K. (2021, June 13). Fire, drought and real estate prices are ending the Californian dream.https://www.abc.net.au/news/2021-06-13/california-dream-is-becoming-a-nightmare/100146900

Duffy, B. E. (2010). Empowerment through endorsement? Polysemic meaning in Dove's user-generated advertising. *Communication, Culture & Critique*, *3*(1), 26–43.

Ellis, E. (1997, Jan 29). *The real dream factory, Australian Financial Review*. Nine Publishing.

Feuer, J. (1995). The self-reflexive musical and the myth of entertainment. *Film Genre Reader*, III, 441–455.

Field, S. (1994). *Screenplay*. Delacorte.

Fiske, J. (1992). Audiencing: A cultural studies approach to watching television. *Poetics*, *21*(4), 345–359.

Fiske, J. (2010). *Understanding popular culture*. Routledge.

Gibson, A. (2011). Flight of the Conchords: Recontextualizing the voices of popular culture 1. *Journal of Sociolinguistics*, *15*(5), 603–626.

Hamel, G. (1999). Bringing silicon valley inside. *Harvard Business Review*, *77*(5), 71.

Healy, G. (2019). 'Fast and furious film-making': YouTube's prospects for budding and veteran producers. *Metro Magazine*, *202*, 100–105.

Hill, G. (2016). La-La land review. http://garryvictorhill.com.au/pdf/La%20La%20Land.pdf

House of Raven (2020, Dec 3). Why we really left LA. [Vlogpost]. https://www.youtube.com/watch?v=oc6FLeF0D30&t=5s

Jacobs, D. (1992). Part III. Westward Ho!. In *Christmas in July: The Life and Art of Preston Sturges by Diane Jacobs, UCP*. (pp. 115–198). University of California Press.

Jarboe, G. (2015, October 12). Why micro moments matter for Facebook, YouTube, and Twitter Video Tubular Insights & Tubular Labs, Inc, California. https://tubularinsights.com/micro-moments-facebook-youtube-twitter/

Jenkins, H., Ford, S., & Green, J. (2013). *Spreadable media*. New York University Press.

Kyncl, R., & Peyvan, M. (2017) *Streampunks: YouTube and the Rebels Remaking Media*. HarperCollins.

Lange, P. (2007). The vulnerable video blogger: Promoting social change through intimacy. The Scholar and Feminist Online. http://sfonline.barnard.edu/blogs/lange_05.htm

Lebret, H. (2017). Equity in startups. https://www.researchgate.net/publication/320820900_Equity_in_Startups

Liu, J. (2019). An empirical study of transformative use in copyright Law. *Stanford Technology Law Review, 22,* 163.

Livingston, P. (2009). Poincaré's 'delicate sieve': On creativity and constraints in the arts. In K. Bardsley, D. Dutton, & M. Krauz (Eds.), *The idea of creativity* (pp. 129–146). Brill.

Lotz, A. D. (2018). *We now disrupt this broadcast: How cable transformed television and the internet revolutionized it all.* MIT Press.

Marcom, J. (1991). Dream factory to the world. Forbes, integrated whale media investments and Forbes family. Forbes magazine April 29, 1991. 98–101.

May, C. (2002). The Venetian moment: New technologies, legal innovation and the institutional origins of intellectual property. *Prometheus, 20*(2), 159–179.

McDavid, J. (2020). The social dilemma. *Journal of Religion and Film, 24*(1), 1–3.

Moore, A., and Himma, K. (2018). Intellectual property. The Stanford encyclopedia of philosophy. https://plato.stanford.edu/archives/win2018/entries/intellectual-property/

Mukherjee, R., & Banet-Weiser, S. (Eds.). (2012). *Commodity activism: Cultural resistance in neoliberal times.* NYU Press.

Murdock, G., & Golding, P. (2016). Political economy and media production: A reply to Dwyer. *Media, Culture & Society, 38*(5), 763–769.

Radner, H. (1999). Introduction: Queering the girl', In H. Radner, & M. Luckett (Eds.), *Swinging single: Representing sexuality in the 1960s.* University of Minnesota Press.

Railton, D., & Watson, P. (2011). Introduction: The Kleenexes of popular culture? In Jamie Sexton, *Music video and the politics of representation.* Edinburgh University Press.

Rieder, B., Coromina, Ò., & Matamoros-Fernández, A. (2020). Mapping YouTube. First Monday.

Robb, J. E. (1998). The archaeology of symbols. *Annual Review of Anthropology, 27*(1), 329–346.

Royal Society for the Arts (2006). *The Adelphi charter. RSA.* www.adelphicharter.org

Santo, A. (2018). AwesomenessTV: Talent management and merchandising on multichannel networks. In Johnson, D. (2018) (Ed.), *From networks to Netflix* (pp. 245–254). Routledge.

Schatz, T. (2013). The *new* Hollywood (pp. 27–56). Routledge.

Screen Australia (2016, July 12). Gender matters: Record-breaking funding for women to be seen and heard. [Media release]. https://www.screenaustralia.gov.au/sa/media-centre/news/2016/07-12-gender-matters-brilliant-stories

Shackleford, S. L. (2016). SketchSHE: From 500 to 500M. Presentation by Shae-lee Shackleford. Real Big Things #13 Conference, Sydney. https://www.youtube.com/watch?v=Adz80K47axY&t=911s

Shackleford, S. L. (2016a). Shae-lee Shackleford: How SketchSHE went viral. https://www.youtube.com/watch?v=Adz80K47axY&t=911s

Shackleford, S. L. (2018, 2019, 2020). Writer/director of SketchSHE; Traffic Jam and Posse! Skype and email interviews with Guy Healy.

Smith, K., & Lawrence, G. (2014). Flooding and food security: A case study of community resilience in Rockhampton. *Rural Society, 23*(3), 216–228.

Tanz, J. (2008) Internet famous: Julia Allison and the secrets of self-promotion. *Wired.* http://www.wired.com/2008/07/howto-allison/

Van der Heyden, A. D. W., Neubauer, L., & van der Heyden, K. (2020). Fridays for future-FFF Europe and beyond. In Claude Henry, Johan Rockström and Nicholas Stern, *Standing up for a sustainable world.* Edward Elgar Publishing.

VerSteeg, R. (2007). Viacom v. Youtube: Preliminary observations. *The North Carolina Journal of Law and Technology,* 9 N.C. J.L. & Tech. 43. https://scholarship.law.unc.edu/ncjolt/vol9/iss1/4.

Vogel, F. G. (2009). Hollywood musicals nominated for best picture. McFarland.

Ward, T.C. (2019, 2020, 2021). Creator, Skype interview with Guy Healy.

Weir, D. (2020, July 1). Submission in response to supporting Australian stories on our screens: Options Paper March 2020, Commonwealth of Australia, Canberra. https://www.communications.gov.au/have-your-say/supporting-australian-stories-our-screens-options-paper

Williams, J. T., & Mandell, C. W. (2013). Winning the battle, but losing the war: Why the second circuit's decision in Viacom Int'l, Inc. v. Youtube, Inc. Is a landmark victory for internet service providers. *AIPLA Quarterly Journal, 41,* 235.

7

EMMY-WINNER JULIE KALCEFF...
NOT SITTING IN A ROOM ON
HER OWN

Kalceff is best known for the low-budget, but high impact web-series, *Starting from Now*, which has achieved 170 million mostly YouTube views to date, after Felicia Day's *The Guild* (2007–2013) (300 million), and Matt Arnold and Freddie Wong's *Video Game High School* (2012–2016) (198 million), comprising the Western world's top three most viewed indie web-series. *Starting From Now (SFN)* built a global audience of the under-represented for itself, especially in the United States, France, Germany, and the United Kingdom, about 80 per cent female and 20 per cent male. Julie Kalceff's methodology, together with her colleagues Susan Miller and Tina Cesa Ward in Chapter 10, provide the richest, most innovative and culturally impactful models for successful global web-series drama in this book. Kalceff and her co-producer on seasons four and five, Rosie Lourde (Figure 7.1), participated in three interviews and one, respectively, with me from 2017 to 2021, so providing the insights which illuminate this case. In addition to popular acclaim, *SFN* was met with critical acclaim winning multiple awards, including: the International Academy of Web Television Award of Recognition at Hollyweb Fest, 2017; the Outstanding Diversity Award at Melbourne WebFest, 2017; and the Audience Award at Sydney's Mardi Gras Film Festival, 2016. Kalceff wrote, directed and co-produced *First Day*, which won the International Emmy Kids Award for Best Live Action Series, 2021.

First, Kalceff's transnational web-series, *SFN*, underlines the critical importance of wise choice of collaborators, in this case, future Netflix director, Rosie Lourde (*Romance on the Menu*, 2021), and writer mentor Amanda Higgs (*Secret Life of Us*, 2001–2005; *Barracuda; Seven Types of Ambiguity; Mustangs FC*); and then on Kalceff's subsequent *First Day* (2020), Epic Films producer Kirsty Stark (*Wastelander Panda*, 2012; *Stateless*, 2020). Second, Kalceff adapted what Smith (2018, p. 54) characterizes as the optimum narrative design for iconic TV series, multiple-storyline plotting, for the low budget web-series. Third, in contrast to the strained

DOI: 10.4324/9781003182481-7

FIGURE 7.1 Kalceff and Lourde collaborate on *SFN*. Photo credit: Ella Mackenzie-Taylor

creative flow experienced by Voigt and Philippou, Kalceff used the web-series to enjoy flow in writing character and relationship-driven stories. Fourth, in contrast to 'very annoying' and 'really bad' experience of participatory storytelling with fans on Emmy-winning, *#7DaysLater* (Ludo, n.d.), Kalceff managed fan participation in such a way as to become instead 'a gift' to the hybrid writer-producer.

Fifth, while not planned this way, the first three seasons of *SFN* effectively acted as an experimental Silicon Valley-style 'proof of concept' to secure modest investment in the final two seasons, in this case Screen Australia funding. Sixth, *SFN* drew on seven of the revenue strategies in Table 2.1, and her IP in the series was ultimately cycled across eight different platforms. Of all creators in these nine case studies, *SFN's* high number of revenue streams and IP cycles are co-equal highest with Miller and Ward on *Anyone But Me (ABM)* (Chapter 10), the world's fourth most highly viewed web-series. Indeed, *SFN* and *ABM's* high numbers set the very high bar for low-budget, culturally impactful web-series. Seventh, *SFN* shows how exceptional web-series can circumvent the symbolic violence directed at marginalized groups in and by many traditional media, and when special resources are focused and sustained, can remake those symbols authentically, and entertainingly, where those audiences are now, in situated online communities.

Background

The literature on screen representation of women, non-white racial and ethnic groups, and queer folk suggests minorities have been marginalized by two egregious mechanisms: invisibility and symbolic violence. For Bourdieu, the political, journalistic, and the social sciences fields struggle to impose the legitimate vision of the social world, principles of vision and division, where the vision seen by the public to be deserving of dominance, 'is charged with symbolic violence' (Benson & Neveu, 2005, p. 37). Classic Hollywood from 1930 to the late 1960s was so opposed to any deviations from heterosexual norms the Motion Picture Production Code forbade 'sex perversion or any inference to it'. The classic Hollywood spectator was not just male, but 'Western, white and straight as well' (White, 1999, p. 12). Extraordinarily, 'visual representations of lesbianism in classical US cinema were censored, not extended the protections of freedom of speech' (White, 1999). Nevertheless, visual and narrative 'traces' enabled women, including lesbian fans, 'to read' and enjoy visual connotations of desire in such a way screen icons like Garbo, Dietrich, and Hepburn are consistently rated their favourite stars (White, 1999, p. 20).

During the Kennedy era, federal communications regulator, Newton Minow (2003, p. 398), was so concerned by the concentrating power of TV networks, and their failure to serve the public interest he critiqued executives to their faces for their 'procession of game shows, violence, audience participation shows, formula comedies about unbelievable families, blood and thunder, mayhem, violence, sadism, murder, Western badmen, Western good men, private eyes, gangsters, more violence and cartoons'. Minow challenged TV executives to tell advertisers the networks were now pursuing high quality programming that promoted 'understanding', and 'if you can find a better place to move automobiles, cigarettes and soap – go ahead and try'. By the time of the Reagan era, Newcomb and Alley (1983, p. 15) argued there was 'an observable, intractable bias' stemming from white male domination of TV, despite female and minority producers creating 'important and high-quality programs'. Since TV was a 'highly charged, symbolic, fictional system', gender parity and minority representation had to be corrected 'if social inequity is to be rectified not only in the television industry, but in American society at large' (Newcomb & Alley, 1983, p. 15).

Australian TV showed the first lesbian kiss in the 1970s, two decades before the first televisual kisses in the United States in 1991, and the United Kingdom in 1993 (Beirne, 2009, p. 26). However, not all Australian representations of lesbians were positive, including one 'fiendish lesbian witch' stripping her flatmate for a sacrificial Black Mass, and another famous *Prisoner* character who was 'a ratbag sadist, corrupt and potentially murderous' (Howes in Beirne, 2009, p. 26). By 2013, gay and lesbian representations were available across a multiplicity of media. However Ng (2013, p. 278) argued anti-LGBT discrimination was still so acute as to require bringing heterosexual allies into a broad movement opposed to violence and injustice.

Between 2014 and 2015, representations of women and other marginalized peoples in over 400 film, broadcast, cable, and digital stories came under formal academic scrutiny in the landmark University of Southern California Annenberg report (2016), prompting calls for urgent diversification-led hiring practices for creator labour in Hollywood. Females were found to hold less than a third of speaking roles in film, and under 40 per cent of speaking roles in streaming, cable and broadcast, (Smith et al. 2016). Of over 4200 directors in the sample, 85 per cent were male and just 15 per cent female. Female writing credits were most likely in broadcast (31.6 per cent), followed by cable (28.5 per cent), streaming (25 per cent), and film (11 per cent). Just two per cent of speaking characters were LGBT-identified and just seven transgender characters appeared in the sample, mostly in the one show. Moreover, characters from under-represented racial/ethnic groups 'are also excluded or erased from mediated storytelling. No platform presents a profile of race/ethnicity matching proportional representation in the United States' (Smith et al., 2016, p. 16). Of the 10 distributors rated on inclusion by Annenberg, comprising 21st century Fox, CBS, NBC Universal, The CW, Walt Disney, TimeWarner, Viacom, Amazon, Hulu, and Netflix, only Hulu was rated fully inclusive on female characters and under-represented characters, followed by Viacom fully inclusive on under-representation and largely inclusive on females, and Walt Disney fully inclusive on females and largely inclusive on under-representation. Smith et al. concluded 'the film industry still functions as a straight, White, boy's club'.

During 2018 the question of the authenticity of who got to play sexually diverse characters in high-profile lead roles, an increasingly frequent discussion in Writers' Rooms, became vexed. Scarlett Johansson withdrew from a fact-based drama, *Rub & Tug*, about a trans crime boss, after an outcry on social media from the trans community. Johansson said while she would have loved to bring the story to life, 'I understand why many feel he should be portrayed by a transgender person'. Months later, conversely, Cate Blanchett, who played a lesbian in *Carol* (2015), said she would 'fight to the death for the right to suspend disbelief and play roles beyond my experience' (BBC, 2018). Overall, 52 straight actors had been Oscar-nominated for representing gay characters, including Blanchett, the BBC reported. By 2021, significant numbers of women were nominated in each category of the BAFTAs, a bankable distinction in its own right. Best Film was most notably won by Chloe Zhao, Frances McDormand, Mollye Asher, Dan Janvey, and Peter Spears for *Nomandland*. At the Oscars, Zhao went onto become the first non-white woman, and second female to win best director (BBC, 2021).

Same-sex love and homosexuality are a reality of history, realities reflected in many nations rewriting laws and rules to be sexuality and gender-neutral. Yet, discrimination-based violence continues to impact young and LGBT people in schools, workplaces, and tragically, sometimes where they congregate for entertainment and solidarity. Whether such relationships were accepted or prosecuted, Morris (2019, p. 2) argues evidence of alternative sexualities have flourished across millennia: 'from the lyrics of same-sex desire inscribed by Sappho in the seventh century BCE, to youths raised as the opposite sex in cultures ranging from Albania to Afghanistan; from the "female husbands" of Kenya, to the Native American "Two Spirit". Morris (2019, p. 2) argues as these realities gradually became known to the West from travellers and others tales, the 'peaceful flowering of early trans or bisexual acceptance in different Indigenous civilizations met with opposition from European and Christian colonizers'.

For Risman (2004, p. 435), gender is conceptualized as a social structure, which means sexism is inherent as children are socialized, in turn producing gender inequality. For the past thirty years, women of colour have been writing about 'intersectionality', leading to a consensus one must always consider 'multiple axes of oppression: to do otherwise presumes the whiteness of women, the maleness of people of colour, and the heterosexuality of everyone'. Crucially, for Risman (2004, p. 445), the next frontier to spur change towards more egalitarian societies, are cognitive biases, and thus 'the interactional or cultural dimension of gender structure'. Homophobic abuse and violence targeting LGBT populations occurs on a regular basis, felt particularly keenly among young people who can suffer vulnerabilities on account of their low incomes, unemployment, low education and poor health and housing (Takács, 2006). LGBT youth experienced most discrimination and/or prejudice at school, with over half of respondents reporting verbal and/or physical violence according to a survey conducted for a key European labour organization (Tákacs, 2006). A decade later, Cornu (2016, p. 7) reported violence in schools was a global problem, with students not conforming to sexual and gender norms being more vulnerable. By this period there were hundreds of scripted web-series 'by and about' black, Latino, Asian American and gay, lesbian, bisexual and transgender people. While Christian (2018, p. 13) has noted most web-series lack the technical sophistication of Hollywood series, community value in terms of better representation, creative autonomy and the opportunity to connect with viewers 'are enough to motivate producers and entrepreneurs'.

Young people have long pleaded for greater understanding from of threats of violence. In 2016, the Pulse nightclub in Orlando, Florida became the site of one the country's worst hate crimes as 49 people attending for sociality and solidarity were killed, and another 53 injured[1]. Overall 90 per cent of the revellers were lesbian, gay, bisexual, and transgender Latin people (Ramirez et al., 2018, p. 579). The constant threat of hate and violence toward LGBT people of colour, and safe spaces being rare, emerged as themes of adult LGBT-POC respondents surveyed following the hate crime (Ramirez et al., 2018, p. 587). Young and distressed people especially turn to the Internet, as a widespread source of confidential health advice bypassing parents and others seen to be compromising, or to avoid embarrassment (Harvey et al., 2007, p. 772). People identifying as lesbian or gay have 'higher rates of depression, anxiety and suicidal ideation' than heterosexuals, while transgender people fare worse, according to the same report. Teachers need to be supported to make classrooms places where contrasting and alternative views can be examined and debated respectfully, to 'recognize, celebrate and affirm diversity of all forms' (Theodore & Stoker, 2021, p. 41).

Audiences are conventionally conceived as passive, but, throughout history, have had surprising degrees of agency regarding the stories they are told. Recently, fan agency has become tightly intertwined with narrative composition. The struggle for the 'people's discourse' in the processes of narrative design has manifested in different ways at different times, according to those situated circumstances. Sixth century BC audiences would negotiate what would be sung with Odyssean poets, how it was to be sung and how well the tales, tailored for kings as much as swineherds, were going (Dalby, 1995, p. 70). Odyssean oratory was tailored to appeal to the genders in different ways, including powerful female patrons (Doherty, 1991, p. 146). The social system of Florentine patrons, guilds and the general populace – via a series of competitions and feedback – has been credited with stimulating the originality of Brunelleschi and Ghiberti in their work on Florence's cathedral making the early Renaissance possible (Csikszentmihalyi, 2014, p. 57). Victorian-era fans suggested plots to Dickens (Jenkins, 1992, p. 28). To build and reinforce bonds of friendship, Australian schoolgirls would re-enact scenes and mimic the characters of their favourite TV soaps, such as *Restless Years* (1977–1981) and *Prisoner* (1979–1986), in the schoolyard (Palmer 1986, p. 40). By the 1990s, the analogue technologies of the photocopier and the post shifted one-way film and TV spectatorship, giving rise to an expressive, female-led, participatory culture, 'textual poaching', that appropriated legacy media narratives, and remixed them as the basis of social exchange (Jenkins, 1992). Later, serialized mythologies like the *X-Files* (1993–2002) and *Buffy* (1997–2003), reached their apotheosis in ABC's *Lost* (2004–2010), 'the greatness' of which Mittell (2007) attributes to four aesthetics: unity-of-purpose, forensic fandom, narrative complexity and the aesthetics of surprise.

The pro-am led drive for narrative distinction has become widespread cultural practice. By the turn of the decade, transmedia storytelling became dominant as every story was exposed to informed consumers, who had their own receptions of stories, but processed them collectively in social networks (Jenkins, 2010, p. 948). Beyond the everyday vernacular UGC, fan fiction sites FF.net and AO3 enabled the evolution of large-scale, amateur, and pro-am narrative production as tens of thousands of fan authors produced over 34,000 original works in response to Hollywood blockbusters, *Batman, The Avengers* and *Inception*. These fans had not been colonized by the major media they consume, argued de Kosnik et al. (2015, p. 148), but were active audiences of media texts who showed 'thoughtfulness, critical thinking and creativity'. Crucially, storytelling is now conducted now in the context of the social web, 'where people perform their identities'. Stories can be reframed in ways unintended by a range of agents in misleading ways so as to avoid AI systems designed to counter 'information disorder'. Misinformation, false content shared by a person who does not realize it is false or misleading, is with disinformation and malinformation, known collectively as information disorder (Wardle & Derakhshan, 2017).

Kalceff Biography

Formative years

'I grew up in the Western suburbs of Sydney. I didn't know anyone who was queer and I certainly didn't have any role models. If there was an LGBTQIA+ character on screen, they were always killed off or they were a plot device and they'd end up being the butt of a joke' (Bailey, 2020). Western Sydney is regarded as one of Australia's most important in terms of its multicultural history, given the role of residents in both 'resisting *and* accommodating' population growth, immigration and multiculturalism (Simic, 2008, p. 233). For Kalceff, film-making is her second career, her first being a high school English teacher. Kalceff feels 'an obligation and responsibility' to the LGBTQIA+ community. Her film-making is driven by the belief 'if you have the privilege of having a voice, then you really need to be mindful of how you use it...you should be the person you needed when you were growing up' (Bailey, 2020). Growing up, TV 'wasn't strong', so her influences were films such as *Thelma & Louise* (1991), characterized as 'a beloved and influential film, for some even a life-altering one' about 'women, men, guns and the fate of women who break the law' (Sturken, 2020). Female-driven stories of female empowerment 'always spoke to me and anything, most queer audiences can identify with this, anything with any semblance of queer content in it, you would seek it out because you didn't see yourself on screen (Kalceff, 2021).

To fulfil her passions, Kalceff left her teaching job and began a masters in screen writing at AFTRS in 2001. Screen industry bible, The Hollywood Reporter has consistently ranked AFTRS as among the world's best film schools, with alumni including Jane Campion (*The Piano*, 1993), Phillip Noyce (*Rabbit-Proof Fence*, 2002), and Sue Maslin (*The Dressmaker*, 2015). Kalceff's fateful change of course is exemplary at multiple levels. First, Kalceff joined the ranks of 'a staggering 42 per cent' of Australian producers with postgraduate qualifications, underlying the fact made by Cameron et al. (2010, p. 98), many new producers – mostly in their forties - arrive with skills, experience and knowledge from their first careers. Second, internationally, the profession shift is typical of the post-industrial economy of the 1990s favouring 'protean' careers, where individuals increasingly managed their own careers in pursuit of promotion, salary, autonomy and personal measures of success (Bridgstock, 2005, p. 40). Third, protean-like career shifts, especially into successful creative professions, require a process of 'encounter, courage and a drive toward form' (May, 1975). While at AFTRS, Kalceff attended a seminar conducted by award-winning screenwriting author and University of Southern California professor Robert McKee. McKee (1997, p. 4) stresses the power of archetypes to drive narrative. Kalceff did a placement in the writing rooms of Channel Seven's *Home & Away*, and was a trainee storyliner on *Neighbours,* but was not passionate enough about those shows to continue working on them. *Neighbours* uses the premise in a suburban 'street where nothing happens, when something does happen it is enormously significant', 'to engage families for as long as we can' (Sergi & Dodds, 2003, p. 74). *Home and Away* (1985–) and *Neighbours* (1988–) are 'reputable', 'soft-sell' Australian soaps representing valuable, 'ready-made' niche audiences of 16–35 females who can be sold to potential advertisers, especially in the United Kingdom (Ward et al., 2010, p. 165). Kalceff had a decade-long period of self-doubt and struggling to 'fit into' the mainstream TV industry given its lack of diversity regarding both sexuality and ethnicity. Ultimately, she got to the point of deciding to either 'put everything into making this work', or cut herself a break and do something else (Kalceff, 2017). Fatefully, Kalceff went all in.

Web-series

After a decade trying to find her place in the industry, the crucial social dynamic underpinning creativity put Kalceff onto the path where she could finally fulfil her creative vision. Future Emmy-nominated script developer, Mike Jones (*Wrong Kind of Black*, 2018), was running the first course on the web-series at AFTRS, where student Natalie Krikowa was starting to create the historically significant, but under-recognized Australian web-series, *Newtown Girls* (2012). Recognizing the shift of audiences online, and the richness of local creative firepower, Screen Australia has presciently supported web-series production with taxpayer funding since about 2012. This resulting combination of talent and modest subvention has made Australia, with Canada, a world-leader in web-series production, dominating the annual International Academy of Web TV awards in Los Angeles (Ward, 2019). Australian series have ranked in the top 10 of the web-series World Cup from 2015 to 2019. However, *Newtown Girls* was ineligible for even the modest subvention available under Skip Ahead, then still in embryo. The proposed distribution method for *Newtown Girls*, the Internet-based Vimeo, YouTube, and ill-fated blip.tv, a crucial monetizing indie platform soon to be absorbed by a series of competing conglomerates and shuttered, ruled it out of available schemes (Keltie, 2017, p. 5). Keltie herself directed and did lighting on *Newtown Girls*. Keltie lauds the 10-part series as 'extremely' empowering application of digital practices, and form of resistance to a dominant culture industry outside institutional control. However, she argues audiences had limited agency in what was supposed to be participatory culture (Keltie, 2017, p. 3), since the team had to rely on crowdfunding, meaning the team had unequal access to production capital.

However, the romantic comedy, centred on the character of Scarlet (Debra Ades) (Figure 7.2), 'a girl determined to find true love in the quirky queer scene of Newtown', and housemate Alex (Renee Lim), would eventually attract 3.3 million views. The series has been watched in 180 countries, especially the United Kingdom, the United States and Saudi Arabia, mostly on YouTube, likely at work and Internet cafes (Keltie, 2017, p. 127). Underscoring the generative potential of collaboration and creative autonomy, Kalceff wrote and directed on the series:

> I saw how you could make content you believed in, and have immediate access to an audience. You didn't have to go through gate-keepers. You didn't have to get approval. That was where the idea to do *SFN* came from.
>
> *Kalceff, 2017*

FIGURE 7.2 Debra Ades pictured in a daydream by her boss on Newtown Girls

Development of Starting From Now (SFN)

From 2014 to 2016, Kalceff drove the story of the lesbian-quadrangle that crossed over to Broadcast VOD (BVOD) on SBS2. Based on her experience with *Newtown Girls*, Kalceff identified a significant market gap in online content: well-scripted, well-acted narratives of appeal to lesbian viewers. Until *SFN*, Kalceff had trained only as a writer, not a director. In the collapse in the division of creative labour in this space highlighted in Chapter 1, Kalceff wrote, directed, and produced the first three seasons of *SFN*. Co-producer and actor Lauren Orrell helped produce the second season. In the humblest beginnings to what would become a transnational web-series, Kalceff revived 'a failed feature' from a drawer she had written years earlier. *SFN* would become writer Kalceff's film-school for directing. *SFN*'s story follows 'four inner-city lesbians as they struggle to work out who they are, find a place where they belong, and maybe even find someone to love along the way'. Kalceff recruited an all-female cast, Sarah de Possesse (Steph), Lauren Orrell (Kristen), Rosie Lourde (Darcy), and Bianca Bradley (Emily) (Figure 7.3). Kalceff self-funded the first two seasons and a crowd-funding campaign raised $10,000 to make Season 3. The subsequent audience build of millions then triggered AU$210,000 subvention to fund the final two seasons, with a combined budget including licensing of AU$322,000. The extra funding enabled higher production values all around and an almost tripling of crew to 42, further heightening logistical challenges. With hindsight, Kalceff explains her web-series style:

> SFN was a big learning curve because it was the equivalent of 30 short films in three years, and we did it on little resources. My focus with directing

FIGURE 7.3 Key cast of SFN from left: Lauren Orrell (Kristen), Rosie Lourde (Darcy), Sarah de Possesse (Steph), and Bianca Bradley (Emily). Photo credit: Julie Kalceff

has always been with the actors. That's what I find most enjoyable. If you have strong performers and a strong story, those are two great building blocks for a great series. Then you get people around you who are good at their jobs, create an environment where they can do their best work, and get out of the way.

Kalceff, 2021

SFN's three most highly viewed episodes were season 2, episode 2 (39 million views) and season 3, episode 1 of 2014 (27 million views), and season four, episode 1 of 2016 (15 million views).

Underlining the intellectual challenge of writing compelling scripts, Kalceff, an AFTRS-trained masters-holder, worked collaboratively with script editor, Amanda Higgs, writer-producer of cult TV serial *Secret Life of Us* (2001–2005):

We had gone from making a series from nothing, to making it with funding which meant we had these funding bodies which had a say in everything. I had Amanda, a wonderful person to work with, an incredible story sense, in my corner because she was someone I could confide in.

Kalceff, 2021

Importantly, Lourde – who at this time was acting on *SFN*, but producing on another project, came on in the third season and co-produced Seasons 3–5 with

Kalceff. Being an older demographic than typically found on YouTube, Kalceff gathered her viewers on Facebook, and from analogue sources, to bring them across to YouTube. Her series resonated among twenty- and thirty-something lesbians in the United States, with 25 million views worldwide, and SBS2, an Australian public service BVOD, commissioned the final two seasons. Underlining the flexibility of the web-series format, they ran as four television half-hours.

Crucially, the evidence from Kalceff shows she was able to write shortform *episodic* narrative for YouTube, a shortform platform, yet enjoy the touchstone artistic experience of flow, as explained in Chapter 1. Importantly, Kalceff also shows how experimental episodic storytelling works when funds, and thus labour-intensive story arcs are limited:

> The beauty of a series is you get to go deeper into character. For me the most interesting thing about storytelling, and the shows I want to watch, are the characters. I do a lot of relationship and character-driven stories. I only ever set out to write one season of *SFN*, and when that went well it was: 'Let's make another season! And then let's make another season. It's not like I had this five-series arc already planned out. Each time it was going deeper and deeper into the characters which was probably the most enjoyable part of it.
>
> *Kalceff, 2021*

Historically, distinctive and compelling characterization is credited with making a success of serial narratives at the top end of mainstream TV in the United States, and in pioneering premium cable such as HBO, FX, and AMC (Mittell, 2015, p. 17; Lotz, 2018, p. 39). Kalceff hit upon the same 'distinctive' approach to complex characters:

> Nothing pulls a viewer out of a narrative more than bad acting. I knew if I could create a decent story, with complex characters, and involve good actors, we'd be doing better than a lot of queer content around then.
>
> *Kalceff, 2017*

While Kalceff enjoyed artistic flow, she did acknowledge a threadbare budget constrained production values. Severe logistical challenges required a fast season shoot:

> We all had other jobs. I was still teaching at film school, part time. All actors and crew were working part time. My focus was scheduling around the actors. We shot the first season (of six episodes) in 10–11 days. I drew up the schedule around them, and found crew among the students I was teaching. We had quite a few DOPs (directors of photography) in that first season, and quite a few sound recordists, but we just had to make it work. Production values suffered. We made the first season for $6000, but we did it. My focus had to be story and acting. I felt something had to give.

By prioritising those things, I was willing to concede production values wouldn't be terribly high.

Kalceff, 2017

In the case of *SFN*, creators and their lead actors expended intense labour by being available to prompt and respond to conversations in the comment streams of the YouTube channels and various social media feeds on which the new narrative was being distributed and promoted (Figure 7.4). Arguably, this interactivity harks back to the earliest proto-web-series, *The Spot* (1995–1997), distributed on personal computers, and where soap characters interacted with fans via message boards and email (Monaghan, 2017, p. 83). This *SFN* case study shows Kalceff synthesized three important principles regarding the exceptional web-series: co-creativity with active audiences, relational labour and proof of concept:

My plan was to make one season, and prove there was an audience. You get such clear analytics from YouTube that demonstrate these shows can be successful. I was confident there was an audience because I was part of that audience.

Kalceff, 2017

Kalceff says she observed intently where the bulk of audience attention lay within the episodes. The first three seasons of *SFN* were written 'in isolation', but an important, circular, time-sensitive audience–creator feedback loop was beginning to form:

I did a lot of work prior to release to build the audience. When we started posting I made sure I read every comment, responded to them. By Season 2, actor Lauren Orrell was helping with production. It was really important once we built the audience, to engage and respond to them. As a creator, I thought it was invaluable to get immediate feedback and be able to respond to feedback.

Kalceff, 2017

Kalceff's characters and storylines were so emotionally compelling an important dialogue, of a playful nature, built up in comment streams:

Most comments were gratitude. People loved being able to access the content, and were really vocal and engaged in the relationships. Some were very much on the side of one couple, and others on the side of another couple. They'd argue about who should be together. Then they'd change their minds and start advocating for the other couple. They were invested in these relationships and played that out online by having discussions among themselves.

Kalceff, 2017

FIGURE 7.4 Feedback loop: Lead characters kiss in SFN, with comments from fans pictured below the scene

FIGURE 7.5 Fans from around the world mixed themselves into the SFN storyworld in this fan video posted on the official SFN YouTube channel in 2016

Kalceff regarded many comments such as these as 'a gift' to her as a writer.

The audience metrics used by National Research Group have reshaped the shoots and endings of dozens of Hollywood movies, with as many as nine out of 10 bearing 'NRG's fingerprints' (Ross, 2010, p. 109). However, Kalceff's co-creativity with her fans is distinguished by its more direct, many-to-one, fans-to-creator feedback loop (figure 7.5). By the end of Season 3, deep observations by the film school-trained, participatory culture eschewing Kalceff, led to an important new and unanticipated dynamic. A direct serendipitous co-creativity evolved regarding the overarching narrative arc of *SFN*'s final two seasons, and was hybridized at the level of narrative design:

> From listening to the audience, I got a very clear sense of which relationship most of them were invested in. I took that feedback into account when scripting Seasons 4 and 5. It made sense to me as a creator to invest more into that relationship because that was where the audience was sitting.
>
> *Kalceff, 2017*

Crucially, Kalceff allowed her vision for *SFN*'s denouement to be redirected by fans, an SME vernacular. In contrast to traditional long-form drama, which is scripted and broadcast in isolation from systematic, real-time fan feedback, the circular-style audience–creator feedback loop evolved during this web-series enabled a synthesis of fan and author creativity in online long-form narrative:

> If I had planned *Starting from Now* as a five-season arc, Steph and Darcy would have ended up together. But because the series was constructed over time,

and the five seasons weren't plotted out from the start, I was able to nimbly respond to what the audience were invested in. When writing Seasons 4 and 5, it made sense to me to make Steph and Emily end up together – not just in terms of audience feedback, but character journeys and story arcs.

Kalceff, 2017

Again, as we saw with Voigt, the networked Muse is apparent. Crucially, in hindsight, the narrative development of *SFN* over five seasons reveals an unanticipated shift in this classically trained creator's mindset. The narrative was freed from a traditional pre-planned structure and adapted to simultaneously reflect character arcs where most audience attention lay, and the author's own creative vision:

I didn't for one-minute think at the start they would be as invested, or I would change my narrative based on what the audience was saying. But I came to see it was really important. It was a gift the audience was giving. They were so open and invested. This immediate feedback was a gift to a creator because you are not sitting in a room on your own. You are engaging with the audience and are able to respond to what it is they are looking for.

Kalceff, 2017

As shown in Table 2.1 (Chapter 2), the most important revenue stream for any creator or producer is sponsorship. *SFN,* and indeed Ward's *Anyone But Me* (2019) in Chapter 10, highlights this dynamic. Importantly, *SFN* foregrounded the issue of same-sex parenting. Traditionally, financial considerations driving product placements in films are suggested as influences on the types of movies made, but can create conflict between sponsors and creators (Ross, 2010, p. 110). In Kalceff's case, the choice of sponsor and product placement was in the control of the creative. For example, one topic in which lesbian couples are interested is assisted reproductive techniques for childbearing, a practice increasingly accepted among practitioners and patients across Europe (Bodri et al., 2017, p. 130). The phenomenon of online consumer backlash against perceived unethical marketing (Uslay, 2017, p. 341), also meant the choice of sponsor had to be strategic, and woven carefully into the storyline:

A mutual friend put Rosie and I in touch with IVF Australia because she thought it would be a good fit. IVF Australia didn't want to impose on the narrative as they were aware being too overt would only alienate the audience. I made minor changes to the script but nothing that wasn't already part of the fabric of the story and the characters. The IVF Australia logo was included at the end of Seasons 4 and 5. IVF Australia were great to partner with. The last thing they wanted was for us to compromise what we were doing.

Kalceff, 2017

Thus Kalceff side-stepped the problem shown in Chapters 5–7, where YouTube's algorithmic bias to freshness was found to be in conflict with labour intensity. Instead, Kalceff was free to focus on engaging storytelling via quality acting and scripting, which built a vibrant online community based on co-creativity. Importantly, the millions of views constituting this community was the tangible proof of concept needed to unlock Screen Australia investment for the final two seasons.

During SFN's fifth season, the Mamamia Women's Network described *SFN* telling stories that are moving, inspiring and perception-shifting, indeed they were 'so real, raw and close-to-home you want to keep watching and turn away at the same time'. Lourde was interviewed and described as a kick-ass advocate of all things important – LGBTIQ rights, Indigenous affairs, community, the environment and human rights (Bishop, 2016). Lourde told Mamamia it was 'incredibly important' to expand the stories told, and characters portrayed:

> Women in film and TV are so often portrayed as mothers or whores. They are often confined to strict stereotypes because it's supposedly easier for the audience to understand quickly. We want our audience to know it doesn't matter who you are, what you identify as or with, or the labels society puts on you. A good human being, in all of that complexity, deserves to be celebrated.
>
> *Bishop, 2016*

During season four, the story of Lourde's character, Darcy, included sexual assault. Lourde said Kalceff had made an important decision to raise the issue in the context of a survivor's story, to help combat complacency around this ongoing crisis.

Meanwhile, the crucible of the all-in *SFN* would prove a direct career accelerator for both Kalceff and Lourde. Screen Australia would again underline its savviness in the web-series space recruiting Kalceff and Lourde for new roles. Kalceff was recruited as a Skip Ahead mentor, delivering workshops in screenwriting and giving feedback on creative documents, a role she would perform for each incoming class until at least 2021. After observing a family friends' struggle with a child's emerging trans identity, Kalceff would soon put a proposal together for the ABC's International Day of the Girl with producer, Kirsty Stark, *First Day* (Figure 7.6). The pair would be commissioned by ABC kids' channel, ABC ME, to create the groundbreaking, multi-award-winning TV episode, which was later commissioned as a series. *First Day* is the journey of 12-year-old transgender actor, Evie Macdonald, who played Hannah Bradford for her first day at high school. Kalceff's aim with *First Day* was to enable trans children to be able to see themselves on screen:

> Our hope was a show like this could start conversations for people who weren't able to talk about these things. We didn't want to convey

FIGURE 7.6   Julie Kalceff and Evie McDonald collaborate on First Day (Photo credit: Ian Routledge)

misinformation and we certainly didn't want to put anything out into the world that could negatively impact transgender children or adults.

Frank, 2020

But above all the original episode and then the series aimed to be relatable, since most people remember their first day of high school with either trepidation or excitement (Kalceff, 2021). *First Day,* the series, was subsequently licensed internationally to broadcast, BVODs, and SVODs, mostly notably Disney-owned Hulu and CBBC in the United Kingdom. *First Day* won the coveted Rose d'Or, an international entertainment award long dominated by Eurovision. At press time, *First Day* was re-commissioned as a second season. Kalceff was looking forward to writing Hannah's continuing journey, by going deeper into her character (Kalceff, 2021).

Meanwhile, Screen Australia recruited Lourde as their new online investment manager, with oversight of Skip Ahead, to replace Mike Cowap, now at Princess Pictures, producing Superwog. Lourde would then go on to direct *Romance on the Menu* for Netflix ANZ, also released internationally by Hallmark as *Hearts Down Under* (Figure 7.7). Lourde explains 'the master-mind' behind *SFN* was Kalceff. Kalceff did not just craft the story and the script, but figure out the intricate logistical challenges of doing the best shoot in the days and locations available, all the while 'not messing with the actors' emotional continuity'. Lourde told me a key argument for attaching her to *Romance on the Menu* was her experience in making a project and a schedule work on a very tight budget:

Sitting with her (Kalceff) as she tried to figure everything out, especially across the final two seasons, was itself a master-class. I've never been to

FIGURE 7.7 Trailer of *Romance on the Menu* from the Netflix ANZ homepage

film school so have always learnt on the job. Thankfully, wonderfully, I have been in the thick of those conversations.

Lourde, 2021

Burning problems

Monetization

SFN was never intended as a direct livelihood earner for Kalceff, instead being an experiment 'to prove there was an audience for LGBT content; to make a show freely available to LGBT audiences' (Kalceff, 2021). Nevertheless, *SFN* (2014–2016) exhibits the same overall pattern of Murdock and Golding's three economies as Voigt in Chapter 2, Superwog in Chapter 3, Racka in Chapter 4, as well as Reardon in Chapter 5, SketchSHE in Chapter 6, Good and Litton-Strain in Chapter 8, and Forster and Rowling in Chapter 9. For example, *SFN* attracted gifting and collaboration (fan participation and crowdfunding); public goods (subvention from Screen Australia and Screen NSW, and Kalceff teaching for AFTRS and mentoring for Screen Australia); and commodities (sponsorship from IVF Australia and queer health organization ACON, investment from Kalceff's production company, Common Language Films, and licensing from SBS2; transaction fees from Vimeo, and AdSense from YouTube). The most important lesson for ambitious web-series makers in subvention countries such as Australia, provided Internet-distribution is eligible, is taxpayer funded grants can be unlocked when web-series first attract views measurable in the multi-millions, the higher the better. Indeed, for policy-makers and activists, the evidence of this book suggests countries aiming to nurture the best online storytelling talent should consider replicating the Skip Ahead model in their own jurisdictions. Google can afford its share of funds in any such private-public partnership.

In terms of the A/B List problem of income inequality for artists, Kalceff sustained herself without teaching with various development grants from late-stage development of the last two seasons of *SFN*. After season five of *SFN* was released, she got some Screen Australia Gender Matters funding to develop a project. This was followed by the original episode of *First Day*.

Platform and algorithmic volatility

Since Kalceff had first made the moral decision to make *SFN* freely available to LGBT audiences, attracting only modest monetization from Vimeo fees and YouTube AdSense, she was shielded from the vagaries of networked video. The collapse of one platform, in her case, Dana, did not affect her personally since *SFN* was available across so many other platforms.

> If those platforms fell over it didn't worry me too much because it was always sitting there on YouTube. It wasn't about making money. It was about making queer content available to people everywhere and proving there is a demand for that content.
>
> *Kalceff, 2021*

Nevertheless, her multi-platform cycling strategy has important implications for writer-producers seeking career sustainability. Crucially, in the same multi-platform cycling phenomena I show with Tina Cesa Ward's *Anyone But Me* (2008–2011) (100 million views) in the final chapter, *SFN* was distributed on YouTube, One More Lesbian, SBS2, Vimeo, Mamamia, IndieFlix, SBS On Demand, and now defunct platform, Dana. This contemporary multi-platform cycling phenomena is paralleled by the second part of the industrial practice dominant in TV series production in an earlier Golden Age of TV, the 1980s US. The networks would pay 80 per cent of the cost of production, using notorious notes to enforce 'traditional morality', with the producer supplying the remaining 20 per cent (Newcomb & Ally, 1983, p. 9). For this upfront funding, the network was guaranteed the exclusive right to the first two appearances of the show, recovering its investment through the sale of commercials. After the first appearances, all rights reverted to the producer, who was free to monetize the series through syndication. If it was a made-for-TV movie, the producer got a license fee, and after the guaranteed showings, was 'free to sell the work to cable television, in foreign markets, and in theatres if possible' (Newcomb & Ally, 1983, p. 9). Importantly for writer-producers seeking sustainable careers, this evolution in remuneration practices over the past 40 years reveals how audience fragmentation and platform proliferation privilege non-exclusivity in license deals, with notable exceptions like exclusivity-requiring Netflix. Crucially, this struggle over advertising sponsor interference and censorship in 1950s US television serials, led to the rise of the 'hyphenate' writer-producer in pursuit of greater creative control (Newcomb & Alley, 1983).

Old and new media

The journeys of writer/director/producer, Kalceff, and her co-producer, Lourde, yield three of the most valuable lessons in this book. First, the fact Lourde spent a significant part of our interview, unprompted, emphasizing the critical importance of choice of collaborators to project success and thus career advancement, speaks volumes. As a former Screen Australia online investment manager including for Skip Ahead, Lourde brings especial insight to this matter. Lourde told us above how important her being 'in the thick of conversations' about logistical challenges with Kalceff on *SFN*, was to her attachment by the Steve Jaggi Company to *Romance on the Menu*: 'Being part of that conversation [about organizing actors and locations on a tight budget] gave me a huge skillset coming into *Romance on the Menu*', shot in just 15 days (Lourde, 2021) (Figure 7.8). Significantly, the fast tempo of Lourde's skillset exactly parallels the 'fast and furious film-making' of RackaRacka in Chapter 4.

Moreover, Lourde said these cross-cultural collaborations, which I termed rapprochement in Chapter 1, also yielded the skillsets necessary to better deal with the rapid evolution of networked video. In an insight into how old and new media labour are blending at the production level, Lourde said people should collaborate beyond their circle of friends, with award-winning writers, DOPs, set designers and script editors who will bring 'the X-Factor' to the project. Unlike many former web-series makers who play down the

FIGURE 7.8 Director Rosie Lourde goes over the script of Romance on the Menu/
Hearts Down Under, with lead actor Cindy Busby. Photo credit: David Fell

web-series as merely formative, Lourde said she was still working on movies and web-series:

> Because the landscape is changing so quickly, no-one can be across all they need to know. All I can do is bring what I know to the table, impart what I know, and keep learning from other people; that's exciting'.
>
> *Lourde, 2021*

While Lourde championed cross-cultural collaboration to help emergent film-makers navigate the many 'hurdles and pot-holes' they will encounter, an important caveat applied. As an 'indie producer' herself, Lourde said she understood why established producers may expect to acquire the IP of a creator in return for their navigation of the project. However, this tension must be managed by a conversation informed by creators' moral rights:

> Producers need to be looked after, but creators have spent years of their lives and literal blood, sweat and tears to build their audiences and brands and their own IP [in characters and storyworlds and tones]. That's a very complex conversation. But in the end, it's a simple one. Creators should keep control their IP.
>
> *Lourde, 2021*

Second, even though neither Kalceff nor Lourde's post-*SFN* projects continued the storyworld of the lesbian love quadrangle, both emphasize a heightened industrial and cultural importance of the web-series. Once a format dismissed as a mere 'stepping stone', the convergence of streaming platforms and more traditional film-makers on the 'shortform episodic space' highlighted its potential as a proof-of-concept for a more ambitious series. For Kalceff:

> The number of streaming platforms actively seeking short-form content highlights this [proof-of-concept], as does the number of more traditional filmmakers looking to move into the short-form episodic space. By making a web series that works, you're demonstrating you have the ability to create a longer, more complex narrative than is possible in a short film. You can also prove you know how to tap into an audience.
>
> *Kornits, 2019*

Similarly, for Lourde, the web-series represents an increasingly necessary tool, depending upon the project and the needs of the producer: 'It's flexible. The web-series can be a calling card or it can be a proof of concept. Some people use the web-series to create IP, to then build it out into a bigger show, and sell that off; some people are doing it to show they can do a thing, and hopefully create opportunities to do something else' (Lourde, 2021).

Third, Kalceff's innovation in using the web-series for storytelling shows screenwriting canon is as important in networked video as ever, but must be economized. We will see a similar phenomenon of economy with online storytelling in Miller and Ward's case in *Anyone But Me* in Chapter 10.

> People need to master the fundamentals of dramatic storytelling first, and then you can look at the specifics of shortform episodic online. I go back to the fundamentals. When I'm working with other creatives, get them to think about how those things apply to their story. Every time I start a new script or story I go back to those concepts. If those building blocks aren't in place, then it's all going to fall over. Who is your protagonist? What's their goal? Who is the antagonist? What are the stakes? Escalating obstacles? Where's the conflict? Every screenwriting book talks about it: if you don't have a protagonist with a goal and an antagonist standing in their way, you have no conflict, and if you have no conflict, you have no drama.
>
> *Kalceff, 2021*

Authenticity and discrimination

The evidence suggests the culture of storytelling is changing in response to changes in social media-driven popular culture, with a heightened emphasis on the ancient principle of authenticity. 'Ethos', the proof established through the character of the speaker; together with 'pathos', established through emotional appeals to the audience; and 'logos', the logical presentation of the facts; are the three most persuasive forms of speech as established by Aristotle (Rapp in Healy & Williams, 2017, p. 151). Ethically and pragmatically, the stakes for storytelling have changed. Kalceff argues new projects should first begin with the writer and producer considering the question of 'authentic representation', in-front of the camera and behind it 'across the board'. Regarding *First Day*, Kalceff and Stark reflected on whether they as cis-gendered women – where a person's identity corresponds to their birth sex – were the right people to tell the story of a 12-year-old trans girl:

> No 12-year-old has the capacity to make a film or TV episode. So our job, once we had cast Evie was to empower her to tell her story, to give her the support she needed. But she is the one who brings authenticity to the story. Give her the support she needed to be on set every day, and carry that show.
>
> *Kalceff, 2021*

A second major factor reinforcing the need for authenticity was the ethical consideration of screen storytelling in the context of discriminatory violence, and the hair-trigger nature of social media brigading, and information disorder.

> The statistics around violence against trans people are high. If you are casting a cis-gendered person in a trans role it leads to misunderstanding and

misinformation, and can perpetuate violence against trans people. There is no excuse to not cast authentically when you are casting trans characters.

Kalceff, 2021

Third, the more authentic a story is behind the camera and in front of the camera, the better it is going to be (Kalceff, 2021).

Finally, convergence between the creatively autonomous storytelling of cable and diversity-recognizing storytelling on SVODs is opening up unprecedented opportunities for authentic storytelling. But they depend upon creative autonomy. Compelling narratives about diverse people are especially valued by the world's largest SVOD, Netflix. The benefits of authenticity in storytelling and not just moral, but increasingly career-enhancing in screen. Authenticity is far more than a buzzword among social media creators. Contrastingly, the evidence of this book, and this chapter, shows creators and writer-producers do their best work, their most authentic and distinctive work, when they grasp creative autonomy with both hands.

Note

1 If you or anyone you know needs help: If this chapter has raised difficult issues for you and you need support, please contact a support service, for example Lesbian, Gay, Bisexual, and Transgender National Hotline 888-843-4564. To find international support services, visit https://findahelpline.com/ and search for your country.

References

Bailey, C. (2020). From one alumnus to another: Claudia Bailey interviews Julie Kalceff [Blogpost]. *AFTRS*, Sydney. https://www.aftrs.edu.au/blog/claudia-bailey-interviews-julie-kalceff-on-queer-australian-storytelling/

BBC (2018, October 20). Cate Blanchett defends straight actors playing LGBT roles. *BBC*, London. https://www.bbc.com/news/newsbeat-45926322

BBC (2021, April 26). Oscars 2021: Audiences turn away as a sluggish ceremony leaves critics cold. *BBC*, London. https://www.bbc.com/news/entertainment-arts-56885646

Beirne, R. (2009) Screening the Dykes of Oz: Lesbian representation on Australian television. *Journal of Lesbian Studies*, *13*(1), 25–34.

Benson, R. & Neveu, E. (2005). Introduction: Field theory as a work in progress. In E. Neveu & R. Benson (Eds.), *Bourdieu and the journalistic field* (pp. 1–25). Polity Press.

Bishop, C. (2016, May 19). Meet the woman breaking all the rules in the lesbian drama that's too hot for TV. [Blogpost], Mamania, Mamamia Women's Network. https://www.mamamia.com.au/why-you-need-to-know-rosie-lourde/

Bridgstock, R. (2005). Australian artists, starving and well-nourished: What can we learn from the prototypical protean career?. *Australian Journal of Career Development*, *14*(3), 40–47.

Bodri, D., Nair, S., Gill, A., Lamanna, G., Rahmati, M., Arian-Schad, M., Smith, V., Linara, E., Wang, J., Macklon, N., & Ahuja, K. K. (2018). Shared motherhood IVF: High delivery rates in a large study of treatments for lesbian couples using partner-donated eggs. *Reproductive Biomedicine Online*, *36*(2), 130–136.

Cameron, A., Verhoeven, D., & Court, D. (2010). Above the bottom line: Understanding Australian screen content producers. *Media International Australia, 136*(1), 90–102.

Christian, A. J. (2018). *Open TV: Innovation beyond Hollywood and the rise of web television* (Vol. 20). NYU Press.

Cornu, C. (2016). Preventing and addressing homophobic and transphobic bullying in education: A human rights–based approach using the United Nations Convention on the Rights of the Child. *Journal of LGBT Youth, 13*(1–2), 6–17.

Csikszentmihalyi, M. (2014). *The systems model of creativity.* Springer.

Dalby, A. (1995). The Iliad, the Odyssey and their audiences. *The Classical Quarterly, 45*(2), 269–279.

De Kosnik, A., El Ghaoui, L., Cuntz-Leng, V., Godbehere, A., Horbinski, A., Hutz, A., Pastel, R. & Pham, V. (2015). Watching, creating, and archiving: Observations on the quantity and temporality of fannish productivity in online fan fiction archives. *Convergence, 21*(1), 145–164.

Doherty, L. E. (1991). The internal and implied audiences of "Odyssey" 11. *Arethusa, 24*(2), 145–176.

Frank, M. (2020, Nov 6). Interview: Hulu Miniseries First Day's Julie Kalceff and Kirsty Stark [Blogpost], Cool Hunting, Captain Lucas Inc., New York City. https://coolhunting.com/culture/interview-hulu-miniseries-first-days-julie-kalceff-and-kirsty-stark/

Harvey, K. J., Brown, B., Crawford, P., Macfarlane, A., & McPherson, A. (2007). 'Am I normal?' Teenagers, sexual health and the internet. *Social Science & Medicine, 65*(4), 771–781.

Healy, G., & Williams, P. (2017). Metaphor use in the political communication of major resource projects in Australia. *Pacific Journalism Review, 23*(1), 150–168.

Jenkins, H. (1992). *Textual poachers: Studies in culture and communication.* Routledge.

Jenkins, H. (2010). Transmedia storytelling and entertainment: An annotated syllabus. *Continuum, 24*(6), 943–958.

Kalceff, J. (2017, 2021). Founder and director of Common Language films. Skype interviews with Guy Healy.

Keltie, E. (2017). *The culture industry and participatory audiences.* Springer.

Kornits, D. (2019, Jan 19) Julie Kalceff: Web series pioneer. [Blogpost], Film Ink, FKP International Exports, Sydney. https://www.filmink.com.au/julie-kalceff-web-series-pioneer/

Lotz, A. D. (2018). *We now disrupt this broadcast: How cable transformed television and the Internet revolutionized.* MIT Press.

Lourde, R. (2021, April 21). Co-producer, Starting From Now; director Romance on the Menu. Facebook Messenger interview with Guy Healy.

Ludo (n.d.). #7DaysLater case study [Blogpost], Ludo Studio, Brisbane, Australia. https://www.infinity2.com.au/project/7-days-later/

May, R. (1975). *The courage to create.* Norton.

McKee, R. (1997). *Story: Style, structure, substance, and the principles of screenwriting.* Harper Collins.

Minow, N. N. (2003). Television and the public interest. *Federal Communications Law Journal, 55*, 395.

Mittell, J. (2007). Lost in a great story. https://justtv.wordpress.com/2007/10/23/lost-in-a-great-story/

Mittell, J. (2015). *Complex TV.* New York University Press.

Monaghan, W. (2017). Starting From… Now and the web series to television crossover: An online revolution?. *Media International Australia, 164*(1), 82–91.

Morris, B. (2019). *History of lesbian, gay, bisexual and transgender social movements*. American Psychological Association.

Newcomb, H., & Alley, R. S. (1983). *The producer's medium: Conversations with creators of American TV* (p. 33). Oxford University Press.

Ng, E. (2013). A "post-gay" era? Media gaystreaming, homonormativity, and the politics of LGBT integration. *Communication, Culture & Critique, 6*(2), 258–283.

Palmer, P. (1986). *Girls & television*. Social Policy Unit, Ministry of Education.

Ramirez, J., Gonzalez, K., & Galupo, M. (2018). "Invisible During My Own Crisis": Responses of LGBT People of Color to the Orlando Shooting. *Journal of Homosexuality, 65*(5), 579–599.

Risman, B. (2004). Gender as a social structure: Theory wrestling with activism. *Gender & Society, 18*(4), 429–450.

Ross, A. G. (2010). Creative decision making within the contemporary Hollywood studios. *Journal of Screenwriting, 2*(1), 99–116.

Sergi, M., & Dodds, P. (2003). How reality bites: the production of Australian soap operas. *Media International Australia, 106*(1), 71–83.

Simic, Z. (2008). 'What are ya?': Negotiating identities in the western suburbs of Sydney during the 1980s. *Journal of Australian Studies, 32*(2), 223–236.

Smith, A. N. (2018). Storytelling industries: Narrative production in the 21st century. Springer.

Smith, S. L., Choueiti, M., & Pieper, K. (2016). Inclusion or invisibility? Comprehensive Annenberg report on diversity in entertainment. *Institute for Diversity and Empowerment at Annenberg, 22*, 1–27.

Sturken, M. (2020). *Thelma & Louise*. Bloomsbury Publishing.

Takács, J. (2006). *Social exclusion of young lesbian, gay, bisexual and transgender (LGBT) people in Europe*. ILGA Europe.

Theodore, P. S., & Stoker, A. (2021). How teachers can reduce bullying of sexual and gender diverse students. In *Violence against LGBTQ+ persons* (pp. 39–49). Springer.

Uslay, C. (2017). The good, bad, and ugly side of entrepreneurial marketing: Is your social media campaign unveiled, incognito, or exposed?. *Rutgers Business Review, 2*(3), 338–349.

Ward, T. C. (2019). Writer-producer, Anyone But Me; Chair, International Academy of Web TV, Los Angeles. Skype interview with Guy Healy.

Ward, S., O'Regan, T., & Goldsmith, B. (2010). From neighbours to packed to the rRafters: Accounting for longevity in the evolution of Aussie soaps. *Media International Australia, 136*(1), 162–176.

Wardle, C., & Derakhshan, H. (2017). Information disorder: Toward an interdisciplinary framework for research and policy making. *Council of Europe, 27*, 1–109.

White, Patricia. (1999). *Uninvited: Classical Hollywood cinema and lesbian representability*. Indiana University Press.

8

ERIN GOOD, TAYLOR LITTON-STRAIN, AND FANTASY-NOIR WEB-PILOT, *JADE OF DEATH*

This book shows the first glimmers of convergence between the international high-end series market popularized by SVODs HBO, Netflix, and Amazon Prime, and the scrappy but innovative world of web-series, *provided* their low budget, short serial narratives are exceptional and have cultural impact. The international series sector is regarded as being in concentration phase with 'fewer projects being made, but each of them require more funds than before to reach the new quality standards' set by the high-end series of these SVOD majors (Baujard et al., 2019, p. 76). This case shows just what is involved for ambitious talented web-series makers to make a mark on this high-end series world and the new standard of excellence to reach those storied heights. This case shows the adaptive potential of the web-series, I argue a hybrid child of film craft from Hollywood, creative autonomy from cable tv, and start-up culture from Silicon Valley. For example, the web-series *Jade of Death* (2015), written by Erin Good and produced by Taylor Litton-Strain, whose career is the focus of this chapter, has achieved the enviable status of both popular and critical acclaim. Viewed over 3.5 million times, it has won over 60 awards including Best Drama Series for the IAWTV in Los Angeles, and Best Digital Series at the C21 Drama Awards, London. LOTL magazine Australia described *Jade of Death (Jade)* as 'dark, funny and hot as hell' (Figure 8.1).

Season One of *Jade* achieved a license deal with CBC's BVOD, Gem, as well as non-exclusive license deals with Wilde.tv in the United States and queer platform, Revry. Jade distinguishes itself as an exemplar that emerged as an avant-garde of filmmakers experimented with cheap but increasingly sophisticated film-making and distribution technologies, stealing a march on their peers still stuck in the career cul de sac of the short film festival era. *Jade* went into production at a crucial turning point in film. The six by 10-minute *Jade*, which was developed over years of intense writing and high-level

DOI: 10.4324/9781003182481-8

FIGURE 8.1   Fan engagement: From left, pioneering web-filmmakers Jordan Cowan (Maya), Erin Good (writer-director Jade of Death), and Bernie Van Tiel (Jade).

mentoring, was released on queer YouTube channel OneMoreLesbian in late 2018. Just some seven months earlier Steven Soderbergh premiered the psychological horror film, *Unsane*, shot entirely on the iPhone 7 Plus, at the Berlin International Film Festival. Erin Good and Litton-Strain had met at AFTRS in Sydney in the early 2010s, around the same time South Korean film-makers Park Chan-wook and Park Chan-kyong shot a fantasy-horror film, *Night Fishing*, on an iPhone 4 (Erbland, 2018). Only a handful of years before, the writers and producers' guilds of America recognized web-first-release narratives in their awards following the screenwriters strike over their share of digital IP rights. Webfests were increasingly being established in the Americas, Australia, Europe, and Russia. In 2016, Californian film-maker scholar John T Caldwell (2016, p. 38) argued that just assuming new technologies 'had cleanly eliminated' old-media labour from new-media labour, was an over-generalization. The assumption 'disregards how old-media labour somehow keeps adapting to new media technologies even as new media entrants disrupt the resulting blended media labour field'. Accordingly, this is one story of what it was like to be young film-makers, fresh out of one of the world's best film schools, during a time of momentous technological and cultural change in film-making.

The origins of fantasy are among the most ancient, as evidenced by the role of 'supernatural aid' – usually an old man or crone – as a formal element of the monomyth documented by Joseph Campbell (1993, p. 69). Mankind's love of the supernatural is driven by the quest for immortality, spiritual, or physical, 'to dispel the terrors of his phenomenality' (Campbell, 1993, p. 143). Supernatural beings are invoked in some of mankind's oldest literature, argues Stephan (2016, 10) such as the utterly compelling *Epic of Gilgamesh* (Campbell, 1993, p. 185), or canonical texts such as *Beowulf*, and *Sir Gawain and the Green Knight*. Contemporary fantasy is world-building genre literature, separately categorized to serious high literature, that 'offers the reader a world estranged from their own, separated by nova (the verisimilar), supernatural or consistent with the marvellous, the dominant tone of which is enchantment, and wonder' (Stephan, 2016, p. 3). However, Vu (2017, p. 278) argues fantasy, based in medieval romance and adventure fiction, manifests a conservative ideology and is understood best as play, and 'the organised escape from the authority of fact'. Fantasy, as seen in blockbuster franchises *Star Wars, Buffy the Vampire Slayer, The Sword of Shannara, Harry Potter, Lord of the Rings,* and *Game of Thrones,* is the reigning genre of the times, courtesy of the richness of audio-visual streaming media, and the genre sophistication of SVOD leader, HBO (Vu, 2017, p. 295). Cross-genre texts have an economic impetus in competing successfully for larger audiences, he notes.

Scholars are quick to draw on Tolkien, who argued fantasy 'starts out with an advantage: arresting strangeness'. Tolkien (1964, p. 60) himself rejected notions of fantasy as mere escape from reality: 'The joy of the happy ending, or more correctly the good catastrophe, the sudden joyous 'turn' (for there is no true end to any fairy tale) this joy is one of the things which fairy-stories can produce supremely well, is not essentially escapist or fugitive. In its fairy-tale – or otherworld setting, it is a sudden and miraculous grace: never to be counted on to recur'. Importantly, however, the suspension of disbelief in the magic must be effective. Tolkein stresses 'the story be taken seriously, neither laughed at or explained away' (Stephan, 2016, p. 11). One important recent franchise is Charlaine Harris's *True Blood* (2008-) described 'as HBO's vampire take on southern US culture, vampire culture and the supernatural'. Significantly, heroine Sookie Stackhouse, able to hear the thoughts of others, 'does not accept nor perform her proper gender roles', rescuing 'out of the coffin' vampire, Civil War hero Bill Compton, from a draining by drug dealers (Boyer, 2011, p. 33).

In counterpoint, film noir is regarded as a distinctly American style of cinema which Thomson (2012, p. 195) argues 'opened up a kind of despair that had found no room for expression in the era of happy endings' pre-World War 11. Deriving from German expressionism and French surrealism, film and TV noir was forever in the shadow of American drama, *Citizen Kane* (1941), produced and directed by Orson Welles and co-written with Herman Mankiewicz. Spurred by the end of the war, noir – which means 'night' in French – meant 'existential agony; not just the underworld as a metaphor for the human fate, but a means of working very economically' (Thomson, 2012,

p. 164). Existential philosophy had distinguished itself in post-war Europe and travelled to US studios with film-makers Billy Wilder (*Double Indemnity*, 1944), Fritz Lang (*Scarlett Street*, 1945) and Otto Preminger (*Anatomy of a Murder*, 1959), who produced 'gripping dramas with a psychological edge' and an element of crime (Sanders, 2008, p. 2). Noir is one of the most enduring American styles – considered a counterweight to blockbusters – with neo-noir cycles epitomized by Arthur Penn's *Bonnie and Clyde* (1967), Francis Ford Coppola's *The Conversation* (1974), David Lynch's *Blue Velvet* (1986), Quentin Tarantino's *Pulp Fiction* (1995), and David Lynch's *Mulholland Drive* (2001) (Sanders, 2008, p. 3). Film noir is characterized by an 'anti-communitarian stance' argues Altman (1984, p. 14). Television noir traces its history back to 'hard-boiled' police procedurals such as *Dragnet* (1951), with more recent 'existential' incarnations such as key episodes of *Miami Vice (1984–1990)*, *The Sopranos* (1999–2007), and *Carnivale* (2003–2005) (Sanders, 2008, p. 5). However, much classic noir film and TV narratives are celebrated for their style, recent approaches have critiqued the genre's schema of the *femme fatale* for its representation of women, and their agency regarding men. For example, analysis of the male protagonists in noir classics, *The Maltese Falcon, Double Indemnity, Out of the Past* and *Scarlett Street* shows a disturbing pattern. Deyo (2020, p. 27) argues 'the orchestration of the man's downfall in all four films is attributable to the femme fatale', who in their first fateful encounter, 'uses (or appears to use) her seductive charms to lure the man into her world of lies, deception and violence'. With the public regarded as possessing, 'self-consciously or not', awareness of the structures and intertextual references binding disparate films into a single genre, studio publicity invokes 'multiple genres' to maximize diverse audiences (Frow, 2014, p. 149).

While critics and scholars have been critiqued for historically regarding genre as 'existing outside the flow of time', as though springing 'full-blown from the head of Zeus', Altman argues genre are mutable. Generic formations have their own discursive power rooted in their interpretive communities. While one Hollywood genre may be borrowed with little change from another medium, a second may evolve before settling into a pattern, while another may go through an extended series of paradigms, none of which may be claimed as dominant (Altman, 1984, p. 8). The genre mash-up of fantasy-noir may evolve as a case in point. One fantasy-noir series regarded to be of singular critical importance is Netflix Original, *Jessica Jones* (2015–2019), produced by showrunner, Melissa Rosenberg, with women writers and co-writers. Krysten Ritter plays Jessica Jones, an abduction and trauma surviving superhuman private detective whose resists Hollywood romance tropes. In sharp contrast to the traditional noir *femme fatale*, Green (2019, p. 179) argues Jessica Jones is notable for the way it upends the noir schema, 'to create a counter-narrative of the gendered superhero'. As an 'unruly' noir anti-hero, female passivity is resisted while 'complex ideological and personal imperatives of power and desire are also acknowledged' (Green, 2019, p. 179). Jade shows just such agency (Figure 8.2)

FIGURE 8.2 Bernie Van Tiel as *Jade* wrestles an attacker to the ground at the Carnival of Darkness

The production of cultural goods – whether high fashion or novels – are fields of struggle characterized by a predisposition 'to function differentially, as instruments of distinction' according to Bourdieu and Nice (1980, p. 277). Originating in Europe in the late 1950s, a film festival circuit emerged principally to circulate film prints around the earth, and offer such a means of distinction: critical acclaim via awards. Even by 2014, the circuit had grown to 'a vast landscape' of over 6000 festivals, but which film professionals might attend or follow 10-15, especially the top tier: the European Film Market held with the Berlinale, and Cannes; and in North America, Toronto, and Sundance. For example, Wim Wenders (*Wings of Desire*, 1987) led the Berline Talent Campus of 2003, when 500 film-makers from 61 countries attended the inaugural event, many hoping 'to close a deal, thereby moving our careers forward' (Ashe, 2003). As Loist (2016, p. 50) explains, these festivals are 'increasingly networked and interconnected, marked by both competition and collaboration over films, talent, sponsors and audiences'. Film professionals, their films and accreditation systems 'equally have agency' within the network. While the arts have traditionally been 'less difficult environments for LGBTQ workers' than other professions (Banks, 2015, p. 24), screenwriters themselves worked in informal but male-dominated Writers' Rooms. While not generally regarded as homophobic, they exhibited a 'heterosexism' which marginalized women and minorities.

Traditionally, the standard pathway for an aspiring screen storyteller was, upon graduation from film-school, makes a 10-minute film and use film festival awards to attract subvention, gradually moving to longer forms and assigning copyright control over their films to distributors, or going into TV (Ryan & Hearn, 2010, p. 138). That 'pathway' began to be further de-structured from the mid-1980s with the advent of the socio-technological phenomenon William Gibson dubbed 'cyberspace', characterized by his axiom from *Burning Chrome* (1986): 'The street finds its own uses for things'. As storytelling became increasingly afforded by technology, Ryan and Hearn (2010) showed how the pathway opened to new means of distribution such as games consoles, YouTube and customized iPhone apps. Culturally diverse, marginalized personalities and performers not only used social media entertainment (SME) to build huge audiences on YouTube (Cunningham & Craig, 2019, p. 4). They built crowdfunded, subscription-based indie channels for queer content such as One More Lesbian (Christian, 2019, 112). About 1000 fans funded this 'lesbian Netflix', paying for comedy westerns such as *Cowgirl Up* and teen dramas such as *The Throwaways*.

The universal human drive to craft narratives – we all tell each other anecdotes for our mutual entertainment – is becoming increasingly public and participatory. Scholarship shows us the history of storytelling is the history of the struggle over whose stories are heard, who gets to tell them, and in what way; a struggle increasingly acute in recent years. Storytelling is so important as to be regarded – alongside creativity itself – as a defining human drive (Lüthi, 1987 p. 75; Niles, 1999, p. 1). This scholarship emphasizes the importance of authenticity. The ancients greatly valued oral storytelling, but their anti-plebian bias led to no records of their training (Scobie, 1979, p. 258). In the 18th to 19th century China, the emphasis was on taking years to learn the craft of storytelling in the context of both doing it oneself and with expert mentoring (McDaniel, 2001, p. 490). In the modern era, Lawrence Lessig (2007) has characterized folk culture as a 'read/write' or remix culture. In 2008, fan fiction writers experienced a sea-change when they realized to protect the health of their passion, they needed to own the means of circulating fan-works such as the servers, the interface, the code, and terms of service (Banet-Weiser et al., 2014, p. 1072). What began as punk-style use of then new technologies, such as cassettes, VHS, and digital downloads, led to the creation of 'an archive of our own' and an organization for transformative works. Today, the commercial potential of this grassroots gifting, collaboration, and remix culture, has led to the encroachment of major commercial platforms such as YouTube, Amazon, LiveJournal, Tumblr, and Wattpad. Fanfiction writers are not homogenous and have competing codes: many do not want to engage with commercialism and feel they should be free to remix on their own terms; while others believe if someone profits from their works, they should be entitled to fair compensation (Banet-Weiser et al., 2014, p. 1073). Just as the acclaim of Broadway musicals acted as proof of concept for musical films (Feuer, 1977, p. 441), some pro-am storytellers who [resonate] on Wattpad have secured film deals, including to Netflix such as *Kissing Booth* (Spangler, 2020; Parnell,

2021, p. 525). Strikingly, the user-generated narrative content phenomenon led by Wattpad has been most embraced by Gen Z's and young Millennials. Started in Canada in just 2008, Wattpad had a global use base of 40 million by 2016, about 40 per cent are 13–17 years old, and 40 per cent 18–30-year-olds (Davies, 2017, p. 52).

Biography

Taylor Litton-Strain's parents tried to dissuade their daughter from pursuing a career in screen because it would be 'too difficult'. Her mother is a former president of the Australian Screen Editors Guild and her parents suggested she try doing something 'easier', like law or the Air Force. 'When I am in the thick of it and running on about three hours' sleep, I do wonder if it might be a little less stressful flying a fighter jet', she said (Hunter, n.d.).

Litton-Strain initially worked as a development executive and freelance producer for Essential Media, and in international sales for SBS TV, Australia's multicultural broadcaster. She completed a postgraduate degree in producing at AFTRS where she began a fateful collaboration with fellow AFTRS postgraduate in directing, Erin Good. Importantly, the pair learnt the problematics of their field by immersing themselves in their respective domains at national and international level. After film school, Good knew she needed to get experience on commercial productions, 'easier said than done'. Good managed to land an internship at Porchlight Films, which ultimately led to directing work. After graduating film school, Litton-Strain joined the international film circuit, traveling first to Europe and Cannes to listen to producers and short film programmers talk, then to London to spend time with the programming team from Sundance. A couple of years later she went to the Palm Springs festival where one of her films was screening.

> I spoke to the programmers from Sundance and Toronto. Short films had exploded so exponentially in recent years the quality was getting to the point festivals had a really tough time curating. They were getting something like 10 per cent of the films submitted worthy of programming, but that was thousands of films. And they could only program say 1 per cent or less of those, even though they were all worthy, and wanted to program them all. That marketplace is saturated.
>
> *Litton-Strain, 2018*

Hard experience with making short films in a hyper-saturated market convinced Good to abandon the traditional rite of passage short film format:

> I was in distribution for a short film, which is a weird time for directors who go from so busy on production and in post, to then waiting for festivals to get back to you. It was my fifth short film so I knew what I was in

for. I just wanted to keep working, but I was also completely done with short films.

Good, in Screen NSW, n.d.

Initially the pair followed the well-worn path for traditional early career screen creatives: they made strong films with festival lives and taught. To support themselves, and as a measure of their technical mastery of their domains, both Litton-Strain and Good would go on to teach at AFTRS. Good did a range of commercial directing work, and in 2014 was recognized by the Australian Directors Guild for her direction of *The Wonderful*. The following year she was recognized by Screen Australia by being accepted into their Talent Escalator program. The YouTube channel of their supernatural thriller project, *Jade*, was established that year and has since been populated with a modest range of teasers, behind-the-scenes videos, and tips on crowdfunding. *Jade* is described as a 'fantasy-noir lesbian web-series about a young woman with supernatural abilities'. Frustrated waiting for distribution of another short film, Good's genesis of the story arose from her work with crayons on butchers' paper where she combined words, pictures, and drawings of what she wanted: a long-running narrative; a story compelling to an audience; something genre; and something quite stylized. 'I combined them all together. Oh! I've got an idea that fits all of this. So, I took an old TV idea and turned it into Jade of Death' (Good, 2017).

Good approached Litton-Strain for feedback on the first drafts of *Jade*. She 'fell in love with the concept immediately' and their collaboration was struck. Good's inversion of the femme fatale trope attracted Litton-Strain:

[Jade's] a really powerful character and she's complex which really excited me about her. I was sick of seeing one-dimensional women characters in genre films and Jade just felt so real even in this heightened supernatural world. Plus she's the one saving the day, not being the damsel in distress.

Admin, 2018

Instead of finding their own 'non-linear pathway' as expected, they evolved an almost scientific six-stage production process and route to hybrid markets for what would become the multi-award-winning *Jade*. First, an investigation was conducted by the creator to understand how her passions for particular TV shows were present online, and to discover a gap in the market:

At the time we were making *Jade,* there was a gap in the market for high production value genre series, with great performances. There were a few great ones out there, and people would find the few that are really great. They talk about them and follow them from one to another because they are being recommended.

Litton-Strain, 2018

Second, a concerted listening process was embarked upon to better understand what audiences were consuming online:

> You should always be considering your audience and the commerciality of your project from the beginning. *Jade* was Erin's really strong idea. But she responded to feedback from me and the marketplace. The research we were doing and stuff we could see. What people were watching. What people wanted. What was missing. What we saw as the market gap.
>
> *Litton-Strain, 2018*

Third, their *Jade of Death* project was entered into and was selected for development as one of just 10 projects via expert workshopping at the Berlinale Short Project Lab, 2016, part of the Berlin International Film Festival. In 2016, Litton-Strain started Last Frame Productions.

> The fact the series was developed in the Berlin Labs already sets it apart. Part of the plan the whole way through was in showing the richness of the storyline by winning these awards.
>
> *Litton-Strain, 2018*

Fourth, the six x 10-minute, multi-genre series, a 'supernatural lesbian drama', was successfully entered into competition for Screen Australia multiplatform funding in 2016. Season one had been made in bursts over an 18-month period characterized by sleepless nights and tireless work by a 'talented and generous group of cast and crew' (Admin, 2018) (figure 8.3). 'Jade has a powerful ability, she can hear when and how people will die, but there's more to her abilities than she knows', read the synopsis. It was just a year after *Jessica Jones* first started to make a name for herself across the Marvel

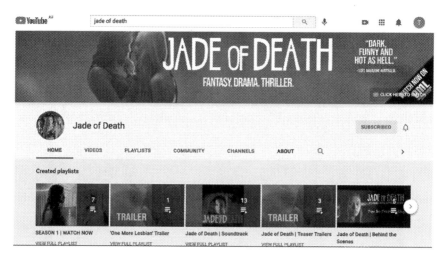

FIGURE 8.3 Banner marketing emphasizes multiple genres to attract larger audiences

FIGURE 8.4   Yoshi Hausler (GEORGE), Jordan Cowan (MAYA), Bernie Van Tiel (JADE)

Cinematic Universe. For a web-series, *Jade* was, at AU$120,000 and in-kind support 'through the roof', an expensive web-series to make, which 'took a lot of time and a lot of favours from different people' (Litton-Strain, 2021) (Figure 8.4). Production was taken 'one step at a time and where we didn't have money we gave time'.

Fifth, their first season was entered into international web festivals, principally the International Academy of Web Television Awards in Los Angeles, winning Best Series, Best Director, and Best Ensemble Cast. *Jade of Death* debuted at the Sydney Mardi Gras Film Festival of 2018. Like the first episode of Julie Kalceff's *Starting from Now*, the first episode of *Jade of Death* surfaced on an Open TV-style YouTube channel, the Silver Play button level One More Lesbian (OML), in September 2018. 'We haven't seen anything like *Jade of Death*, it's a perfect fit for OML, and *Jade* is mesmerizing', OML founder Shirin Papillon said at the time. In the background, the pair left the comfort zone of above-the-line cinema creatives and did relational labour:

> We replied [to comments] as a *Jade of Death* channel. We tried to reply to all comments because they were so wonderful and we wanted to speak to fans that way.
>
> *Litton-Strain, 2021*

Sixth, the creators endured a long period in the wilderness, with Erin Good teaming with co-writer, Huna Amweero, in developing a second season of *Jade* with the ABC, Australia's national public service broadcaster. The script development process underscores the hybrid, adaptive nature of the web-series:

> Erin and Huna are both amazing screenwriters and they developed the second season in a more traditional TV process. We did Writers' Rooms.

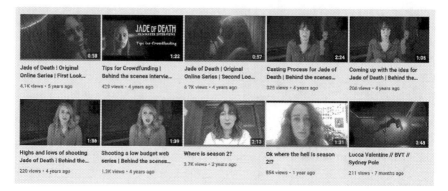

FIGURE 8.5   From left on the Jade YouTube channel, Bernie Van Tiel as *Jade*, ...Erin Good and Taylor Litton-Strain

> We had script feedback. We had a cast read-through. We were also developing it with the ABC, so we had a traditional feedback process with the ABC, and myself as a producer with different script changes. It was a more traditional TV process, but still for a web-series format.
>
> *Litton-Strain, 2021*

By then *Jade of Death* had been seen over three million times online, with the second season in development for a potential TV adaptation with the ABC's BVOD, iView, if things panned out. Their project was also supported by Create NSW. Season 1 was to be distributed internationally by French-based agent Rockzeline.

However, in a 'devastating' development shared with fans in late 2018, Good announced 'some of the financing had fallen through' (Figure 8.5). After almost five years of hard work, their meticulously designed passion project struck two obstacles beyond the creatives control: first, platform volatility meant they were not able to find an international partner to help finance the series, and were not able to finance it from Australia alone. Second, they were inadvertently caught up in the history wars, a rear-guard struggle 'to influence the representation and public understanding of Australian history', still dragging on Australia from the mid-1990s. Neo-conservativism imported from the United States, the political interests of re-elected Coalition governments and their conservative leaders had led to sustained criticism of the taxpayer-funded ABC (Bonnell & Crotty, 2008, p. 149). A fractious leadership change at the ABC, widely regarded as a national treasure, occurred while *Jade* was in second season development. In the fall-out, much development was halted, including on *Jade*, and the pair had to endure a nerve-wracking struggle over their hard-earnt IP. Good attributed the situation to two factors: first, declining arts funding in Australia. Indeed, Abbott/Turnbull government cuts to Screen Australia's budget amounting to AU$51.5 million since 2014/2015 were critiqued by screen trade press as 'not just an attack on funding, but a restriction on the space in which to discuss and critique public support for storytelling in the national conversation' (Harris, 2017, p. 123). Second, the fact Season Two of series was more ambitious and thus more expensive.

> *Jade* was a micro-version of TV and we wanted to retain the high production values, and the ensemble cast we established in season one – but that was going to be expensive for a webseries. We intended to finance the webseries similarly to how you would finance a television series, with a patch work of finance, albeit on a smaller scale. The first season was built on a lot of in-kind support and over a long period of time. We knew we couldn't sustain that again for the next season. But we wouldn't have developed it as big if we didn't think financing it was a possibility. But sadly, the platforms we thought would be perfect partners suddenly were closing down and others we had hoped to pitch to as well were tightening purse strings and financing less than they were before.
>
> *Litton-Strain, 2021*

While the scripts for the second season had been written, and they would 'work our arses off' to make Season 2 happen, Good appealed to fans to share Season 1 far and wide: 'The more Season 1 is viewed, the more that will help us make Season 2' (Good, 2018). Like her SME counterpart Reardon in Chapter 5, Good directly links high views in the millions to greater sustainability. Underlining the vision of Australian screen agencies regarding the fragile script development process, Create NSW had agreed to fund a long-form TV pilot of *Jade of Death*. In the background, Litton-Strain was living the advice of Screen Producers Australia chief executive, Matt Deaner: producers should have 10 projects on the slate at any one time, with the expectation only one or two of them will get up (Litton-Strain, 2018). In 2019, Taylor's company produced *Inner Demons*, a documentary by Hawanatu Bangura for the With Her in Mind Network (WHIMN). She was in development on a small slate of film, TV, and online projects: the crime-mystery TV series *The Forgotten*, one of eight projects selected for Bunya Productions' Genre Masterclass run by Raelle Tucker (*Jessica Jones, True Blood*) and Jeremy Podeswa (*Game of Thrones, The Handmaid's Tale*). Digital series, *Kara: Infected*, withdrawn for obvious reasons; a short VR film, *Aloft*, has since been made, while *The Forgotten* is still in development.

Jade was sold to the Canadian Broadcasting Corporation, to stream on CBC's OTT platform, GEM, from July 2019. The pair co-own the rights to sell internationally. Canada hosts one of the world's oldest webfests, Reelworld, dedicated to socially engaged storytelling, and established in 2002, followed by Toronto webfest in 2013. CBC has exclusive rights to *Jade* in Canada, but has also been licensed to platforms Wilde.tv and REVRY. In a pattern new to scholarship we see in Chapters 7–10, creators assert and secure non-exclusive license deals with multiple distributors:

> With Canada we gave them exclusive rights to Canada, but same thing [with *Starting From Now, Flunk* and *Anyone But Me*]. We negotiated non-exclusive license deals with every other platform. We wanted to keep it

on YouTube. We wanted to keep it accessible to fans so we had it on the One More Lesbian channel. Even today we are getting new views and new comments which is a joy to see.

Litton-Strain, 2021

By 2019, Litton-Strain was working as a producer's assistant on *The Invisible Man* for Universal Studios. Her post-Jade trajectory underlines the flexible role of the web-series as proof-of-concept, as evidenced by its attracting development funding for longform; and as a calling card for personnel:

> *Jade* been such a fantastic part of my career there's no way to distinguish how its helped and not helped. I worked on *The Invisible Man* as a producer's assistant. It was fantastic experience working with Kylie du Fresne who is a really brilliant producer. Then off the back I established a relationship with the US producer, Beatriz Sequeira [Executive Producer] from Blumhouse Productions. Then I went onto work with Bea in Toronto and LA on *The Craft,* working as a producers attachment there, supported by Screen Australia. The work on *Jade* has given me credibility. While it doesn't quite cross-over in terms of your skills on big stuff, it's enough to show your capacity and interest.

Litton-Strain, 2021

Meanwhile Good (2020) had taken to *Jade* YouTube channel to announce Season Two scripts were complete but had not been able to attract finance. In the meantime, in order to satisfy fan desires about what happened to the characters, and invite feedback, the six new scripts had been posted to Wattpad. After a long struggle, Good turned back to the fans to help rebuild momentum to get Season Two produced:

> A lot of shifts happened in the marketplace. We didn't quite get the finance to make the series in the way we wanted to. But we didn't want to leave fans in the lurch. So, we thought publishing the scripts on Wattpad would be a great way to do that. And now we have the superfans who have read it and given us feedback which has been really nice.

Litton-Strain, 2021

Litton-Strain's mentors include Bunya Production's Greer Simpkin (*Mystery Road; Sweet Country*), and Blumhouse's Bea Sequeira (*The Craft; Us; Get Out*).

Burning problems

Monetization

Good and Litton-Strain epitomize the real struggle over high cultural identity, and the obstacles they overcame in the post-TV ecology to achieve career mobility. They found pragmatism necessary for traditional producers to embrace SME and quickly adapt to the social network to hybrid digital service pathway.

By hard experience at what they found to be costly, highly saturated traditional short film festivals that left filmmakers in a career cul de sac, and subsequent trial and error, they showed a pathway for professionals to use a hybrid business model to secure licence deals. To support themselves in the run-up and while making *Jade of Death*, they drew on five of the revenue strategies detailed in Table 2.1: teaching at their alma mater, AFTRS; off-platform commercial jobs in the screen industry; crowdfunding; subvention from Screen Australia's Online Production Fund; and licensing. The pair thus drew on Murdock and Goldings three cultural economies of public goods, gifting and collaboration and the market. However, to be frank, even then the licences from CBC Gem and Wilde. tv did not cover production costs, their labour and that of their cast and crew:

> Definitely not; we have been able to share some sales revenue with our cast and crew, but making this web-series was much more than a financial opportunity. Jade was a big series to create, and everyone involved knew that. They were committed to making something that was going to be standout series to showcase skills, and to showcase a great story. Our in-kind budget for *Jade* was through the roof, but everyone got something out of it other the money: key being career escalation. That was why Screen Australia supported it, because it was a career escalation for everyone involved.
>
> *Litton-Strain, 2021*

Coping with volatility

Good and Litton-Strain's prioritization of achieving distinction for *Jade of Death* via character and storyworld-building meant they side-stepped the two big problems besetting social media entertainers: algorithmic volatility, and an upload regime inimical to good creative work. Algorithmic culture was actually a boon for Good and Litton-Strain since they were able to build a niche audience for themselves online, and attract strong views on make-or-break social analytics from YouTube. We saw the same use of strong social analytics as literal proof-of-concept with SuperWog in Chapter 3 and RackaRacka in Chapter 4. However, Good and Litton-Strain's pursuit of license deals on post-TV SVOD networks left them – and indeed Forster and Rowland in Chapter 9, and Miller and Ward in Chapter 10 – vulnerable to platform volatility. As Litton-Strain told me:

> Platform volatility! These platforms coming and going! 100% was the biggest challenge with *Jade* and financing a second season. The challenge in financing a series is it can take a long time to develop. You are having conversations with players who are coming in and out of the market suddenly. Also, there's no clear benchmark on the level of finance you should be seeking for a web-series. It's as though because it is a web-series it must be as cheap as possible; it must be bottom–dollar. That wasn't what we were

exploring on *Jade*. We were looking at the higher quality series. A few have been made with financing like that but they are few and far between.

Litton-Strain, 2021

Old and new media divide

I argue the web-series is a hybrid genre especially adapted from these streaming defined times, precisely because it originally emerged from cyberspace in the mid-1990s. In terms of its affordances to the careers of contemporary screen storytellers, *Jade* showed itself to be both performing the traditional shortfilm function of a calling card to the screen industry, but also, crucially, as a proof-of-concept, depending upon the situated needs of the writers, producers and directors at the time:

> *Jade* is a calling card in that it showcases my skills as a producer, Erin's skills as a writer-director, it showcases the cinemaphotographer's skills, the editor's skills, all the cast and crew's skills. We have pitched the web-series as a proof of concept, and Erin wrote a pilot script for a TV series version of the idea, but even as a TV series – as a genre show with an ensemble cast it's still a complex project to pitch and finance…the people commenting on YouTube are saying make this into a Netflix series! But TV development takes a long time and requires multiple partners, whereas web-series is fast and driven by creators without gatekeepers and that was part of the reason we did it.
>
> *Litton-Strain, 2021*

I argue that web-series require characters journeying through storyworlds; if compelling, this gives rise to the opportunity to go straight to developing creator-sustaining IP for hybrid digital services. Not only do they offer a discoverable, demonstrable skill-set to mainstream TV gatekeepers who might commission bigger and better projects, but the new IP can be directly licensed, so countering precariousness:

> Despite the quality of your short film, the struggle is greater than it ever was before. That's why I am moving to web-series. Web-series are like a mini-TV series. You also have direct access to audience. Even though web-series are becoming saturated, there's so many opportunities to create content that will find its audience.
>
> *Litton-Strain, 2018*

> A web-series has returnability. It continues. It's something the market is responding to. It's not one little short-film and then you can't continue with it because it's such an isolated project. Whereas with web-series, you are building characters and building story. You have elements you can return to in another season, or as a larger TV series.
>
> *Litton-Strain, 2018*

Discrimination and authenticity

What has been authentic for one intersection of the audience, is inauthentic to another. These cases suggest that discrimination and authenticity, at this stage of history as socio-technologies have diversified and democratized cultural production, are two sides of the same coin. For example, Hollywood studios and production companies have been increasingly and rightly critiqued over the past five years for what Smith et al. (2019, p. 14) describe as 'doing little' to fix the 'historic and discriminatory approach' to hiring in directors, writers and producers. Among the directors across the top 100 films from 2007 to 2018, the total unique number of men is 657. The total number of female directors was just 47. More recently, of above the line creatives, female producers faired 'best'. The male to female gender ratio for directors in 2018 was 21.4 to 1; for writers it was 6 to 1; and just 3.8 males to 1 female producer. Inevitably then, just 12.3 per cent of films were assessed as having balanced casts, with the ratio of males to females of 2.2 to 1. Almost 40 per cent of the top 100 films in 2018 showed a female lead or co lead, but just 11 female actors were from under-represented racial/ethnic groups, and just 11 were 45 years or older (Smith et al., 2019, p. 1).

Given the popular and critical acclaim of *Jade*, Good and Litton-Strain's mode of address resonated deeply with their online audiences. Indeed, for Litton-Strain, now teaching at AFTRS full-time, the fate of a web-series rises or falls on its authenticity:

> You can't just market it broadly. You have to be talking to an audience in an authentic way for them to come on the journey and find the show, and not just find it, but fall in love with it, and want to support it.
>
> *Litton-Strain, 2021*

But for Good, however, much *Jade* met the needs and desires of its audiences, her Writers' Room remained sacrosanct:

> We didn't have people sending us messages, 'We want this!' We were trying to be aware of what was out there. But you must do that authentically as a writer. I can't go out and look at everything audiences are loving right now and make a monster of a thing that builds on pieces of all the other successful shows. It must be genuine and come from a cohesive place.
>
> *Good, 2018*

The quality of authenticity, a quality possibly as old as storytelling itself, remains as crucial as ever to cut-through the hyper-saturation of content enjoyed by contemporary audiences.

References

Admin (2018, February 15). Jade of death interview – Producer Taylor Litton-strain, impulse gamer [Blog]. https://www.impulsegamer.com/jade-death-interview-producer-taylor-litton-strain/

Altman, R. (1984). A semantic/syntactic approach to film genre. *Cinema Journal, 23*(3), 6–18.

Ashe, F. (2003). Berlinale talent campus. Retrieved from: https://www.berlinale.de/en/archive/jahresarchive/2003/08

Banet-Weiser, S., Baym, N. K., Coppa, F., Gauntlett, D., Gray, J., Jenkins, H., & Shaw, A. (2014). Participations: Dialogues on the participatory promise of contemporary culture and politics—part 1: Creativity. *International Journal of Communication, 8,* 1069–1088.

Aldridge, L. (2017). *Miranda J. Banks, The Writers: A History of American Screenwriters and Their Guild.* Michigan Publishing, University of Michigan Library.

Banks, Miranda. (2015). *The writers: A history of American screenwriters and their guild.* Rutgers University Press.

Baujard, T., Tereszkiewicz, R., & de Swarte, A. (2019). *Entering the new paradigm of artificial intelligence and series. A Study commissioned by the Council of Europe and Eurimages.* Peacefulfish.

Bonnell, A., & Crotty, M. (2008). Australia's history under Howard, 1996-2007. *The ANNALS of the American Academy of Political and Social Science, 617*(1), 149–165.

Bourdieu, P., & Nice, R. (1980). The production of belief: Contribution to an economy of symbolic goods. *Media, Culture & Society, 2*(3), 261–293.

Boyer, S. (2011). Thou shalt not crave thy neighbor: True blood, abjection, and otherness. *Studies in Popular Culture, 33*(2), 21–41.

Caldwell, J. T. (2016). 3. Spec world, craft world, brand world. In Curtin, M., & Sanson, K. (Eds.) *Precarious creativity* (pp. 33–48). University of California Press.

Campbell, J. (1993). *The hero with a thousand faces.* Fontana Press.

Christian, A. J. (2019). *Open TV.* New York University Press.

Cunningham, S., & Craig, D. (2019). *Social media entertainment.* New York University Press.

Davies, R. (2017). Collaborative production and the transformation of publishing: The case of Wattpad. In Gandini, A., & Graham, J. Collaborative production in the creative industries (p. 240). University of Westminster Press.

Deyo, N. (2020). The Maltese Falcon, Double Indemnity, Scarlet Street, and Out of the Past: Paradigm cases. In Gibbs, J., & Pye, D. (Eds.), Film Noir and the possibilities of hollywood (pp. 25–46). Palgrave Close Readings in Film and Television.

Erbland, K. (2018, March 21). 11 Movies shot on iPhones, from 'Tangerine' to a charming short. Indiewire, Penske Media, Los Angeles. https://www.indiewire.com/2018/03/movies-shot-on-iphones-unsane-tangerine-shorts-1201941565/

Feuer, J. (1977). The self-reflective musical and the myth of entertainment. Quarterly Review of Film & Video, 2(3), 313–326.

Frow, J. (2014). System and history. *Genre* (pp. 134–167). Routledge.

Gibson, W. (1986). *Burning Chrome.* Orion Publishing.

Good, E. (2017, February 15). Coming up with the idea for Jade of Death | Behind the scenes interview. [Vlog], Jade of Death channel. https://www.youtube.com/watch?v=JfQjBt9Ixt0

Good, E. (2018). Producer, Jade of Death, January 2018. Skype interview with Guy Healy.

Good, E. (2020). Ok where the hell is season 2!? [blog] Jade of Death, 15 February. https://www.youtube.com/watch?v=GWT7f_-rDhU

Green, S. (2019). Fantasy, gender and power in Jessica Jones. *Continuum, 33*(2), 173–184.

Harris, L. C. (2017). What are our stories worth? Value, the culture wars and the Screen Currency report. *Industry Perspectives, Metro Magazine, 192,* 120–123.

Hunter, B. (n.d.). Erin good jade of death interview, Female.com.au, Trellian P/L, Australia. https://www.female.com.au/erin-good-jade-of-death-interview.htm

ImpulseGamer (2018). Jade of death interview – Producer Taylor Litton-Strain [Blog]. https://www.impulsegamer.com/jade-death-interview-producer-taylor-litton-strain/

Lessig, L. (2007). How creativity is being strangled by the law (TED). https://www.youtube.com/watch?v=t5pHeV3jF48

Litton-Strain, T. (2018 & 2021). Producer, jade of death. Skype interviews with Guy Healy.

Loist, S. (2016). The film festival circuit: Networks, hierarchies, and circulation. *Film Festivals: History, Theory, Method, Practice,* 49–64. In de Valck, M., Kredell, B., & Loist, S. (Eds.). (2016). Film Festivals: History, Theory, Method, Practice (1st ed.). Routledge. https://doi.org/10.4324/9781315637167.

Lüthi, M. (1987). *The fairytale as art form and portrait of man* (Vol. 420). Indiana University Press.

McDaniel, L. (2001). "Jumping the Dragon Gate" storytellers and the creation of the Shanghai identity. *Modern China, 27*(4), 484–507.

Niles, J. D. (1999). *Homo Narrans: The poetics and anthropology of oral literature.* University of Pennsylvania Press.

Parnell, C. (2021). Mapping the entertainment ecosystem of Wattpad: Platforms, publishing and adaptation. *Convergence, 27*(2), 524–538.

Ryan, M. D., & Hearn, G. (2010). Next-generation 'filmmaking': New markets, new methods and new business models. *Media International Australia, 136*(1), 133–145.

Sanders, S. M. (2008). An introduction to the philosophy of TV Noir. In Sanders, S., and Skoble, A. (Eds.), *The Philosophy of TV Noir* (pp. 1–29). University Press of Kentucky.

Scobie, A. (1979). Storytellers, storytelling, and the novel in Graeco-Roman antiquity. *Rheinisches Museum für Philologie, 122*(H. 3/4), 229–259.

Screen NSW (n.d.). Erin good is bringing the web to life with Jade of Death. NSW Government, Sydney. Retrieved from: https://www.screen.nsw.gov.au/news/erin-good-is-bringing-the-web-to-life-with-jade-of-death

Smith, S. L., Choueiti, M., Pieper, K., Yao, K., Case, A., & Choi, A. (2019). Inequality in 1,200 popular films: Examining portrayals of gender, race/ethnicity. LGBTQ & disability from 2007 to 2018. Annenberg Inclusion Initiative.

Stephan, M. (2016). Do you believe in magic? The potency of the fantasy genre. *Coolabah, 18,* 3–15.

Telecompaper (2019, April 12). Short-video platform Blackpills closes down app to focus on content production, Telecompaper. https://www.telecompaper.com/news/short-video-platform-blackpills-closes-down-app-to-focus-on-content-production–1288642

Thomson, D. (2012). *The big screen: The story of the movies.* Macmillan.

Tolkien, J. R. R. (1964). On fairy stories. *Tree and leaf* (pp. 11–70). Unwin Books.

Spangler, T. (2020). How Wattpad's Aron Levitz mines user-generated stories for movie, TV Hits, Variety, Penske Media Corporation. https://variety.com/2020/digital/news/wattpad-studios-aron-levitz-user-stories-movies-shows-1234779399/Wattpad

Vu, R. (2017). Fantasy after representation: D&D, game of thrones, and postmodern world-building. *Extrapolation, 58*(2/3), 273–276.

9

BENDING ALGORITHMIC CULTURE TO SERVE POST-TV STORYTELLING

This case is the only stand-alone study of one of the Skip Ahead producer-mentors. Of all the established Skip Ahead producers considered in this book, Forster, a film school graduate and expatriate Englishman, is the most hybrid; his web design and online video practice the most ambitious and advanced; and his pathway to sustainability via the participatory web-series, ultimately licensed to an SVOD, one of the most significant (Healy, 2019, p. 115). This was clearly his ambition all along. When I first spoke to Forster in 2017, he described doing a self-funded web-series as 'the first step in having a broadcaster like Netflix pay for it. A dream assignment' (Forster, 2017). Indeed, as I showed in Chapter 1, a major finding of my longitudinal investigation is the tendency for more Skip Ahead creators to pursue longer formats off YouTube – particularly in the hybrid digital services of BVODs and SVODs – the longer they are exposed to algorithmic volatility on the short-form dominated platform of YouTube. Recent developments have further underlined this finding. The above-the-line narrative labour of two key Skip Ahead creatives quoted earlier in this book have since been featured on SVOD Netflix: Rosie Lourde's direction of *Romance on the Menu* (2020), and the Van Vuuren's writing credits on two episodes of *New Legends of Monkey* (2020). Since then, YouTubers and Skip Aheaders' Aunty Donna, have also transitioned to Netflix with their absurdist series, *Big Ol' House of Fun* (2020). That the Emmy award-winning short form series *'After Forever'*, on which web-series maker, Tina Cesa Ward (*Anyone But Me*, 100 million views), was a director, has been licensed Amazon Prime and has an advertising deal with Hulu, underlines the new democratizing path web-series makers have blazed to BVODs and SVODs, a central finding of my five-year investigation. This pathway is only likely to become wider as SVODs try to capture the audience zeitgeist hard-won by narratively-gifted YouTubers.

DOI: 10.4324/9781003182481-9

Forster, working in the traditional home of the TV soap opera, Melbourne Australia, is arguably one of the most significant, independent, and earliest adapters of TV storytelling to algorithmic culture internationally. When I first interviewed the former *Hollyoaks* storyliner in 2017, he was Senior Social and Digital Producer at FremantleMedia Australia. Fremantle produces the long-running *Neighbours,* one of Australia's most successful TV exports, which has become a cultural staple of British TV audiences, airing on BBC One and Channel 5. With TV broadcasters worldwide facing the existential threats of a media environment characterized by increasing audience fragmentation, and an accompanying increase in audience autonomy and cultural appropriation (Napoli, 2003, p. 12; Webster & Ksiazek, 2012, p. 40), Forster led the extension of the storyworld of *Neighbours* onto YouTube under Skip Ahead. With this adaptation, Forster was placed on the fault line between traditional and new media and opted for a cross-cultural, intergenerational collaboration with veteran YouTuber and musician, Louna Maroun (6.8 million views). Together the pair created the official web-series, *Neighbours vs Zombies* (hereafter *Zombies)* (2014), which celebrated the disruptive remix culture accelerated in popularity by YouTube. The web-series was backed by Fremantle. Its genre mashing of the web-series drew on the spirit of remix, an experimental and participatory production style credited as a new form of sense-making for the young (Lessig, 2004, p. 970) that helps people 'keep up with a genre that moves too quickly to be captured' by traditional technologies (Katz, 2008, p. 22). As William Gibson (2005) wrote: 'Today's audience is not listening, but participating … The record, not the remix, is the anomaly today. The remix is the very nature of the digital'. Forster's passion project was queer teen drama, *Flunk,* he was about to launch independently to such impact in a series of entrepreneurial experiments in 'multiplatform labour' (Healy, 2019, p. 117), across rival social media: Twitter, Google's YouTube, and the Mark Zuckerberg-owned Instagram. The synopsis for *Flunk* centres on sixteen-year-old Ingrid, 'who starts to explore her sexuality whilst struggling to cope with the pressures of a country high school and her conservative Chinese-Australian family' (Screen Australia, 2021). Forster flagged with me the question of how to monetize the web-series as the great dilemma for online screenwriters, the first of the burning problem addressed in Chapter 1. In the meantime, he practised fast, low-cost filmmaking:

> There's this thing with web-series: Step 1, make the web-series. Step 3 is profit. No one knows what the Step 2 is? You make a web-series, great! You spend your money. Make six eps. Are you now expecting an ABC to come along and buy it? A lot of creators think that. I had thought that. I'll make *LOL*. I'll do 20 eps. Industry might throw me the lifeline. But you can't look at it like that. It's amazing if it happens. Can you make the content quickly enough at a cost per minute of video low enough? Very hard in drama. That's why YouTube is full of vlogs. You can make it for next to nothing.

Forster, 2017

By the time I interviewed him again in late 2019, Forster had answered the question continuing to bedevil the screen industry and online creators worldwide: how to monetize online content (Kramer in Caldwell, 2004, p. 41; Judah, 2015, p. 123). Forster had licensed the critically acclaimed *Flunk,* which has now attracted 52 million views worldwide, to Here TV and built a large, monetized audience to YouTube. The exact methodology Forster used to solve his 'Step 2', the problem of monetization and sustainability, is elaborated in this final case. At the Melbourne WebFest, now one of 25 international web festivals worldwide (Bassaget & Burkholder, 2019), *Flunk* was nominated for Best Australian Drama, Best Cinemaphotography and Best Director. The season 1 super-High Definition, longform web-series was structured as eight broadcast half-hours, or 40 by five minutes on YouTube.

Forster is the exception to the overall finding of this investigation that collaborations between YouTubers and established TV producers are characterized by an even balance of skillset cross-fertilization as creators and producers help each other adapt to their respective screen cultures. Overall, established TV producer mentors were exposed to the 'fast and furious film-making' of their younger YouTube collaborators under Skip Ahead (Healy, 2019). In Forster's case, this established TV producer and Skip Ahead mentor had already been making successful web-series long before meeting *Zombies* collaborator, Maroun. Forster was a pioneer as early as any peer in the US, except Zarakin's proto-web-series *The Spot* from the mid-1990s. For example, Forster's first web-series, *LOL,* was produced in 2008, the same period as pioneering touchstone series such as *Lonelygirl15* (2006–2008) and *The Guild* (2007–2013).

I previously foreshadowed the themes of rapprochement, blended labour, and enhanced diversity in screen labour in Chapter 1. Accordingly, this case centres on Forster's most important younger collaborators, YouTuber Maroun, and his producer on *Flunk,* Melanie Rowland. This case reveals important and striking parallels regarding participatory, co-creativity with fans, with the innovative audience-building techniques used to such effect by Julie Kalceff in her *Starting From Now,* the world's third most highly viewed independent web-series elaborated in Chapter 10. Crucially, this case shows the skillsets of YouTube-launched web-series writer-producers map coherently against those of TV showrunners, as elaborated in Chapter 1, differing only regarding factors of less experience of traditional TV production. A critical point of tension in this regard is the freedom web-series makers enjoy from notorious 'production notes' used by TV executives to 'discipline' creatives (Caldwell, 2013, p. 161), and make 'changes on series and episodes' (Lotz, 2017, p. 13). Above all, this case underlines the continuing, even increasing importance of 'deliberate experimentation' to generative creativity (Livingston, 2009, p. 11), especially in algorithmic culture, so nurturing the garden in YouTube's machine.

In terms of continuity and change, what is striking is the degree to which this audience participation, and even powerful agency in the web-series narratives of *Flunk, Starting From Now* and to a lesser extent, *Anyone But Me,* is mirrored in the proto web-series, The Spot (1995–1997), decades ago. Audience reaction to particular actors in *Anyone But Me* (2008–2001), and their romantic couplings, was used to 'boost the presence of those actors in the series, and keep writing more stuff for their characters' Ward (2020) told me. Scott Zakarin's *Spot* was delivered online via desktop computers with the characters appearing in short videos and photographs, and where fans were encouraged to write in via message boards and email. As Zakarin said of his series:

> We are able to put things out there television never could. You can get inside our characters souls … you can then turn around and email a character and give them advice. They'll write back to you and you can find out you affected the story.
>
> *Monaghan, 2017, p. 83*

Biography

Forster studied film and TV at Bournemouth University in the United Kingdom and Ryerson University in Canada in the early 2000s, and had made 'lots of shorts'. He aimed to work in the Story Room of long-running, award-winning British soap opera *Hollyoaks*, produced by Lime Pictures for Channel Four (Forster, 2017). He achieved the first rung of his dream, starting work as a storyliner for Lime Pictures in 2008 on *Hollyoaks*. Under the Director Training Scheme at Lime, upcoming writers and directors at the company were given access to the production facilities: 'Use the sets, use the equipment, come in on weekends and produce. I was doing the digital content, but wanted to get into narrative' (Forster, 2017).

That year, Forster also opened his YouTube channel and has thus been in a position to safely observe at least five of YouTube's algorithm changes (as discussed in Chapter 1). However, since he was a traditional employee with a stable income, he was not vulnerable to algorithmic volatility. Yet we will see below he was still vulnerable to platform volatility, as US conglomerates tend to subsume competing outlets and 'upstart' disrupters (Lanham, 2011, p. 9; Downes & Nunes, 2013, p. 46), a problem endemic to platformed creation. During 2008 and 2009, he produced behind-the-scenes pieces for *Hollyoaks,* the Sci Fi Channel and BBC series. As a sign of his prescience, Forster created his first web-series, the edgy teen drama *LOL* (20 by two- to five-minute episodes) in 2008, the same year YouTube's star-making potential was first demonstrated. Justin Bieber – who once had the most viewed video on YouTube – first broke out on the platform in 2008, as did Portuguese songwriter, Mia Rose (Burgess & Green, 2018, p. 33).

As foreshadowed in Chapter 1, Forster's case exemplifies the way some web-series writer-producers have been stealing a march on most of their peers, who are still trying to stand out by making short films for the 'saturated', 6000-strong international film festival circuit (Loist, 2016, p. 49), or writing 'calling card' scripts (Ashton, 2011, p. 49). *LOL* dealt with sex, drugs, and social media-driven

FIGURE 9.1 Forster taps YouTube's bedroom culture

peer pressure among young people. Research suggests these topics are salient for young people with the age of first sexual intercourse declining over the past three decades to about 16 (Forsyth & Rogstad, 2015, p. 448). Young people are increasingly concerned about bullying, drug addiction, and alcohol consumption among their peers (Horowitz & Graf, 2019), and a majority regarding social media as doing more harm than good (Deloitte, 2019, p. 20). Arguably these participatory web-series are not merely compelling entertainment, but an important, emergent public sphere for youth. The first webisodes were shot in high definition on the *Hollyoaks* backlots in Liverpool: 'Most people made shorts; instead I made the first three eps of *LOL*' (Forster, 2017) (Figure 9.1). Season 2 of *LOL* was nominated for Best British Webseries at Raindance Webfest 2014. *Hollyoaks* itself won the British Soap Awards twice, in 2014 and 2019, beating out long-standing award rivals *EastEnders* and *Coronation Street*.

Forster mainly launched *LOL* on the now defunct Blip.tv, parlaying his new reputation as a web-series creator into the *Hollyoaks* Story Room at Channel Four (Forster, 2017). Blip.tv was one of just a handful of Web 2.0 sites highlighted by Lessig (2006), for upholding the ethics of the web of 'true sharing', creator freedom, and remix. By 2011, Forster had joined Fremantle Media's team producing iconic Australian soap opera *Neighbours*, as a trainee storyliner (Figure 9.2). MTV reached out to make a US version of *LOL*, but things did not pan out. Nevertheless, *LOL* put Forster on MTV's radar. Later he joined MTV as an associate producer and worked on their new YouTube originated crossover, *The Janoskians MTV Sessions*. In 2012, the Janoskians were high profile Melbourne-based YouTube pranksters with a Beatle-esque following, who largely inspired Skip Ahead (Cowap, 2017). Skip Ahead itself began as an experiment in trying

FIGURE 9.2   Ric Forster goes over lines with Neighbours' actors

to understand how 'young talent was finding audiences on YouTube that TV was unable to match' (Cowap, 2017). Forster could not have been unaware of the disruptive cultural power of these YouTubers, especially when coupled with cheap, networked production technology in the hands of fans. The youthful exuberance of fans is shared in their participatory mix videos, best captured in *Janoskians Meet & Greet 2012 Sydney* and *Janoskians Meet & Greet 2012 Luna Park (rachmichellee, 2012; Charlotte Beth, 2012).* The Melbourne event had to be shut down and ambulances called after fans mobbed the young YouTubers. From 2013, Forster was employed to extend the storyworld of *Neighbours* online for *Neighbours'* and TEN's YouTube channels – for example, *Neighbours Backstage, Neighbours: Steph in Prison* and *Neighbours: Brennan on the Run.* Forster says his brief was 'to export/ explore *Neighbours* multi-platform content, and get as much rich video as we could' (Forster, 2017).

In 2014, in the first class of Skip Ahead, Forster collaborated with Maroun to produce the genre-mashing *Neighbours VS Zombies*, which would go onto be a nominated finalist for Best Drama at Raindance Webfest in 2015. Forster's work in this regard represented the first significant renovation to *Neighbours* since van Vuuren et al. (2013, p. 36) reported on a periodic renovation over a decade ago to stay in touch with the broadcasters' priority audience: 16- to 35-year-old females. Forster left Fremantle in early 2019 to work on his original productions full time, specifically his *Flunk*, with producer Melanie Rowland. But to achieve this crossover success from YouTube to a subscription-based global streamer such as Here

TV, Forster first had to get a lesson in spreadability and even faster film-making from Maroun. Forster and Maroun fatefully met and struck up a collaboration under Skip Ahead, 'the point at which YouTube culture meets Australian screen culture most directly' (Cunningham & Craig, 2019, p. 255), five years earlier.

Skip Ahead

Forster had three key learnings from his experience of Skip Ahead: first, how to adapt the weeknightly or 'strip programming' of *Neighbours* for a fragmenting demographic via appeals to remix culture for FremantleMedia; second, acquiring the know-how of Audience Growth Hacking, the use of platform affordances to grow online audiences, from Maroun; and third, acquiring faster, lower-cost filmmaking production skillsets.

Firstly, the idea for *Neighbours VS Zombies (Zombies)* was Forster's own, drawing on the inspiration of the BBC's own earlier experiment in engaging participatory culture with charity event Children in Need's two-part *EastEnders/Doctor Who* crossover, *Dimensions in Time* (McKee, 2004, p. 14):

> Working at Fremantle, we had tried a few different shapes and sizes of web-series, but for all of them, *Zombies* was the biggest, shiniest one we have done. We had the question of 'What's the craziest thing we can do? It's such an 'out there' idea: a zombie invasion of *Neighbours*. Not without precedent. *EastEnders* had a *Doctor Who* crossover in the 90s; all kinds of crazy.
>
> *Forster, 2017*

FIGURE 9.3 YouTuber, Louna Maroun (pictured) singing the official song she wrote to help keep Neighbours relevant to a younger generation

In *Zombies*, we again see the role of Gibson's zeitgeist of 'genre-bending' – in this case, a soap and sci-fi mash-up. RackaRacka also did genre-bending in its Skip Ahead project, *Stunt Gone Wrong LIVE*, as seen in Chapter 4. *Zombies* combines contemporaneous and ancient traditions, and is thus a hybrid transnational product that draws on both the popularity of Halloween with teens, and ancient, symbol-laden ritual. The series was launched in October, the global Halloween season historically originating with the Celts celebrating the end of harvest and remembering the dead.

Second, Forster was able to learn an audience growth-hacking skillset from Maroun – especially what he described as their 'power of cross-pollination', their collaborative networks and knowledge of cultural references:

> It's the power of cross-pollination. With *Zombies* we did a playlist of 10 to 12 vids, a trailer and five ep's (episodes). That's on our Fremantle *Neighbours* channel. In the same playlist, Louna has BTS (behind-the-scenes) content and a music video of her *Zombies* theme cover she wrote and performed. Hopefully Louna would receive views from *Neighbours* fans. *Neighbours* would have got views from her fans.
>
> *Forster, 2017*

Forster observed a 'rat-pack' dynamic of YouTubers collaborating by appearing in each other's videos, and in *Zombies* as minor characters. I explain the rat pack-like nature of the creative practice of the most successful YouTubers by their face-to-face sociality, especially regarding collaboration videos. The original 'rat pack' was the creative collaboration led by Frank Sinatra who called together a group of friends to make *Ocean's 11* (1960). As Forster explains:

> I didn't realise this until I met with her. There's a real creators community in Melbourne. If you watch her stuff, a lot of them pop up in each other's videos. It's hard as a viewer to subscribe to just one of them. You end up subscribing to them all. That was an interesting learning.
>
> *Forster, 2017*

Maroun has said being part of a peer circle to help each other and create – especially to do 'collabs' – was the essence of audience growth: 'The more people you collaborate with, the greater the potential to grow your channel through audience exposure' (Maroun, 2015). Indeed, recent face-recognition-based research of YouTube videos by Koch et al. (2018, p. 28), confirms Maroun's hard-won insight. The most collaborations occur among YouTubers with between 100,000 and 1 million subscribers as they leverage each other's popularity, with popularity growth of 100 per cent overall for collaborating channels. This socially based phenomenon of YouTuber video collaboration is in the direct tradition of Northern Californian youth observed by Lange (2007, p. 9), who became acquainted by making YouTube videos at first for 'fun, and we just started hanging out after that, and then we started making movies as well'. At the level of creativity, Csikszentmihalyi (2014, p. 77) emphasizes the salience of social interaction – especially before and after 'the moment of creative insight' – to better integrate creative products into the symbolic domains of relevant social groups, and address the most interesting questions as defined by the relevant discipline. Forster observes this phenomenon in Maroun's practice:

> Louna was bringing an audience across. They say when you are a brand working with a YouTuber, they know that audience best. Absolutely true. She has a certain demographic that's different from the *Neighbours* demographic. The ideas she had for things we could do in the narrative; callbacks to zombie movies; little moments empowering young characters more – they worked really well. Important to really listen to them when you are working with them; they know what the audience want.
>
> *Forster, 2017*

Third, audience growth hacking and tapping the cultural zeitgeist were not the only important learnings from Maroun. I argue these concepts of co-creativity and spreadability as prefigured in Chapter 1, parallel the Silicon Valley concept of growth hacking: 'making the experience of sharing the product with others must-have' (Ellis & Brown, 2017). Forster was exposed to the contemporaneous version of what Kaufman and Mohan (2008, p. 2) describe as the 'new vernacular', the 'new tools of speech' enabled by video in every phone, and editing software in most laptops. At this time digital anthropologist, Michael Wesch (2010) argued YouTube enabled the revolutionary moment of 'universal film-making', where 'millions of little cameras have been linked together for the first time in history'.

The five burning questions and the multi-platform labour of Flunk

Three key lessons emerge from this case: first, *Flunk*, along with Kalceff's *Starting From Now*, and Ward's *Anyone But Me,* each among the most highly viewed web-series to date, all share a distinctive, iterative, participatory web-series production methodology with fans; second, a multiplatform approach to social media was essential to audience-building; and third, an ethos of experimentation in production and distribution was essential to the rare achievement of Forster and Rowland being able to make a living from their web-series. This new mapping is important because 15 years ago Angela McRobbie (2004) considered the issue of artists as pioneers of the new economy, and the need for a better understanding of how the small business model works in practice. McRobbie's provocation asked, 'To what extent is it a fully effective (or merely half-baked) entrepreneurialism? How exactly are the artistic careers conducted as small businesses?' McRobbie (2016, p. 17) has since posited a shift from first- to second-wave 'cultural entrepreneurialism' and argues interrogating this issue is more necessary than ever, given the displacement of 'a politics of the workplace' by 'speeded up' work in the cultural sector. Moreover, given 'the countless young women utilising social media in the hopes of monetizing their passion projects', Duffy (2015, p. 2) says more scholarship is needed to understand the 'cultural experiences of female social media producers in their own voices'.

Monestization, sustainability, and the A/B list

After film school, Forster left the security of Fremantle in 2019, to focus on original productions such as *Flunk* fulltime. Forster did not use SME to make 'a decent middle-class living', and instead funded his post-Fremantle web-series via an experimental combination of modest subvention, YouTube ads, merchandise, transaction fees on Vimeo, licensing of his web-series to a major SVOD, and fan gifting and participatory collaboration. My analysis shows *Flunk* drew on each of Murdock and Golding's three cultural economies: 'It doesn't happen overnight though…(But) there comes a point where YouTube revenue alone covers production and living costs – that's what you want to achieve'. Their funding deal with Here Now TV 'gave us confidence and some funding to continue (Forster, 2020). Significantly, Forster invoked the more than decade old concept of the 'superfan' in helping secure their living via *Flunk*, which has now achieved 34 million views.

Cultural divide

In Chapter 1, I identified the cultural divide was contributing to a systematic knowledge transfer blockage, especially for those under 45. Younger producers and new media creators consistently report feeling blocked in finding people to share jealously guarded industry know-how (Cameron et al., 2010, p. 99; Ryan et al, 2012, p. 7). Moreover, this blockage is occurring as traditional mentoring and expertise-sharing mechanisms had broken down during 'craft disaggregation' (Banks, 2010, p. 316; Caldwell, 2010, p. 222). However in the case of *Flunk*, Forster has Rowland producing. Rowland makes a qualitative differentiation between the traditional TV production career route, and the web-series:

> I had worked on TV series and features in the production department but wanted to make the leap into producing. It can be hard to get opportunities to step up to the next rung on the career ladder without the experience. Web-series offer an opportunity for creators to go direct to audience with no middleman - there are no gatekeepers. You don't need to be greenlit or get the approval from someone else. If you want to produce a feature film or a web-series, you just go out and do it - you learn so much along the way.

Rowland, 2020

Volatility in algorithmic culture and doing good work

Producers were shielded from algorithmic volatility by the different emphasis in their revenue streams, especially various forms of modest subvention. Aside from the protection of a day job in teaching (Throsby & Zednik, 2011, p. 9), or working for a cultural organization or creative talent 'embedded' in other industries (Higgs et al., 2008, p. 3), the best protection against algorithmic volatility is a strong and supportive online fan base. In his former core creative roles in the United Kingdom and at Fremantle, Forster was able to observe the vagaries of algorithm change – and the havoc they can wreak on creator incomes (Weiss, 2017) from relative safety. These changes were detailed in Chapter 1. Data analytics curated by algorithms mean the days when creators had to either imagine an audience or see 'presence cues' limited to friends lists, general facts about the audience, or their feedback capabilities (Litt, 2012, p. 337) are long gone. Contemporary YouTube creators have access to 20 data analytic tools, including but not limited to Watch Time in minutes and average view duration, impressions, audience retention, demographics, top geographics, playback locations, traffic sources, devices, interaction reports, subscribers, likes and dislikes, comments, sharing and gender, all in near real-time. Like all the creators and producers I interviewed, Forster can tell you exactly where his main markets are: the United States, South East Asia, and South America being the strongest, Australia less so. Algorithm-driven social analytics, together with the qualitative comment streams, are most important for creators, as they stand in for applause. 'You will see comments on episodes in a variety of languages. Reaching viewers across the world has been one of the highlights of the project so far' (Forster, 2020).

In terms of whether these creators can do good creative work on digital platforms such as YouTube, I found SME-originating creators were overwhelmingly negative and professional-origin producers were pragmatically positive. The difference is explained by the fact the latter, unlike the former, are not stuck in the algorithm for their daily bread. As I showed in Chapter 2, for Sennett (2008, p. 9), the 'desire to do a job well for its own sake' is an 'enduring human impulse', but social and economic conditions 'often stand in the way of the craftsman's discipline and commitment'. Moreover, Bourdieu (2005, p. 45) and Csikszentmihalyi (2014, p. 68) both contend periods of idleness and leisure are essential to the quality of creativity. SME-origin creators Voigt and Philippou both reported good creative work *once could be* conducted on YouTube, but algorithm change had 'killed' (Voigt) and 'assassinated' (Philippou) creativity (Chapters 2 and 4, respectively). Time-poor creators Reardon and Shackleford told me the make-or-break YouTube Recommender had become increasingly hard to predict and incoherent over time, stressing their creativity. In terms of their scripted work, the algorithm change effectively suppressed higher quality, labour-intensive content in favour of longer, but *easier-to-produce* videos that promoted longer total session times among online audiences. YouTube veteran Voigt made precisely the same observation in Chapter 2. On the reverse side of the coin, I showed in Chapter 8 none of the professionals complained of not being able to do good creative work, despite the prevalence of fast shoots.

Maroun is an exception among the creatively stressed social media entertainers. True to generations of creatives before her, Maroun emphasizes the importance of her creative autonomy and 'flow'. In observing the creative experience, Csikszentmihalyi (2014, p. 173) coins the term 'flow' to describe the motivating feelings analogue artists report when their skills become so adept they come naturally, and their focus becomes so intense as to lose track of time. Says Maroun:

> There's two industries. What I do now is just very free flowing. I noticed that working with *Neighbours*. There were a lot of contracts and people about you telling you what to change and what to do. But I like having creative control over what I am doing. I'm hesitant about going into a structured industry format. Maybe we are pioneering a new method of film.
>
> *Maroun, 2015*

Authenticity

Authenticity is tied into the diversity that characterizes successful web-series, especially the participatory, iterative web-series of Kalceff, Ward and Forster. Hollywood was always concerned with authenticity (Custen & Custen, 1992, p. 7), but it was top down for mass markets worldwide. The role of diversity in screen storytelling is not mere political correctness. Words and representations matter. The more diverse and inclusive the creators and writer-producers, the more diverse stories can be authentically told and heard. The latest compact filming hardware, and Kalceff-style co-creativity, was used to invite the audience to participate in *Flunk* (Figure 9.4). The production model was less a traditional model of a six-week shoot and more a flexible model, which directly gave rise to the circular feedback phenomenon that helped characterize the success of *Starting from Now*, discussed in Chapter 9. Rowland said the Blackmagic Design allowed a low-cost, fast shoot that 'democratized' filmmaking:

> We've been able to make the show, put it out there, get the feedback from our audience, what they like and what they don't like and adjust as we make it. They're getting a product they enjoy a lot more and wouldn't be possible if we were having to rent equipment every time we shot.
>
> *Kornits, 2019*

Kalceff evolved her co-creative practice of the five seasons of *Starting from Now*, adapting the couples' storylines in response to viewer consensus, and ultimately attributes this 'listening' – and the acting – to the transnational success of the

FIGURE 9.4 Lighter gear opening up film-making to women: Rowland attributes the Ursa Mini Pro and Pocket Cinema light Pocket Camera 4K (pictured) to enabling significant co-creativity

series (Kalceff, 2017). However as pictured in the comment stream here below, Forster appears to have pre-absorbed Kalceff's hard-won learning, and jumps straight to asking viewers to inform the series about who would make 'a good couple'. Forster too is active in the comment streams, inviting the audience to participate in the storyworld of *Flunk* (Figure 9.5).

Forster told me in developing his version of iterative, participatory narrative-making, he did not look specifically at other web-series. Rather, he drew on his past experience of managing social channels – and granular-level social analytics – to learn when the audience tells you something, you should listen:

> The audience shaped the narrative. We quickly learned which characters and storylines were more popular - in our case, Ingrid's journey of self-discovery and exploration of same sex relationships. There was an opportunity for the show to lean into the storylines and give the audience more of what they were responding to. Given the show appeared on YouTube as roughly 5-minute episodes, we were also able to see on a minute by minute basis which parts of episodes were more popular and learn which moments got viewers hooked.
>
> *Forster, 2020*

Underlining 'the garden in the machine' phenomenon extant in the vibrant community spaces of these participatory web-series, fans 'write themselves' into the storyworlds of their favourite creators, via remixes on the most popular social media for young women, Instagram. Arguably, this produsage shows how 'teens write their community into being' (boyd, 2006, p. 2). This trend of fans writing themselves into online entertainment – we also saw in the case of Voigt (Chapter 2), Racka (Chapter 4), and SketchSHE (Chapter 6), has also been provoked by the characters and storytelling in *Flunk*:

flunk new love episiode 26

Flunk Series 2 years ago
Can't wait to see more Flunk? Watch the full 23 minute episode NOW on Vimeo and find out what happens between Ingrid and Dani: https://bit.ly/2NNuOCE - Don't forget to post a comment letting us know what you think of the new romance!

👍 46   💬   REPLY

▾ View 6 replies from Flunk Series and others

2 years ago
Dani is super cool, Ingrid will be fine with her💜💜💜💜Stella dies of jealousy🙈

👍 273   💬   🗨   REPLY

1 year ago
AHHH QUE LINDA MANO SOCORRO
cê merece Ingridinha 🙈

👍 6   💬   REPLY

2 years ago
I would like to see Ingrid and Dani, together. I think that they will be a good couple.

👍 149   💬   🗨   REPLY

2 years ago
I ship it 100% time for Ingrid to find herself some happiness and have fun

👍 55   💬   🗨   REPLY

2 years ago (edited)
I love Dani!! She's so cute!! Ugh I wish I could pay Vimeo bc waiting will be hard🙈.

FIGURE 9.5 Flunk actors perform, and beneath in the comment streams, Flunk fans express adoration for the actors

Like Kalceff and Ward before him, Forster reported these fan remixes and mashup videos were created by fans around key couples in the show:

> The audience invested in the storylines – you can see it in the comments where they fiercely argue for one couple versus another...We are so grateful they enjoy the show enough to want to support it [through merchandise sales], and help spread the word.
>
> *Forster, 2020*

Democratization of filmmaking has given rise to new diverse voices, but also a new set of algorithmic gatekeepers. Former *Neighbours* producer Peter Dodds argues the meaning of any particular *Neighbours* episode 'is best understood as being filtered by the constraints governing production and direction', especially the 'G' classification (Sergi and Dodds, 2003, p. 75). It was a source of frustration for Dodds the mass demographic of *Neighbours* provided a valuable forum for young people, yet the show's classification constrained coverage of health topics such as teenage drinking, pre-marital sex or condom use. By contrast, *Flunk* is reported to 'proudly explore sexuality, substance abuse and identity, issues facing teens daily, but rarely explored in mainstream media the way it is here' (Kornits, 2019). Indeed, the vision of greater diversity reflected on democratized media was one of the most important aspects of Screen Australia's original vision for the MPF (Cowap, 2017):

> Filmmakers can make stuff themselves and don't have to wait permission or money from anyone. We are seeing something much more reflective of Australia's rich diverse society and multiculturalism, LGBT. They don't have to wait for a conservative broadcaster to come around to the fact there's an audience for this content – they can do it themselves. That's something we have been proud to respond to.
>
> *Cowap, 2017*

Indeed, Forster is alive to the meaningful problem-solving engendered by some web-series:

> One of the real highlights was receiving heartfelt messages and comments from viewers speaking about how the show helped them in some way – they were dealing with similar issues to the characters and they found the show a source of comfort. Some were very humbling.
>
> *Forster, 2020*

References

Ashton, P. (2011). *The calling card script: A writer's toolbox for screen, Stage and Radio*. Bloomsbury Publishing Plc.

Banks, M. (2010). Craft labour and creative industries. *International Journal of Cultural Policy, 16*(3), 305–321.

Burgess, J., & Green, J. (2018). *YouTube: Online video and participatory culture.* John Wiley & Sons.

Bassaget, J., & Burkholder, M. (2019). *Short, narrative & serialized: A complete guide to the web series phenomenon.* Kindle Edition. https://www.amazon.com.au/Short-Narrative-Serialized-complete-phenomenon-ebook/dp/B07SX4Z991

Bourdieu, P. (2005). The political field, the social science field, and the journalistic field. In E. Neveu & R. Benson (Eds.), *Bourdieu and the journalistic field.* Polity Press.

boyd, danah (2006). Friends, Friendsters, and MySpace Top 8: Writing Community into Being on Social Network Sites. First Monday 11:12, December. http://www.firstmonday.org/issues/issue11_12/boyd/index.html

Caldwell, J. (2004). Convergence television: Aggregating form and repurposing content in the culture of conglomeration. In J. Olsson, & L. Spigel (Eds), *Television after TV* (pp. 35–74). Duke University Press.

Caldwell, J. T. (2010). Breaking ranks: Backdoor workforces, messy workflows, and craft disaggregation. *Popular Communication, 8*(3), 221–226.

Caldwell, J. T. (2013). Para-industry: Researching Hollywood's Blackwaters. *Cinema Journal, 52*(3), 157–165.

Cameron, A., Verhoeven, D., & Court, D. (2010). Above the bottom line: Understanding Australian screen content producers. *Media International Australia, 136,* 90–102.

Cowap, M. (2017). Screen Australia multi-platform investment manager. Phone interview with Guy Healy, Brisbane, March.

Cunningham, S., & Craig, D. (2019). *Social media entertainment.* New York University Press.

Creator Academy (n.d.) *How is my channel doing?* [Blog]. YouTube, San Bruno. https://creatoracademy.youtube.com/page/lesson/using-analytics

Csikszentmihalyi, M. (2014). *The systems model of creativity.* Springer.

Custen, G. F., & Custen, G. (1992). *Bio/pics: How Hollywood constructed public history.* Rutgers University Press.

Deloitte (2019). *The Deloitte global millennial survey 2019.* Deloitte Touche Tohmatsu Limited.

Downes, L., & Nunes, P. (2013). Big bang disruption. *Harvard Business Review, Mar 1,* 44–56.

Duffy, E. (2015). The labour of visibility: Gendered self-expression in the social media imaginary. *Selected papers of the 16th annual meeting of the association of internet researchers.* AoIR. https://spir.aoir.org/ojs/index.php/spir/article/view/9040.

Ellis, S., & Brown, M. (2017). *Hacking growth: How today's fastest-growing companies drive breakout success.* Currency Press.

Forster, R. (2017, 2019, 2020, 2021). Skype interviews, and email with then Fremantle Media writer-producer-director Ric Forster, with Guy Healy, Brisbane.

Forsyth, S., & Rogstad, K. (2015). Sexual health issues in adolescents and young adults. *Clinical Medicine, 15*(5), 447.

Gibson, W. (2005). God's little toys, WIRED. Conde Nast, San Francisco. Retrieved from: https://www.wired.com/2005/07/gibson-3/

Healy, G. (2019). Fast and furious filmmaking: YouTube's prospects for budding and veteran screen content producers. *Metro Magazine: Media & Education Magazine, 202,* 114–120.

Higgs, P., Cunningham, S., & Bakhshi, H. (2008). Beyond the creative industries: Mapping the creative economy in the United Kingdom, NESTA (formerly the National Endowment for Science, Technology and the Arts), London.

Horowitz, J. M., & Graf, N. (2019). *Most US teens see anxiety and depression as a major problem among their peers.* Pew Research Center, February, 20.

Judah, S. (2015). Place your bets: Unknown odds at the 2014 screen forever conference. *Metro, 184*(Autumn), 123.

Kalceff, J. (2017, 2020). Founder and director of Common Language Films. Skype interview with Guy Healy.

Kaufman, P., & Mohan, J. (2008). *The economics of independent film and video distribution in the digital age.* Tribeca Film Institute.

Katz, M. (2008). Recycling copyright: Survival & (and) growth in the remix age. *Intellectual Property Law Bulletin, 13*(1), 21–62.

Koch, C., Lode, M., Stohr, D., Rizk, A., & Steinmetz, R. (2018). Collaborations on YouTube: From unsupervised detection to the impact on video and channel popularity. *ACM Transactions on Multimedia Computing, Communications, and Applications (TOMM), 14*(4), 1–28.

Kornits, D. (2019). Melanie Rowland: Top grade. FilmInk, 23 April. https://www.filmink.com.au/melanie-rowland-top-grade

Lange, P. G. (2007). Fostering friendship through video production: How youth use YouTube to enrich local interaction. In *Proceedings of Annual Meeting of the International Communication Association* (Vol. 27). ICA.

Lanham, R. A. (2011). The two markets. *Library Resources & Technical Services, 52*(2), 3–11.

Lessig, L. (2004). Free(ing) culture for remix. *Utah Law Review, 2004*(4), 961–976.

Lessig, L. (2006, Oct 20). The Ethics of Web 2.0: YouTube vs. Flickr, Revver, Eyespot, blip.tv, and even Google [Blog] Retrieved from: https://www.lessig.org/2006/10/the-ethics-of-web-20-youtube-v/

Litt, E. (2012). Knock, knock. Who's there? The imagined audience. *Journal of Broadcasting & Electronic Media, 56*(3), 330–345.

Livingston, P. (2009). Poincaré's 'delicate sieve': On creativity and constraints in the arts. In K. Bardsley, D. Dutton, & M. Krauz (Eds.), *The idea of creativity* (pp. 126–146). Brill.

Loist, S. (2016). The film festival circuit: Networks, hierarchies, and circulation. In M. de Valck, B. Kredell, & S. Loist (Eds.), *Film Festivals: History, Theory, Method, Practice* (pp. 49–64). Routledge.

Lotz, A. D. (2017). *Portals: A treatise on internet-distributed television.* Michigan Publishing, University of Michigan Library.

Maroun, L. (2015). Creator (LunaMaroun). Interview with Stuart Cunningham and Andrew Golledge, 23 March.

McKee, A. (2004). How to tell the difference between production and consumption: A case study in *Doctor Who* fandom. In S. Gwenllian-Joes & R. E. Pearson (Eds.), *Cult television.* University of Minnesota Press.

McRobbie, A. (2004). 'Everyone is creative': Artists as pioneers of the new economy. In E. Silva & T. Bennett (Eds.), *Contemporary culture and everyday life.* Routledge-Cavendish.

McRobbie, A. (2016). *Be creative: Making a living in the new culture industries.* Polity Press.

Monaghan, W. (2017). Starting From… Now and the web series to television crossover: An online revolution?. *Media International Australia, 164*(1), 82–91.

Napoli, P. M. (2003). *Audience economics: Media institutions and the audience marketplace.* Columbia University Press.

Rowland, M. (2020). Producer, Flunk, personal communication with Guy Healy, Brisbane.

Ryan, M., Cunningham, S., & Verhoeven, D. (2012). 2nd Australian producer survey 2012: understanding Australian screen content producers: wave 2.

Screen Australia (2021). Flunk [blog]. Screen guide, Screen Australia, Sydney. https://www.screenaustralia.gov.au/the-screen-guide/t/flunk-2021/38328/

Sennett, R. (2008). *The craftsman*. Yale University Press.

Sergi, M., & Dodds, P. (2003). How reality bites: The production of Australian soap operas. *Media International Australia, 106*, 71–83.

Throsby, D., & Zednik, A. (2011). Multiple job-holding and artistic careers: Some empirical evidence. *Cultural Trends, 20*(1), 9–24.

Van Vuuren, K., Ward, S., & Coyle, R. (2013). Revisiting the greening of prime-time television soap operas. *Media International Australia, 146*(1), 35–47.

Ward, T. C. (2019, 2020, 2021). Creator, anyone but me; Skype interviews with Guy Healy.

Webster, J. G., & Ksiazek, T. B. (2012). The dynamics of audience fragmentation: Public attention in an age of digital media. *Journal of Communication, 62*(1), 39–56.

Weiss, G. (2017, May 4). Here's how the YouTube 'Adpocalypse' is affecting top creators. Tubefilter Inc, Los Angeles. https://www.tubefilter.com/2017/05/04/how-youtube-adpocalypse-affected-top-creators/

Wesch, M. (2010). Lessons from YouTube [web-video]. https://www.youtube.com/watch?v=lNwvPauwbFg&t=43s

10

TINA CESA WARD

The New York film director
who fell into web-series

Veteran film-makers say films are not made but forced into existence; so goes the exceptional web-series. Previous cases elaborated the publication trajectories of new media creatives, many of them onto North American BVOD and SVOD platforms. This final case centres on a writer-producer-director raised in the hardest, most competitive school for filmmakers, the United States itself. The journey of Tina Cesa Ward dramatizes the momentous forces reshaping the increasingly promising production, but chaotic distribution environment for screen creatives. Crucially, to make a living from her screen storytelling centred on drama, Ward bypassed legacy TV to monetize platforms paradigmatic to the post-TV-broadcast era, AVOD platforms like YouTube, and SVOD platforms like Hulu and Amazon Prime, via her strategy of 'non-exclusive' licensing and uploading (Ward, 2019, 2020). Kalceff exhibited the same non-exclusive IP cycling strategy to diverse platforms in Chapter 7 with *Starting From Now*; and Forster in Chapter 9 with *Flunk*. The case also underlines the importance of sociality and collaboration to successful makers as they adapt to persistent disruption, especially in distribution.

Ward's storytelling career spans film school in Chicago, and the oldest of the performing arts, theatre, to her early pivot to new media on Strike.tv, and the algorithmic culture of social media, especially Twitter and YouTube, to the streamer for Hollywood studios, Hulu. Together with Guggenheim Fellow and two-time Obie winning playwright Susan Miller (*My Left Breast; The L Word; thirtysomething*), the pair wrote and produced *Anyone But Me* (*ABM*) (2008–2012, 2019), which won them the Writers Guild of America (WGA) inaugural Award for Original New Media in 2011 (Figure 10.1). This chapter draws on longitudinal interviews with Ward in 2019 and 2020 and an interview with Miller in late 2020. In addition to critical acclaim, *ABM* has attracted about 100 million views to 2020, making it one of the world's top five most watched web-series together

DOI: 10.4324/9781003182481-10

FIGURE 10.1   Susan Miller and Tina Cesa Ward executive produced *Anyone But Me* together, which won them the Writers Guild of America (WGA) inaugural Award for Original New Media in 2011 (Photo: Michael Seto)

with Felicia Day's *The Guild* (300 million views), Freddie Wong Productions' *Video Game High School* (2012–2014) (148 million views), Kalceff's *Starting from Now* (170 million views), and Hank Green and Bernie Su's *Lizzie Bennet Diaries* (2006–2013) (89 million views). *Anyone But Me*, the second oldest big impact web-series after the ground-breaking *The Guild,* 'broke barriers' as one of the 'few diverse indie series' to reach a distribution agreement with Hulu (Christian, 2018, p. 132). As such, this case epitomizes the transition of the web-series from the era of the 'handheld video camera, very low budget...deferred payment', to fully 'professional' endeavours (Miller in Kallas, 2014, p. 145).

This book suggests makers using the web-series format for their diverse new stories have been engaged in a 20-year struggle to win legitimacy from the traditional industry in the United States. America On Line (AOL) established the Webby's in the mid-1990s at the time of the proto-web-series, Scott Zakarin's *The Spot.* Web categories were only added to the mainstream TV industry's highest honour, the Prime-Time Emmys, in 2016. I argue even while the web-series format appears stigmatized in some Hollywood quarters, over the past seven years, the most innovative of the SVODs have been quietly acquiring or commissioning series from top makers operating in these littoral spaces, further burnishing these SVODs' credentials for diversity of the authentic kind

(Healy, forthcoming). For example, James Bland's *Giants* (2017–), premiered on Issa Rae's YouTube channel, won an audience of over five million, picked up an IAWTV award, and an Emmy, and crossed over to CleoTV, a subscriber channel 'for millennial women of color'.[1] Crucially for one of the overarching arguments of this book, this trajectory from littoral to formal platforms is precisely the same Hollywood and TV network-bypassing, creative autonomy-pursuing path beaten to these North American platforms by the cross-over Skip Aheaders and professional-origin makers, as foregrounded in my previous chapters.

Ward is an innovator in both storytelling and burgeoning distribution technologies. In the first section of this case, Biography, I trace Ward's early influences and emergence as a traditional creative, but her frustration with legacy media. We see her pivot to new media, and break-out with *ABM,* and her continued experimentation with diverse storytelling media. We consider Ward's efforts to get veteran Hollywood producers, The Caucus (Payne, 2017), to recognize the still marginalized community of many talented web-series storytellers as worthy collaborators; as well as her influential role as Chair of the International Academy of Web TV (IAWTV) in bridging the divide between the worlds of Hollywood and web-series makers. Indeed, these Los Angeles-based IAWTV awards have since allowed two web-series teams to distinguish themselves and attract cross-over deals with the most historically innovative premium cable companies, HBO and Showtime, via *A Whole New Irving* and *Flatbush Misdemeanours,* respectively (Ward, 2020). By late 2019, Ward had directed the second season of the multi-Emmy Award winning web-series, *After Forever.* Finally, in what may be her most impactful web-series advocacy yet, Ward (2020) foreshadows her efforts to package together some of the world's best web-series for her new channel to be launched via smart TVs this year.

Biography

Tina Cesa Ward grew up in Ohio, where she attended high school in Painesville. 'It's not a diverse area, to say the least. I don't know what it was, but I always kind of believed in activism and equal rights for everybody' (Payne, 2017). Ward describes Spike Lee's comedy-drama, '*Do the Right Thing*' (1989) as a career catalyst. Lee's film – 'a hard swift punch to the multi-headed beast of racism' (Lee & Jones, 1989, p. 16) – made her realize 'movies could be more – and do more – than big budget Hollywood productions' (Payne, 2017). To help fulfil her dream of being a director, she attended film school at Columbia College in Chicago, but left there a year later. She encountered the powerful traditional imaginary continues to drive short-filmmakers worldwide to this day, and indeed herself until 2008: 'You are always taught you just need one big short, and that will put you on your way'. While there, Ward remembers Max Rubenstein (*Hot Resort,* 1985), as a great screenwriting teacher who 'was listening to my voice, while still trying to teach me'. Rubenstein wanted to know why she wrote about 'such heavy dark stuff, social and political issues'. Ward says while her early work is social justice-driven, her later work is relationship-driven (Payne, 2017). Importantly for screenwriters frustrated by the dominant narrative heuristic of the hero's journey[2], Kalceff was also seen to prioritize character-driven storytelling in Chapter 7. Ward fell into theatre, directing for the stage, especially on *Freak Show*, and attracted her first acclaim, the Jean Dalrymple award for Best Director. From theatre, Ward learnt 'blocking', the choreography of actors, crew, sets, and equipment that must move harmoniously together to produce a scene of live performance. 'You are stripped away from worrying about camera angles; working just with actors, and the text' (Ward, 2020).

Like most aspiring screen creatives, she made a handful of short films, especially the eight-minute, minimalist drama for the traditional festival circuit, *In Their Absence* (2003) (Figure 10.2). The silent film explored themes of 'love, loneliness, loss and need'. The film was shot in one location in just two and a half days and was entered into numerous traditional film festivals. 'A period piece set in the 1940s about two lesbians may not be the short film that's going to put you over, and get you hired by the mainstream. But it helped me creatively and personally, especially the response to it' (Ward, 2020). Importantly, like HBO's long-standing strategy of attracting press 'buzz' around new titles (Lotz, 2018, p. 41), *In Their Absence* attracted like-minded, niche media attention – in this case from Curve magazine – which made it discoverable by niche audiences. Meanwhile, Ward adapted a play she had directed into her first feature film, *Red Molly* (2006), the last longform she would make before turning to her life's work, adapting shortform episodic narrative to different combinations of creator-oriented socio-technological platforms.

FIGURE 10.2   The silent film, *In Their Absence* (2003)

Ward then tried to pull another feature together, but it was 'one of those heartbreaking things where you do all the right things, but it fell apart' (Ward, 2020). Fatefully, the spark for *ABM* was struck when a friend suggested Ward 'do something for the web'. This suggestion 'was completely outrageous at the time, because all we knew about YouTube was cat videos' (Ward, 2020). Indeed, the *New York Times* has wryly described cat videos as an essential 'building block' of the Internet (Willis, 2014). Ward had been focused on 'cinematic' longform narrative, not episodic storytelling, and the idea of doing scripted storytelling on YouTube 'seemed ridiculous'. However, in the end, her love of The WB's *Buffy the Vampire Slayer* (1997–2003), and ambition 'to make something as good as that' tipped her over to making episodic entertainment (Payne, 2017). Indeed, as Caldwell (2006, p. 112) observes, just like the audiences they serve, creatives are also consumers of cultural products, which informs their practice. Then, the *New York Times* and TIME declared 2006 'the year brought to you by you', especially 'the people's network' of YouTube, with all its unruly verisimilitude and individualism (Grossman, 2006; Pareles, 2006). Highlighting Miller and Ward's achievement in adapting scripted storytelling to new media, this was the time Hollywood and traditional media first attempted to marketize participatory culture, especially proto-social networks such as News Corp's $580 million buy, MySpace, via the low-budget web-series. News Corp and former Disney CEO Michael Eisner teamed up for *Prom Queen*, David Katzenberg and CBS Internet TV made *Clark & Michael* with A-List actor, Michael Cera, Blake Calhoun produced *Pink*, and then Producers Guild of America president, Marshall Herskovitz, and collaborator, Edward Zwick, made *Quarterlife*.

Breakout

Miller and Ward were seasoned theatre dramatists, who had to get expert advice on what web-series were. Fortunately, the web-series community was 'lovely' as regards their keenness 'to learn from and help each other' (Miller, 2020). Miller and Ward were also quick studies. Ward paid just $3500 for the first two episodes of *ABM* and quickly raised more for the next episodes. They were overjoyed when the first attracted 500 views in a day (Kallas, 2014). The pair helped sustain themselves through the notorious, labour intensive, 'valley-of-death' script production period freelancing on Miller's branded series, *Bestsellers,* released in 2011. In production from 2008 to 2012, *ABM's* views were the first of a coming 100 million for its life of three seasons (Ward, 2020). Eleven of their episodes went onto attract a minimum of 1 million views each, four of them a minimum of 5 million, and one, '*Welcome to the Party*' (Figure 10.3), 20 million views and counting. The fan base for this multi-platform-based web-series spread globally to comprise the UK, Germany, the Netherlands, France, China, South America, and Canada, becoming necessarily international enough to attract decent monetization. Importantly, these web-series do not exhibit transmedia storytelling, where Jenkins (2010, p. 944) says key elements 'of a fiction get dispersed systematically

Anyone But Me Season One: Ep. 7 "Welcome to the Party, Now Clean Up the Mess."

0:28 / 7:19

FIGURE 10.3 Rachael Hip-Flores (Vivian) and Nicole Pacent (Aster) in *Anyone But Me*. This episode alone achieved over 19 million views on YouTube as of 2021

across multiple delivery channels for the purpose of creating a unified and coordinated entertainment experience'. Instead, under the multiplatform creative labour of the successful web-series maker (Healy, 2019), writer-producers use diverse social media for informal distribution and online community building. As the community is built, attention is directed to the priority platforms where the episodic shortform narrative is windowed, and thus monetized via modest, multiple revenue streams. For example, *ABM* has now been up, and attracting revenue from multiple platforms for over a decade:

> Blip.tv were a huge advocate for us. I loved them. Blip was out of New York; our main platform. But we would be wherever we could be. YouTube was always our third platform in terms of pushing. Hulu was only domestic at the time, and not a ton of people subscribed. But Hulu had great prestige because your show was on next to *Scandal* (2012-2018), and that was great for us …It's accurate to say over Blip.tv, Hulu, Amazon Prime and YouTube, from which we have 75 million views, we are nearing 100 million views'.
>
> *Ward, 2020*

I attribute the break-out success of *Anyone But Me* to three key elements working in unison: first, the creative product was story-driven, and rooted in authenticity; second; Miller and Ward's experiment-driven mastery of the volatile forces dominating post-broadcast TV; and third; their hybrid model of creative autonomy slipped the bonds of controlling studio executives.

First, their story concerns 'the daughter of a NYC firefighter, Vivian, who has no choice but to leave the city with her Dad after health problems he suffered trying to save people on September 11th force him to retire'. In another example of the socially inspired nature of novel creativity, this story arose out of Ward and Miller's experience of the post-9-11 streets of where they lived. Ward told me:

> I realized all these kids growing up in 2007, even teenagers had never seen New York prior to 9-11. They can't get out of the subway without seeing, 'See Something, Say Something'. There's random checks, there's military. I was curious to explore. But these kids are: 'whatever. It's every day' But for us it was 'oooh'.

Ward, 2019

Policing in New York became increasingly paramilitary (Murray, 2005, p. 354) in the wake of the 'asymmetrical' terror attacks in the United States, which upended the world order (Williams & Taylor, 2003, p. 26).

Ward wanted to tell stories 'about identity and the struggles of figuring out who you are when you're a kid, so more characters came into play from every background, race, gender and sexual orientation' (Eckerling, 2010). Underlining the story-enabling affordance of the web, Ward (2020) told me she 'likes making heavy Bergman-esque dramas, so the web gave me the chance to do it'. Influential Swedish film-maker, Ingmar Bergman, best known for films such as *The Seventh Seal* (1957) and *Persona* (1966), has a dark, 'troublesome' quality to his works which 'revel in human frailty, in every crisis capable of disrupting life', according to Livingston (1982, p. 15). Making *Anyone But Me* and her later *Good People in Love* (2014), reinforced Ward's drive to write drama, and hold fast to this vision for herself: 'I've always known I wanted to work in drama. I've found this is the world for me. I don't care what anyone tells me it's not going to fly; I am going to stick with it because eventually it will' (Ward, 2020). Drama itself is regarded as the purgative, cathartic process involved in 'the clearing up of the vision of the soul by the removal of obstacles...for truly or correctly knowing' (Nussbaum in Winston, 1996, p. 193). Miller attributes the success of the series to their 'beautifully talented (and beautiful!) cast' and evolving the scripting of the characters in a well-planned and 'strict' fashion (Lipkin, 2009; Miller, 2020). Ward says a mix of genres was also important to the show: 'a teenage drama mixed with quirky romantic comedy'. Arguably, Miller and Ward – steeped in film and theatre history – adapted dramatic storytelling for the algorithmically based, multi-platform society, via 'economising, getting at something essential' with the dialogue (Miller, 2020). For Ward, 'I like to say a lot on every inch of the page. That's a big reason why I love doing web-series. Every word, every action in every episode of *ABM* counts' (Ward, 2009). As Csikszentmihalyi (2015, p. 280) found, the best artists are obsessed with the past achievements of their domain, but also a desire after the new possibilities of the future, to express them in the present.

Second, of all the cases in this book, *ABM* cycled its IP across the highest number of platforms: one social media giant YouTube; two rival global streamers, Hulu and Amazon Prime; three niche longform narrative platforms long since shuttered, Strike.tv, Blip.tv, and Koldcast; and one YouTube-born, multi-channel network, Fullscreen. Miller's social, and professional contacts in New York opened valuable doors for *ABM* in regard to Strike.tv and Blip.tv. *ABM* also streamed on niche culture site, Lesbian Nation's AfterEllen. *ABM* launched first on WGA writer, Peter Hyoguchi's Strike.tv, before moving to Blip.tv, proving its deep resonance with audiences for the eventual advertising revenue deal with Hulu (Ward, 2019). Strike.tv – born of the WGA's 100-day strike in 2008 to secure a fair share of royalties for online streaming – proved a crucial turning point in the development of the web-series. Long suffering screenwriters historically subjected to studio production notes, multiple authorship and horror stories during script 'development hell' that marginalized their creativity (Conor, 2014, p. 74), finally glimpsed an opportunity for creative freedom. In the preceding years, Miller herself had sold four original screenplays to Fox, Universal, Disney and Warner Bros – a rare feat in itself, 'but they were never produced' (Kallas, 2014, p. 144). Dozens of web-series went into production on Strike.tv, but, of them all, Joss Whedon's *Dr Horrible's Sing-Along Blog* and *Anyone But Me* distinguished themselves (Christian, 2018, p. 38). Miranda J. Banks (2010, p. 26) notes Whedon was 'among the most prominent striking WGA members', being best known as the showrunner of The WB's acclaimed TV series, *Buffy: The Vampire Slayer* (1997–2003).

Third, the development of the narrative arc of *ABM* was an important hybrid that slipped the constraints of Hollywood production notes, to revel in the newfound creative autonomy afforded by the web-series, generatively informed by live theatre-style audience feedback. In his ultimately successful pitch to striking creatives at the time, Strike.tv chief executive, Peter Hyoguchi said: 'For 100 years creative professionals have wanted to create their own content and own it, and control it, but haven't been able to do that' (Christian, 2018, p. 176). Crucially, Miller agrees, telling me: 'The most important thing, and one of the best experiences of my life, and I am sure Tina (Cesa Ward) agrees, was *Anyone But Me*, because we owned it'.

When I asked Ward (2020) to account for the success of *ABM*, she said – just like the boisterous reception that greeted Julie Kalceff's *Starting From Now* – *ABM* fans were vocal about which characters they wanted to be lovers, and which characters were right and wrong for each other. Fans were especially vocal on Twitter, where Miller and Ward engaged fans 'in an all-out and constant effort', some of which continues to this day (Miller, 2020; Ward, 2020). However, unlike the style of narrative co-creativity elaborated by Kalceff and Forster in Chapters 7 and 9, Miller and Ward stress they stopped short of allowing the audience to 'break stories' with them, Hollywood jargon for plot twists and turns:

> We had a big reaction to Nicole who played Aster right off the bat. 'Wow, we thought we have to make sure Aster is in each show. It's not as if Aster

wasn't a significant part, it suddenly just became much more of Vivian and Aster's series, just because of the reaction. Nicole was so wonderful we just wanted to keep writing more stuff for her. We wanted to see her on screen. Both her and Rachael Hip-Flores who played Vivian, were so great together. Writing it, then seeing them together, then seeing the reaction certainly expanded their relationship on screen, and in the story itself. [But] people would also want this, that, or the other. But we thought, 'No, we are sticking to what we are going to do'. Sometimes they always wanted them (Vivian and Aster) together. But then once again, like everybody said, 'Once they are together, what do you do?' They always have to have strife; otherwise, what sort of drama is this?

Ward, 2020

When web-series resonate with online fans, Miller (in Kallas, 2014, p. 149) likens the audience to the ancient Greek chorus, the 'informed audiences' of Athenian citizens who came together to fulfil their civic duties in open air theatre (Arnott, 1991 p. 23). Feedback from fans is 'instant…which is a lot like theatre…I see them as the chorus, our fans on Twitter and Facebook. They participate, it's communal, but we don't invite them to tell us how the story should go' (Miller in Kallas, 2014).

During 2011, Ward made her most experimental web-series, the five-part *Good People in Love*, distributed on Vimeo, YouTube, and Out TV in Canada, but also on the now defunct Blip (Figure 10.4). The series – which would go onto win Best Dialogues at the Rome Web Awards in 2014 – sought, successfully, to test the proposition a web-series could be made 'for practically nothing' (Landa, 2011).

FIGURE 10.4   Good People in Love (2011), 'made for practically nothing' one weekend

But again, it had to be fast filmmaking: the series was made for US$1100 over a weekend (Ward, 2019). Set on the eve of New York's approval for same-sex marriage, the series focuses on an engagement party where two couples, one gay, one straight, explore what Ward believed was gap in the conversation about committed relationships: 'We've gone through life thinking we don't have that option, and what happens when we do have that option?' Moreover, Ward conceived the series 'to test the waters for what the web is willing to watch. It's a drama you need to engage in; it's not a simple little story' (Ward, 2019). Paralleling the unrelenting film style of one of her Muses, Ingmar Bergman, her *Good People in Love* is 'hard-hitting' since she wanted to have 'those classic elements you saw more of in the 1970's…I wanted to make something that didn't pull any punches' (Ward, 2019). The 1970s was best known for a slew of films that finally demolished the 1930s era, 'Hays code' that had controlled what sex and violence could, and could not, be depicted on American theatre screens, now known as 'New Hollywood': *Wanda* (1970), *Straw Dogs* (1971), *Dog Day Afternoon* (1975), *Taxi Driver* (1976) and *Norma Rae* (1979) (Thomson, 2012, p. 430). Digiday described the series 'as good as any drama on television', and crucially included *ABM* hyperlinks in their story, enhancing its discoverability. Shackleford – in Chapter 6 – said the tactic was among those crucial to the spreadability of her content. Ward's series also experiments with characters sometimes narrating the story themselves, so breaking the fourth wall. The fourth wall is a narrative device that sustains 'the illusion of the story world', the destruction of which, depending upon context, either risks shattering this illusion, or can 'intensify our relationship with the drama' (Brown, 2013). Rachael Hip-Flores returns in *Good People in Love* to play Sarah, one of the characters who also narrates.

By 2013, Ward had returned in *Producing Juliet*, an 11-part web-series about playwright Juliet, who was in love with a gay man, and her friend Rebecca, in an open relationship. Underlining the importance of ad and license fee income to web-series makers, the new series was 'made on her own dime', being partly funded from her *ABM* royalties (Ward, 2019). The series premiered at the Raindance Film Festival in September 2013 attracted three 2014 Indie Series Award nominations including Best direction. In 2015, Ward won the IAWTV award for Best Writing (Drama). Still true to her 'economical' scripting style from *ABM* we saw above, Ward told AfterEllen (2013) she 'always liked the idea of saying something that means everything in as few words as possible, so I think the medium is fitting'. Story and medium are seen to shape each other: 'I love language because of the characters that inhabit this world. I really start to move in this direction with *Good People in Love*, and now I am excited to go further down that path'. Another telling aspect of Ward's methodology is her foregrounding of not just under-represented identities, but topics most important to their community: 'I often like to dive into issues that affect our lives as gay and lesbians no one really talks about' (Piccoli, 2013). We saw this same 'identification of an important gap' strategy by Erin Good and Taylor Litton-Strain in their *Jade of Death* in Chapter 8. Ward tells niche media and blogger audiences if they want to see a second season, 'big numbers' of views are needed for the first season (Piccoli, 2013), so priming audiences to participate by sharing her content with their friends. This aspect of relational labour parallels exemplar entrepreneurial cellist, Zoe Keating, who is vocal on social media that she lives on album sales, and fans choosing not to pay, 'might actually hurt them' (Baym, 2018).

After dealing with many web-series colleagues on the West Coast for many years, Ward made the decision to return to Los Angeles, and live, this time as a seasoned operator. Artists have longed shifted from city to city to best exploit market conditions where they can pursue their work 'with the least hinderance' (Csikszentmihalyi, 2014, p. 113). From 2015 to 2018, the irrepressible storyteller in Ward was exhibited when she turned her attention to digital comics with *Delegates* and *Guards of Dagmar,* the latter about 'a world of monsters, heroes and mysteries'. Ward started writing scripts for comic books as submission pieces, and explains with the digital age, 'we now have our chance to get our work out into the world without gatekeepers' (Vasseur, 2018). Her inspiration for *Delegates,* co-created with Bin Lee, was again character-driven: 'I was always interested in how characters made decisions in the world we created. A lot of our story was driven by the desire to get our characters in a particular situation and see how they would react (Vasseur, 2018). During 2015, Miller and Ward returned to *ABM* releasing *The Lost Scenes* on Hulu and YouTube, an episode of which attracted views in the millions. The episode Miller wrote attracted a WGA award nomination. Ward established a company to work as a self-employed executive producer, writer, director, and consulting developer. In 2016, she joined the IAWTV's board, rising to Chair shortly thereafter: 'I've always loved the web world so much. I feel it's given me so much, I wanted to do something to help others make things as well' (Ward, 2019).

As Chair, Ward responded positively to overtures from the small but prestigious group of progressive Hollywood TV writers, producers, and directors, known as The Caucus, who style themselves 'the creative conscience' of Hollywood. In a significant development for rapprochement between the worlds of Hollywood and web-series makers in 2017, the IAWTV became the New Media division of The Caucus. Strikingly, as a I showed in previous chapters, the two worlds falling towards each other's skillsets was paralleled in Australia under Skip Ahead, but in a structured, modestly funded way driven by Google and Screen Australia. Screen Australia itself assumed both the cultural and commercial responsibilities of the peak agencies from which it was formed in 2008, with an emphasis on convergent audio-visual industries of film, TV and online (Trevisanut, 2019, p. 380). Arguably, in the IAWTV and Caucus case, each world has what the other lacks, but most requires. For the web-series makers, they most need seed capital, political know-how to deal with what Ward (2019) describes as 'the big Hollywood machine', and, above all, discoverability. On the reverse of the coin, post the 2007–2008 Writers strike, Banks (2010, p. 20) observed many veteran Hollywood producers were 'deep in a process of modifying their skills' to produce content for the new platforms, so concerned were they about the 'death of Hollywood' film and TV. Indeed, Ward (2020) says The Caucus recognized the need to embrace the other world of new media to 'blend' their craft labour with digital creative labour, in Caldwell's sense, as I showed in Chapter 2.

> Every press outlet had the same Top 10 web-series. There was only a small percentage of amazing web storytellers who would get noticed, when there's tons of people making amazing stuff. The idea was to bring The Caucus, a veteran organisation of TV producers, directors and writers, together with IAWTV, and hope to bridge the gap between traditional and new media. Now Hollywood knows how to get hold of us should they want and go and make shortform (episodic) content, by bridging the gap with the IAWTV awards. Hopefully through The Caucus they'll say, 'Hey, here's some money, go and make some content.
>
> *Ward, 2019*

In 2019 Miller and Ward released an hour-long 10th anniversary special of ABM, again via Hulu and later YouTube. Ward directed the second season of the multi-Emmy Award winning web-series, *After Forever*, which went onto to stream on Amazon Prime and Australian OTT, Binge Figure 10.5. The following year, Ward won an Indie Series Award for Directing in a Drama, while *After Forever* won Best Drama Series.

> The story itself fits my proclivities: a middle-aged gay man dealing with the death of his husband. That's not a story I've seen anywhere, and I loved being a part of that.
>
> *Ward, 2021*

FIGURE 10.5 Ward directed the second season of the multi-Emmy Award winning shortform series, *After Forever*

By 2020, Ward was again positioned ahead of the curve. She advocated for the success of the US$1 billion Quibi venture led by Hollywood veterans Jeffrey Katzenberg and Meg Whitman. Quibi, short for 'quick bites', promised 'the next generation of film narrative': shortform serialised narratives formatted for smart-phones, but made by Hollywood A-Listers (Shambler, 2019). However, Quibi, billed as 'Netflix for the Instagram and Tik Tok generation' (Shambler, 2019), announced in October 2020 it was shutting down after just six months with 500,000 subscribers, far short of its seven million subscriber target.

> I was really pushing for Quibi to do well. To have that platform that was open to shortform – under 15 minutes – would have been set up for us. I was hoping with Quibi it would liven up the idea of shortform episodic.
>
> *Ward, 2020*

As an artist, Ward was working in a domain being buffeted by the transformation of TV to the post-network TV era, but a domain drawing oxygen away from broadcast TV as niche online audiences in the multi-millions were attracted to web-series that spoke their identities in ways important to them. Accordingly, Ward has been building a distribution arm capable of bringing shortform epi-sodic the discovery she argues the format desperately needs:

> If you look at it now, we have so many OTT's; you have Samsung putting out content; Vizio putting out content; all these folks putting out content, but you need to have a decent amount, at least 50 hours of content to get on with those, so I am working on bringing some of these great shows together and putting them on there.
>
> *Ward, 2020*

Most recently, Ward had turned her hand to writing a column on same sex mar-riage, and continued to develop new shows to pitch to networks and streamers for her day job at Trifecta in Los Angeles. Ward continues to work on *Delegates* as its illustrated and released.

Burning problems

Monetization, sustainability, and the A/B List

In the United States, cable TV has a reputation for heightened creativity, but budgets can be so stressed the issue for showrunners is Writers' Room creatives 'are more worried about going broke than about creating the story' (Curtin & Sanson, 2017, p. 29). The go-to model for financing ultra-low budget features and documentaries has been 'the use of credit cards and loans from family and friends' (de Roeper & Luckman, 2009, p. 11), often supplemented, usually very modestly, by crowdfunding platforms such as Kickstarter or Patreon (Shapiro &

Aneja, 2017, p. 8). But in the United States overall, the lack of resources or private investment or state subvention available for web-series, has meant 'you can only tell one kind of story' (Ward, 2020), mainly, much like Europe, autobiographies (Knol & Trostrum, 2014). As a principle of creativity, Csikszentmihalyi (2015, p. 113) found subsistence societies – which arguably parallel the tough economic conditions faced by emergent storytellers – have 'fewer opportunities to encourage and reward novelty, especially if it is expensive to produce'. Indeed, bankers and financiers regard investments in the cultural industries as a 'high-risk, low-profit' proposition (La Torre, 2016, p. 2).

In Murdock and Golding (2016) terms, *ABM,* being in the United States without a subvention culture, was only able to draw on markets and gifting and collaboration. At the creator level, the distribution ecology means the very high bar of multiple seasons of an extremely popular web-series being put up or licensed to multiple AVODs and SVODs, but on 'a non-exclusive basis' that favours the creator, says Ward. On *ABM*, the whole US$250,000 cost of the series was raised from a combination of 'an angel investor', crowdsourcing from fans, and from advertising and licensing revenue from YouTube, Blip, Hulu, Amazon, and other platforms at different times (Ward, 2020). Importantly, while 'not a huge amount', this ad revenue paid for *The Lost Scenes* and the *10th Anniversary Special* of *ABM* (Ward, 2021). The tendency for individual consumers to silo themselves on one platform, with one subscription meant multiplatform labour had to be maximized:

> You have to make sure you are on a platform that gives you decent revenue. You are trying to find more revenue streams because monetization is not huge for us. Most of the time you are doing advertising revenue from AVODs such as YouTube and Vimeo-on-Demand, and SVODs such as Hulu and Amazon'.
>
> *Ward, 2020*

Even so, Ward is frank her income does not match the US$100,000 income defined – rather aspirationally – as 'middle-class' by YouTube business officer, Robert Kyncl, as elaborated in Chapter 2. Ward says $100,000 'is a great middle class', and while *ABM* has done better than most in revenue over the past 12 years, 'I am in no way coming close to that figure (Ward, 2020). Ward says she and Miller are still repaying their angel investor, but they are happy they can continue to repay, 'even if it's taken a decade so far, and will probably take many more years to repay completely'.

Algorithmic and platform volatility

Overall, volatility is driven by the struggles over subscriber and transaction share among important US demographics between the newly dominant streamers, Netflix, Hulu, and Amazon in order, and the older mediums of cable and satellite (Liesman, 2018). The struggle over valuable telecommunications IP also drives volatility as giants such as Google make acquisitions to shape the market on favourable terms (Downes & Nunes, 2013). In contrast to many traditional creatives, web-series makers such as Ward are audience-centric, in the way only those whose livelihoods depend upon it are. As Ward says:

> They don't call it the world wide web for nothing. There's a lot of content out there and you have to know who your audience is, because not only are you going to be the writer, but you are also going to have to market the hell out of your series to get viewers.
>
> *Ward in Eckerling, 2010*

The streaming video platform business is also wracked with creative destruction. At the creator level, Ward (2020) told me to avoid being 'hurt', no web-series maker should take an exclusive deal, since to find audiences, it was necessary 'to be on as many platforms as you can' to get as many revenue streams as possible Figure 10.6. This combination was necessary to best exploit the industry's distribution structure: monetization offered by ad-supported platforms, or AVODs, and license fee income from platforms behind paywalls, such as SVODs, or pay-per-view outlets such as TVODs. As Joseph Schumpeter (1942, p. 84) has observed, the essential fact about capitalism is the 'incessant' destruction of the old economic structure and creation of the new from within, 'a perennial gale of creative destruction'. Highlighting the platform volatility confronting any

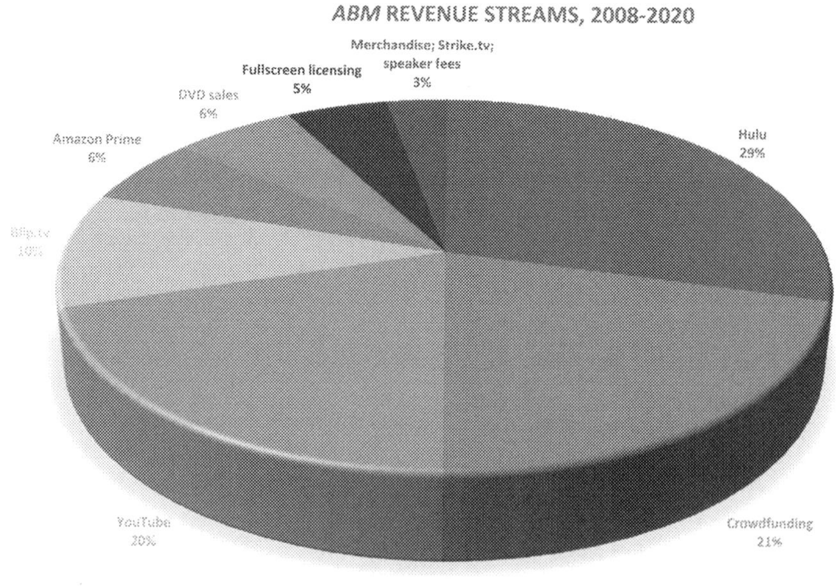

ABM REVENUE STREAMS, 2008-2020

Merchandise; Strike.tv; speaker fees 3%
Fullscreen licensing 5%
DVD sales 6%
Amazon Prime 6%
Blip.tv 10%
YouTube 20%
Hulu 29%
Crowdfunding 21%

FIGURE 10.6 ABM revenue streams, 2008–2020 (supplied by Tina Cesa Ward, 2021)

successful web-series maker, almost half the platforms *ABM* played on shut down due to adverse economic conditions beyond the makers' control.

For example, Strike.tv shuttered when striking creatives went back to work (Christian, 2015); and serialized originals platform Koldcast, lost millions of dollars and shut down (Scott, 2014). We saw Forster use Blip.tv, highlighted in the last chapter for upholding the ethics of the web of 'true sharing', creator freedom, and remix (Lessig, 2006). But Blip.tv too was shuttered after it was acquired by Disney-owned Maker Studios in 2013, ostensibly for its independent distribution platform, to allow creators 'to escape YouTube's sub-optimal revenue streams' (Gutelle, 2013).

The very paradigm shift identified by the *New York Times* and TIME in 2006, from traditional one-way media production to the power of You-based interactivity, can be leveraged by the individual web-series maker to mitigate platform volatility. 'Clicks or views are the lifeblood of the web-series' Ward (2009) blogged in a call to action to her fans; since advertisers used this 'lifeblood' to determine how much they would spend on series. Directly drawing on the power of the paradigm shift, Ward blogged to her fans the web-series represented 'an important step forward in entertainment that is more individualized. *Anyone But Me* is a series made for you. Not the mass-audience, watered down version of you, but the naturally complicated, not easily labelled version of you' (Ward, 2009). Fans responded in kind Figure 10.7. Fans generated significant levels of their own fan art and video remixes that celebrated their entry into the *ABM*

FIGURE 10.7   Remixed by you: Miller and Ward allowing what would normally be copyright-infringing remix such as this fan-generated interactive content, *Vivian & Aster Music Video* (above), itself seen over 4000 times

storyworld online. They raised US$50,000 to help fund the series and made new content to help raise more. Like we saw with Kalceff's *Starting From Now* in Chapter 7, Ward said while she and Miller always had high aspirations for *ABM*, they were surprised at how big it got, and how richly meaningful their online storytelling became for fans:

> The fandom around it; how everyone, Jeez, so dedicated to it, the emails and the posts we'd get all the time, exciting for us. Hard for me to even understand fully how much it meant to people, even though they voice us, I am just wow, I can't even just take that.
>
> *New Media Weekly, 2012*

This rich participatory experience around *ABM* also served another crucial purpose: engaging YouTube's collaborative-filtering-based algorithms – as introduced in Chapter 1. Makers creating such compelling content people must share it with their friends is the basis of Audience Growth Hacking. This algorithmic traction sets up a virtuous circle as fans participate by remixing and sharing, so making the original creators' content more and more discoverable. The gift of fan videos shows the power of social network markets to solve the burning problem of creator discoverability in a hyper-saturated market:

> The numbers may not be there for the fan videos – we have counted at least 20 – but in the YouTube ecosystem, the more videos with *Anyone But Me* in the title certainly helps the algorithms. To be able to fill the right side of the YouTube page with more *ABM* vids is a great thing. YouTube is all about quantity, so even if those fan videos didn't do a ton of numbers, they do help. And I think 10 years ago, they may have helped even more.
>
> *Ward, 2020*

Cultural divide

The cultural divide may seem an abstract concept far removed from the challenges of creative livelihoods, but, as I showed in Chapter 1, is implicated in a knowledge transfer blockage, cruelling the advance of younger creatives. However, there are now five signs the divide is being bridged. First, Ward is bullish on the web-series, likening the movement to the low budget independent movement of the 1990s known as the 'cinema of cool', which nearly every major studio rushed to emulate:

> So, the whole web-series movement reminds me of the independent movement of the 90s. There was this influx of independent films we had never seen before. Suddenly the film world was opening up to everybody. Partially because the technology afforded us the way to make cheaper films, but also once independent stuff came along, everybody, and the

studios took notice: 'Wow, there's like other stories out there!' Which is what the web-series has done for TV. It's given people who have their own voices and stories an option to be seen by TV, and then move into TV if they want, or stay shortform episodic on the web.

Ward, 2020

For example, Perren (2012, p. 17) credits the break-out success of Stephen Soderbergh's *sex, lies and videotape* (1989), followed by *Clerks* (1994), *Pulp Fiction, Sling Blade* (1996), and *Good Will Hunting* (1997), theatrically distributed in the United States by Miramax, as ushering in 'a quality American indie aesthetic'. Importantly for the 1990s US indie movement, Miramax did not immediately become a major studio player, being only a 'marginal' operation during the 1980s, having emerged from 'a turbulent industrial environment'.

Second, as aforementioned, the IAWTV awards have attracted enough attention the most historically innovative premium cable companies, HBO and Showtime, have inked in at least two development deals for indie web-series makers (Ward, 2020). Third, the Skip Ahead evidence for the 19 Skip Ahead teams I tracked, shows 17 of these web-series or storyworlds crossed over to BVODs and SVODs – 9 of which had established producers or above-the-line creators (see Appendix 1). As I showed in Chapter 1, rapprochement is important since it is strongly correlated with platforming beyond YouTube to streamers. Fourth, as I mentioned in Chapter 1, aside from initiatives such as Skip Ahead, some creative teams have the nous to form cross-culturally to maximize the success of their pitches to BVOD gatekeepers. The ABC's former Head of Comedy, Rick Kalowski (2018) told me he had observed collaborations between professional producers and new YouTube creators had emerged as an important strategy at grass-roots levels in their TV pilot pitches to him, the former ABC gatekeeper. Fifth, and most hopefully for younger generations, Ward indicated the cultural divide may be breaking down due to the sheer weight of generational change:

Web-series can be a transition to work in TV, rather than on web-series. Web-series is about what stories you want to tell. TV is about you trying to figure out what to sell TV. The crossover which is nice to see have been times I've reached out to executives from different networks from Amazon to SyFy. It's fun to run into them and its: 'Oh my God! I loved *Anyone But Me*!' They were these young adult fans, and now they are these executives who can say yes or no to your project. It's fascinating.

Ward, 2020

Discrimination, diversity, and authenticity

At one level, my argument Latinos, African Americans, Asian Americans, and queer folk are exemplar creators in the United States web-series community is the most straightforward matter to explain: participatory culture enabled by low-barrier technological advance, has arisen as US demographics increasingly diversify. Even mainstream audiences themselves can no longer be considered 'simply white' in a post-TV broadcast era (Ramón & Hunt, 2019, p. 304), where the US population is 61.6 per cent White, 17.6 per cent Hispanic, 13 per cent African American, and 5.6 per cent Asian American (Dhoest, 2020, p. 298). But demographic increase does not necessarily translate to political enfranchisement. For Turner (2010, p. 20), the gains in demographic access to media representation and accompanying diversity, are 'not of itself intrinsically democratic', nor politically enfranchising, but merely, 'demotic' or colloquial. Murdock (2010, p. 225) suggests meaningful cultural change is cruelled by the longstanding dominance of advertisers over TV broadcasters, restricting 'diversity of expression' since they believe only the most popular themes and genres must be used to gather mass audiences in front of their TVs. Concerns about advertiser influence over networks date back at least 60 years when US Federal Communications Commissioner, Newton Minow (2003, p. 398), indicted broadcasters of the day, face-to-face, for serving up 'a vast wasteland'. For mass audiences, Silverstone (1993, p. 575) argues broadcast TV provides order amid the chaos of life, where narratives stimulate and disturb, pacify and reassure, reinforcing the 'containing temporalities of the everyday'. For Hollywood field ethnographer, Caldwell (2013, p. 159) even the progressive parts of the industry that celebrated inclusion were 'racialized' with 'diversity hires' 'herded' into departmental 'ghettos', far from 'a sanctum defined by white (male) privilege'. At a deeper, problematic level, some accounts suggest minority populations – black women in particular – have suffered the 'symbolic violence' of racialized screen representations (Warner, 2016).

Who the storytellers are, shapes the stories they tell. In 2016, the WGA West found job growth in TV was so strong it reflected a 'renaissance in TV production' from 2008 to 2014. Even so, the longstanding dominance of white male jobs and pay continued (Hunt, 2016). Women and minorities remained 'severely underrepresented among the corps of TV writers, by a factor of nearly 2 to 1, and 3 to 1, respectively (Hunt, 2016, p. 30). Curtin and Sanson (2017) suggest despite numerous high-profile diversity initiatives from Hollywood, 'deep structural obstacles' prevent meaningful multiculturalism in above-the-line creatives, especially blocking employer and union gatekeepers, hyper-commercialism, sexism, and non-childcare-friendly workplaces. By 2020, the Academy of Motion Picture Arts and Sciences released new representation and inclusion standards for Best Picture in Oscars 2022, 'designed to encourage equitable representation on and off screen in order to better reflect the diversity of the movie-going audience'. But Variety's Davis (2020), immediately critiqued the new rules as 'purposefully vague', 'divisive', 'utterly confusing', and as 'easy to qualify' for. The stakes remain high for cultural progress and human flourishing. For Hunt (2016), Hollywood continued to play a major role in the process by which a nation circulates stories about itself.

However, the publication trajectories of the digital avant-garde elaborated in these nine cases are reflected in the predictions of scholarship. Echoing the inter-generational struggle Bourdieu identified that opens this book, Williams (2013, p. xii) dedicated his reflections to the 'young radical professionals in TV and video', in their 'steady ambition of innovation and excellence', while 'fully sharing a sense of what they are up against'. For Mark Banks (2010, p. 316), the 'communitarian basis' of screencraft clashed with increasingly individual- ized creative industries, but at least authentic storytelling should win out, since consumers continued to demand it. For Gripsrud (2010, p. 12), Internet-TV enhanced the development of diverse group identities 'as sub-altern counter- publics and for talking back to authorities and institutions of power'. By the end of the second decade of the 21st century, important signs, centred on the world's largest SVOD, showed Netflix was valuing diverse characters and storylines, and sometimes, behind-the-scenes talent. Shimpach (2020, p. 3) pointed to the globally dispersed, 'ethnically and sexually diverse characters' of *Sense8* (2015–2018), to highlight how the SVOD used algorithmically based 'taste clusters', rather than traditional demographics, to keep its globally diverse subscribers satisfied. Similarly, Dhoest (2020, p. 300) argues Netflix's *Orange is the New Black* (2013–2019) – based on its 'daring representations of gender and sexuality', rendered the traditional TV mass audience business model irrelevant, with the global streamer able to replace the legacy model by finding 'a large niche audience'.

Ward argues a correspondence between on-screen representation and the background of writers is increasingly essential to authenticity, especially to cap- ture the nuances of social injustice:

> Networks like Disney's FreeForm and The CW have been inclusive for a while, which I very much appreciate. Hollywood is starting to recognise they need that voice. It's not good enough to just have a show with a black lead, and then a whole bunch of non-black people writing it. It's important to have the above-the-line people, the writers and producers and directors, all have their voice to tell authentic stories. It shouldn't be just a check-box.
> *Ward, 2020*

Just as all the Australian creators and writer-producers in previous cases valorized the creative autonomy afforded by web-series, Ward too says the same is true for US web-series makers:

> That's always been the case on the web, because we have had the lovely luxury of being able to tell our stories. We all gravitated to it because it was so important to tell those stories. I feel online we have always been telling very authentic stories, for example James Bland's *Giants*³ which I love. Landing on Issa Rea's YouTube channel helped set *Giants* up for success. I hope people continue to make stuff for the web, because it will be a while

before we see some authenticity in Hollywood. I don't think they know how to do it yet.

Ward, 2020

Nevertheless, white male power finds a way to persist at the level of screen narratives.

It's a good time for women. But as much as inclusivity is a huge part of it, there's still certain stories people are dedicated to telling. You can get hired as a woman, but you are still telling this male kind of story.

Ward, 2020

Or the story just does not get made. Ward relates the story of her pitch with a female colleague to a male Hollywood executive a few years ago about a digital series. The story was about the second wave of the women's movement:

We would sit with this executive and talk about the series. But he would still say it has to be this particular way. He kept telling us as a man what women viewers would want to watch. It was astounding! That series never took off because we would butt heads. We'd say you have two of them (women), sitting in from of you right now telling you what we think. But it didn't matter. He has been making entertainment for women forever, so why wouldn't he think that? Because, until recently, women haven't had the chance to make that entertainment for themselves.

Ward, 2020

Notes

1 Giants went onto Viacom's BETNetwork's, a self-described 'black culture streamer'.
2 Chapter 4 on RackaRacka elaborates the hero's journey.
3 Giants surfaced on Issa Rae's YouTube channel, attracting 2.2 million views, before crossing over to cable, CleoTV, picking up 11 Emmy nominations (Hall, 2019), and an Emmy.

References

Arnott, P. D. (1991). *Public and performance in the Greek theatre*. Routledge.
Banks, M. J. (2010). The picket line online: Creative labor, digital activism, and the 2007–2008 writers guild of America strike. *Popular Communication, 8*(1), 20–33.
Banks, M. (2010). Craft labour and creative industries. *International Journal of Cultural Policy, 16*(3), 305–321.
Baym, N. K. (2018). *Playing to the crowd: Musicians, audiences, and the intimate work of connection* (Vol. 14). NYU Press.
Brown, T. (2013). *Breaking the fourth wall*. Edinburgh University Press.
Caldwell, J. (2006). Cultural studies of media production: Critical industrial practices. In W. Mimi & J. Schwoch (Eds.), *Questions of method in cultural studies* (pp. 109–153). Blackwell.

Caldwell, J. T. (2013). Para-industry: Researching Hollywood's blackwaters. *Cinema Journal, 52*(3), 157–165.

Christian, A. J. (2015). *Web TV networks challenge linear business models.* Carsey-Wolf Center Media Industries Project.

Christian, A. J. (2018). *Open TV: Innovation beyond Hollywood and the rise of web television.* New York University Press.

Conor, B. (2014). *Screenwriting: Creative labor and professional practice* (p. 164). Taylor & Francis.

Csikszentmihalyi, M. (2015). *The systems model of creativity: The collected works of Mihaly Csikszentmihalyi.* Springer.

Curtin, M., & Sanson, K. (2017). *Voices of labor.* University of California Press.

Davis, C. (2020, September 10). The New Oscars inclusion rules explained. Variety, Variety Media, Los Angeles. https://variety.com/2020

De Roeper, J., & Luckman, S. (2009). Future audiences for Australian stories: Industry responses in a post-Web 2.0 world. *Media International Australia, 130*(1), 5–16.

Dhoest, A. (2020). Televisual identities: The case of flemish TV drama. In S.Shimpach (Ed.), *The Routledge companion to global television* (pp. 294–303). Routledge.

Downes, L., & Nunes, P. (2013). Big bang disruption. *Harvard Business Review,* Mar 1, 44–56.

Eckerling, D. (2010, May 4). Author Q&A: Webisode writer/director Tina Cesa Ward, "Anyone But Me". [Blogpost]. http://writeononline.com/2010/05/04/author-qa-webisode-writerdirector-tina-cesa-ward-anyone-but-me/

Gripsrud, J. (Ed.). (2010). *Relocating television: Television in the digital context.* Routledge.

Grossman, L. (2006, December 25). You – Yes, You – Are TIME's person of the year. *Time Magazine,* New York. http://content.time.com/time/magazine/article/0,9171,1570810,00.html

Gutelle, S. (2013, August 21). Maker studios will buy blip to give its creators a home off YouTube. Tubefilter Inc, Los Angeles. https://www.tubefilter.com/2013/08/21/maker-studios-blip-purchase/

Hall, M.N. (2019, April 29). 'GIANTS': The team behind the 11-time Emmy nominated series shares one critical secret to their success. Shadow and Act, Blavity, Los Angeles. https://shadowandact.com/giants-series-james-bland-emmy-nominations-interview

Healy, G. (2019). 'Fast and furious film-making': YouTube's prospects for budding and veteran producers. *Metro Magazine, 202,* 100–105.

Hunt, D. (2016). The 2016 Hollywood writers report: Renaissance in reverse? Writers Guild of America West.

Jenkins, H. (2010). Transmedia storytelling and entertainment: An annotated syllabus. *Continuum, 24*(6), 943–958.

Kallas, C. (2014). *Inside the writers' room: Conversations with American TV writers.* Macmillan International Higher Education.

Kalowski, R. (2018). Then Head of ABC Comedy. Skype interview with Guy Healy.

Knol, M., & Trostrum, (2014). Berlinale Talents 2014: Finding delight in storytelling. Berlinale, Germany. https://www.berlinale.de/en/archiv/jahresarchive/2014/06b_berlinale_themen_2014/berlinale_talents_2014.html

Landa, C. (2011, December 6). 'Anyone but me' director finds drama in 'good people in love', [Blogpost] Tubefilter, Los Angeles. https://www.tubefilter.com/2011/12/06/good-people-in-love/

La Torre, M. (2016). The economics of the audiovisual industry: Financing TV, Film and Web. Springer.

Lee, S., & Jones, L. (1989). *Do the right thing: A Spike Lee joint.* Simon and Schuster.

Liesman, S. (2018 March 29). Nearly 60% of Americans are streaming and most with Netflix: CNBC survey. https://www.cnbc.com/2018/03/29

Lipkin, J. (2009, January 14). Playwright Susan Miller brings drama to the Net, Windy City Times, Chicago. https://www.windycitytimes.com/m/APPredirect.php?AID=20448

Livingston, P. (1982). *Ingmar Bergman and the rituals of art*. Cornell University Press.

Lessig, L. (2006). The ethics of Web 2.0: YouTube vs Flickr, Revver, Eyespot, blip.tv, and even Google. Lessig Blog. https://www.lessig.org/?s=

Lotz, A. D. (2018). *We now disrupt this broadcast: how cable transformed television and the internet revolutionized it all*. MIT Press.

Miller, S. (2020). Playwright, co-creator of *ABM*; interview with Guy Healy, Brisbane.

Minow, Newton N. (2003). Television and the Public Interest. *Federal Communications Law Journal, 55*(3), 395–406, Article 4.

Murdock, G. (2010). Networking the commons: Convergence culture and the public interest. In J. Gripsrud, (Ed.), *Relocating television* (pp. 224–237). Routledge.

Murdock, G., & Golding, P. (2016). Political economy and media production: A reply to Dwyer. *Media, Culture & Society, 38*(5), 763–769.

Murray, J. (2005). Policing terrorism: A threat to community policing or just a shift in priorities?. *Police Practice and Research, 6*(4), 347–361.

New Media Weekly (2012, April 8). Marc Cuevas interview with Tina Cesa Ward (anyone but me, good people in love), Pt 1. Web Blog, New Media Weekly, Los Angeles. https://www.youtube.com/watch?v=zTsxK0-0png&t=8s

Pareles, J. (2006, December 10). 2006, Brought to you by you. New York Times, New York. https://www.nytimes.com/2006/12/10/arts/music/10pare.html

Payne, S. (2017). The Caucus features...Tina Cesa Ward, Caucus/IAWTV Member. IAWTV, Los Angeles.https://archive.caucus.org/newsletter/news/vol8no1/17spr_tcward.html:

Perren, A. (2012). *Indie, Inc.: Miramax and the transformation of Hollywood in the 1990s*. University of Texas Press.

Piccoli, D. (2013, September 11). Tina Cesa Ward talks about 'Producing Juliet'. [Blogpost]. AfterEllen, Lesbian Nation, California. https://afterellen.com/people

Ramón, A. C., & Hunt, D. (2019). The future is now: Evolving technology, shifting demographics, and diverse TV content. In S. Shimpach (Ed.), The Routledge Companion to Global Television (pp. 304–319). Routledge.

Scott, R. (2014, March 10). Web video pioneer KoldCast TV shutters after loss of millions, [Blogpost]. Entertainment Technology Centre, University of Southern California. https://www.etcentric.org/web-video-pioneer-koldcast-tv-shutters-after-loss-of-millions/

Schumpeter, J. (1942). *Capitalism, socialism, and democracy*. Harper & Bros.

Shambler, T. (2019, November 5). Meet Quibi: Netflix for the Instagram and TikTok generation. Esquire, New York. https://www.esquireme.com/content/40691-meet-quibi-the-netflix-for-the-instagram-story-generation

Shapiro, R., & Aneja, S. (2017). Unlocking the gates: America's new creative economy. Recreate Coalition, p 1-99. http://www.recreatecoalition.org

Shimpach, S. (Ed.). (2020). *The Routledge companion to global television*. Routledge.

Silverstone, R. (1993). Television, ontological security and the transitional object. *Media, Culture and Society, 15*, 573–598.

Thomson, D. (2012). *The big screen: The story of the movies*. Macmillan.

Trevisanut, A. M. (2019). How Screen Australia, the ABC and SBS have shaped film and television convergence. *A Companion to Australian Cinema, 37*, 389.

Turner, G. (2010). *Ordinary people and the media: The demotic turn*. Sage Publications.

Vasseur, R. (2018, April 15). Rich interviews: Tina Cesa Ward co-creator/co-writer for delegates [Blog], First Comics News, California. https://www.firstcomicsnews.com

Ward, T. C. (2009, July 15). Power to the people – How fans really, really make a difference. [Blogpost]. Official ABM website. http://anyonebutmeseries.blogspot.com/2009/

Ward, T. C. (2019, 2020, 2021). IAWTV chair and creator, ABM; interviews and personal communication with Guy Healy, Brisbane.

Warner, K. J. (2016). Strategies for success?: Navigating Hollywood's "postracial" labor practices. In *Precarious Creativity*, 13, 172–184. University of California Press.

Williams, R. (2013). *Raymond Williams on television (Routledge Revivals): Selected writings*. Routledge.

Williams, C., & Taylor, B. (Eds.). (2003). Countering terror: New directions post'911' (No. 147). Strategic and Defence Studies Centre.

Willis, D. (2014, July 22). What the internet can see from your cat pictures. *New York Times*, New York. https://www.nytimes.com/2014/07/23/upshot/what-the-internet-can-see-from-your-cat-pictures.html

Winston, J. (1996). Emotion, reason and moral engagement in drama. *Research in Drama Education*, 1(2), 189–200.

11

THE GARDEN IN YOUTUBE'S MACHINE

I started the research for this book as a PhD candidate at QUT's Digital Media Research Centre in 2016. I did not know where it would lead, but aimed to better understand how storytelling and creativity itself were faring in the new media ecology of post-broadcast TV. I did not expect in these dark times, I would have a such a hopeful story to share. But it is no fairy tale. This book presents the first longitudinal study of veteran YouTubers and established TV producers making transnational web-series together and maps the professional outcomes from their rapprochement and evolution of two-way mentoring. This book argues women, ethnic and racial minorities, queer folk, and those from hardscrabble backgrounds are bending algorithmic culture to their needs, becoming exemplars in the adaptive new genre of low budget, high cultural impact web-series, disrupting longstanding white male domination of the film and TV industries. Overall, this study showed most teams parlayed highly viewed web-series into non-exclusive license deals with digital broadcasters and online streamers, and thus potentially sustainable careers. This strategy parallels that Chalaby (2010, p. 686) found among UK super-indies who fought to retain their IP and ultimately were found to 'sweat their assets to the last drop'. Based on this reinvigoration of storytelling via diversity, this book posits the theory of the garden in YouTube's machine.

The major findings from the nine cases are sevenfold. First, modest subvention to creators and writer-producers of about just AU$100,000, in concert with TV producers and screenwriting mentors, is enough for the most determined and talented creatives to make low-budget web-series with high cultural impact. Further in a majority of cases, these collaborations, funded by the globally rare AU$3 million Google-Screen Australia initiative, Skip Ahead, resulted in these web-series or their creators crossing over not to broadcast TV as expected, but their edgier online variants, broadcast-video-on-demand (BVOD), and

DOI: 10.4324/9781003182481-11

subscription-video-on-demand (SVOD) in Australia and the United States (Appendix 1). In contrast to longstanding white male domination of Western film and TV, the Australian web series cohort exhibited striking gender, racial, ethnic, sexual, and socio-economic diversity. These creative journeys are mapped in cases 1–5. For example, more than half the producers involved in the cohort were female, almost half the creators were culturally and linguistically diverse, one was transgender, and some were from hardscrabble backgrounds. To qualify for the competitive funds, each YouTuber who had already achieved a minimum of 50,000 subscribers and have a killer pitch for a narrative web-series. The suggestion the YouTuber collaborate with an established TV producer became increasingly strong over time as Screen Australia absorbed the lessons of 'two-way mentoring', yielded by such cross-generational collaborations. For the 19 Skip Ahead teams I tracked, 17 of these web-series or storyworlds crossed over to BVODs and SVODs – 9 of which had established producers or above-the-line creators – including SBS Viceland, ABC iView, Stan, and Foxtel in Australia; Netflix, Discovery Channel, PBS Digital, and YouTube Originals in the United States[1]. Not all rapprochements are necessarily aimed at cross-over. Most of those not mentored escalated to better screen industry jobs. Four collaborations – despite their quality and niche appeal – have recorded no sales yet. The Skip Ahead mentors, Julie Kalceff and Rosie Lourde (Chapter 7), Mike Jones (Chapter 3), and Mike Cowap, published to Netflix, BBC Children's, Hulu, Adult Swim, and public broadcasters across Scandinavia. The reverse of the coin; outcomes for film school graduates and established professionals launching web-series in social network markets were mapped in cases 6–9. Of the film school graduates/professionals leveraging YouTube and niche OTTs such as Vimeo in cases 6–9, their web-series crossed over to SBS Viceland in Australia and CBC Gem in Canada and Wilde.TV, Here.TV on Amazon Prime, Hulu and Amazon Prime in the United States. Significantly, the variegated trajectories of the creatives in my study parallel previous findings by Csikszentmihalyi (2014, p. 21) among art school graduates.

Second, these outcomes were achieved by a multiplatform labour that these creatives evolved over about six years, some of the most distinguished of whom used audience-centric co-creativity to secure make-or-break audience engagement. Co-creativity with online audiences – which was a cultural bridge too far for some classically trained writers such as Erin Good (*Jade of Death*, Chapter 8) – manifested on a spectrum: from video-sharing of creators performances, fan-provided locations, and vlog-style reaction videos (RackaRacka, Chapter 4), co-composition of song lyrics (GreasyTales, Chapter 2), participatory meme videos (SketchSHE), fan art (Susan Miller and Tina Cesa Ward, Chapter 10), and online community comment streams that influence narrative arcs (Julie Kalceff, Chapter 7; Ric Forster, Chapter 9). Where multiplatform labour was best practice, it resulted in increasing career mobility of storytellers across Caldwell's three blended labour systems of spec world, craft world, and brand world. Moreover, most cases drew, consciously or not, on Murdock and Golding's three cultural economies: traditional markets, public goods, and gifting and collaboration, which enabled seven of the nine cases to achieve at least a middle-class living. Future research on creative labour could test whether the congruent mapping of their schema exhibited in the nine cases is playing a role in the sustainability of online creative labour in local jurisdictions more broadly. Indeed, competitive grants to local streampunk storytellers could initiate a pipeline of talent to develop their own IP and cross-over to the burgeoning international series market, that Baujard et al. (2019, p. 32) value at tens of billions of dollars.

Third, in contrast to the long criticized 'individualized' model of cultural production, exemplified by the lone YouTube vlogger model, this multiplatform labour was characterized by a collaborative 'rock band' model of production of networked video. Crucially, I argue Skip Ahead has become an adaptive mechanism for the knowledge transfer lacking in the traditional industry, cruelling its progress to sustainability, as identified in comprehensive surveys of producers introduced in Chapter 1. Contrastingly, I argue the problem of knowledge transfer – in the context of adapting to ongoing digital screen disruption – is respect for each other's accomplishments as creators and producers, and like-minded humour. Importantly, these different generations of creatives respond with what *Who Do You Think You Are?* producer and Skip Ahead mentor, Margie Bryant, describes as 'two-way mentoring'. I advance the notion of hybridity through rapprochement, where SME and professionally trained narrative storytellers fell towards each other's skill-sets, and learnt new collaborative strategies to cross over from YouTube to the high-profile hybrid digital outlets named above, and achieve greater sustainability. The development of IP-able content and the transitions involved are fully elaborated based on the accounts of the collaborating professionals, particularly official Screen Australia mentors Julie Kalceff and Mike Jones.

Fourth, I found as creators are exposed to algorithmic volatility over the medium-to-long term, more of them gravitate to IP-recognizing, license-fee-paying BVODs and SVODs. Among the Skip Ahead creatives, the average time to achieve at least the 50,000 subscribers to qualify for the stunningly successful initiative was six years. Most of the hard-driving film-school graduates had achieved significant industry milestones about six years after risking all to bet on a web-series. Traditionally, screenwriters take up to 15 years to achieve 'overnight success' (Field, 1994, p. 256). Now, in about a third of the time, creative entrepreneurs can use multiplatform labour to distinguish themselves via an exceptional web-series and parlay the resulting IP[2] and audience into sales and licensing on a BVOD or SVOD (Healy, 2019, p. 116). Traditional producers had as much to learn from the YouTubers, as younger YouTubers had to learn from the TV industry collaborators and mentors, who themselves had been marginalized by the TV industry. In terms of skillsets, the two sides of the divide fell towards each other: the established producers learnt about the 'audience growth hacking' know-how hard won by their younger YouTube collaborators, while they in turn were inducted into the craft skills of storytelling critical to short form episodic narrative. Audience growth hacking, based on the Silicon Valley concept of 'growth hacking', comprises non-instrumental community-building techniques that encourage audiences to share compelling content with their friends via their own social media feeds. For example, the factors producers learnt from creators included:

- exemplifying creative entrepreneurship,
- knowing your audience (compared with traditional cultural and business practice),
- creativity under severe cost constraint – the cost structure of the business,
- a work ethic,
- reaching a youth sensibility and demographic,
- global reach of content.

Fifth, depending upon whether they were born-online social media entertainers or film school graduates, a striking difference was thrown up regarding the priority experience sought by all creatives: the sacrosanct principle of flow. Flow is the optimal creative experience described by artists in observations by Mihaly Csikszentmihalyi, where an artist's skills are so developed 'everything one does seems to come naturally, and when concentration is so intense one loses track of time'. While all the YouTubers were passionate about their labour-intensive careers, all – with the notable exception of Louna Maroun (Chapter 9) – observed highly adverse experiences regarding flow. Veteran YouTube animation storyteller Chris Voigt, now on Emmy-winning *Bluey* (Chapter 2), bluntly told me: 'Creativity gets killed' (Voigt, 2017). Moreover, Danny Philippou (Chapter 4) said good creative work *once could be* conducted on a digital platform such as YouTube, but since then creativity has been 'assassinated'. Similarly, Ann Reardon aka How To Cook That and Shae-lee Raven (formerly SketchSHE director) both told me the algorithmic reward system of YouTube – which is increasingly hyper-saturated over time – has become increasingly incoherent, problematizing their labour and their livelihoods.

Sixth, effective experimentation with genres – which Todorov said function as 'horizons of expectation' for readers and 'models of writing' for authors – has proven essential to ensure cut-through on a hyper-saturated platform such as YouTube, which Tubefilter's Hale (2019) calculates ingests at least 82 years of video per day. For example in Chapter 2, Voigt was seen to exhibit exquisitely animated absurdist narratives; in Chapter 4, RackaRacka showed novel innovation seamlessly blending the traditional three-act structure into at least three distinct genres: faux livestream, thriller and horror for *Stunt Gone Wrong*, and did culture-jamming with the distinctive *Flex*; in Chapter 8, Good and Litton-Strain adapted fantasy-noir drama to networked video; while in Chapter 10, Ward says a mix of genres was also important to *ABM*: 'a teenage drama mixed with quirky romantic comedy'.

Seventh, the development with the most profound implications for social change, via networked counter-power (Castells 2007, p. 248; Slaughter 2017, p. 163), was seen as the creators and writer-producers in the nine cases used socio-technologies to reclaim the power of authentic representation free of the traditional repressive and hegemonic representations that had marginalized them. For example, SuperWog (Chapter 3) exemplifies this power shift as talented minorities hold up racial and other stereotypes to the 'disinfectant of sunlight', and so invalidate them. Ann Reardon, with almost five million subscribers, in Chapter 5, was shown to share her networked attention with small independent social and health entrepreneurs to drive change regarding some of the world's most pressing problems such as hunger, poverty, and disease, later turning to debunking COVID misinformation. In Chapter 6, Shae Raven too shared her attention from millions of fans with peer creators to encourage greater self-acceptance, collective responses, and celebrate 'girl power' in 2018, a year marked by an upsurge in collective activism as citizens took to the streets worldwide. Future Emmy-winner, Julie Kalceff (Chapter 7), showed how an exceptional web-series such as *Starting From Now* can circumvent the symbolic violence directed at marginalized groups by some powerful traditional media. Diverse web-series writer-producers can remake those symbols authentically, and entertainingly, on their own representational terms, for where those audiences are now, in writers' own online communities. Similarly, Ric Forster and Melanie Rowland in queer teen web-soap *Flunk* (Chapter 9) showed how co-creativity can not only secure greater engagement but also better tap into the zeitgeist, further enhancing creator sustainability. Moreover, Miller and Ward with *Anyone But Me* (Chapter 10) showed how irrepressible storytellers can resist subjugation by traditional gatekeepers, and using persistent experimentation, exploit new platforms, even as they rise and fall, to monetize and distribute new narratives that find deep niche audiences online.

It remains an irony and paradox that an exemplar of capitalism, an unruly child of Silicon Valley, YouTube, has nevertheless provided the means – which the platform has done little to support – for collectivist approaches by creatives in service of themselves and the greater good. Lingering scepticism shown towards the initial promise of democratization and diversification of cultural production (Napoli, 2016, p. 342: Duffy et al., 2019, p. 4), needs re-evaluation. A lively, participatory long tail was shown to play a crucial role in creator sustainability. This is explained by the phenomena identified by William Gibson in *Burning Chrome* (1986): 'The street finds its own uses for things'.

Four Internet years on, the findings of my peers who conducted ethnographic-style research, but in North America ending about 2017, Drs Emilia Zboralska and Jean Aymar Christian, hold up very well indeed. For web-series maker and scholar Christian (2018), the web-series format was an innovative space in screen storytelling in the United States, especially its potential for new IP generation in either pitches and 'calling cards' or pilots sold on a non-exclusive license basis to distributors. The main value of the web-series to these producers lays in the creative autonomy used by marginalized communities to create their own representations of themselves in online communities. The producers 'lived the dream, or, at least, some form of the dream', but 'what was missing from the dream was what only large institutions could provide: sustainability and legitimacy'. Christian found a sustainable indie web-series market was not then present in the United States, but, legacy distributors could develop a sustainable indie market, 'if they extend ownership rights, license indie series with healthy fees, and open development' indeed. Significantly, the web-series makers Christian interviewed wanted 'a more sustainable and less "viral" way to fund non-corporate content: a sustainable market for independent web video by skilled professionals'. Similarly for Canadian web-series maker and scholar, Zboralska (2018), aspirants had turned to entrepreneurial approaches to use the web-series as 'a calling card' and for 'web-to-tv-adaptations'. Zboralka's interviews among Canadian creators and writers and producers revealed 'a deep desire to break free from, and to break up the status quo', with effective web-series acting as a career accelerator. Absolutely. While their success was 'neither even nor universal', Canadian web creators, via entrepreneuring, developed 'a breadth of new, tangible, and meaningful storytelling and production skills where opportunities to do so were few'. Nevertheless, like Christian, Zboralska reported overall 'sustainability thus remained a dream, rather than reality' for most creators.

In contrast, the research presented in this book is not based on a snapshot of multiple creators and writers and producers at one time in their careers. The nine cases are all longitudinal, tracking creator journeys over their adult lives – both from a perspective of their external careers, but also their subjective creative experiences of those journeys. In contrast also are the journeys of high-value creators born-online, and high-value writer-producers and directors transitioning to license deals, with this mapping revealing the pathway from the exceptional web-series to sustainability with BVODs and SVODs and middle-class livings. Sustainability is defined as being able to make a reasonable, if gritty and hardworking living, and being able to attract seed funding for a slate of ongoing narrative projects. In terms of industrial, cultural, and social value, the cases showed the low-budget but high cultural impact web-series was, depending on the situated needs of the creatives at various times on their journeys, a calling card, a Silicon Valley-style 'proof-of-concept' for a longer series aimed at BVODs and SVODs, or, simply a joyous and beloved series of online artefacts that enabled marginalized communities to engage in identity formation, often characterized by fan art. In terms of sustainability four years on from Christian and Zboralska's important studies, the nine cases showed the increasing career mobility of storytellers across Caldwell's three blended labour systems of spec world, craft world and brand world. Moreover, the role of Murdock and Golding's three media economies: traditional markets, public goods, and gifting and collaboration, in enabling them to do so. For example, Canadian and Australian makers – hosted in countries with subvention cultures and socio-technologies able to bypass international borders – are lead performers in both Los Angeles' IAWTV awards and Germany's

Web Series World Cup. For policy-makers, this fact is telling regarding the enabling role of modest but competitive subvention for low-budget productions. Creators told Christian they wanted a less 'viral' way to make indie web-series. This is a fantasy contradicted by the harsh realities of the networked video ecology. Cases 3, 7, 9, and 10, the Saiddens, Kalceff, Forster, and Miller and Ward especially show the role of spreadable episodes – supported by audience growth hacking – in distinguishing creators sufficiently to attract private and public seed funding. For example, a single standout episode of *Anyone But Me*, 'Welcome to the Party', (Chapter 10), has attracted 20 million views and counting, while a *Starting from Now* episode (Chapter 7) has attracted at least 39 million views. This is the unprecedented power of the previously unrepresented deep niche in action online.

Sixty years after Minow excoriated broadcast TV for not trying hard enough to do better than serving up 'a vast wasteland', storytelling in the post-broadcast era is at a cross-roads. If Big Tech, especially YouTube and Facebook, offered to extend the Skip Ahead model worldwide in private-public partnerships with interested national screen agencies, these mega-platforms could begin to restore their long faded social license to operate. For example, social media 'does more harm than good' say a majority of over 16,000 Millennials and Gen Z's, in Deloitte's Global Millennial Survey of 2019. Given just $3.5 million under Skip Ahead has achieved the bang for buck revealed in this book, costs would be modest. Indeed Baujard et al. (2019, p. 77) have suggested to the Council of Europe an ideal place to start on the continent is improved subvention: 'The development phase [for high end series] does not receive enough public funding, even as the phase where it could be most efficient and where private investments are lacking because of high risk'. Baujard was referring to the strong international market in high-end-series; however, as these nine cases have shown, the most determined and talented creatives are using the exceptional web-series as proof-of-concept for higher end series. The nascent market of web-series and high-end series is becoming increasingly porous, especially as SVODs' needs for diverse narratives and brilliant showrunners, meet rising numbers of talented and diverse web-series makers such as those in this book. Effective showrunners are already in short supply (Andreeva, 2014; Hadas, 2017, p. 89) in this, the Golden Age of SVODs. This dynamic suggests porosity between the worlds of exceptional web-series and SVODs and BVODs will open further. However, at the cross-roads two threats loom: first from what Murdock (2011, p. 26) describes as 'the corporate push to enclose digital gifting'; and second, from the intermediaries and institutions Baym (in Banet-Weiser et al., 2014, p. 1078) warns have made 'some creations easy, and others hard, and how they reward some players and not others'. The late Don Valentine, the founder of Sequoia Capital, has provided the gold standard for what I suggest is a much-needed IP sharing convention between streampunk web-series makers and financiers/distributors: 'We'll put up all the money, you put up all the blood, sweat and tears, and we'll split the company' (Lebret, 2017). Web-series makers are the creatives building a new scripted, networked art world and emergent market. But without lighthouse structures such as YouTube and Screen Australia's Skip Ahead, indie creators and start-up platforms are most exposed to the gales of hyper-capitalism. In distribution deals, creators deserve to retain at least half their IP for their blood, sweat, and tears.

Equality of representation in screen storytelling is one of the most longstanding, most burning, and increasingly problematic issues raised in these pages. In the 1980s, in their foundational series of interviews with the showrunners of the then Golden Age of TV, Newcomb and Ally (1983, p. 16) formally apologized for only including male producers. They said despite women and minority producers creating important and high-quality programmes, the structure of American TV, like the structure of American society, 'has been dominated by white males'. Given television was 'the most powerful and the most pervasive replication of capitalism yet developed in American society', its 'highly charged, symbolic, fictional system' demanded scrutiny. Limited producer diversity had to be corrected to rectify social inequity 'not only in the television industry, but in American society at large', Newcomb and Ally wrote. More recently, Robert Kyncl (2017, p 90), the business chief of YouTube, acknowledged in his book, *Streampunks,* that unless algorithms were built with strong input from diverse perspectives, 'they risk mirroring existing biases in our society'. The ideals of an open and democratic platform YouTube strove to be, a theme of his book, meant anyone should be able to find equal opportunity to share his or her voice, Kyncl asserted. By 2019, showrunner Javier Grillo-Marxuach, who wrote on the first two seasons what many consider to be broadcast TV's finest hours, ABC's *Lost* (2004–2010), laid down a marker for when there would be enough representation: 'There will have been enough representation when a female writer or a person-of-color doesn't remember a time when they felt unrepresented' (Gordon, 2019).

Indeed in his famous riff on popular culture, Stuart Hall (2018, p 360) spoke about the struggle between the culture of the people and the culture of the power-bloc. Hall argued popular culture was one of the places where socialism might be constituted. 'That is why popular culture matters. Otherwise, to tell you the truth, I don't give a damn about it', Hall said. None of the 40 odd creators or writer-producers I interviewed over the past five years described themselves as 'socialist'. But they all nevertheless exemplified collaborative, collectivist approaches for the greater public good. If Hall was still with us, I would humbly suggest to him the cases of these determined, talented, and diverse web-series creatives elaborated in these pages are one aspect of popular culture he might give a damn about.

Millennials and Gen Zs face real and disruptive challenges, from automated decision-making to climate breakdown to income inequality and uncontrolled AI, amid more recent threats such as the global pandemic. The stakes, argues Oxford University risk analyst and author, Toby Ord (2021), are the 'live possibilities' that 'may include the global collapse of civilization, or even the extinction of humanity'. Bluntly, given how much stories help constitute our beings as *homo narrans*, prudence alone demands we now draw on the full depth of humanity's storytelling talent, in all our glorious diversity. Moreover, deliberative decision-making needs to be better informed by science, or otherwise at our peril. After all, zoonotic experts warned us over a decade ago research funding into and surveillance of bat-borne viruses in Asia, Africa, and elsewhere had to be prioritized to prevent pandemics (Healy, 2009). Work is changing rapidly, but the future is unclear. For example, a third of Millennial and Gen Z respondents expect evolving technologies to replace all or part of their jobs, while a majority expect these technologies to 'augment' their roles, freeing them to pursue 'creative, human and value-added work' (Deloitte, 2018, p. 23). The attention of these generations has shifted to YouTube and the hybrid digital services of public service broadcaster 'catch-up' and subscription streamers. Younger generations especially deserve access to participatory, high-quality, highly informative web-series made by well-trained and remunerated creators to help them cope with future adversity, together. In many ways, these creators are closer to their audiences and the zeitgeist than previous generations of storytellers. As Nathan Saidden says of SuperWog fans: 'The best feedback is when fans write to tell us our videos have got them through rough times in their lives' (Burke, 2018). Representative, sustainable voices matter now more than ever.

Note

1 We saw with Susan Miller and Tina Cesa Ward in Chapter 10 that retaining their IP in the hit web-series, *Anyone But Me*, is one of their proudest achievements.

References

Andreeva, N. (2014). Showrunners wanted: Networks grapple with lack of experienced writing producers. Deadline. http://www.deadline.com/2014/05/

Baujard, T., Tereszkiewicz, R., & de Swarte, A. (2019). *Entering the new paradigm of artificial intelligence and series. A Study Commissioned by the Council of Europe and Eurimages.* Peacefulfish.

Banet-Weiser, S., Baym, N. K., Coppa, F., Gauntlett, D., Gray, J., Jenkins, H., & Shaw, A. (2014). "Participations| Part 1: CREATIVITY." *International Journal of Communication, 8*, 1069–1088.

Burke, J. (2018, November 13). Brothers Saidden usher in zombie apocalypse. *The Australian*, News Corp Australia.

Castells, M. (2007). Communication, power and counter-power in the network society. *International Journal of Communication, 1*, 238–266.

Chalaby, J. K. (2010). The rise of Britain's super-indies: Policy-making in the age of the global media market. *International Communication Gazette, 72*(8), 675–693.

Christian, A. J. (2018). *Open TV.* New York University Press.

Csikszentmihalyi, M. (2014). *The systems model of creativity: The collected works of Mihaly Csikszentmihalyi.* Springer.

Deloitte (2018). *Deloitte millennial survey: Millennials disappointed in business, Unprepared for Industry 4.0.* Deloitte.

Deloitte (2019). *Deloitte millennial survey.* Deloitte Touche Tohmatsu.

Duffy, B. E., Poell, T., & Nieborg, D. B. (2019). Platform practices in the cultural industries: Creativity, labor, and citizenship. Social Media+ Society, 5(4), 2056305119879672.

Field, S. (1994). *Screenplay: The foundations of screenwriting*. Dell Publishing.

Gordon, D. (2019, Aug 10). Television Writer, Producer Javier Grillo-Marxuach on the Toxic Culture Behind Many TV Shows, *Wisconsin Public Radio*, US. https://www.wpr.org/television-writer-producer-javier-grillo-marxuach-toxic-culture-behind-many-tv-shows

Hadas, L. (2017). From the workshop of JJ Abrams: Bad robot, networked collaboration, and promotional authorship. In Gandini, A., & Graham, J. (Eds), *Collaborative production in the creative industries* (pp 87–105). University of Westminster Press.

Hale, J. (2019, July 5). More than 500 hours of content are now being uploaded to YouTube every minute. Tubefilter, Tubefilter Inc, Los Angeles. https://www.tubefilter.com/2019/05/07/number-hours-video-uploaded-to-youtube-per-minute/

Hall, S. (2018). 11. Notes on Deconstructing "the Popular" [1981]. In Stuart Hall, *Essential Essays, Volume 1: Foundations of Cultural Studies* (pp. 347–361). Duke University Press.

Healy, G. (2009). Cross-species diseases proliferating in the wild, The Australian, Higher Education. News Corp Australia, Sydney.

Healy, G. (2019). 'Fast and furious film-making': YouTube's prospects for budding and veteran producers. *Metro Magazine*, *202*, 100–105.

Kyncl, R., & Peyvan, M. (2017). *Streampunks: YouTube and the rebels remaking media*. HarperCollins.

Lebret, H. (2017). Equity in startups. https://www.researchgate.net/publication/320820900_Equity_in_Startups

Murdock, G. (2011) Political economies as moral economies: Commodities, gifts and public goods. In J. Wasko, G. Murdock, & H. Sousa (Eds.), *The Blackwell handbook of the political economy of communication* (pp. 13–40). Wiley-Blackwell.

Napoli, P. M. (2016). Requiem for the long tail: Towards a political economy of content aggregation and fragmentation. *International Journal of Media & Cultural Politics*, *12*(3), 341–356.

Newcomb, H., & Alley, R. S. (1983). *The producer's medium: Conversations with creators of American TV* (p. 33). Oxford University Press.

Ord, T. (2021, March 23). *Covid-19 has shown humanity how close to the edge we are*. The Guardian, The Guardian Philanthropic Trust.

Slaughter, A. M. (2017). *The chessboard and the web*. Yale University Press.

Voigt, C. (2017, 2018, 2019, 2021). Creator of SexuaLobster channel. Interviews and personal communications with Guy Healy.

Zboralska, E. (2018). *Telling our stories on the web: Canadian English-language web series and the production of culture online* [Doctoral dissertation, York University].

Appendix 1

CAREER MOBILITY PATHS OF SKIP AHEAD ALUMNI, 2014–2019

Established Producer	Channel	Title	Class	of Episodes	Post-Skip Ahead destinations
1/Bryan Moses (Eurovision Aust)	Axis of Awesome	Axis All Areas	2014	4	Dormant; Lee Naimo now heads Skip Ahead
2/No producer	Mighty Car Mods	Lend Us a Ride	2014	6 + trailer	2.79M subs; 461M views
3/No producer	SexuaLobster	Fernandos legitimate business enterprise	2014	7	Storyboarder for Emmy-winning Ludo Studios on Bluey (ABC/BBC)
4/Noted cinematographer Pierce Cook	Veritasium	This Will Revolutionize Education	2014	1 × 7mns	Correspondent on Bill Nye's Netflix series; Presenter Vitamania on SBS/YouTube Movies
5/Ric Forster (Hollyoaks; Neighbours)	Neighbours	Neighbours vs Zombies	2014	5 + trailer	Work with Fremantle Media; Flunk
6/No producer	Roundabout Crew	Australiana Hostel	2015	3 + trailer	Tom Armstrong worked for Seven West Media
7/Nel Minchin (Blood, Sweat & Takeaways)	Aunty Donna	1999	2015	10+ trailer + outtakes	Trendies on Comedy Channel; ABC iView pilot; Chaperones onto Stan; Big 'Ol House of Fun (Netflix)

(Continued)

Established Producer	Channel	Title	Class of Episodes	Post-Skip Ahead destinations
8/Drew Bailey (Miracle Fish)	SketchSHE	Traffic Jam	2015 4	Gender Matters grant; Awesomeness TV grant; Posse TV pilot; Foxtel's The Slot
9/Jos Brooks Kate Taylor-Marsden	Draw with Jazza	*The Tale Teller*	2015 1 × 8.50mns + trailer	3.2M subs; 415M views
10/Unidentified producer	How To Cook That	*The Sweetest Thing*	2015 4	3.48M subs; 569M views
11/Paul Walton (*Heartbeat; Touch of Frost*)	SuperWog	The SuperWog Show	2016 1 × 23mns	ABC Comedy's first scripted series, SuperWog; The Slot
12/Nadine Bates (*Sesame Street*)	Charli's Crafty Kitchen	*Crafty Kingdom*	2016 3 + BTS	Dormant
13/Julie Byrne (*McLeod's Daughters; Babadook*)	RackaRacka	*Stunt Gone Wrong (Live)*	2016 1 × 41mns	ABC iView Deadlock; The Slot; The Racka series in development with Triptych & Ludo
14/Margie Bryant (*Who Do You Think You Are?*)	BrainCraft	*Mutant Menu*	2016 1 × 36mns	PBS Digital's first longform video, Mutant Menu; Attention Wars funded by S.Aust & PBS Digital Studios
9 producers	14 creator teams			
15/Laura Clelland (Network Ten)	Study w Jess	*Life of Jess*	2017 6 × 5 mns	Seeking a streamer for Life of Jess
16/Nick Boshier; Christiaan Van Vuuren; (*Bondi Hipsters*)	Van Vuuren Bros	*Over & Out*	2017 6 × 5 mns	Canneseries Best Short Series for Over & Out; Screen Australia Premium Fund grant for Over & Out; Dom and Adrian, A Sunburnt Christmas on Stan.
17/No producer	Timtimfed	*Rebooted*	2017 20mns	Shown at @ Flickerfest
18/No producer	Skit Box	*Skit Box*	2017 22mns	Sale not recorded
19/Walton/ Cowap	Wengie	*Parked*	2017 15mins	Shown on Pinterest

Source: Table 4.1 Healy's original analysis. Teams that went off-platform to BVODs, SVODS, and mainstream jobs in bold.

Appendix 2

THREE KEYS TO SUSTAINABILITY FOR WEB-SERIES MAKERS, 2005–2021, BASED ON MURDOCK AND GOLDINGS' (2016, P. 764) THREE ECONOMIES

	Commodities, central to capitalism	Public goods paid from taxation, especially government's grants	Gifting generated by voluntary collaboration activities
Ch 2: Voigt	YouTube, AdSense, and freelance commissions	Skip Ahead	Co-creative crowdwriting, and crowdfunding (Patreon)
Ch 3: SuperWog	AdSense; appearance fees from live comedy; licensing to BVOD iView and ABC	Skip Ahead	YouTube reaction videos; fan feedback
Ch 4: RackaRacka	Sponsorships especially Netflix, Warner Bros Games, Village Roadshow Pictures	Screen Australia development and talent grants, inc Skip Ahead	YouTube 'superchat' gifts; remix and reaction videos; set locations
Ch 5: Reardon	Sponsorship especially Breville and Wix	Skip Ahead	Patreon; fan requests for recipe ideas; fan suggestions for debunking targets
Ch 6: Shackleford	Sponsorship such as HP Spectre, Canesten, Vibe Israel	Skip Ahead and Screen Australia Gender Matters	Tribute and mashup videos; crowdfunding
Ch 7: Kalceff	IVF Australia, queer health organization ACON, licensing from SBS2, transaction fees from Vimeo, AdSense	Screen Australia grants, and mentor employment, AFTRS teaching, Screen NSW grant	Co-creativity with fans that shaped narrative arc of SFN; fan tribute videos

(Continued)

	Commodities, central to capitalism	Public goods paid from taxation, especially government's grants	Gifting generated by voluntary collaboration activities
Ch 8: Litton-Strain & Good	Licenses from CBC's Gem (Canada); Wilde. tv (US)	Teaching at AFTRS; Screen Australia online production	Extensive fan comments on various platforms promoted sharing
Ch 9: Forster & Rowland	License deal to Here Now.tv which sits on SVOD Amazon Prime; Vimeo; merchandise	Screen Australia online development and production funds; Film Victoria grant	Co-creativity with fans that shaped character arcs; fan comments on various platforms promoted sharing
Ch 10: Miller & Ward	Angel investor; ad and license revenue from YouTube, Blip, Hulu, Amazon	–	Crowdfunding and crowdsourcing

Source: Healy's own original analysis.

INDEX